ISBN: 9781314538533

Published by:
HardPress Publishing
8345 NW 66TH ST #2561
MIAMI FL 33166-2626

Email: info@hardpress.net
Web: http://www.hardpress.net

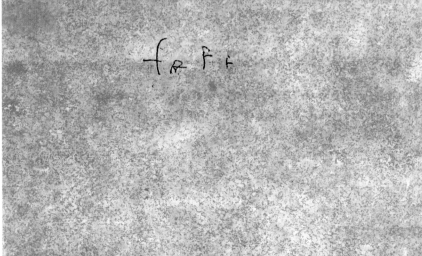

THE

REDSKINS;

OR,

INDIAN AND INJIN:

BEING THE CONCLUSION OF THE

Littlepage Manuscripts.

BY J. FENIMORE COOPER.

In every work regard the writer's end;
None e'er can compass more than they intend.—*Pope.*

COMPLETE IN ONE VOLUME.

NEW EDITION.

NEW YORK:
STRINGER AND TOWNSEND.
1857.

THE REDSKINS.

48922

PREFACE.

THIS book closes the series of the Littlepage Manuscripts, which have been given to the world, as containing a fair account of the comparative sacrifices of time, money and labour, made respectively by, the landlord and the tenants, on a New York estate; together with the manner in which usages and opinions are changing among us; as well as certain of the reasons of these changes. The discriminating reader will probably be able to trace in these narratives the progress of those innovations on the great laws of morals which are becoming so very manifest in connection with this interest, setting at naught the plainest principles that God has transmitted to man for the government of his conduct, and all under the extraordinary pretence of favouring liberty! In this downward course, our picture embraces some of the proofs of that looseness of views on the subject of certain species of property which is, in a degree perhaps, inseparable from the semi-barbarous condition of a new settlement; the gradation of the squatter, from him who merely makes his pitch to crop a few fields in passing, to him who carries on the business by wholesale; and last, though not least in this catalogue of marauders, the anti-renter.

It would be idle to deny that the great principle which lies at the bottom of anti-rentism, if principle

(iii)

it can be called, is the assumption of a claim that the interests and wishes of numbers are to be respected, though done at a sacrifice of the clearest rights of the few. That this is not liberty, but tyranny in its worst form, every right-thinking and right-feeling man must be fully aware. Every one who knows much of the history of the past, and of the influence of classes, must understand, that whenever the educated, the affluent and the practised, choose to unite their means of combination and money to control the political destiny of a country, they become irresistible; making the most subservient tools of those very masses who vainly imagine *they* are the true guardians of their own liberties. The well-known election of 1840 is a memorable instance of the power of such a combination; though that was a combination formed mostly for the mere purposes of faction, sustained perhaps by the desperate designs of the insolvents of the country. Such a combination was necessarily wanting in union among the affluent; it had not the high support of principles to give it sanctity, and it affords little more than the proof of the power of money and leisure, when applied in a very doubtful cause, in wielding the masses of a great nation, to be the instruments of their own subjection. No well-intentioned American legislator, consequently, ought ever to lose sight of the fact, that each invasion of the right which he sanctions is a blow struck against liberty itself, which, in a country like this, has no auxiliary so certain or so powerful as justice.

The State of New York contains about 43,000 square miles of land; or something like 27,000,000 of acres. In 1783, its population must have been about 200,000 souls. With such a proportion between people and surface it is unnecessary to prove that the husbandman was not quite as dependent on the landholder, as the landholder was dependent on the husbandman. This would have been true, had the State been an island; but we all know it was surrounded by many other communities similarly situated, and that nothing else was so abundant as land. All notions of exactions and monopolies, therefore, must be untrue, as applied to those two interests at that day.

In 1786–7, the State of New York, then in possession of all powers on the subject, abolished entails, and otherwise brought its law of real estate in harmony with the institutions. At that time, hundreds, perhaps thousands, of the leases which have since become so obnoxious, were in existence. With the attention of the State drawn directly to the main subject, no one saw anything incompatible with the institutions in them. *It was felt that the landlords had bought the tenants to occupy their lands by the liberality of their concessions,* and that the latter were the obliged parties. Had the landlords of that day endeavoured to lease for one year, or for ten years, no tenants could have been found for wild lands; but it became a different thing, when the owner of the soil agreed to part with it for ever, in consideration of a very low rent, granting six or eight years free from any charge whatever, and consenting to receive the product of the soil itself in lieu of money. Then, indeed, men were not only willing to come into the terms, but eager; the best evidence of which is the fact, that the same tenants might have bought land,

out and out, in every direction around them, had
they not preferred the easier terms of the leases.
Now, that these same men, or their successors, have
become rich enough to care more to be rid of the
encumbrance of the rent than to keep their money,
the rights of the parties certainly are not altered.

In 1789, the Constitution of the United States went
into operation; New York being a party to its creation
and conditions. By that Constitution, the State deliberately deprived itself of the power to touch the
covenants of these leases, without conceding the
power to any other government; unless it might be
through a change of the Constitution itself. As a
necessary consequence, these leases, in a legal sense,
belong to the institutions of New York, instead of
being opposed to them. Not only is the spirit of the
institutions in harmony with these leases, but so is
the letter also. Men must draw a distinction between
the " spirit of the institutions" and their own " spirits;" the latter being often nothing more than a
stomach that is not easily satisfied. It would be just
as true to affirm that domestic slavery is opposed to
the institutions of the United States, as to say the
same of these leases. It would be just as rational to
maintain, because A. does not choose to make an associate of B., that he is acting in opposition to the
"spirit of the institutions," inasmuch as the Declaration of Independence advances the dogmas that men
are born equal, as it is to say it is opposed to the
same spirit, for B. to pay rent to A. according to his
covenant.

It is pretended that the durable leases are feuda.
in their nature. We do not conceive this to be true

but, admitting it to be so, it would only prove that feudality, to this extent, is a part of the institutions of the State. What is more, it would become a part over which the State itself has conceded all power of control, beyond that which it may remotely possess as one, out of twenty-eight communities. As respects this feudal feature, it is not easy to say where it must be looked for. It is not to be found in the simple fact of paying rent, for that is so general as to render the whole country feudal, could it be true; it cannot be in the circumstance that the rent is to be paid " in kind," as it is called, and in labour, for that is an advantage to the tenant, by affording him the option, since the penalty of a failure leaves the alternative of paying in money. It must be, therefore, that these leases are feudal because they run for ever! Now the length of the lease is clearly a concession to the tenant, and was so regarded when received; and there is not probably a single tenant, under lives, who would not gladly exchange his term of possession for that of one of these detestable durable leases !

Among the absurdities that have been circulated on this subject of feudality, it has been pretended that the well-known English statute of "*quia emptores*" has prohibited fines for alienation; or that the quarter-sales, fifth-sales, sixth-sales, &c. of our own leases were contrary to the law of the realm, when made. Under the common law, in certain cases of feudal tenures, the fines for alienation were an incident of the tenure. The statute of *quia emptores* abolished that general principle, but it in no manner forbade parties *to enter into covenants of the nature of quarter-sales,* did they see fit. The common law gives all the real estate to the eldest son. Our statute divides the real estate among the nearest of kin, without regard even to sex. It might just as well be pretended that the father cannot devise all his lands to his eldest son, under our statute, as to say that the law of Edward I. prevents parties from *bargaining* for quarter-sales. Altering a provision of the common law does not preclude parties from making covenants similar to its ancient provisions.

Feudal tenures were originally divided into two great classes; those which were called the military tenures, or knight's service, and *soccage.* The first tenure was that which became oppressive in the progress of society. Soccage was of two kinds; free and villian. The first has an affinity to our own system, as connected with these leases; the last never existed among us at all. When the knight's service, or military tenures of England were converted into free soccage, in the reign of Charles II., the concession was considered of a character so favourable to liberty as to be classed among the great measures of the time; one of which was the *habeas corpus* act!

The only feature of our own leases, in the least approaching " villian soccage," is that of the " day's works." But every one acquainted with the habits of American life, will understand that husbandmen, in general, throughout the northern States, would regard it as an advantage to be able to pay their debts in this way; and the law gives them an option, since a failure to pay " in kind," or in " work," merely incurs the forfeiture of paying what the particular thing is worth, in money. In point of fact, money has always been received for these "day's works," and at a stipulated price.

But, it is pretended, whatever may be the equity of these leasehold contracts, they are offensive to the tenants, and ought to be abrogated, for the peace of the State. The State is bound to make all classes of men respect its laws, and in nothing more so than in the fulfilment of their legal contracts. The greater the number of the offenders, the higher the obligation to act with decision and efficiency. To say that these disorganizers *ought* not to be put down, is to say that crime is to obtain impunity by its own extent; and to say that they *cannot* be put down " under our form of government," is a direct admission that the government is unequal to the discharge of one of the plainest and commonest obligations of all civilized society. If this be really so, the sooner we get rid of the present form of government the better. The notion of remedying *such* an evil by concession, is as puerile as it is dishonest. The larger the concessions become, the greater will be the exactions of a cormorant cupidity. As soon as quiet is obtained by these means, in reference to the leasehold tenures, it will be demanded by some fresh combination to attain some other end.

When Lee told Washington, at Monmouth, " Sir, your troops will not stand against British grenadiers," Washington is said to have answered, " Sir, you have never tried them." The same reply might be given to those miserable traducers of this republic, who, in order to obtain votes, affect to think there is not sufficient energy in its government to put down so bare-faced an attempt as this of the anti-renters

1

to alter the conditions of their own leases to suit their own convenience. The county of Delaware has, of itself, nobly given the lie to the assertion, the honest portion of its inhabitants scattering the knaves to the four winds, the moment there was a fair occasion made for·them to. act. A single, energetic proclamation from Albany, calling a "spade a spade," and not affecting to gloss over the disguised robbery of these anti-renters, and laying just principles fairly before the public mind, would of itself have crushed the evil in its germ. The people of New York, in their general capacity, are not the knaves their servants evidently suppose.

The assembly of New York, in its memorable session of 1846, has taxed the rents on long leases ; thus, not only taxing the same property twice, but imposing the worst sort of income-tax, or one aimed at a few individuals. It has "thimble-rigged" in its legislation, as Mr. Hugh Littlepage not unaptly terms it ; endeavouring to do that indirectly, which the Constitution will not permit it to do directly. In other words, as it can pass no direct law "impairing the obligation of contracts," while it *can* regulate descents, it has enacted, so far as one body of the legislature has power to enact anything, that on the *death* of a landlord the tenant may convert his lease into a mortgage, on discharging which he shall hold his land in fee !

We deem the first of these measures far more tyrannical than the attempt of Great Britain to tax her colonies, which brought about the revolution. It is of the same general character, that of unjust taxation ; while it is attended by circumstances of aggravation that were altogether wanting in the policy of the mother country. This is not a tax for revenue, which is not needed; but a tax to "choke off" the landlords, to use a common American phrase. It is clearly taxing *nothing*, or it is taxing the same property twice. It is done to conciliate three or four thousand voters, who are now in the market, at the expense of three or four hundred who, it is known, are not to be bought. It is unjust in its motives, its means and its end. The measure is discreditable to civilization, and an outrage on liberty.

But, the other law mentioned is an atrocity so grave, as to alarm every man of common principle in the State, were it not so feeble in its devices to cheat the Constitution, as to excite contempt. This extraordinary power is exercised because the legislature *can* control the law of descents, though it cannot "impair the obligation of contracts!" Had the law said at once that on the death of a landlord each of his tenants should *own* his farm in fee, the *ensemble* of the fraud would have been preserved, since the "law of descents" would have been so far regulated as to substitute one heir for another; but changing the *nature* of a contract, with a party who has nothing to do with the succession at all, is not so very clearly altering, or amending, the law of descents! It is scarcely necessary to say that every reputable court in the country, whether State or Federal, would brand such a law with the disgrace it merits.

But the worst feature of this law, or attempted law, remains to be noticed. It would have been a premium on murder. Murder *has* already been committed by these anti-renters, and that obviously to effect their ends; and they were to be told that whenever you shoot a landlord, as some have already often shot *at* them, you can convert your leasehold tenures into tenures in fee! The mode of valuation is so obvious, too, as to deserve a remark. A master was to settle the valuation on testimony. The witnesses of course would be " the neighbours," and a whole patent could swear for each other!

As democrats we protest most solemnly against such bare-faced frauds, such palpable cupidity and covetousness being termed anything but what they are. If they come of any party at all, it is the party of the devil. Democracy is a lofty and noble sentiment. It does not rob the poor to make the rich richer, nor the rich to favour the poor. It is just, and treats all men alike. It does not " impair the obligations of contracts." It is not the friend of a canting legislation, but, meaning right, dare act directly. There is no greater delusion than to suppose that true democracy has anything in common with injustice or roguery.

Nor is it an apology for anti-rentism, in any of its aspects, to say that leasehold tenures are inexpedient. The most expedient thing in existence is to do right. Were there no other objection to this anti-rent movement than its corrupting influence, that alone should set every wise man in the community firmly against it. We have seen too much of this earth, to be so easily convinced that there is any disadvantage, nay that there is not a positive advantage in the existence of large leasehold estates, when they carry with them no political power, as is the fact here. The common-place argument against them, that they defeat the civilization of a country, is not sustained by fact. The most civilized countries on earth are under this system; and this system, too, not entirely free from grave objections which do not exist among ourselves. That a poorer class of citizens have originally leased than have purchased lands in New York, is probably true; and it is equally probable that the effects of this poverty, and even of the tenure· in the infancy of a country, are to be traced on the estates. But this is taking a very one-sided view of the matter. The men who became tenants in moderate but comfortable circumstances, would have been mostly labourers on the farms of. others; but for these leasehold tenures. That is the benefit of the system in a new country, and the ultra friend of humanity, who decries the condition of a tenant, should remember that if he had not been in this very condition, he might have been in a worse. It is, indeed, one of the proofs of the insincerity of those who are decrying leases, on account of their aristocratic tendencies, that their destruction will necessarily condemn a numerous class of agriculturists, either to fall back into the ranks of the peasant or day-labourer, or to migrate, as is the case with so many of the same class in New England. In point of fact, the relation of landlord and tenant is one entirely natural and salutary, in a wealthy community, and one that is so much in accordance with the necessities of men, that no legislation can long prevent it. A state of things which will not encourage the rich to hold real estate would not be desirable, since it would be diverting their money, knowledge, liber-

1 *

ality, feelings and leisure, from the improvement of the soil, to objects neither so useful nor so praise-worthy.

The notion that every husbandman is to be a free-holder, is as Utopian in practice, as it would be to expect that all men were to be on the same level in fortune, condition, education and habits. As such a state of things as the last never yet did exist, it was probably never designed by divine wisdom that it should exist. The whole structure of society must be changed, even in this country, 'ere it could exist among ourselves, and the change would not have been made a month before the utter impracticability of such a social fusion would make itself felt by all.

We have elsewhere imputed much of the anti-rent feeling to provincial education and habits. This term has given the deepest offence to those who were most obnoxious to the charge. Nevertheless, our opinion is unchanged. We know that the distance between the cataract of Niagara and the Massachusetts line is a large hundred leagues, and that it is as great between Sandy Hook and the 45th parallel of lati-tude. Many excellent things, moral and physical, are to be found within these limits, beyond a ques-tion; but we happen to know by an experience that has extended to other quarters of the world, for a term now exceeding forty years, that more are to be found beyond them. If "honourable gentlemen" at Albany fancy the reverse, they must still permit us to believe they are too much under the influence of provincial notions.

THE REDSKINS.

CHAPTER I.

"Thy mother was a piece of virtue, and
She said—Thou wert my daughter; and thy father
Was duke of Milan; and his only heir
A princess;—no worse issued."

Tempest.

My uncle Ro and myself had been travelling together in the East, and had been absent from home fully five years, when we reached Paris. For eighteen months neither of us had seen a line from America, when we drove through the barriers, on our way from Egypt, viâ Algiers, Marseilles, and Lyons. Not once, in all that time, had we crossed our own track, in a way to enable us to pick up a straggling letter; and all our previous precautions to have the epistles meet us at different bankers in Italy, Turkey, and Malta, were thrown away.

My uncle was an old traveller—I might almost say, an old resident—in Europe; for he had passed no less than twenty years of his fifty-nine off the American continent. A bachelor, with nothing to do but to take care of a very ample estate, which was rapidly increasing in value by the enormous growth of the town of New York, and with tastes early formed by travelling, it was natural he should seek those regions where he most enjoyed himself. Hugh Roger Littlepage was born in 1786—the second son of my grandfather, Mordaunt Littlepage, and of Ursula Malbone, his wife. My own father, Malbone Littlepage, was the eldest child of that connexion; and he would have inherited the property of Ravensnest, in virtue of his birthright, had

he survived his own parents; but, dying young, I stepped
into what would otherwise have been his succession, in my
eighteenth year.   My uncle Ro, however, had got both
Satanstoe and Lilacsbush; two country-houses and farms,
which, while they did not aspire to the dignity of being
estates, were likely to prove more valuable, in the long run,
than the broad acres which were intended for the patrimony
of the elder brother.   My grandfather was affluent; for not
only had the fortune of the Littlepages centred in him, but
so did that of the Mordaunts, the wealthier family of the
two, together with some exceedingly liberal bequests from
a certain Col. Dirck Follock, or Van Valkenburgh; who,
though only a very distant connexion, chose to make my
great-grandmother's, or Anneke Mordaunt's, descendants
his heirs.   We all had enough; my aunts having handsome
legacies, in the way of bonds and mortgages, on an estate
called Mooseridge, in addition to some lots in town; while
my own sister, Martha, had a clear fifty thousand dollars in
money.   I had town-lots, also, which were becoming productive; and a special minority of seven years had made
an accumulation of cash that was well vested in New York
State stock, and which promised well for the future.   I say
a "special" minority; for both my father and grandfather,
in placing, the one, myself and a portion of the property,
and the other the remainder of my estate, under the guar-
dianship and ward of my uncle, had made a provision that
I was not to come into possession until I had completed my
twenty-fifth year.

I left college at twenty; and my uncle Ro, for so Martha and myself always called him, and so he was always
called by some twenty cousins, the offspring of our three
aunts;—but my uncle Ro, when I was done with college,
proposed to finish my education by travelling. 'As this was
only too agreeable to a young man, away we went, just
after the pressure of the great panic of 1836–7 was over,
and our "lots" were in tolerable security, and our stocks
safe.   In America it requires almost as much vigilance to
take care of property, as it does industry to acquire it.

Mr. Hugh Roger Littlepage—by the way, I bore the same
name, though I was always called Hugh, while my uncle
went by the different appellations of Roger, Ro, and Hodge,

among his familiars, as circumstances had rendered the associations sentimental, affectionate, or manly—Mr. Hugh Roger Littlepage, Senior, then, had a system of his own, in the way of aiding the scales to fall from American eyes, by means of seeing more clearly than one does, or can, at home, let him belong where he may, and in clearing the specks of provincialism from off the diamond of republican water. He had already seen enough to ascertain that while " our country," as this blessed nation is very apt on all occasions, appropriate or not, to be called by all who belong to it, as well as by a good many who do not, could teach a great deal to the old world, there was a possibility.—just a *possibility*, remark, is my word—that it might also learn a little. With a view, therefore, of acquiring knowledge seriatim, as it might be, he was for beginning with the hornbook, and going on regularly up to the belles-lettres and mathematics. The manner in which this was effected deserves a notice.

Most American travellers land in England, the country farthest advanced in material civilization ; then proceed to Italy, and perhaps to Greece, leaving Germany, and the less attractive regions of the north, to come in at the end of the chapter. My uncle's theory was to follow the order of time, and to begin with the ancients and end with the moderns ; though, in adopting such a rule, he admitted he somewhat lessened the pleasure of the novice ; since an American, fresh from the fresher fields of the western continent, might very well find delight in memorials of the past, more especially in England, which pall on his taste, and appear insignificant, after he has become familiar with the Temple of Neptune, the Parthenon, or what is left of it, and the Coliseum. I make no doubt that I lost a great deal of passing happiness in this way, by beginning at the beginning, or by beginning in Italy, and travelling north.

Such was our course, however ; and, landing at Leghorn, we did the peninsula effectually in a twelvemonth ; thence passed through Spain up to Paris, and proceeded on to Moscow and the Baltic, reaching England from Hamburg. When we had got through with the British isles, the antiquities of which seemed flat and uninteresting to me, after having seen those that were so much more *antique*, we returned to Paris, in order that I might become a man of the world, if possible, by rubbing off the provincial specks that had unavoidably adhered to the American diamond while in its obscurity.

My uncle Ro was fond of Paris, and he had actually become the owner of a small hotel in the faubourg, in which he retained a handsome furnished apartment for his own use. The remainder of the house was let to permanent tenants; but the whole of the first floor, and of the *entresol*, remained in his hands. As a special favour, he would allow some American family to occupy even his own apartment— or rather *appartement*, for the words are not exactly synonymous—when he intended to be absent for a term exceeding six months, using the money thus obtained in keeping the furniture in repair, and his handsome suite of rooms, including a *salon, salle à manger, ante-chambre, cabinet,* several *chambres à coucher,* and a *boudoir*—yes, a male *boudoir!* for so he affected to call it—in a condition to please even his fastidiousness.

On our arrival from England, we remained an entire season at Paris, all that time rubbing the specks off the diamond, when my uncle suddenly took it into his head that we ought to see the East. He had never been further than Greece, himself; and he now took a fancy to be my companion in such an excursion. We were gone two years and a half, visiting Greece, Constantinople, Asia Minor, the Holy Land, Petra, the Red Sea, Egypt quite to the second cataracts, and nearly the whole of Barbary. The latter region we threw in, by way of seeing something out of the common track. But so many hats and travelling-caps are to be met with, now-a-days, among the turbans, that a well-mannered Christian may get along almost anywhere without being spit upon. This is a great inducement for travelling generally, and ought to be so especially to an American, who, on the whole, incurs rather more risk now of suffering this humiliation at home, than he would even in Algiers. But the animus is everything in morals.

We had, then, been absent two years and a half from Paris, and had not seen a paper or received a letter from America in eighteen months, when we drove through the barrier. Even the letters and papers received or seen pro-viously to this last term, were of a private nature, and contained nothing of a general character. The "twenty millions"—it was only the other day they were called the "twelve millions"—but, the "twenty millions," we knew, had been looking up amazingly after the temporary depression of the moneyed crisis it had gone through; and the bankers had paid our drafts with confidence, and without extra charges, during the whole time we had been absent. It is true, Uncle Ro, as an experienced traveller, went well fortified in the way of credit—a precaution by no means unnecessary with Americans, after the cry that had been raised against us in the old world.

And here I wish to say one thing plainly, before I write another line. As for falling into the narrow, self-adulatory, provincial feeling of the American who has never left his mother's apron-string, and which causes him to swallow, open-mouthed, all the nonsense that is uttered to the world in the columns of newspapers, or in the pages of your yearling travellers, who go on "excursions" before they are half instructed in the social usages and the distinctive features of their own country, I hope I shall be just as far removed from such a weakness, in any passing remark that may flow from my pen, as from the crime of confounding principles and denying facts in a way to do discredit to the land of my birth and that of my ancestors. I have lived long enough in the "world," not meaning thereby the south-east corner of the north-west township of Connecticut, to understand that we are a vast way behind older nations, in *thought* as well as deed, in many things; while, on the opposite hand, they are a vast way behind us in others. I see no patriotism in concealing a wholesome truth; and least of all shall I be influenced by the puerility of a desire to hide anything of this nature, because I cannot communicate it to my countrymen without communicating it to the rest of the world. If England or France had acted on this narrow principle, where would have been their Shakspeares, their Sheridans, their Beaumonts and Fletchers, and their Molieres! No, no! great national truths are not to be treated as the gossiping surmises of village crones. He who reads what I *write*, therefore, must expect to find what I *think* of matters and things, and not exactly what he may happen to

think on the same subjects. Any one is at liberty to com
pare opinions with me; but I ask the privilege of possessing
some small liberty of conscience in what is, far and near,
proclaimed to be the *only* free country on the earth. By
" far and near," I mean from the St. Croix to the Rio
Grande, and from Cape Cod to the entrance of St. Juan de
Fuca, and a pretty farm it makes, the " interval" that lies
between 'these limits! One may call it " far and near"
without the imputation of obscurity, or that of vanity.

Our tour was completed, in spite of all annoyances; and
here we were again, within the walls of magnificent Paris!
The postilions had been told to drive to the hotel, in the rue
St. Dominique; and we sat down to dinner, an hour after
our arrival, under our own roof. My uncle's tenant had
left the apartment a month before, according to agreement;
and the porter and his wife had engaged a cook, set the
rooms in order, and prepared everything for our arrival.

" It must be owned, Hugh," said my uncle, as he finished
his soup that day, " one *may* live quite comfortably in Paris,
if he possess the *savoir vivre*. Nevertheless, I have a
strong desire to get a taste of native air. One may say and
think what he pleases about the Paris pleasures, and the
Paris *cuisine,* and all' that sort of things; but " home is
home, be it ever so homely." A ' d'Inde aux truffes' is capital eating; so is a turkey with cranberry sauce. I sometimes think I could fancy even a pumpkin pie, though there
is not a fragment of the rock of Plymouth in the granite of
my frame."

" I have always told you, sir, that America is a capital
eating and drinking country, let it want civilization in
other matters, as much as it may."

" Capital for eating and drinking, Hugh, if you can keep
clear of the grease, in the first place, and find a real cook,
in the second. There is as much difference between the
cookery of New England, for instance, and that of the
Middle States, barring the Dutch, as there is between that
of England and Germany. The cookery of the Middle
States, and of the Southern States, too, though that savours
a little of the West Indies—but the cookery of the Middle
States is English, in its best sense; meaning the hearty,
substantial, savoury dishes of the English in their true do-

mestic life, with their roast-beef underdone, their beefsteaks done to a turn, their chops full of gravy, their mutton-broth, legs-of-mutton, *et id omne genus.* We have some capital things of our own, too; such as canvass-backs, reedbirds, sheepshead, shad, and blackfish. The difference between New England and the Middle States is still quite observable, though in my younger days it was *patent.* I suppose the cause has been the more provincial origin, and the more provincial habits, of our neighbours. By George! Hugh, one could fancy clam-soup just now, eh!"

"Clam-soup, sir, well made, is one of the most delicious soups in the world. If the cooks of Paris could get hold of the dish, it would set them up for a whole season."

"What is ' crême de Bavière,' and all such nick-nacks, boy, to a good plateful of clam-soup? Well made, as you say—made as a cook of Jennings' used to make it, thirty years since. Did I ever mention that fellow's soup to you before, Hugh?"

"Often, sir. I have tasted very excellent clam-soup, however, that he never saw. Of course you mean soup just flavoured by the little hard-clam—none of your vulgar *potage* à la soft-clam?"

"Soft-clams be hanged! they are not made for gentlemen to eat. Of course I mean the hard-clam, and the small clam, too—

> Here 's your fine clams,
> As white as snow; ·
> On Rockaway
> These clams do grow.

The cries of New York are quite going out, like everything else at home that is twenty years old. Shall I send you some of this eternal *poulet à la Marengo?* I wish it were honest American boiled fowl, with a delicate bit of shoat-pork alongside of it. I feel amazingly *homeish* this evening, Hugh!"

"It is quite natural, my dear uncle Ro; and I own to the ' soft impeachment' myself. Here have we both been absent from our native land five years, and half that time almost without hearing from it. We know that Jacob"— this was a free negro who served my uncle, a relic of the

2

old domestic system of the colonies, whose name would have been Jaaf, or Yop, thirty years before—" has gone to our banker's for letters and papers; and that naturally draws our thoughts to the other side of the Atlantic. I dare say we shall both feel relieved at breakfast to-morrow, when we shall have read our respective despatches."

" Come, let us take a glass of wine together, in the good old York fashion, Hugh. Your father and I, when boys, never thought of wetting our lips with the half-glass of Madeira that fell to our share, without saying, ' Good health, Mall!' ' Good health, Hodge!' "

" With all my heart, uncle Ro. The custom was getting to be a little obsolete even before I left home; but it is almost an American custom, by sticking to us longer than to most people."

" Henri !"

This was my uncle's maitre d'hotel, whom he had kept at board-wages the whole time of our absence, in order to make sure of his ease, quiet, taste, skill, and honesty, on his return.

" Monsieur !"

" I dare say"—my uncle spoke French exceedingly well for a foreigner; but it is better to translate what he said as we go—" I dare say this glass of vin de Bourgogne is very good; it *looks* good, and it came from a wine-merchant on whom I can rely; but Mons. Hugh and I are going to drink together, à l'Américaine, and I dare say you will let us have a glass of Madeira, though it is somewhat late in the dinner to take it."

" Tres volontiers, Messieurs—it is my happiness to oblige you."

Uncle Ro and I took the Madeira together; but I cannot say much in favour of its quality.

" What a capital thing is a good Newtown pippin !" exclaimed my uncle, after eating a while in silence. " They talk a great deal about their *poire beurrée*, here at Paris; but, to my fancy, it will not compare with the Newtowners we grow at Satanstoe, where, by the way, the fruit is rather better, I think, than that one finds across the river, at Newtown itself."

" They are capital apples, sir; and your orchard at Satanstoe is one of the best I know, or rather what is left of it ; for I believe a portion of your trees are in what is now a suburb of Dibbletonborough ?"

" Yes, blast that place ! I wish I had never parted with a foot of the old neck, though I did rather make money by the sale. But money is no compensation for the affections."

" *Rather* make money, my dear sir ! Pray, may I ask what Satanstoe was valued at, when you got it from my grandfather ?"

" Pretty well up, Hugh ; for it was, and indeed *is*, a first-rate farm. Including sedges and salt-meadows, you will remember that there are quite five hundred acres of it, altogether."

" Which you inherited in 1829 ?"

" Of course ; that was the year of my father's death. Why, the place was thought to be worth about thirty thousand dollars at that time ; but land was rather low in Westchester in 1829."

" And you sold two hundred acres, including the point, the harbour, and a good deal of the sedges, for the moderate modicum of one hundred and ten thousand, cash. A tolerable sale, sir !"

" No, not cash. I got only eighty thousand down, while thirty thousand were secured by mortgage."

" Which mortgage you hold yet, I dare say, if the truth were told, covering the whole city of Dibbletonborough. A city ought to be good security for thirty thousand dollars ?"

" It is not, nevertheless, in this case. The speculators who bought of me in 1835 laid out their town, built a hotel, a wharf, and a warehouse, and then had an auction. They sold four hundred lots, each twenty-five feet by a hundred regulation size, you see, at an average of two hundred and fifty dollars, receiving one-half, or fifty thousand dollars, down, and leaving the balance on mortgage. Soon after this, the bubble burst, and the best lot at Dibbletonborough would not bring, under the hammer, twenty dollars. The hotel and the warehouse stand alone in their glory, and will thus stand until they fall, which will not be a thousand years hence, I rather think."

" And what is the condition of the town-plot ?"

"Bad enough. The landmarks are disappearing, and it would cost any man who should attempt it, the value of his lot, to hire a surveyor to find his twenty-five by a hundred"

"But your mortgage is good?"

"Ay, good in one sense; but it would puzzle a Philadelphia lawyer to foreclose it. Why, the equitable interests in that town-plot, people the place of themselves. I ordered my agent to commence buying up the rights, as the shortest process of getting rid of them; and he told me in the very last letter I received, that he had succeeded in purchasing the titles to three hundred and seventeen of the lots, at an average price of ten dollars. The remainder, I suppose, will have to be absorbed."

"Absorbed! That is a process I never heard of, as applied to land."

"There is a good deal of it done, notwithstanding, in America. It is merely including within your own possession, adjacent land for which no claimant appears. What can I do? No owners are to be found; and then my mortgage is always a title. A possession of twenty years under a mortgage is as good as a deed in fee-simple, with full covenants of warranty, barring minors and *femmes covert*."

"You did better by Lilacsbush?"

"Ah, *that* was a clean transaction, and has left no drawbacks. Lilacsbush being on the island of Manhattan, one is sure there will be a town there, some day or other. It is true, the property lies quite eight miles from the City Hall; nevertheless, it has a value, and can always be sold at something near it. Then the plan of New York is made and recorded, and one can find his lots. Nor can any man say when the town will not reach Kingsbridge."

"You got a round price for the Bush, too, I have heard, sir?"

"I got three hundred and twenty-five thousand dollars, in hard cash. I would give no credit, and have every dollar of the money, at this moment, in good six per cent. stock of the States of New York and Ohio."

"Which some persons in this part of the world would fancy to be no very secure investment."

"More fools they. America is a glorious country, after all, Hugh; and it is a pride and a satisfaction to belong to it. Look back at it, as I can remember it, a nation spit upon by all the rest of Christendom——"

"You must at least own, my dear sir," I put in, somewhat pertly, perhaps, "the example might tempt other people; for, if ever there was a nation that is assiduously spitting on itself, it is our own beloved land."

"True, it has that nasty custom in excess, and it grows worse instead of better, as the influence of the better mannered and better educated diminishes; but this is a spot on the sun—a mere flaw in the diamond, that friction will take out. But what a country—what a glorious country, in truth, it is! You have now done the civilized parts of the old world pretty thoroughly, my dear boy, and must be persuaded, yourself, of the superiority of your native land."

"I remember you have always used this language, uncle Ro; yet have you passed nearly one-half of your time *out* of that glorious country, since you have reached man's estate."

"The mere consequence of accidents and tastes. I do not mean that America is a country for a bachelor, to begin with; the means of amusement for those who have no domestic hearths, are too limited for the bachelor. Nor do I mean that society in America, in its ordinary meaning, is in any way as well-ordered, as tasteful, as well-mannered, as agreeable, or as instructive and useful, as society in almost any European country I know. I have never supposed that the man of leisure, apart from the affections, could ever enjoy himself half as much at home, as he may enjoy himself in this part of the world; and I am willing to admit that, intellectually, most gentlemen in a great European capital live as much in one day, as they would live in a week in such places as New York, and Philadelphia, and Baltimore."

"You do not include Boston, I perceive, sir."

"Of Boston I say nothing. They take the mind hard there, and we had better let such a state of things alone. But as respects a man or woman of leisure, a man or woman of taste, a man or woman of refinement generally, I am willing enough to admit that, *cæteris paribus*, each can find far more enjoyment in Europe than in America. But the philosopher, the philanthropist, the political economist—in

2 *

a word, the patriot, may well exult in such elements of profound national superiority as may be found in America.".

- "I hope these elements are not so profound but they can
be dug up at need, uncle Ro?"

"There will be little difficulty in doing that, my boy.
Look at the equality of the laws, to begin with. They are
made on the principles of natural justice, and are intended
for the benefit of society—for the poor as well as the rich."

"Are they also intended for the rich as well as the poor?"

"Well, I will grant you a slight blemish is beginning to
appear, in that particular. It is a failing incidental to humanity, and we must not expect perfection. There is certainly a slight disposition to legislate for numbers, in order
to obtain support at the polls, which has made the relation
of debtor and creditor a little insecure, possibly; but prudence can easily get along with that. It is erring on the
right side, is it not, to favour the poor instead of the rich,
if either is to be preferred?"

"Justice would favour neither, but treat all alike. I have
always heard that the tyranny of numbers was the worst
tyranny in the world."

"Perhaps it is, where there is actually tyranny, and for
a very obvious reason. One tyrant is sooner satisfied than
a million, and has even a greater sense of responsibility. I
can easily conceive that the Czar himself, if disposed to be
a tyrant, which I am far from thinking to be the case with
Nicholas, might hesitate about doing that, under his undivided responsibility, which one of our majorities would do,
without even being conscious of the oppression it exercised,
or caring at all about it. But, on the whole, we do little of
the last, and not in the least enough to counterbalance the
immense advantages of the system."

"I have heard very discreet men say that the worst symptom of our system is the gradual decay of justice among
us. The judges have lost most of their influence, and the
jurors are getting to be law-makers, as well as law-
breakers."

"There is a good deal of truth in that, I will acknowledge, also; and you hear it asked constantly, in a case of
any interest, not which party is in the right, but *who* is on
the jury. But I contend for no perfection; all I say is, that

he country is a glorious country, and that you and I have every reason to be proud that old Hugh Roger, our predecessor and namesake, saw fit to transplant himself into it, a century and a half since."

"I dare say now, uncle Ro, it would strike most Europeans as singular that a man should be proud of having been born an American—Manhattanese, as you and I both were."

"All that may be true, for there have been calculated attempts to bring us into discredit of late, by harping on the failure of certain States to pay the interest on their debts. But all that is easily answered, and more so by you and me as New Yorkers. There is not a nation in Europe that would pay its interest, if those who are taxed to do so had the control of these taxes, and the power to say whether they were to be levied or not."

"I do not see how that mends the matter. These countries tell us that such is the effect of your *system* there, while we are too honest to allow such a system to *exist* in this part of the world."

"Pooh! all gammon, that. They prevent the existence of our system for very different reasons, and they coerce the payment of the interest on their debts that they may borrow more. This business of repudiation, as it is called, however, has been miserably misrepresented; and there is no answering a falsehood by an argument. No American State has repudiated its debt, that I know of, though several have been unable to meet their engagements as they have fallen due."

"*Unable*, uncle Ro?"

"Yes, *unable*—that is the precise word. Take Pennsylvania, for instance; that is one of the richest communities in the civilized world; its coal and iron alone would make any country affluent, and a portion of its agricultural population is one of the most affluent I know of. Nevertheless, Pennsylvania, owing to a concurrence of events, *could* not pay the interest on her debt for two years and a half, though she is doing it now, and will doubtless continue to do it. The sudden breaking down of that colossal moneyed institution, the *soi-disant* Bank of the United States, after it ceased to be in reality a bank of the government, brought about such a state of the circulation as rendered payment, by any of the ordinary means known to government, *impossible.* I know what I say, and repeat *impossible.* It is well known that many persons, accustomed to affluence, had to carry their plate to the mint, in order to obtain money to go to market. Then something may be attributed to the institutions, without disparaging a people's honesty. Our institutions are popular, just as those of France are the reverse; and the people, they who were on the spot—the home creditor, with his account unpaid, and with his friends and relatives in the legislature, and present to aid him, contended for his own money, before any should be sent abroad."

" Was that exactly right, sir?"

" Certainly not ; it was exactly wrong, but very particularly natural. Do you suppose the King of France would not take the money for his civil list, if circumstances should compel the country to suspend on the debt for a year or two, or the ministers their salaries? My word for it, each and all of them would prefer themselves as creditors, and act accordingly. Every one of these countries has suspended in some form or other, and in many instances balanced the account with the sponge. Their clamour against us is altogether calculated with a view to political effect."

" Still, I wish Pennsylvania, for instance, had continued to pay, at every hazard."

" It is well enough to wish, Hugh; but it is wishing for an impossibility. Then you and I, as New Yorkers, have nothing to do with the debt of Pennsylvania, no more than London would have to do with the debt of Dublin or Quebec. *We* have always paid *our* interest, and, what is more, paid it more honestly, if honesty be the point, than even England has paid hers. When *our* banks suspended, the State paid its interest in as much paper as would buy the specie in open market ; whereas England made paper legal tender, and paid the interest on her debt in it for something like five-and-twenty years, and, that, too, when her paper was at a large discount. I knew of one American who held near a million of dollars in the English debt, on which he had to take unconvertible paper for the interest for a long series of years. No, no! this is all gammon, Hugh, and is not to be regarded as making us a whit worse than our neighbours. The. equality of our laws is the fact in which I glory !"

" If the rich stood as fair a chance as the poor, uncle Ro."

" There *is* a screw loose there, I must confess ; but it amounts to no great matter.".

" Then the late bankrupt law ?"

"Ay, that was an infernal procedure—that much I will acknowledge, too. It was special legislation enacted to pay particular debts, and the law was repealed as soon as it had done its duty. That is a much darker spot in our history than what is called repudiation, though perfectly honest men voted for it."

" Did you ever hear of a farce they got up about it at New York, just after we sailed ?"

" Never ; what was it, Hugh ? though American plays are pretty much all farces."

" This was a little better than common, and, on the whole, really clever. It is the old story of Faust, in which a young spendthrift sells himself, soul and body, to the devil. On a certain evening, as he is making merry with a set of wild companions, his creditor arrives, and, insisting on seeing the master, is admitted by the servant. He comes on, club-footed and behorned, as usual, and betai'ed, too, I believe ; but Tom is not to be scared by trifles. He insists on his guest's being seated, on his taking a glass of wine, and then on Dick's finishing his song. But, though the rest of the company had signed no bonds to Satan, they had certain outstanding book-debts, which made them excessively uncomfortable ; and the odour of brimstone being rather strong, Tom arose, approached his guest, and desired to know the nature of the particular business he had mentioned to his servant. ' This bond, sir,' said Satan, significantly. ' This bond ? what of it, pray ? It seems all right.' ' Is not that your signature ?' ' I admit it.' ' Signed in your blood ?' 'A conceit of your own ; I told you at the time that ink was just as good in law.' ' It is past due, seven minutes and fourteen seconds.' ' So it is, I declare ! but what of that ?' ' I demand payment.' ' Nonsense ! no one thinks of paying now-a-days. Why, even Pennsylvania and Maryland don't pay.' ' I insist on payment.

'Oh! you do, do you?' Tom draws a paper from his pocket, and adds, magnificently, ' There, then, if you 're so urgent—there is a discharge under the new bankrupt law, signed Smith Thompson.' This knocked the devil into a cocked-hat at once."

My uncle laughed heartily at my story ; but, instead of taking the matter as I had fancied he might, it made him think better of the country than ever.

" Well, Hugh, we have wit among us, it must be confessed," he cried, with the tears running down his cheeks, " if we have some rascally laws, and some rascals to administer them. But here comes Jacob with his letters and papers—I declare, the fellow has a large basket-full."

Jacob, a highly respectable black, and the great-grandson of an old negro named Jaaf, or Yop, who was then living on my own estate at Ravensnest, had just then entered, with the porter and himself lugging in the basket in question. There were several hundred newspapers, and quite a hundred letters. The sight brought home and America clearly and vividly before us ; and, having nearly finished the dessert, we rose to look at the packages. It was no small task to sort our mail, there being so many letters and packages to be divided.

" Here are some newspapers I never saw before," said my uncle, as he tumbled over the pile ; " ' The Guardian of the Soil'—that must have something to do with Oregon."

" I dare say it has, sir. Here are at least a dozen letters from my sister."

"Ay, *your* sister is single, and can still think of her brother ; but mine are married, and one letter a-year would be a great deal. This is my dear old mother's hand, however ; that is something. Ursula Malbone would never forget her child. Well, *bon soir*, Hugh. Each of us has enough to do for one evening."

"*Au revoir*, sir. We shall meet at ten to-morrow, when we can compare our news, and exchange gossip."

CHAPTER II.

" Why droops my lord, like over-ripen'd corn,
Hanging the head at Ceres' plenteous load?"
King Henry VI.

I DID not get into my bed that night until two, nor was I ou of it until half-past nine. It was near eleven when Jacob came to tell me his master was in the *salle à manger,* and ready to eat his breakfast. I hastened up stairs, sleeping in the *entresol,* and was at table with my uncle in three minutes. I observed, on entering, that he was very grave, and I now perceived that a couple of letters, and several American newspapers, lay near him. His " Good morrow, Hugh," was kind and affectionate as usual, but I fancied it sad.

" No bad news from home, I hope, sir!" I exclaimed under the first impulse of feeling. " Martha's last letter is of quite recent date, and she writes very cheerfully. I *know* that my grandmother was perfectly well, six weeks since."

" I know the same, Hugh, for I have a letter from herself, written with her own blessed hand. My mother is in excellent health for a woman of fourscore; but she naturally wishes to see us, and you in particular. Grandchildren are ever the pets with grandmothers."

" I am glad to hear all this, sir; for I was really afraid, on entering the room, that you had received some unpleasant news."

"And is all your news pleasant, after so long a silence?"

" Nothing that is disagreeable, I do assure you. Patt writes in charming spirits, and I dare say is in blooming beauty by this time, though she tells me that she is generally thought rather plain. *That* is impossible; for you know when we left her, at fifteen, she had every promise of great beauty."

"As you say, it is impossible that Martha Littlepage should be anything but handsome; for fifteen is an age when, in America, one may safely predict the woman's appearance. Your sister is preparing for you an agreeable surprise. I have heard old persons say that she was very like my mother at the same time of life; and Dus Malbone was a sort of toast once in the forest."

"I dare say it is all as you think; more especially as there are several allusions to a certain Harry Beekman in her letters, at which I should feel flattered, were I in Mr. Harry's place. Do you happen to know anything of such a family as the Beekmans, sir?"

My uncle looked up in a little surprise at this question. A thorough New Yorker by birth, associations, alliances and feelings, he held all the old names of the colony and State in profound respect; and I had often heard him sneer at the manner in which the new-comers of my day, who had appeared among us to blossom like the rose, scattered their odours through the land. It was but a natural thing that a community which had grown in population, in half a century, from half a million to two millions and a half, and that as much by immigration from adjoining communities as by natural increase, should undergo some change of feeling in this respect; but, on the other hand, it was just as natural that the true New Yorker should not.

"Of course you know, Hugh, that it is an ancient and respected name among us," answered my uncle, after he had given me the look of surprise I have already mentioned. "There is a branch of the Beekmans, or Bakemans, as we used to call them, settled near Satanstoe; and I dare say that your sister, in her frequent visits to my mother, has met with them. The association would be but natural; and the other feeling to which you allude is, I dare say, but natural to the association, though I cannot say I ever experienced it."

"You will still adhere to your asseverations of never having been the victim of Cupid, I find, sir."

"Hugh, Hugh! let us trifle no more. There *is* news from home that has almost broken my heart."

I sat gazing at my uncle in wonder and alarm, while he placed both his hands on his face, as if to exclude this wicked world, and all it contained, from his sight. I did not speak, for I saw that the old gentleman was really affected, but waited his pleasure to communicate more. My impatience was soon relieved, however, as the hands were removed, and I once more caught a view of my uncle's handsome, but clouded countenance.

" May I ask the nature of this news ?" I then ventured to inquire.

" You may, and I shall now tell you. It is proper, indeed, that you should hear all, and understand it all; for you have a direct interest in the matter, and a large portion of your property is dependent on the result. Had not the manor troubles, as they were called, been spoken of before we left home ?"

" Certainly, though not to any great extent. We saw something of it in the papers, I remember, just before we went to Russia; and I recollect you mentioned it as a discreditable affair to the State, though likely to lead to no very important result."

" So I then thought; but that hope has been delusive. There were some reasons why a population like ours should chafe under the situation of the estate of the late Patroon that I thought natural, though unjustifiable; for it is unhappily too much a law of humanity to do that which is wrong, more especially in matters connected with the pocket."

" I do not exactly understand your allusion, sir."

" It is easily explained. The Van Rensselaer property is, in the first place, of great extent—the manor, as it is still called and once was, spreading east and west eight-and-forty miles, and north and south twenty-four. With a few immaterial exceptions, including the sites of three or four towns, three of which are cities containing respectively six, twenty and forty thousand souls, this large surface was the property of a single individual. Since his death, it has become the property of two, subject to the conditions of the leases, of which by far the greater portion are what are called durable."

" I have heard all this, of course, sir, and know something of it myself. But what is a durable lease ? for I believe we have none of that nature at Ravensnest."

" No ; your leases are all for three lives, and most of them renewals at that. There are two sorts of 'durable leases,' as we term them, in use among the landlords of New York. Both give the tenant a permanent interest

2

being leases for ever, reserving an annual rent, with the
right to distrain, and covenants of re-entry.   But one class
of these leases gives the tenant a right at any time to demand a deed in fee-simple, on the payment of a stipulated
sum ; while the other gives him no such privilege.   Thus
one class of these leases is called ' a durable lease with a
clause of redemption ;' while the other is a simple ' durable
lease.' "

"And are there any new difficulties in relation to the
manor rents ?"

" Far worse than that ; the contagion has spread, until
the greatest ills that have been predicted from democratic
institutions, by their worst enemies, seriously menace the
country.   I am afraid, Hugh, I shall not be able to call
New York, any longer, an exception to the evil example of
a neighbourhood, or the country itself a glorious country."

" This is so serious, sir, that, were it not that your looks
denote the contrary, I might be disposed to doubt your
words."

" I fear my words are only too true.   Dunning has written me a long account of his own, made out with the precision of a lawyer ; and, in addition, he has sent me divers
papers, some of which openly contend for what is substantially a new division of property, and what in effect would
be agrarian laws."

" Surely, my dear uncle, you cannot seriously apprehend
anything of that nature from our order-loving, law-loving,
property-loving Americans !"

" Your last description may contain the secret of the
whole movement.   The love of property may be so strong
as to induce them to do a great many things they ought not
to do.   I certainly do not apprehend that any direct attempt
is about to be made, in New York, to divide its property ;
nor do I fear any open, declared agrarian statute ; for what
I apprehend is to come through indirect and gradual innovations on the right, that will be made to assume the delusive aspect of justice and equal rights, and thus undermine
the principles of the people, before they are aware of the
danger themselves.   In order that you may not only understand me, but may understand facts that are of the last
importance to your own pocket, I will first tell you what

has been done, and then tell you what I fear is to follow. The first difficulty——or, rather, the first difficulty of recent occurrence——arose at the death of the late Patroon. I say of recent occurrence, since Dunning writes me that, during the administration of John Jay, an attempt to resist the payment of rent was made on the manor of the Livingstons ; but *he* put it down *instanter*."

".Yes, I should rather think that roguery would not be apt to prosper, while the execution of the laws was entrusted to such a man. The age of such politicians, however, seems to have ended among us."

"It did not prosper. Governor Jay met the pretension as we all know such a man would meet it ; and the matter died away, and has been nearly forgotten. It is worthy of remark, that *he* PUT THE EVIL DOWN. But this is not the age of John Jays. To proceed to my narrative : When the late Patroon died, there was due to him a sum of something like two hundred thousand dollars of back-rents, and of which he had made a special disposition in his will, vesting the money in trustees for a certain purpose. It was the attempt to collect this money which first gave rise to dissatisfaction. Those who had been debtors so long, were reluctant to pay. In casting round for the means to escape from the payment of their just debts, these men, feeling the power that numbers ever give over right in America, combined to resist with others who again had in view a project to get rid of the rents altogether. Out of this combination grew what have been called the ' manor troubles.' Men appeared in a sort of mock-Indian dress, calico shirts thrown over their other clothes, and with a species of calico masks on their faces, who resisted the bailiffs' processes, and completely prevented the collection of rents. These men were armed, mostly with rifles ; and it was finally found necessary to call out a strong body of the militia, in order to protect the civil officers in the execution of their duties."

"All this occurred before we went to the East. I had supposed *those* anti-renters, as they were called, had been effectually put down."

" In appearance they were. But the very governor who called the militia into the field, referred the subject of the

'*griefs*' of the tenants to the legislature, as if they were
actually aggrieved citizens, when in truth it was the landlords, or the Rensselaers, for at that time the ' troubles' were
confined to their property, who were the aggrieved parties.
This false step has done an incalculable amount of mischief,
if it do not prove the entering wedge to rive asunder the
institutions of the State."

" It is extraordinary, when such things occur, that any
man can mistake his duty. Why were the tenants thus
spoken of, while nothing was said beyond what the law
compelled in favour of the landlords ?"

" I can see no reason but the fact that the Rensselaers
were only two, and that the disaffected tenants were proba
bly two thousand. With all the cry of aristocracy, and
feudality, and nobility, neither of the Rensselaers, by the
letter of the law, has one particle more of political power,
or political right, than his own coachman or footman, if the
last be a white man ; while, in practice, he is in many things
getting to be less protected."

" Then you think, sir, that this matter has gained force
from the circumstance that so many votes depend on it ?"

" Out of all question. Its success depends on the violations of principles that we have been so long taught to hold
sacred, that nothing short of the over-ruling and corrupting
influence of politics would dare to assail them. If there
were a landlord to each farm, as well as a tenant, universal
indifference would prevail as to the griefs of the tenants ;
and if two to one tenant, universal indignation at their
impudence."

" Of what particular griefs do the tenants complain ?"

" You mean the Rensselaer tenants, I suppose ? Why,
they *complain* of such covenants as they can, though their
deepest affliction is to be found in the fact that they do not
own other men's lands. The Patroon had quarter sales on
many of his farms—those that were let in the last century."

" Well, what of that ? A bargain to allow of quarter
sales is just as fair as any other bargain."

" It is fairer, in fact, than most bargains, when you come
to analyze it, since there is a very good reason why it should
accompany a perpetual lease. Is it to be supposed that a
landlord has no interest in the character and habits of his

tenants? He has the closest interest in it possible, and no prudent man should let his lands without holding some sort of control over the assignment of leases. Now, there are but two modes of doing this; either by holding over the tenant a power through his interests, or a direct veto dependent solely on the landlord's will."

"The last would be apt to raise a pretty cry of tyranny and feudality in America!"

"Pretty cries on such subjects are very easily raised in America. More people join in them than understand what they mean. Nevertheless, it is quite as just, when two men bargain, that he who owns every right in the land before the bargain is made, should retain this right over his property, which he consents to part with only with limitations, as that he should grant it to another. These men, in their clamour, forget that, until their leases were obtained, they had no right in their lands at all, and that what they have got is through those very leases of which they complain; take away the leases, and they would have no rights remaining. Now, on what principle can honest men pretend that they have rights beyond the leases? On the supposition, even, that the bargains are hard, what have governors and legislators to do with thrusting themselves in between parties so situated, as special umpires? I should object to such umpires, moreover, on the general and controlling principle that must govern all righteous arbitration—your governors and legislators are not *impartial;* they are political or party men, one may say, without exception; and such umpires, when votes are in the question, are to be sorely distrusted. I would as soon trust my interests to the decision of feed counsel, as trust them to such judges."

"I wonder the really impartial and upright portion of the community do not rise in their might, and put this thing down—rip it up, root and branch, and cast it away, at once."

"That is the weak point of our system, which has a hundred strong points, while it has this besetting vice. Our laws are not only made, but they are administered, on the supposition that there are both honesty and intelligence enough in the body of the community to see them *well* made, and *well* administered. But the sad reality shows

3 *

that good men are commonly passive, until abuses become
intolerable; it being the designing rogue and manager who
is usually the most active.   Vigilant philanthropists *do* exist,
I will allow; but it is in such small numbers as to effect
little on the whole, and nothing at all when opposed by the
zeal of a mercenary opposition.   No, no—little is ever to
be expected, in a political sense, from the activity of virtue;
while a great deal may be looked for from the activity of
vice."

"You do not take a very favourable view of humanity,
sir."

"I speak of the world as I have found it in both hemispheres, or, as your neighbour the magistrate 'Squire Newcome has it, the ' four hemispheres.'   Our representation is,
at the best, but an average of the qualities of the whole
community, somewhat lessened by the fact that men of real
merit have taken a disgust at a state of things that is not
very tempting to their habits or tastes.   As for a quarter
sale, I can see no more hardship in it than there is in paying the rent itself; and, by giving the landlord this check
on the transfer of his lands, he compels a compromise that
maintains what is just.   The tenant is not obliged to sell,
and he makes his conditions accordingly, when he has a
good tenant to offer in his stead.   When he offers a bad
tenant, he ought to pay for it."

"Many persons with us would think it very aristocratic,"
I cried, laughingly, "that a landlord should have it in his
power to say, I will not accept this or that substitute for
yourself."

"It is just as aristocratic, and no more so, than it would
be to put it in the power of the tenant to say to the landlord,
you *shall* accept this or that tenant at my hands.   The
covenant of the quarter sale gives each party a control in
the matter; and the result has ever been a compromise that
is perfectly fair, as it is hardly possible that the circumstance should have been overlooked in making the bargain;
and he who knows anything of such matters, knows that
every exaction of this sort is always considered in the
rent.   As for feudality, so long as the power to alienate
exists at all in the tenant, he does not hold by a feudal
tenure.   He has bought himself from all such tenures by

his covenant of quarter sale; and it only remains to say whether, having agreed to such a bargain in order to obtain this advantage, he should pay the stipulated price or not."

"I understand you, sir. It is easy to come at the equity of this matter, if one will only go back to the original facts which colour it. The tenant had no rights at all until he got his lease, and can have no rights which that lease does not confer."

"Then the cry is raised of feudal privileges, because some of the Rensselaer tenants are obliged to find so many days' work with their teams, or substitutes, to the landlord, and even because they have to pay annually a pair of fat fowls! *We* have seen enough of America, Hugh, to know that most husbandmen would be delighted to have the privilege of paying their debts in chickens and work, instead of in money, which renders the cry only so much the more wicked. But what is there more feudal in a tenant's thus paying his landlord, than in a butcher's contracting to furnish so much meat for a series of years, or a mail contractor's agreeing to carry the mail in a four-horse coach for a term of years, eh? No one objects to the rent in wheat; and why should they object to the rent in chickens? Is it because our republican farmers have got to be so *aristocratic* themselves, that they do not like to be thought poulterers? This is being aristocratic on the other side. These dignitaries should remember that if it be plebeian to furnish fowls, it is plebeian to receive them; and if the tenant has to find an individual who has to submit to the degradation of tendering a pair of fat fowls, the landlord has to find an individual who has to submit to the degradation of taking them, and of putting them away in the larder. It seems to me that one is an offset to the other."

"But, if I remember rightly, uncle Ro, these little matters were always commuted for in money."

"They always must lie at the option of the tenant, unless the covenants went to forfeiture, which I never heard that they did; for the failure to pay in kind at the time stipulated, would only involve a payment in money afterwards. The most surprising part of this whole transaction is, that men among us hold the doctrine that these leasehold estates are opposed to our institutions, when, being guarantied *by* the institutions, they in truth form a part of them. Were it not for these very institutions, to which they are said to be opposed, and of which they virtually form a part, we should soon have a pretty kettle of fish between landlord and tenant."

" How do you make it out that they form a part of the institutions, sir ?"

" Simply. because the institutions have a solemn profession of protecting property. There is such a parade of this, that all our constitutions declare that property shall never be taken without due form of law ; and to read one of them, you would think the property of the citizen is held quite as sacred as his person. Now, some of these very tenures existed when the State institutions were framed ; and, not satisfied with this, we of New York, in common with our sister States, solemnly prohibited ourselves, in the constitution of the United States, from ever meddling with them ! Nevertheless, men are found hardy enough to assert that a thing which in fact belongs to the institutions, is opposed to them."

" Perhaps they mean, sir, to their spirit, or to their tendency."

"Ah ! there may be some sense in that, though much less than the declaimers fancy. The spirit of institutions is their legitimate object ; and it would be hard to prove that a leasehold tenure, with any conditions of mere pecuniary indebtedness whatever, is opposed to any institutions that recognise the full rights of property. The obligation to pay rent no more creates political dependency, than to give credit from an ordinary shop ; not so much, indeed, more especially under such leases as those of the Rensselaers ; for the debtor on a book-debt can be sued at any moment, whereas the tenant knows precisely when he has to pay. There is the great absurdity of those who decry the system as feudal and aristocratic ; for they do not see that those very leases are more favourable to the tenant than any other."

" I shall have to ask you to explain this to me, sir, being too ignorant to comprehend it."

" Why, these leases are perpetual, and the tenant cannot be dispossessed. The longer a lease is, other things being equal, the better it is for the tenant, all the world over. Let us suppose two farms, the one leased for five years, and the other for ever: Which tenant is most independent of the political influence of his landlord, to say nothing of the impossibility of controlling votes in this way in America, from a variety of causes? Certainly he who has a lease for ever. He is just as independent of his landlord, as his landlord can be of him, with the exception that he has rent to pay. In the latter case, he is precisely like any other debtor—like the poor man who contracts debts with the same storekeeper for a series of years. As for the possession of the farm, which we are to suppose is a desirable thing for the tenant, he of the long lease is clearly most independent, since the other may be ejected at the end of each five years. Nor is there the least difference as to acquiring the property in fee, since the landlord may sell equally in either case, if so disposed; and if NOT DISPOSED, NO HONEST MAN, UNDER ANY SYSTEM, OUGHT TO DO ANYTHING TO COMPEL HIM SO TO DO, either directly or indirectly; AND NO TRULY HONEST MAN WOULD."

I put some of the words of my uncle Ro in small capitals, as the spirit of the *times*, not of the *institutions*, renders such hints necessary. But, to continue our dialogue:

. "I understand you now, sir, though the distinction you make between the *spirit* of the institutions and their *tendencies* is what I do not exactly-comprehend."

"It is very easily explained. The spirit of the institutions is their *intention ;* their tendencies is the natural direction they take under the impulses of human motives, which are always corrupt and corrupting. The 'spirit' refers to what things *ought* to be; the 'tendencies,' to what they *are*, or are *becoming*. The 'spirit' of all political institutions is to place a check on the natural propensities of men, to restrain them, and keep them within due bounds; while the tendencies *follow* those propensities, and are quite often in direct opposition to the spirit. That this outcry against leasehold tenures in America is following the tendencies of our institutions, I am afraid is only too true; but that it is in any manner in compliance with their *spirit*, I utterly deny."

"You will allow that institutions have their spirit, which

ought always to be respected, in order to preserve har·
mony?"

"Out of all question. The first great requisite of a political system is the means of protecting itself; the second, to
check its tendencies at the point required by justice, wisdom
and good faith. In a despotism, for instance, the spirit of
the system is to maintain that one man, who is elevated
above the necessities and temptations of a nation—who is
solemnly set apart for the sole purpose of government, fortified by dignity, and rendered impartial by position—will
rule in the manner most conducive to the true interests of
his subjects. It is just as much the theory of Russia and
Prussia that their monarchs reign not for their own good,
but for the good of those over whom they are placed, as it
is the theory in regard to the President of the United States.
We all know that the tendencies of a despotism are to abuses
of a particular character; and it is just as certain that the
tendencies of a republic, or rather of a democratic republic
—for republic of itself means but little, many republics having had kings—but it is just as certain that the tendencies
of a democracy are to abuses of another character. Whatever man touches, he infallibly abuses; and this more in
connection with the exercise of political power, perhaps, than
in 'the management of any one interest of life, though he
abuses all, even to religion. Less depends on the nominal
character of institutions, perhaps, than on their ability to
arrest their own tendencies at the point required by everything that is just and right. Hitherto, surprisingly few
grave abuses have followed from our institutions; but this
matter looks frightfully serious; for I have not told you
half, Hugh."

"Indeed, sir! I beg you will believe me quite equal to
hearing the worst."

"It is true, anti-rentism did commence on the estate of
the Rensselaers, and with complaints of feudal tenures, and
of days' works, and fat fowls, backed by the extravagantly
aristocratic pretension that a ' manor' tenant was so much
a privileged being, that it was beneath his dignity, as a free
man, to do that which is daily done by mail-contractors,
stage-coach owners, victuallers, and even by themselves in
their passing bargains to deliver potatoes, onions, turkeys

and pork, although they had solemnly covenanted with their landlords to pay the fat fowls, and to give the days' works. The feudal system has been found to extend much further, and ' troubles,' as they are called, have broken out in other parts of the State. Resistance to process, and a cessation of the payment of rents, has occurred on the Livingston property, in Hardenberg—in short, in eight or ten counties of the State. Even among the *bonâ fide* purchasers, on the Holland Purchase, this resistance has been organized, and a species of troops raised, who appear disguised and armed wherever a levy is to be made. Several men have already been murdered, and there is the strong probability of a civil war."

" In the name of what is sacred and right, what has the government of the State been doing all this time ?"

." In my poor judgment, a great deal that it ought not to have done, and very little that it ought. You know the state of politics at home, Hugh ; how important New York is in all national questions, and how nearly tied is her vote —less than ten thousand majority in a canvass of near half a million of votes. When this is the case, the least-principled part of the voters attain an undue importance—a truth that has been abundantly illustrated in this question. The natural course would have been to raise an armed constabulary force, and to have kept it in motion, as the anti-renters have kept their ' Injins' in motion, which would have soon tired out the rebels, for rebels they are, who would thus have had to support one army in part, and the other altogether. Such a movement on the part of the State, well and energetically managed, would have drawn half the ' Injins' at once from the ranks of disaffection to those of authority ; for all that most of these men want is to live easy, and to have a parade of military movements. Instead of that, the legislature substantially did nothing, until blood was spilt, and the grievance had got to be not only profoundly disgraceful for such a State and such a country, but utterly intolerable to the well-affected of the revolted counties, as well as to those who were kept out of the enjoyment of their property. Then, indeed, it passed the law which ought to have been passed the first year of the ' Injin' system—a law which renders it felony to appear armed and disguised ; but

Dunning writes me this law is openly disregarded in Delaware and Schoharie, in particular, and that bodies of 'Injins,' in full costume and armed, of a thousand men, have
appeared to prevent levies or sales.   Where it will end,
Heaven knows!"

"Do you apprehend any serious civil war?"

. "It is impossible to say where false principles may lead,
when they are permitted to make head and to become widely
disseminated, in a country like ours.   Still, the disturbances,
as such, are utterly contemptible, and could and would be put
down by an energetic executive in ten days after he had time
to collect a force to do it with.   In some particulars, the present incumbent has behaved perfectly well; while in others,
in my judgment, he has inflicted injuries on the right that
it will require years to repair, if, indeed, they are ever repaired."

"You surprise me, sir; and this the more especially, as
I know you are generally of the same way of thinking, on
political subjects, with the party that is now in power."

"Did you ever know me to support what I conceived to
be wrong, Hugh, on account of my political affinities?"
asked my uncle, a little reproachfully as to manner.   "But
let me tell you the harm that I conceive has been done by
all the governors who have had anything to do with the
subject; and that includes one of a party to which I am
opposed, and two that are not.   In the first place, they have
all treated the matter as if the tenants had really some cause
of complaint; when in truth all their griefs arise from the
fact that other men will not let them have their property
just as they may want it, and in some respects on their own
terms."

"That is certainly a grief not to be maintained by reason
in a civilized country, and in a christian community."

"Umph! Christianity, like liberty, suffers fearfully in
human hands; one is sometimes at a loss to recognise either.
I have seen ministers of the gospel just as dogged, just as
regardless of general morality, and just as indifferent to the
right, in upholding *their* parties, as I ever saw laymen;
and I have seen laymen manifesting tempers, in this respect,
that properly belong to devils.   But our governors have
certainly treated this matter as if the tenants actually had

griefs; when in truth their sole oppression is in being obliged to pay rents that are merely nominal, and in not being able to buy other men's property contrary to their wishes, and very much at their own prices. One governor has even been so generous as to volunteer a mode of settling disputes with which, by the way, he has no concern, there being courts to discharge that office, that is singularly presuming on his part, to say the least, and which looks a confounded sight more like aristocracy, or monarchy, than anything connected with leasehold tenure."

"Why, what can the man have done?"

"He has kindly taken on himself the office of doing that for which I fancy he can find no authority in the institutions, or in their spirit—no less than advising citizens how they may conveniently manage their own affairs so as to get over difficulties that he himself substantially admits, while giving this very advice, are difficulties that the law sanctions!"

"This is a very extraordinary interference in a public functionary; because one of the parties to a contract that is solemnly guarantied by the law, chooses to complain of its *nature*, rather than of its *conditions*, to pretend to throw the weight of his even assumed authority into the scales on either side of the question!"

"And that in a popular government, Hugh, in which it tells so strongly against a man to render him unpopular, that not one man in a million has the moral courage to resist public opinion, even when he is right. You have hit the nail on the head, boy; it is in the last degree presuming, and what would be denounced as tyrannical in any monarch in Europe. But he has lived in vain who has not learned that they who make the loudest professions of a love of liberty, have little knowledge of the quality, beyond submission to the demands of numbers. Our executive has carried his fatherly care even beyond this; he has actually suggested the terms of a bargain by which he thinks the difficulty can be settled, which, in addition to the gross assumption of having a voice in a matter that in no manner belongs to him, has the palpable demerit of recommending a pecuniary compromise that is flagrantly wrong as a mere pecuniary compromise."

4

" You astonish me, sir! What is the precise nature of his recommendation?"

" That the Rensselaers should receive such a sum from each tenant as would produce an interest equal to the value of the present rent. Now, in the first place, here is a citizen who has got as much property as he wants, and who wishes to live for other purposes than to accumulate. This property is not only invested to his entire satisfaction, as regards convenience, security and returns, but also in a way that is connected with some of the best sentiments of his nature. It is property that has descended to him through ancestors for two centuries; property that is historically connected with his name—on which he was born, on which he has lived, and on which he has hoped to die; property, in a word, that is associated with all the higher feelings of humanity. Because some interloper, perhaps, who has purchased an interest in one of his farms six months before, feels an *aristocratic* desire not to have a landlord, and wishes to own a farm in fee; that in fact he has no other right to than he gets through his lease, the governor of the great State of New York throws the weight of his official position against the old hereditary owner of the soil, by solemnly suggesting, in an official document that is intended to produce an effect on public opinion, that he should sell that which he does not wish to sell, but wishes to keep, and that at a price which I conceive is much below its true pecuniary value. We have liberty with a vengeance, if these are some of its antics!"

" What makes the matter worse, is the fact that each of the Rensselaers has a house on his estate, so placed as to be convenient to look after his interests; which interests he is to be at the trouble of changing, leaving him his house on his hands, because, forsooth, one of the parties to a plain and equitable bargain wishes to make better conditions than he covenanted for. I wonder what his Excellency proposes that the landlords shall do with their money when they get it? Buy new estates, and build new houses, of which to be dispossessed when a new set of tenants may choose to cry out against aristocracy, and demonstrate their own love for democracy by wishing to pull others down in order to shove themselves into their places?"

"You are right again, Hugh; but it is a besetting vice of America to regard life as all means, and as having no end, in a worldly point of view. I dare say men may be found among us who regard it as highly presuming in any man to build himself an ample residence, and to announce by his mode of living that he is content with his present means, and does not wish to increase them, at the very moment they view the suggestions of the governor as the pink of modesty, and excessively favourable to equal rights! I like that thought of yours about the house, too; in order to suit the ' spirit' of the New York institutions, it would seem that a New York landlord should build on wheels, that he may move his abode to some new estate, when it suits the pleasure of his tenants to buy him out."

" Do you suppose the Rensselaers would take their money, the principal of the rent at seven per cent., and buy land with it, after their experience of the uncertainty of such possessions among us ?"

" Not they," said my uncle Ro, laughing. " No, no! they would sell the Manor-House, and Beverwyck, for taverns ; and then any one might live in them who would pay the principal sum of the cost of a dinner ; bag their dollars, and proceed forthwith to Wall street, and commence the shaving of notes—that occupation having been decided, as I see by the late arrivals, to be highly honourable and praiseworthy. Hitherto they have been nothing but drones ; but, by the time they can go to the quick with their dollars, they will become useful members of society, and be honoured and esteemed accordingly."

What next might have been said I do not know, for just then we were interrupted by a visit from our common banker, and the discourse was necessarily changed.

CHAPTER III.

"O, when shall I visit the land of my birth,
   The loveliest land on the face of the earth?
When shall I those scenes of affection explore,
      Our forests, our fountains,
      Our hamlets, our mountains,
With the pride of our mountains, the maid I adore?"
                                        MONTGOMERY.

IT was truly news for an American, who had been so
long cut off from intelligence from home, thus suddenly to
be told that some of the scenes of the middle ages—scenes
connected with real wrongs and gross abuses of human
rights—were about to be enacted in his own land; that
country which boasted itself, not only to be the asylum
of the oppressed, but the conservator of the right. I was
grieved at what I had heard, for, during my travels, I had
cherished a much-loved image of justice and political excel-
lence, that I now began to fear must be abandoned. My
uncle and myself decided at once to return home, a step
that indeed was required by prudence. I was now of an
age to enter into the full possession of my own property (so
far as "new laws and new lords" would permit); and the
letters received by my late guardian, as well as certain
newspapers, communicated the unpleasant fact that a great
many of the tenants of Ravensnest had joined the association, paid tribute for the support of "Injins," and were getting to be as bad as any of the rest of them, so far as
designs and schemes to plunder were concerned, though
they still paid their rents. The latter circumstance was
ascribed by our agent to the fact that many leases were
about to fall in, and it would be in my power to substitute
more honest and better disposed successors for the present
occupants of the several farms. Measures were taken accordingly for quitting Paris as soon as possible, so that we
might reach home late in the month of May.

"If we had time, I would certainly throw in a memorial
or two to the legislature," observed my uncle, a day or two

before we proceeded to Havre to join the packet. "I have a strong desire to protest against the invasion of my rights as a freeman that is connected with some of their contemplated laws. I do not at all like the idea of being abridged of the power of hiring a farm for the longest time I can obtain it, which is one of the projects of some of the ultra reformers of free and equal New York. It is wonderful Hugh, into what follies men precipitate themselves as soon as they begin to run into exaggerations, whether of politics, religion, or tastes. Here are half of the exquisite philanthropists who see a great evil affecting the rights of human nature in one man's hiring a farm from another for as long a term as he can obtain it, who are at the very extreme in their opinions on free trade! So free-trade are some of the journals which think it a capital thing to prevent landlords and tenants from making their own bargains, that they have actually derided the idea of having established fares for hackney-coaches, but that it would be better to let the parties stand in the rain and higgle about the price, on the free-trade principle. Some of these men are either active agents in stimulating the legislature to rob the citizen of this very simple control of his property, or passive lookers-on while others do it."

"Votes, sir, votes."

"It is, indeed, votes, sir, votes; nothing short of votes could reconcile these men to their own inconsistencies. As for yourself, Hugh, it might be well to get rid of that canopied pew——"

"Of what canopied pew? I am sure I do not understand you."

"Do you forget that the family-pew in St. Andrew's Church, at Ravensnest, has a wooden canopy over it—a relic of our colonial opinions and usages?"

"Now you mention it, I do remember a very clumsy, and, to own the truth, a very ugly thing, that I have always supposed was placed there, by those who built the church, by way of ornament."

"That ugly thing, by way of ornament, was intended for a sort of canopy, and was by no means an uncommon distinction in the State and colony, as recently as the close of the last century. The church was built at the expense of

4 *

my grandfather, Gen. Littlepage, and his bosom friend and kinsman, Col. Dirck Follock, both good Whigs and gallant defenders of the liberty of their country. They thought it proper that the Littlepages should have a canopied pew, and that is the state in which they caused the building to be presented to my father. The old work still stands ; and Dunning writes me that, among the other arguments used against your interests, is the fact that your pew is thus distinguished from those of the rest of the congregation."

" It is a distinction no man would envy me, could it be known that I have ever thought the clumsy, ill-shaped thing a nuisance, and detestable as an ornament. I have never even associated it in my mind with personal distinction, but have always supposed it was erected with a view to embellish the building, and placed over our pew as the spot where such an excrescence would excite tho least envy."

" In all that, with one exception, you have judged quite naturally. Forty years ago, such a thing might have been done, and a majority of the parishioners would have seen in it nothing out of place. But that day has gone by ; and you will discover that, on your own estate, and in the very things created by your family and yourself, you will actually have fewer rights of any sort, beyond those your money will purchase, than any man around you. The simple fact that St: Andrew's Church was built by your great-grandfather, and by him presented to the congregation, will diminish your claim to have a voice in its affairs with many of the congregation."

" This is so extraordinary, that I musk ask the reason."

" The reason is connected with a principle so obviously belonging to human nature generally, and to American nature in particular, that I wonder you ask it. It is envy. Did that pew belong to the Newcomes, for instance, no one would think anything of it."

" Nevertheless, the Newcomes would make themselves ridiculous by sitting in a pew that was distinguished from those of their neighbours. The absurdity of the contrast would strike every one."

. " And it is precisely because the absurdity does not exist in your case, that your seat is envied. No one envies absurdity. However, you will readily admit, Hugh, that a church, and a church-yard, are the two last places in which human distinctions ought to be exhibited. All are equal in the eyes of Him we go to the one to worship, and all are equal in the grave. I have ever been averse to everything like worldly distinction in a congregation, and admire the usage of the Romish Church in even dispensing with pews altogether. Monuments speak to the world, and have a general connexion with history, so that they may be tolerated to a certain point, though notorious liars."

" I agree with you, sir, as to the unfitness of a church for all distinctions, and shall be happy on every account to get rid of my canopy, though that has an historical connexion, also. I am quite innocent of any feeling of pride while sitting under it, though I will confess to some of shame at its quizzical shape, when I see it has attracted the eyes of intelligent strangers."

" It is but natural that you should feel thus ; for, while we may miss distinctions and luxuries to which we have ever been accustomed, they rarely excite pride in the possessor, even while they awaken envy in the looker-on.".

" Nevertheless, I cannot see what the old pew has to do with the rents, or my legal rights."

, " When a cause is bad, everything is pressed into it that it is believed may serve a turn. No man who had a good legal claim for property, would ever think of urging any other ; nor would any legislator who had sound and sufficient reasons for his measures—reasons that could properly justify him before God and man for his laws—have recourse to slang to sustain him. If these anti-renters were right, they would have no need of secret combinations, of disguises, blood-and-thunder names, and special agents in the legislature of the land. The right requires no false aid to make it appear the right ; but the wrong must get such support as it can press into its service. Your pew is called aristocratic, though it confers no political power ; it is called a patent of nobility, though it neither gives nor takes away , and it is hated, and you with it, for the very reason that you can sit in it and not make yourself ridiculous. I suppose you have not examined very closely the papers I gave you o read ?"

" Enough so to ascertain that they are filled with trash."

' Worse than trash, Hugh; with some-of the locses, principles, and most atrocious feelings, that degrade poor human nature.   Some of the reformers propose that no man shall hold more than a thousand acres of land, while others lay down the very intelligible and distinct principle that nc man ought to hold more than he can use.   Even petitions to that effect, I have been told, have been sent to the legislature."

" Which has taken care not to allude to their purport, either in debate or otherwise, as I see nothing to that effect in the reports."

"Ay, I dare say the slang-whangers of those honourable bodies will studiously keep all such enormities out of sight, as some of them doubtless hope to step into the shoes of the present landlords, as soon as they can get the feet out of them which are now in.   But these are the projects and the petitions in the columns of the journals, and they speak for themselves.   Among other things, they say it is nobility to be a landlord."

" I see by the letter of Mr. Dunning, that they have petitioned the legislature to order an inquiry into my title. Now, we hold from the crown——"

" So much the worse, Hugh.   Faugh! hold from a crown in a republican country! I am amazed you are not ashamed to own it.   Do you not know, boy, that it has been gravely contended in a court of justice that, in obtaining our national independence from the King of Great Britain, the people conquered all his previous grants, which ought to be declared void and of- none effect?"

" That is an absurdity of which I had not heard," I answered, laughing; " why, the people of New York, who held all their lands under the crown, would in that case have been conquering them for other persons!   My good grandfather and great-grandfather, both of whom actually fought and bled in the revolution, must have been very silly thus to expose themselves to take away their own estates, in order to give them to a set of immigrants from New England and other parts of the world!"

" Quite justly said, Hugh," added my uncle, joining in the laugh.   " Nor is this half of the argument.   The State, too, in its corporate character, has been playing swindler all his time. You may not know the fact, but I as your guardian do know, that the quit-rents reserved by the crown when it granted the lands of Mooseridge and Ravensnest, were claimed by the State; and that, wanting money to save the people from taxes, it commuted with us, receiving a certain gross sum in satisfaction of all future claims."

"Ay, *that* I did not know.. Can the fact be shown?"

" Certainly—it is well known to all old fellows like myself, for it was a very general measure, and very generally, entered into by all the landholders. In our case, the receipts are still to be found among the family-papers. In the cases of the older estates, such as those of the Van Rensselaers, the equity is still stronger in their favour, since the conditions to hold the land included an obligation to bring so many settlers from Europe within a given time; conditions that were fulfilled at great cost, as you may suppose, and on which, in truth, the colony had its foundation."

" How much it tells against a people's honesty to wish to forget such facts, in a case like this !"

" There is nothing forgotten, for the facts were probably never known to those who prate about the conquered rights from the crown. As you say, however, the civilization of a community is to be measured by its consciousness of the existence of all principles of justice, and a familiarity with its own history. The great bulk of the population of New York have no active desire to invade what is right in this anti-rent struggle, having no direct interests at stake ; *their* crime is a passive inactivity, which allows those who are either working for political advancement, or those who are working to obtain other men's property, to make use of them, through their own laws." .

" But is it not an embarrassment to such a region as that directly around Albany, to have such tenures to the land, and for so large a body of people to be compelled to pay rent, in the very heart of the State, as it might be, and in situations that render it desirable to leave enterprise as unshackled as possible ?"

" I am not prepared to admit this much, even, as a general principle. One argument used by these anti-renters is, for instance, that the patroons, in their leases, reserved the mill-seats. Now, what if they did? Some one must own the mill-seats; and why not the Patroon as well as another? To give the argument any weight, not as law, not as morals, but as mere expediency, it must be shown that the patroons would not let these mill-seats at as low rents as any one else; and my opinion is that they would let them at rents of not half the amount that would be asked, were they the property of so many individuals, scattered up and down the country. But, admitting that so large an estate of this particular sort has some inconveniences in that particular spot, can there be two opinions among men of integrity about the mode of getting rid of it? Everything has its price, and, in a business sense, everything is entitled to its price. No people acknowledge this more than the Americans, or practise on it so extensively. Let the Rensselaers be tempted by such offers as will induce them to sell, but do not let them be invaded by that most infernal of all acts of oppression, special legislation, in order to bully or frighten them from the enjoyment of what is rightfully their own. If the State think such a description of property injurious in its heart, let the State imitate England in her conduct towards the slave-holders—*buy* them out; not *tax* them out, and *wrong* them out, and *annoy* them out. But, Hugh, enough of this at present; we shall have much more than we want of it when we get home. Among my letters, I have one from each of my other wards."

" ' Still harping on my daughter,' sir !" I answered, laughing. " I hope that the vivacious Miss Henrietta Coldbrooke, and the meek Miss Anne Marston, are both perfectly well ?'

" Both in excellent health, and both write charmingly. I must really let you see the letter of Henrietta, as I do think it is quite creditable to her : I will step into my room and get it."

I ought to let the reader into a secret here that will have some connexion with what is to follow. A dead-set had been made at me, previously to leaving home, to induce me to marry either of three young ladies—Miss Henrietta Coldbrooke, Miss Anne Marston,-and Miss Opportunity Newcome. The advances in the cases of Miss Henrietta Coldbrooke and Miss Anne Marston came from my uncle Ro who, as their guardian, had a natural interest in their making

what he was pleased to think might be a good connexion for
either; while the advances on account of Miss Opportunity
Newcome came from herself. · Under such circumstances,
it may be well to say who these young ladies actually
were.

Miss Henrietta Coldbrooke was the daughter of an Englishman of good family, and some estate, who had emigrated
to America and married, under the impulse of certain theories in politics which induced him to imagine that this was
the promised land. I remember him as a disappointed and
dissatisfied widower, who was thought to be daily growing
poorer under the consequences of indiscreet investments,
and who at last got to be so very English in his wishes and
longings, as to assert that the common Muscovy was a better bird than the canvas-back! He died, however, in time
to leave his only child an estate which, under my uncle's
excellent management, was known by me to be rather more
than one hundred and seventy-nine thousand dollars, and
which produced a nett eight thousand a-year. This made
Miss Henrietta a belle at once; but, having a prudent friend
in my grandmother, as yet she had not married a beggar.
I knew that uncle Ro went quite as far as was proper, in
his letters, in the way of hints touching myself; and my
dear, excellent, honest-hearted, straightforward old grand
mother had once let fall an expression, in one of her letters
to myself, which induced me to think that these hints had
actually awakened as much interest in the young lady's
bosom, as could well be connected with what was necessarily nothing but curiosity.

Miss Anne Marston was also an heiress, but on a very
diminished scale. She had rather more than three thousand
a-year in buildings in town, and a pretty little sum of about
sixteen thousand dollars laid by out of its savings. She
was not an only child, however, having two brothers, each
of whom had already received as much as the sister, and
each of whom, as is very apt to be the case with the heirs of
New York merchants, was already in a fair way of getting
rid of his portion in riotous living. Nothing does a young
American so much good, under such circumstances, as to
induce him to travel. It makes or breaks at once. If a
downright fool, he is plucked by European adventurers in

so short a time, that the agony is soon over. If only vain
and frivolous, because young and ill-educated, the latter
being a New York endemic, but with some foundation of
native mind, he lets his whiskers grow, becomes fuzzy about
the chin, dresses better, gets to be much better mannered,
soon loses his taste for the low and vulgar indulgences of
his youth, and comes out such a gentleman as one can only
make who has entirely thrown away the precious moments
of youth. If tolerably educated in boyhood, with capacity
to build on, the chances are that the scales will fall from his
eyes very fast on landing in the old world—that his ideas
and tastes will take a new turn—that he will become what
nature intended him for, an intellectual man; and that he
will finally return home, conscious alike of the evils and
blessings, the advantages and disadvantages, of his own
system and country—a wiser, and it is to be hoped a better
man. How the experiment had succeeded with the Marstons, neither myself nor my uncle knew; for they had paid
their visit while we were in the East, and had already returned to America. As for Miss Anne, she had a mother
to take care of her mind and person, though I had learned
she was pretty, sensible and discreet.

Miss Opportunity Newcome was a belle of Ravensnest,
a village on my own property; a rural beauty, and of rural
education, virtues, manners and habits. As Ravensnest was
not particularly advanced in civilization, or, to make use of
the common language of the country, was not a very "aristocratic place," I shall not dwell on her accomplishments,
which did well enough for Ravensnest, but would not essentially ornament my manuscript.

Opportunity was the daughter of Ovid, who was the son
of Jason, of the house of Newcome. In using the term
"house," I adopt it understandingly; for the family had
dwelt in the same tenement, a leasehold property of which
the fee was in myself, and the dwelling had been associated
with the name of Newcome from time immemorial; that is,
for about eighty years. All that time had a Newcome been
the 'enant of the mill, tavern, store and farm, that lay nearest the village of Ravensnest, or Little Nest, as it was commonly called; and it may not be impertinent to the moral
of my narrative if I add that, for all that time, and for

something longer, had I and my ancestors been the landlords. I beg the reader to bear this last fact in mind, as
there will soon be occasion to show that there was a strong
disposition in certain persons to forget it.

As I have said, Opportunity was the daughter of Ovid.
There was also a brother, who was named Seneca, or
Sene*ky*, as he always pronounced it himself, the son of
Ovid, the son of Jason, the first of the name at Ravensnest.
This Seneca was a lawyer, in the sense of a license granted
by the Justices of the Supreme Court, as well as by the
Court of Common Pleas, in and for the county of Washington. As there had been a sort of hereditary education
among the Newcomes for three generations, beginning with
Jason, and ending with Seneca; and, as the latter was at
the bar, I had occasionally been thrown into the society of
both brother and sister. The latter, indeed, used to be fond
of visiting the Nest, as my house was familiarly called,
Ravensnest being its true name, whence those of the " patent" and village; and as Opportunity had early manifested
a partiality for my dear old grandmother, and not less dear
young sister, who occasionally passed a few weeks with me
during the vacations, more especially in the autumns, I had
many occasions of being brought within the influence of her
charms—opportunities that, I feel bound to state, Opportunity did not neglect. I have understood that her mother,
who bore the same name, had taught Ovid the art of love
by a very similar demonstration, and had triumphed. That
lady was still living, and may be termed Opportunity the
Great, while the daughter can be styled Opportunity the
Less. There was very little difference between my own
years and those of the young lady; and, as I had last
passed through the fiery ordeal at the sinister age of twenty,
there was not much danger in encountering the risk anew,
now I was five years older. But I must return to my uncle
and the letter of Miss Henrietta Coldbrooke.

" Here it is, Hugh," cried my guardian, gaily ; " and a
capital letter it is! I wish I could read the whole of it to
you ; but the two girls made me promise never to show their
letters to any one, which could mean only you, before they
would promise to write anything to me beyond common-
places. Now, I get their sentiments freely and naturally

5

and the correspondence is a source of much pleasure to me.
I think, however, I might venture just to give you one
extract."

"You had better not, sir; there would be a sort of
treachery in it, that I confess I would rather not be acces-
sary to. If Miss Coldbrooke do not wish me to read what
she writes, she can hardly wish that you should read any
of it to me."

Uncle Ro glanced at me, and I fancied he seemed dissatisfied with my *nonchalance*. He read the letter through to
himself, however, laughing here, smiling there, then muttering " capital !" " good !" " charming girl !" " worthy of
Hannah More !" &c. &c., as if just to provoke my curiosity.
But I had no desire to read " Hannah More," as any young
fellow of five-and-twenty can very well imagine, and I stood
it all with the indifference of a stoic. My guardian had to
knock under, and put the letters in his writing-desk.

" Well, the girls will be glad to see us," he said, after a
moment of reflection, " and not a little surprised. In my
very last letter to my mother, I sent them word that we
should not be home until October; and now we shall see
them as early as June, at least."

"Patt will be delighted, I make no doubt. As for the
other two young ladies; they have so many friends and
relations to care for, that I fancy our movements give them
no great concern."

. " Then you do both injustice, as their letters would prove.
They take the liveliest interest in our proceedings, and
speak of my return as if they look for it with the greatest
expectation and joy."

I made my uncle Ro a somewhat saucy answer; but fair-
dealing compels me to record it.

" I dare say they do, sir," was my reply; " but what
young lady does not look with ' *expectation* and joy' for the
return of a friend, who is known to have a long purse,
from Paris !"

" Well, Hugh, you deserve neither of those dear girls;
and, if I can help it, you shall have neither."

" Thank 'ee, sir !"

" Poh ! this is worse than silly—it is rude. I dare say
neither would accept you, were you to offer to-morrow."

" I trust not, sir, for her own sake. It would be a singularly palpable demonstration were either to accept a man
she barely-knew, and whom she had not seen since she was
fifteen."

Uncle Ro laughed, but I could see he was confoundedly
vexed; and, as I loved him with all my heart, though I did
not love-match-making, I turned the discourse, in a pleasant
way, on our approaching departure.

" I 'll tell you what I 'll do, Hugh," cried my uncle, who
was a good deal of a boy in some things, for the reason, I
suppose, that he was an old bachelor; " I 'll just have wrong
names entered on board the packet, and we 'll surprise all
our friends. Neither Jacob nor your man will betray us,
we know; and, for that matter, we can send them both
home by the way of England. Each of us has trunks in
London to be looked after, and let the two fellows go by the
way of Liverpool. That is a good thought, and occurred
most happily."

" With all my heart, sir. My fellow is of no more use to
me at sea than an automaton would be, and I shall be glad
to get rid of his rueful countenance. He is a capital servant on terrâ firma, but a perfect Niobe on the briny main."

The thing was agreed on; and, a day or two afterwards,
both our body-servants, that is to say, Jacob the black and
Hubert the German, were on their way to England. My
uncle let his apartment again, for he always maintained I
should wish to bring my bride to pass a winter in it; and
we proceeded to Havre in a sort of incognito. There was
little danger of our being known on board the packet, and
we had previously ascertained that there was not an acquaintance of either in the ship. There was a strong family
resemblance between my uncle and myself, and we passed
for father and son in the ship, as old Mr. Davidson and
young Mr. Davidson, of Maryland—or Myr-r-land, as it is
Doric to call that State. We had no concern in this part
of the deception, unless abstaining from calling my supposed father " uncle," as one would naturally do in strange
society, can be so considered.

The passage itself—by the way, I wish all landsmen
would be as accurate as I am here, and understand that a
" voyage" means " out" and " home," or " thence" and

" back again," while a " passage" means from place to place—but our passage was pregnant with no events worth recording. We had the usual amount of good and bad weather, the usual amount of eating and drinking, and tho usual amount of ennui. The latter circumstance, perhaps, contributed to the digesting of a further scheme of my uncle's, which it is now necessary to state.

A re-perusal of his letters and papers had induced him to think the anti-rent movement a thing of more gravity, even, than he had first supposed. The combination on the part of the tenants, we learned also from an intelligent New Yorker who was a fellow-passenger, extended much further than our accounts had given us reason to believe; and it was deemed decidedly dangerous for landlords, in many cases, to be seen on their own estates. Insult, personal degradation, or injury, and even death, it was thought, might be the consequences, in many cases. The blood actually spilled had had the effect to check the more violent demonstrations, it is true; but the latent determination to achieve their purposes was easily to be traced among the tenants, in the face of all their tardy professions of moderation, and a desire for nothing but what was right. In this case, what was right was the letter and spirit of the contracts; and nothing was plainer than the fact that these were not what was wanted.

Professions pass for nothing, with the experienced, when connected with a practice that flatly contradicts them. It was only too apparent to all who chose to look into the matter, and that by evidence which could not mislead, that the great body of the tenants in various counties of New York were bent on obtaining interests in their farms that were not conveyed by their leases, without the consent of their landlords, and insomuch that they were bent on doing that which should be discountenanced by every honest man in the community. The very fact that they supported, or in any manner connived at, the so-called " Injin" system, spoke all that was necessary as to their motives; and, when we come to consider that these " Injins" had already proceeded to the extremity of shedding blood, it was sufficiently plain that things must soon reach a crisis.

My uncle Roger and myself reflected on all these matters

calmly, and decided on our course, I trust, with prudence. As that decision has proved to be pregnant with consequences that are likely to affect my future life, I shall now briefly give an outline of what induced us to adopt it.

It was all-important for us to visit Ravensnest in person, while it might be hazardous to do so openly. The Nest house stood in the very centre of the estate, and, ignorant as we were of the temper of the tenants, it might be indiscreet to let our presence be known; and circumstances favoured our projects of concealment. We were not expected to reach the country at all until autumn, or " fall," as that season of the year is poetically called in America; and this gave us the means of reaching the property unexpectedly, and, as we hoped, undetected. Our arrangement, then, was very simple, and will be best related in the course of the narrative.

The packet had a reasonably short passage, as we were twenty-nine days from land to land. It was on a pleasant afternoon in May when the hummock-like heights of Navesink were first seen from the deck; and, an hour later, we came in sight of the tower-resembling sails of the coasters which were congregating in the neighbourhood of the low point of land that is so very appropriately called *Sandy* Hook. The light-houses rose out of the water soon after, and objects on the shore of New Jersey next came gradually out of the misty back-ground, until we got near enough to be boarded, first by the pilot, and next by the news-boat; the first preceding the last for a wonder, news usually being far more active, in this good republic, than watchfulness to prevent evil. My uncle Ro gave the crew of this news-boat a thorough scrutiny, and, finding no one on board her whom he had ever before seen, he bargained for a passage up to town.

We put our feet on the Battery just as the clocks of New York were striking eight. A custom-house officer had examined our carpet-bags and permitted them to pass, and we had disburthened ourselves of the effects in the ship, by desiring the captain to attend to them. Each of us had a town-house, but neither would go near his dwelling; mine being only kept up in winter, for the use of my sister and an aunt who kindly took charge of her during the season, while my uncle's was opened principally for his mother.

5 *

At that season, we had reason to think neither was tenanted but by one or two old family servants; and it was our cue also to avoid them. But "Jack Dunning," as my uncle always called him, was rather more of a friend than of an agent; and he had a bachelor establishment in Chamber Street that was precisely the place we wanted. Thither, then, we proceeded, taking the route by Greenwich Street, fearful of meeting some one in Broadway by whom we might be recognised.

<hr>

CHAPTER IV.

Cit. "Speak, speak."
1 *Cit.* "You are all resolved rather to die than to famish?"
Cit. "Resolved, resolved."
1 *Cit.* "First you know, Caius Marcus is chief enemy to the people."
Cit. "We know 't, we know 't."
1 *Cit.* "Let 's kill him, and we 'll have corn at our own price. Is 't a verdict?"

                                    Coriolanus.

THE most inveterate Manhattanese, if he be anything of a man of the world, must confess that New York is, after all, but a Rag-Fair sort of a place, so far as the eye is concerned. I was particularly struck with this fact, even at that hour, as we went stumbling along over an atrociously bad side-walk, my eyes never at rest, as any one can imagine, after five years of absence. I could not help noting the incongruities; the dwellings of marble, in close proximity with miserable, low constructions in wood; the wretched pavements, and, above all, the country air, of a town of near four hundred thousand souls. I very well know that many of the defects are to be ascribed to the rapid growth of the place, which gives it a sort of hobbledehoy look; but, being a Manhattanese by birth, I thought I might just as well own it all, at once, if it were only for he information of a particular portion of my townsmen, who may have been under a certain delusion on the subject. As for comparing the Bay of New York with that of Naples on the score of beauty, I shall no more be guilty of any such folly, to gratify the cockney feelings of Broadway and Bond street, than I should be guilty of the folly of comparing the commerce of the ancient Parthenope with that of *old* New York, in order to excite complacency in the bosom of some bottegajo in the Toledo, or on the Chiaja. Our fast-growing Manhattan is a great town in its way—a wonderful place—without a parallel, I do believe, on earth, as a proof of enterprise and of the accumulation of business; and it is not easy to make such a town appear ridiculous by any jibes and innuendoes that relate to the positive things of this world, though nothing is easier than to do it for itself by setting up to belong to the sisterhood of such places as London, Paris, Vienna and St. Petersburg. There is too much of the American notion of the omnipotence of numbers among us Manhattanese, which induces us to think that the higher rank in the scale of places is to be obtained by majorities. No, no; let us remember the familiar axiom of " ne sutor ultra crepidum." New York is just the queen of " business," but not yet the queen of the world. Every man who travels ought to bring back something to the common stock of knowledge; and I shall give a hint to my townsmen, by which I really think they may be able to tell for themselves, as by feeling a sort of moral pulse, when the town is rising to the level of a capital. When simplicity takes the place of pretension, is one good rule; but, as it may require a good deal of practice, or native taste, to ascertain this fact, I will give another that is obvious to the senses, which will at least be strongly symptomatic; and that is this: When *squares* cease to be called *parks;* when horse-bazaars and fashionable streets are not called Tattersalls and Bond street; when *Washington* Market is rechristened *Bear* Market, and Franklin and Fulton and other great philosophers and inventors are plucked of the unmerited honours of having shambles named after them; when *commercial* is not used as a prefix to emporium; when people can return from abroad without being asked " if they are reconciled to their country," and strangers are not interrogated at the second question, " how do you like *our*

city?"· then may it be believed that the town is beginning
to go alone, and that it may set up for itself.

·Although New York is, out of all question, decidedly
provincial, labouring under the peculiar vices of provincial
habits and provincial modes of thinking, it contains many
a man of the world, and some, too, who have never quitted
their own firesides. Of this very number was the Jack
Dunning, as my uncle Ro called him, to whose house in
Chamber street we were now proceeding.

" If we were going anywhere but to Dunning's," said my
uncle, as we turned out of Greenwich street, " I should
have no fear of being recognised by the servants; for no
one here thinks of keeping a man six months. Dunning,
however, is of the old school, and does not like new faces;
so he will have no Irishman at his door, as is the case with
two out of three of the houses at which one calls, now-a-
days."

In another minute we were at the bottom of Mr. Dunning's " stoup"—what an infernal contrivance it is to get in
and out at the door by, in a hotty-cold climate like ours!—
but, there we were, and I observed that my uncle hesitated.

" *Parlez au* SUISSE," said I ; " ten to one he is fresh
from some Bally-this, or Bally-that."

· " No, no ; it must be old Garry the nigger"—my uncle
Ro was of the old school himself, and *would* say " nigger"—
" Jack can never have parted with Garry."

" Garry" was the diminutive of Garret, a somewhat common Dutch christian name among us.

We rang, and the door opened—in about five minutes.
Although the terms " aristocrat" and " aristocracy" are
much in men's mouths in America just now, as well as those
of " feudal" and the " middle ages," and this, too, as applied
to modes of living as well as to leasehold tenures, there is
but one porter in the whole country ; and he belongs to the
White House, at Washington. I am afraid even that per-
sonage, royal porter as he is, is often out of the way ; and
the reception he gives when he *is* there, is not of the most
brilliant and princely character. When we had waited three
minutes, my uncle Ro said—

· " I am afraid Garry is taking a nap by the kitchen-fire ;
I 'll try him again."

Uncle Ro did try again, and, two minutes later, the door opened.

"What is your pleasure?" demanded the *Suisse*, with a strong brogue.

My uncle started back as if he had met a sprite; but he asked if Mr. Dunning was at home.

"He is, indeed, sir."

"Is he alone, or is he with company?"

"He is, indeed."

"But *what* is he, indeed?"

"He is *that*."

"Can you take the trouble to explain which *that* it is? Has he company, or is he alone?"

"Just *that*, sir. Walk in, and he'll be charmed to see you. A fine gentleman is his honour, and pleasure it is to live with him, I'm sure!"

"How long is it since you left Ireland, my friend?"

"Isn't it a mighty bit, now, yer honour!" answered Barney, closing the door. "T'irteen weeks, if it's one day."

"Well, go ahead, and show us the way. This is a bad omen, Hugh, to find that Jack Dunning, of all men in the country, should have changed his servant—good, quiet, lazy, respectable, old, grey-headed Garry the nigger—for such a bogtrotter as that fellow, who climbs those stairs as if accustomed only to ladders."

Dunning was in his library on the second floor, where he passed most of his evenings. His surprise was equal to that which my uncle had just experienced, when he saw us two standing before him. A significant gesture, however, caused him to grasp his friend and client's hand in silence; and nothing was said until the *Swiss* had left the room, although the fellow stood with the door in his hand a most inconvenient time, just to listen to what might pass between the host and his guests. At length we got rid of him, honest, well-meaning fellow that he was, after all; and the door was closed.

"My last letters have brought you home, Roger?" said Jack, the moment he *could* speak; for feeling, as well as caution, had something to do with his silence.

"They have, indeed. A great change must have come over the country, by what I hear; and one of the very worst symptoms is that you have turned away Garry, and got an Irishman in his place."

"Ah! old men must die, as well as old principles, I find. My poor fellow went off in a fit last week, and I took that Irishman as a *pis. aller*. After losing poor Garry, who was born a slave in my father's house, I became indifferent, and accepted the first comer from the intelligence office."

" We must be careful, Dunning, not to give up too soon. But hear my story, and then to other matters."

My uncle then explained his wish to be incognito, and his motive. Dunning listened attentively, but seemed uncertain whether to dissent or approve. The matter was discussed briefly, and then it was postponed for further consideration.

"But how comes on this great moral dereliction, called anti-rentism? Is it on the wane, or the increase?"

"On the wane, to the eye, perhaps; but on the increase, so far as principles, the right, and facts, are concerned. The necessity of propitiating votes is tempting politicians of all sides to lend themselves to it; and there is imminent danger now that atrocious wrongs will be committed under the form of law."

"In what way *can* the law touch an existing contract? The Supreme Court of the United States will set that right."

"That is the only hope of the honest, let me tell you. It is folly to expect that a body composed of such men as usually are sent to the State Legislature, can resist the temptation to gain power by conciliating numbers. *That is out of the question.* Individuals of these bodies may resist; but the tendency there will be as against the few, and in favour of the many, bolstering their theories by clap-traps and slang political phrases. The scheme to tax the rents, under the name of quit-rents, will be resorted to, in the first place."

"That will be a most iniquitous proceeding, and would justify resistance just as much as our ancestors were justified in resisting the taxation of Great Britain."

"It would more so, for here we have a written covenant to render taxation equal. The landlord already pays one tax on each of these farms—a full and complete tax, that is reserved from the rent in the original bargain with the tenant; and now the wish is to tax the rents themselves;

and this not to raise revenue, for that is confessedly not wanted, but most clearly with a design to increase the inducements for the landlords to part with their property. If that can be done, the sales will be made on the principle that none but the tenant must be, as indeed no one else *can* be, the purchaser; and then we shall see a queer exhibition— men parting with their property under the pressure of a clamour that is backed by as much law as can be pressed into its service, with a monopoly of price on the side of the purchaser; and all in a country professing the most sensitive love of liberty, and where the prevailing class of politicians are free-trade men !"

" There is no end of these inconsistencies among politicians."

" There is no end of knavery when men submit to ' noses,' instead of principles. Call things by their right names, Ro, as they deserve to be. This matter is so plain, that he who runs can read."

" But will this scheme of taxation succeed ? It does not affect us, for instance, as our leases are for three lives."

" Oh ! that is nothing ; for you they contemplate a law that will forbid the letting of land, for the future, for a period longer than five years. Hugh's leases will soon be falling in, and then he can't make a slave of any man for a longer period than five years."

" Surely no one is so silly as to think of passing such a law, with a view to put down aristocracy, and to benefit the tenant !" I cried, laughing.

"Ay, you may laugh, young sir," resumed Jack Dunning; " but such *is* the intention. I know very well what will be your course of reasoning ; you will say, the longer the lease, the better for the tenant, if the bargain be reasonably good ; and landlords cannot ask more for the use of their lands than they are really worth in this country, there happening to be more land than there are men to work it No, no ; landlords rather get less for their lands than they are worth, instead of more, for that plain reason. To compel the tenant to take a lease, therefore, for a term as short as five years, is to injure him, you think ; to place him more at the control of his landlord, through the little interests connected with the cost and trouble of moving, and through the natural desire he may possess to cut the meadows he has seeded, and to get the full benefit of manure he has made and carted.   I see how you reason, young sir; but you are behind the age—you are sadly behind the age."

"The age is a queer one, if I am!   All over the world it is believed that long leases are favours, or advantages, to tenants; and nothing can make it otherwise, *cæteris paribus*.   Then what good will the tax do, after violating right and moral justice, if not positive law, to lay it?   On a hundred dollars of rent, I should have to pay some fifty-five cents of taxes, as I am assessed on other things at Ravensnest; and does anybody suppose I will give up an estate that has passed through five generations of my family, on account of a tribute like that!"

"Mighty well, sir—mighty well, sir! · This is fine talk; but I would advise you not to speak of *your* ancestors at all. Landlords can't name *their* ancestors with impunity just now."

"I name mine only as showing a reason for a natural regard for my paternal acres."

"That you might do, if you were a tenant; but not as a landlord.   In a landlord, it is aristocratic and intolerable pride, and to the last degree offensive—as Dogberry says, ' tolerable and not to be endured.' "

"But it is a *fact*, and it is natural one should have some feelings connected with it."

"The more it is a fact, the less it will be liked.   People associate social position with wealth and *estates*, but not with farms; and the longer one has such things in a family, the worse for them!"

"I do believe, Jack," put in my uncle Ro, "that the rule which prevails all over the rest of the world is reversed here, and that with us it is thought a family's claim is lessened, and not increased, by time."

"To be sure it is!" answered Dunning, without giving me a chance to speak. "Do you know that you wrote me a very silly letter once, from Switzerland, about a family called de Blonay, that had been seated on the same rock, in a little castle, some six or eight hundred years, and the sort of respect and veneration the circumstance awakened? Well, all that was very foolish, as you will find when you

pay your incognito visit to Ravensnest. I will not anticipate the result of your schooling; but, go to school."

" As the Rensselaers and other great landlords, who have
estates on durable leases, will not be very likely to give
them up, except on terms that will suit themselves, for a tax
as insignificant as that mentioned by Hugh," said my uncle,
" what does the legislature anticipate from passing the law?"

" That its members will be called the friends of the people, and not the friends of the landlords. Would any man
tax his friends, if he could help it?"

" But what will that portion of the people who compose
the anti-renters gain by such a measure?"

" Nothing; and their complaints will be just as loud, and
their longings as active, as ever. Nothing that can have
any effect on what they wish, will be accomplished by any
legislation in the matter. One committee of the assembly
has actually reporfed, you may remember, that the State
might assume the lands, and sell them to the tenants, or
some one else; or something of the sort."

" The constitution of the United States must be Hugh's
ægis."

"And that alone will protect him, let me tell you. But
for that noble provision of the constitution of the Federal
Government, his estate would infallibly go for one-half its
true value. There is no use in mincing things, or in affect-
ing to believe men more honest than they are—AN INFERNAL
FEELING OF SELFISHNESS IS SO MUCH TALKED OF, AND
CITED, AND REFERRED TO, ON ALL OCCASIONS, IN THIS
COUNTRY, THAT A MAN ALMOST RENDERS HIMSELF RIDICU-
LOUS WHO APPEARS TO REST ON PRINCIPLE."

" Have you heard what the tenants of Ravensnest aim
at, in particular?"

" They want to get Hugh's lands, that's all; nothing
more, I can assure you."

" On what conditions, pray?" demanded I.

"As you 'light of chaps,' to use a saying of their own.
Some even profess a willingness to pay a fair price.'

" But I do not wish to sell for even a fair price. I have
no desire to part with property that is endeared to me by
family feeling and association. I have an expensive house
and establishment on my estate, which obtains its principal

6

value from the circumstance that it is so placed that I can
look after my interests with the least inconvenience to myself.   What can I do with the money but buy another
estate? and I prefer this that I have."

"Poh! boy, you can shave notes, you'll recollect," said
uncle Ro, drily. "The calling is decided to be honourable
by the highest tribunal; and no man should be above his
business."

"You have no right, sir, in a free country," returned the
caustic Jack Dunning, "to prefer one estate to another,
more especially when other people want it.   Your lands are
leased to honest, hard-working tenants, who can eat their
dinners without silver forks, and whose ancestors——"

"Stop!" I cried, laughing; "I bar all ancestry.   No
man has a right to ancestry in a free country, you'll remember!"

"That means landlord-ancestry; as for tenant-ancestry,
one can have a pedigree as long as the Maison de Levis.
No, sir; every tenant you have has every right to demand
that his sentiment of family feeling should be respected.
His father planted that orchard, and he loves the apples
better than any other apples in the world——"

"And my father procured the grafts, and made him a
present of them."

"His grandfather cleared that field, and converted its
ashes into pots and pearls——"

"And my grandfather received that year ten shillings of
rent, for land off which his received two hundred and fifty
dollars for his ashes."

"His great-grandfather, honest and excellent man—nay,
super-honest and confiding creature—first 'took up' the land
when a wilderness, and with his own hands felled the timber, and sowed the wheat."

"And got his pay twenty-fold for it all, or he would not
have been fool enough to do it.   I had a great-grandfather,
too; and I hope it will not be considered aristocratic if I
venture to hint as much.   He—a dishonest, pestilent knave,
no doubt—leased that very lot for six years without any
rent at all, in order that the 'poor, confiding creature' might
make himself comfortable, before he commenced paying his
sixpence or shilling an acre rent for the remainder of three

lives, with a moral certainty of getting a renewal on the most liberal terms known to a new country; and who knew, the whole time, he could buy land in fee, within ten miles of his door, but who thought *this* a better bargain than *that*."

" Enough of this folly," cried uncle Ro, joining in the laugh; " we all know that, in our excellent America, he who has the highest claims to anything, must affect to have the least, to stifle the monster envy; and, being of one mind as to principles, let us come to facts. What of the girls, Jack, and of my honoured mother?"

" She, noble, heroic woman! she is at Ravensnest at this moment; and, as the girls would not permit her to go alone, they are all with her."

"And did you, Jack Dunning, suffer them to go unattended into a part of the country that is in open rebellion?" demanded my uncle, reproachfully.

" Come, come! Hodge Littlepage, this is very sublime as a theory, but not so clear when reduced to practice. I did not go with Mrs. Littlepage and her young fry, for the good and substantial reason that I did not wish to be ' tarred and feathered.' "

" So you leave them to run the risk of being ' tarred and feathered' in your stead?"

" Say what you will about the cant of freedom that is becoming so common among us, and from which we were once so free; say what you will, Ro, of the inconsistency of those who raise the cry of ' feudality,' and ' aristocracy,' and ' nobility,' at the very moment they are manifesting a desire for exclusive rights and privileges in their own persons; say what you will of dishonesty, envy, that prominent American vice, knavery, covetousness, and selfishness; and I will echo all you can utter;—but do not say that a woman can be in serious danger among any material body of Americans, even if anti-renters, and mock-redskins in the bargain."

' I believe you are right there, Jack, on reflection. Pardon my warmth; but I have lately been living in the old world, and in a country in which women were not long since carried to the scaffold on account of their politics."

" Because they meddled with politics. Your mother is in

no serious danger, though it needs nerve in a woman to be able to think so. There are few women in the State, and fewer of her time of life anywhere, that would do what she has done ; and I give the girls great credit for sticking by her. Half the young men in town are desperate at the thought of three such charming creatures thus exposing themselves to insult. · Your mother has only been sued."

- "Sued! Whom does she owe, or what can she have done to have brought this indignity on her?"

"You know, or ought to know, how it is in this country, Littlepage ; we must have a little law, even when most bent on breaking it. A downright, straight-forward rascal, who openly sets law at defiance, is a wonder. Then we have a great talk of liberty when plotting to give it the deepest stab ; and religion even gets to share in no small portion of our vices. Thus it is that the anti-renters have dragged in the law in aid of their designs. I understand one of the Rensselaers has been sued for money borrowed in a ferry-boat to help him across a river under his own door, and for potatoes bought by his wife in the streets of Albany !"

"But neither of the Rensselaers need borrow money to cross the ferry, as the ferry-men would trust him ; and no lady of the Rensselaer family ever bought potatoes in the streets of Albany, I 'll answer for it."

"You have brought back some knowledge from your travels, I find !" said Jack Dunning, with comic gravity. "Your mother writes me that *she* has been sued for twenty-seven pairs of shoes furnished her by a shoemaker whom she never saw, or heard of, until she received the summons !"

"This, then, is one of the species of annoyances that has been adopted to bully the landlords out of their property?"

"It is ; and if the landlords have recourse even to the covenants of their leases, solemnly and deliberately made, and as solemnly guarantied by a fundamental law, the cry is raised of ' aristocracy' and ' oppression' by these very men, and echoed by many of the creatures who get seats in high places among us—or what *would* be high places, if filled with men worthy of their trusts."

"I see you do not mince your words, Jack."

"Why should I? Words are all that is left me. I am of no more weight in the government of this State than that Irishman, who let you in just now, will be, five years hence —less, for he will vote to suit a majority; and, as I shall vote understandingly, my vote will probably do no one any good."

Dunning belonged to a school that mingles a good deal of speculative and impracticable theory, with a great deal of sound and just principles; but who render themselves useless because they will admit of no compromises. He did not belong to the class of American *doctrinaires*, however, or to those who contend—no, not *contend*, for no one does *that* any longer in this country, whatever may be his opinion on the subject—but those who *think* that political power, as in the last resort, should be the property of the few; for he was willing New York should have a very broad constituency. Nevertheless, he was opposed to the universal suffrage, in its wide extent, that does actually exist; as I suppose quite three-fourths of the whole population are opposed to it; in their hearts, though no political man of influence, now existing, has the moral calibre necessary to take the lead in putting it down. Dunning deferred to principles, and not to men. He well knew that an infallible whole was not to be composed of fallible parts; and while he thought majorities ought to determine many things, that there are rights and principles that are superior to even such *unanimity* as man can manifest, and much more to their majorities. But Dunning had no selfish views connected with his political notions, wanting no office, and feeling no motive to affect that which he neither thought nor wished. He never had quitted home, or it is highly probable his views of the comparative abuses of the different systems that prevail in the world would have been essentially modified. Those he saw had unavoidably a democratic source, there being neither monarch nor aristocrat to produce any other; and, under such circumstances, as abuses certainly abound, it is not at all surprising that he sometimes a little distorted facts, and magnified evils.

"And my noble, high-spirited, and venerable mother has actually gone to the Nest to face the enemy!" exclaimed my uncle, after a thoughtful pause.

6 *

" She has, indeed ; and the noble, high-spirited, though not venerable, young ladies have gone with her," returned Mr. Dunning, in his caustic way.

"All three, do you mean ?"

" Every one of them—Martha, Henrietta, and Anne."

" I am surprised that the last should have done so. Anne Marston is such a meek, quiet, peace-loving person, that I should think *she* would have preferred remaining, as she naturally might have done, without exciting remark, with her own mother."

" She has not, nevertheless. Mrs. Littlepage *would* brave the anti-renters, and the three maidens *would* be her companions. I dare say, Ro, you know how it is with the gentle sex, when they make up their minds ?"

" My girls are all good girls, and have given me very little trouble," answered my uncle, complacently.

" Yes, I dare say that may be true. You have only been absent from home five years, this trip."

"An attentive guardian, notwithstanding, since I left you as a substitute. Has my mother written to you since her arrival among the hosts of the Philistines ?"

" She has, indeed, Littlepage," answered Dunning, gravely ; " I have heard from her three times, for she writes to urge my not appearing on the estate. I did intend to pay her a visit ; but she tells me that it might lead to a violent scene, and can do no good. As the rents will not be due until autumn, and Master Hugh is now of age and was to be here to look after his own affairs, I have seen no motive for incurring the risk of the tarring and feathering. We American lawyers, young gentleman, wear no wigs."

" Does my mother write herself, or employ another ?" inquired my uncle, with interest.

" She honours me with her own hand. Your mother writes much better than you do yourself, Roger."

" That is owing to her once having carried chain, as she would say herself. Has Martha written to you ?"

" Of course. Sweet little Patty and I are bosom friends, as you know."

" And does she say anything of the Indian and the negro ?"

" Jaaf and Susquesus ? To be sure she does. Both are

living still, and both are well. I saw them myself, and even ate of their venison, so lately as last winter."

" Those old fellows must have each lived a great deal more than his century, Jack. They were with my grandfather in the old French war, as active, useful men—older, then, than *my* grandfather !"

. "Ay! a nigger or a redskin, before all others, for holding on to life, when they have been temperate. Let me see— that expedition of Abercrombie's was about eighty years since ; why, these fellows must be well turned of their hundred, though Jaap is rather the oldest, judging from appearances."

" I believe no one knows the age of either. A hundred each has been thought, now, for many years. Susquesus was surprisingly active, too, when I last saw him—like a healthy man of eighty." -

" He has failed of late, though he actually shot a deer, as I told you, last winter. Both the old fellows stray down to the Nest, Martha writes me ; and the Indian is highly scandalized at the miserable imitations of his race that are now abroad. I have even heard that he and Yop have actually contemplated taking the field against them. Seneca Newcome is their especial aversion."

" How is Opportunity ?" I inquired. " Does she take any part in this movement ?"

"A decided one, I hear. She is anti-rent, while she wishes to keep on good terms with her landlord ; and that is endeavouring to serve God and Mammon. She is not the first, however, by a thousand, that wears two faces in this business."

" Hugh has a deep admiration of Opportunity," observed my uncle, " and you had needs be tender in your strictures. The modern Seneca, I take it, is dead against us ?"

" Seneky wishes to go to the legislature, and of course he is on the side of votes. Then his brother is a tenant at the mill, and naturally wishes to be the landlord. He is also interested in the land himself. One thing has struck me in this controversy as highly worthy of notice ; and it is the *naïveté* with which men reconcile the obvious longings of covetousness with what they are pleased to fancy the principles of liberty ! When a man has worked a farm a certain number of years, he boldly sets up the doctrine that the fact itself gives him a high moral claim to possess it for ever. A moment's examination will expose the fallacy by which these sophists apply the flattering unction to their souls. They work their farms under a lease, and in virtué of its covenants. Now, in a moral sense, all that time can do in such a case, is to render these covenants the more sacred, and consequently more binding; but these worthies, whose morality is all on one side, imagine that these time-honoured covenants give them a right to fly from their own conditions during their existence, and to raise pretensions far exceeding anything they themselves confer, the moment they cease."

"Poh, poh! Jack; there is no need of refining at all, to come at the merits of such a question. This is a civilized country, or it is not. If it be a civilized country, it will respect the rights of property, and its own laws; and if the reverse, it will not respect them. As for setting up the doctrine, at this late day, when millions and millions are invested in this particular species of property, that the leasehold tenure is opposed to the *spirit* of institutions of which it has substantially formed a part, ever since those institutions have themselves had an existence, it requires a bold front, and more capacity than any man at Albany possesses, to make the doctrines go down. Men may run off with the notion that the *tendencies* to certain abuses, which mark every system, form their spirit; but this is a fallacy that a very little thought will correct. Is it true that proposals have actually been made, by these pretenders to liberty, to appoint commissioners to act as arbitrators between the landlords and tenants, and to decide points that no one has any right to raise?"

"True as Holy Writ; and a regular 'Star Chamber' tribunal it would be! It is wonderful, after all, how extremes do meet!"

"That is as certain as the return of the sun after night. But let us now talk of our project, Jack, and of the means of getting among these self-deluded men—deluded by their own covetousness — without being discovered; for I am determined to see them, and to judge of their motives and conduct for myself."

" Take care of the tar-barrel, and of the pillow-case of feathers, Roger !"

" I shall endeavour so to do."

We then discussed the matter before us at length and leisurely. I shall not relate all that was said, as it would be going over the same ground twice, but refer the reader to the regular narrative. At the usual hour, we retired to our beds, retaining the name of Davidson, as convenient and prudent. Next day Mr. John Dunning busied himself in our behalf, and made himself exceedingly useful to us. In his character of an old bachelor, he had many acquaintances at the theatre ; and through his friends of the green-room he supplied each of us with a wig. Both my uncle and myself spoke German reasonably well, and our original plan was to travel in the characters of immigrant trinket and essence pedlars. But I had a fancy for a hand-organ and a monkey ; and it was finally agreed that Mr. Hugh Roger Littlepage, senior, was to undertake this adventure with a box of cheap watches and gilded trinkets ; while Mr. Hugh Roger Littlepage, junior, was to commence his travels at home, in the character of a music-grinder. Modesty will not permit me to say all I might, in favour of my own skill in music in general ; but I sang well for an amateur, and played, both on the violin and flute, far better than is common.

Everything was arranged in the course of the following day, our wigs of themselves completely effecting all the disguises that were necessary. As for my uncle, he was nearly bald, and a wig was no great encumbrance ; but my shaggy locks gave me some trouble. A little clipping, however, answered the turn ; and I had a hearty laugh at myself, in costume, that afternoon, before Dunning's dressing-room glass. We got round the felony law, about being armed and disguised, by carrying no weapons but our tools in the way of trade.

CHAPTER V.

"And she hath smiles to earth unknown—
Smiles, that with motion of their own
Do spread, and sink, and rise;
That come and go with endless play,
And ever, as they pass away,
Are hidden in her eyes."
                                    WORDSWORTH

I WAS early in costume the following morning. I question if my own mother could have known me, had she lived
long enough to see the whiskers sprout on my cheeks, and
to contemplate my countenance as a man. I went into
Dunning's library, drew the little hurdy-gurdy from its
hiding-place, slung it, and began to play St. Patrick's Day
in the Morning, with spirit, and, I trust I may add, with
execution. I was in the height of the air, when the door
opened, and Barney thrust his high-cheeked-bone face into
the room, his mouth as wide open as that of a frozen
porker.

"Where the divil did ye come from?" demanded the new
footman, with the muscles of that vast aperture of his working from grin to grim, and grim to grin again. "Yee's
wilcome to the tchune; but how comes ye here?"

"I coomes vrom Halle, in Preussen. Vat isht your
vaterland?"

"Be yees a Jew?"

"Nein—I isht a goot Christian. Vilt you haf Yankee
Tootle?"

"Yankee T'under! Ye'll wake up the masther, and
he'll be displais'd, else ye might work upon t'at tchune till
the end of time. That I should hear it here, in my own
liberary, and ould Ireland t'ree thousand laigues away!"

A laugh from Dunning interrupted the dialogue, when
Barney vanished, no doubt anticipating some species of
American punishment for a presumed delinquency. Whether the blundering, well-meaning, honest fellow really
ascertained who we were that breakfasted with his master,

I do not know; but we got the meal and left the house without seeing his face again, Dunning having a young yellow fellow to do the service of the table.

I need scarcely say that I felt a little awkward at finding myself in the streets of New York in such a guise; but the gravity and self-possession of my uncle were a constant source of amusement to me. He actually sold a watch on the wharf before the boat left it, though I imputed his success to the circumstance that his price was what a brother dealer, who happened to be trading in the same neighbour-hood, pronounced " onconscionably low." We took a comfortable state-room between us, under the pretence of locking-up our property, and strolled about the boat, gaping and looking curious, as became our class.

" Here are at least a dozen people that I know," said my uncle, as we were lounging around—loafing around, is the modern Doric—about the time that the boat was paddling past Fort Washington; " I have reconnoitred in all quarters, and find quite a dozen. I have been conversing with an old school-fellow, and one with whom I have ever lived in tolerable intimacy, for the last ten minutes, and find my broken English and disguise are perfect. I am confident my dear mother herself would not recognise me."

" We can then amuse ourselves with my grandmother and the young ladies," I answered, " when we reach the Nest. For my part, it strikes me that we had better keep our own secret to the last moment."

" Hush! As I live, there is Seneca Newcome this moment! He is coming this way, and we must be Germans again.".

Sure enough, there was 'Squire Seneky, as the honest farmers around the Nest call him; though many of them must change their practices, or it will shortly become so absurd to apply the term " honest" to them, that no one will have the hardihood to use it. Newcome came slowly towards the forecastle, on which we were standing; and my uncle determined to get into conversation with him, as a means of further proving the virtue of our disguises, as well as possibly of opening the way to some communications that might facilitate our visit to the Nest. With this view, the pretended pedlar drew a watch from his pocket, and, offer-

ing it meekly to the inspection of the quasi lawyer, he
said—

"Puy a vatch, shentlemans?"

"Hey! what? Oh! a watch," returned Seneca, in that
high, condescending, vulgar key, with which the salt of the
earth usually affect to treat those they evidently think much
beneath them in intellect, station, or some other great essential, at the very moment they are bursting with envy, and
denouncing as aristocrats all who are above them. "Hey!
a watch, is it? What countryman are you, friend?"

"A Charmans—ein Teutscher."

"A German—ine Tycher is the place you come from, I
s'pose?"

"Nein—ein Teutscher isht a Charman."

"Oh, yes! I understand. How long have you been in
Ameriky?"

"Twelf moont's."

"Why, that's most long enough to make you citizens.
Where do you live?"

"Nowhere; I lifs jest asht it happens—soometimes here,
ant soometimes dere."

"Ay, ay! I understand—no legal domicile, but lead a
wandering life. Have you many of these watches for sale?"

"Yees—I haf asht many as twenty. Dey are as sheep
as dirt, and go like pig clocks."

'And what may be your price for this?"

"Dat you can haf for only eight tollars. Effery poty
wilt say it is golt, dat doesn't know petter."

"Oh! it isn't gold then — I swan!"—what this oath
meant I never exactly knew, though I suppose it to be a
puritan mode of saying "I swear!" the attempts to cheat
the devil in this way being very common among their pious
descendants, though even "Smith Thompson" himself can
do no man any good in such a case of conscience—"I
swan! you come plaguy near taking even me in! Wil.
you come down from that price any?"

"If you wilt gif me some atfice, perhaps I may. You
look like a goot shentlemans, and one dat woultn't sheat a
poor Charmans; ant effery poty wants so much to sheat de
poor Charmans, dat I will take six, if you will drow in some
atfice."

"Advice? You have come to the right man for that! Walk a little this way, where we shall be alone. What is the natur' of the matter—action on the case, or a tort?"

"Nein, nein! it isht not law dat I wants, put atfice."

"Well, but advice leads to law, ninety-nine times in a nundred."

"Ya, ya!" answered the pedlar, laughing; "dat may be so; put it isht not what I vants—I vants to know vere a Charman can trafel wit' his goots in de coontry, and not in de pig towns."

"I understand you—six dollars, hey! That sounds high for such a looking watch"—he had just before mistaken it for gold—"but I'm always the poor man's friend, and despise aristocracy"—what Seneca hated with the strongest hate, he ever fancied he *despised* the most, and by aristocracy he merely understood gentlemen and ladies, in the true signification of the words—"why, I'm always ready to help along the honest citizen. If you could make up your mind, now, to part with this one watch for nawthin', I think I could tell you a part of the country where you might sell the other nineteen in a week."

"Goot!" exclaimed my uncle, cheerfully. "Take him—he ist your broberty, and wilcome. Only show me de town where I canst sell de nineteen udders."

Had my uncle Ro been a true son of peddling, he would have charged a dollar extra on each of the nineteen, and made eleven dollars by his present liberality.

"It is no town at all—only a township," returned the literal Seneca. "Did you expect it would be a city?"

"Vat cares I? I woult radder sell my vatches to goot, honest, country men, dan asht to de best burghers in de land."

"You're my man! The right spirit is in you. I hope you're no patroon—no aristocrat?"

"I don't know vat isht badroon, or vat isht arishtocrat."

"No! You are a happy man in your ignorance. A patroon is a nobleman who owns another man's land; and an aristocrat is a body that thinks himself better than his neighbours, friend."

"Well den, I isht no badroon, for I don't own no land

7

at all, not even mine own; and I ishn't petter asht no poty at all."

"Yes, you be; you 've only to think so, and you 'll be the greatest gentleman of 'em all."

"Well, den, I will dry and dink so, and be petter asht de greatest shentlemans of dem all. But dat won't do, nudder, as dat vilt make me petter dan you; fon you are one of de greatest of dem all, shentlemans."

"Oh! as for me, let me alone. I scorn being on their level. I go for 'Down with the rent!' and so 'll you, too, afore you 've been a week in our part of the country."

"Vat isht de rent dat you vants to git down?"

"It 's a thing that 's opposed to the spirit of the institutions, as you can see by my feelin's at this very moment. But no matter! I 'll keep the watch, if you say so, and show you the way into that part of the country, as your pay."

"Agreet, shentlemans. Vat I vants is atfice, and vat you vants is a vatch."

Here uncle Ro laughed so much like himself, when he ought clearly to have laughed in broken English, that I was very much afraid he might give the alarm to our companion; but he did not. From that time, the best relations existed between us and Seneca, who, in the course of the day, recognised us by sundry smiles and winks, though I could plainly see he did not like the anti-aristocratic principle sufficiently to wish to seem too intimate with us. Before we reached the islands, however, he gave us directions where to meet him in the morning, and we parted, when the boat stopped alongside of the pier at Albany that afternoon, the best friends in the world.

"Albany! dear, good old Albany!" exclaimed my uncle Ro, as we stopped on the draw of the bridge to look at the busy scene in the basin, where literally hundreds of canal-boats were either lying to discharge or to load, or were coming and going, to say nothing of other craft; "dear, good old Albany! you are a town to which I ever return with pleasure, for you at least never disappoint me. A first-rate country-place you are; and, though I miss your quaint old Dutch church, and your rustic-looking old *Eng-*

lish church from the centre of your principal street, almost every change *you* make is respectable. I know nothing that tells so much against you as changing the name of Market street by the paltry imitation of Broadway; but, considering that a horde of Yankees have come down upon you since the commencement of the present century, you are lucky that the street was not called the Appian Way. But, excellent old Albany! whom even the corruptions of politics cannot change in the core, lying against thy hill-side, and surrounded with thy picturesque scenery, there is an air of respectability about thee that I admire, and a quiet prosperity that I love. Yet, how changed since my boyhood! Thy simple stoups have all vanished; thy gables are disappearing; marble and granite are rising in thy streets, too, but they take honest shapes, and are free from the ambition of mounting on stilts; thy basin has changed the whole character of thy once semi-sylvan, semi-commercial river; but it gives to thy young manhood an appearance of abundance and thrift that promise well for thy age!"

The reader may depend on it that I laughed heartily at this rhapsody; for I could hardly enter into my uncle's feelings. Albany is certainly a very good sort of a place, and relatively a more respectable-looking town than the "*commercial* emporium," which, after all, externally, is a mere huge expansion of a very marked mediocrity, with the pretension of a capital in its estimate of itself. But Albany lays no claim to be anything more than a provincial town and in that class it is highly placed. By the way, there is nothing in which "*our* people," to speak idiomatically, more deceive themselves, than in their estimate of what composes a capital. It would be ridiculous to suppose that the representatives of such a government as this could impart to any place the tone, opinions, habits and manners of a capital · for, if they did, they would impart it on the novel principle of communicating that which they do not possess in their own persons. Congress itself, though tolerably free from most shackles, including those of the constitution, is not up to that. In my opinion, a man accustomed to the world might be placed blindfolded in the most finished quarter of New York, and the place has new quarters in which the incongruities I have already mentioned do not exist, and,

my life on it, he could pronounce, as soon as the bandage
was removed, that he was not in a town where the tone of
a capital exists. The last thing to make a capital is trade.
Indeed the man who hears the words " business" and " the
merchants" ringing in his ears, may safely conclude, *de
facto*, that he is not in a capital. Now, a New-York village
is often much less rustic than the villages of the most advanced country of Europe ; but a New-York town is many
degrees below any capital of a large State in the old world.

Will New York ever be a capital? . Yes—out of all question, yes. But the day will not come until after the sudden
changes of condition which immediately and so naturally
succeeded the revolution, have ceased to influence ordinary
society, and those above again impart to those below more
than they receive. This restoration to the natural state of
things must take place, as soon as society gets settled ; and
there will be nothing to prevent a town living under our
own institutions—spirit, *tendencies* and all—from obtaining
the highest tone that ever yet prevailed in a capital. The
folly is in anticipating the natural course of events. Nothing will more hasten these events, however, than a literature that is controlled, not by the lower, but by the higher
opinion of the country ; which literature is yet, in a great
degree, to be created.   :   .

I had dispensed with the monkey, after trying to get
along with the creature for an hour or two, and went around
only with my music. I would rather manage an army of
anti-renters than one monkey. With the hurdy-gurdy slung
around my neck, therefore, I followed my uncle, who actually sold another watch before we reached a tavern. Of
course we did not presume to go to Congress Hall, or the
Eagle, for we knew we should not be admitted. This was
the toughest part of our adventures. I am of opinion my
uncle made a mistake; for he ventured to a second-class
house, under the impression that one of the sort usually
frequented by men of our supposed stamp might prove too
coarse for us, altogether. I think we should have been
better satisfied with the coarse fare of a coarse tavern, than
with the shabby-genteel of the house we blundered into.
In the former, everything would have reminded us, in a way
we expected to be reminded, that we were out of the com

mon track; and we might have been amused with the
change, though it is one singularly hard to be endured. I remember to have heard a young man, accustomed from childhood to the better habits of the country, but who went to sea a
lad, before the mast, declare that the coarseness of his ship-
mates, and there is no vulgarity about a true sailor, even
when coarsest, gave him more trouble to overcome, than all
the gales, physical sufferings, labour, exposures and dangers, put together. I must confess, I have found it so, too,
in my little experience. While acting as a strolling musician, I could get along with anything better than the coarse
habits which I encountered at the table. Your silver-fork-
isms, and your purely conventional customs, as a matter of
course, no man of the world attaches any serious importance to; but there are conventionalities that belong to the
fundamental principles of civilized society, which become
second nature, and with which it gets to be hard, indeed, to
dispense. I shall say as little as possible of the disagree-
ables of my new trade, therefore, but stick to the essentials.

The morning of the day which succeeded that of our
arrival at Albany, my uncle Ro and I took our seats in the
train, intending to go to Saratoga, viâ Troy. I wonder the
Trojan who first thought of playing this travestie on Homer,
did not think of calling the place Troyville, or Troybo-
rough! That would have been semi-American, at least,
whereas the present appellation is so purely classical! It
is impossible to walk through the streets of this neat and
flourishing town, which already counts its twenty thousand
souls, and not have the images of Achilles, and Hector, and
Priam, and Hecuba, pressing on the imagination a little
uncomfortably. Had the place been called Try, the name
would have been a sensible one; for it is trying all it can
to get the better of Albany; and, much as I love the latter
venerable old town, I hope Troy may succeed in its trying
to prevent the Hudson from being bridged. By the way, I
will here remark, for the benefit of those who have never
seen any country but their own, that there is a view on the
road between Schenectady and this Grecian place, just
where the heights give the first full appearance of the valley
of the Hudson, including glimpses of Waterford, Lansing-
burg and Albany, with a full view of both Troys, which

7 *

gives one a better idea of the affluence of European scenery
than almost any other,spot I can recall in America. To my
hurdy-gurdy : .

I made my first essay as a musician in public beneath the
windows of the principal inn of Troy. I cannot say much
in favour of the instrument, though I trust the playing itself
was somewhat respectable. This I know full well, that I
soon brought a dozen fair faces to the windows of the inn,
and that each was decorated with a smile. Then it was
that I regretted the monkey. Such an opening could not
but awaken the dormant ambition of even a ",patriot" of
the purest water, and I will own I was gratified.'

· Among the curious who thus appeared, were two whom
I at once supposed to be father and daughter. The former
was a clergyman, and, as I fancied by something in his air
of " the Church," begging pardon of those who take offence
at this exclusive title, and to whom I will just give a hint in
passing. Any one at all acquainted with mankind, will at
once understand that no man who is certain of possessing
any particular advantage, ever manifests much sensibility
because another lays claim to it also. In the constant
struggles of the jealous, for instance, on the subject of that
universal source of jealous feeling, social position, the man
or woman who is conscious of claims never troubles himself or herself about them. For them the obvious fact is
sufficient. If it be answered to this that the pretension of
" the Church" is exclusive, I shall admit it is, and "conclusive," too. It is not exclusive, however, in the sense
urged, since no one denies that there are many branches to
" the Church," although those branches do not embrace
everything. I would advise those who take offence at " our"
styling " ourselves" " the Church," to style themselves " the
Church," just as they call all their parsons bishops, and see
who will care about it. That is a touchstone which will
soon separate the true metal from the alloy.

My parson, I could easily see, was a *Church* clergyman
—not a *meeting*-house clergyman. How I ascertained that
fact at a glance, I shall not reveal ; but I also saw in his
countenance some of that curiosity which marks simplicity
of character : it was not a vulgar feeling, but one which
induced him to beckon me to approach a little nearer. I did

so, when he invited me in. It was a little awkward, at first, I must acknowledge, to be beckoned about in this manner; but there was something in the air and countenance of the daughter that induced me not to hesitate about complying. I cannot say that her beauty was so *very* striking, though she was decidedly pretty; but the expression of her face, eyes, smile, and all put together, was so singularly sweet and feminine, that I felt impelled by a sympathy I shall not attempt to explain, to enter the house, and ascend to the door of a parlour that I saw at once was public, though it then contained no one but my proper hosts.

"Walk in, young man," said the father, in a benevolent tone of voice. "I am curious to see that instrument; and my daughter here, who has a taste for music, wishes it as much as I do myself. What do you call it?"

"Hurty-gurty," I answered.

"From what part of the world do you come, my young friend?" continued the clergyman, raising his meek eyes to mine still more curiously. -

"Vrom Charmany; vrom Preussen, vere did reign so late de good Koenig Wilhelm."

"What does he say, Molly?"

So the pretty creature bore the name of Mary! I liked the Molly, too; it was a good sign, as none but the truly respectable dare use such familiar appellations - in these ambitious times. Molly sounded as if these people had the *aplomb* of position and conscious breeding. Had they been vulgar, it would have been Mollissa.

"It is not difficult to translate, father," answered one of the sweetest voices that had ever poured its melody on my ear, and which was rendered still more musical by the slight laugh that mingled with it. "He says he is from Germany —from Prussia, where the good King William lately reigned."

I liked the "father," too—that sounded refreshing, after passing a night among a tribe of foul-nosed adventurers in humanity, every one of whom had done his or her share towards caricaturing the once pretty appellatives of "Pa" and "Ma." A young lady may still say "Papa," or even "Mamma," though it were far better that she said

" Father," and " Mother ;" but as for " Pa" and " Ma," they are now done with in respectable life. They will not even do for the nursery.

"And this instrument is a hurdy-gurdy?" continued the clergyman. " What have we here—the name spelt on it?"

" Dat isht de maker's name—*Hochstiel fecit.*"

" Fecit!" repeated the clergyman ; " is that German?"

" Nein—dat isht Latin ; *facio, feci, factum, facere— feci, feciste,* FECIT. It means make, I suppose you know.

The parson looked at me, and at my dress and figure with open surprise, and smiled as his eye glanced at his daughter. If asked why I made this silly display of lower-form learning, I can only say that I chafed at being fancied a mere every-day street musician, that had left his monkey at home, by the charming girl who stood gracefully bending over her father's elbow, as the latter examined the inscrip-tion that was stamped on a small piece of ivory which had been let into the instrument. I could see that Mary shrunk back a little under the sensitive feeling, so natural to her sex, that she was manifesting too much freedom of manner for the presence of a youth who was nearer to her own class than she could have supposed it possible for a player on the hurdy-gurdy to be. A blush succeeded ; but the glance of the soft blue eye that instantly followed, seemed to set all at rest, and she leaned over her father's elbow again.

" You understand Latin, then?", demanded the parent, examining me over his spectacles from head to foot.

"A leetle, sir—just a ferry leetle. In my coontry, efery mans isht obliget to be a soldier some time, and them t'at knows Latin can be made sergeants and corporals."

" That is Prussia, is it?"

" Ya—Preussen, vere so late did reign de goot Koenig Wilhelm."

"And is Latin much understood among you? I have heard that, in Hungary, most well-informed persons even speak the tongue."

" In Charmany it isht not so. We all l'arnts somet'ing, but not all dost l'arn efery t'ing."

I could see a smile struggling around the sweet lips of that dear girl, after I had thus delivered myself, as I fancied, with a most accurate inaccuracy; but she succeeded in repressing it, though those provoking eyes of hers continued to laugh, much of the time our interview lasted.

"Oh! I very well know that in Prussia the schools are quite good, and that your government pays great attention to the wants of all classes," rejoined the clergyman; "but I confess some surprise that *you* should understand anything of Latin. Now, even in this country, where we boast so much——"

"Ye-e-s," I could not refrain from drawling out, "dey does poast a great teal in dis coontry!"

Mary actually laughed; whether it was at my words, or at the somewhat comical manner I had assumed—a manner in which simplicity was *tant soit peu* blended with irony—I shall not pretend to say. As for the father, his simplicity was of proof; and, after civilly waiting until my interruption was done, he resumed what he had been on the point of saying.

"I was about to add," continued the clergyman, "that even in this country, where we boast so much"—the little minx of a daughter passed her hand over her eyes, and fairly coloured with the effort she made not to laugh again —"of the common schools, and of their influence on the public mind, it is not usual to find persons of your condition who understand the dead languages."

"Ye-e-s," I replied; "it isht my condition 'dat misleats you, sir. Mine fat'er wast a shentlemans, and he gifet me as goot an etication as de Koenig did gif to de Kron Prinz."

Here, my desire to appear well in the eyes of Mary caused me to run into another silly indiscretion. How I was to explain the circumstance of the son of a Prussian gentleman, whose father had given him an education as good as that which the King of his country had given to its Crown Prince, being in the streets of Troy, playing on a hurdy-gurdy, was a difficulty I did not reflect on for a moment. The idea of being thought by that sweet girl a mere uneducated boor, was intolerable to me; and I threw it off by this desperate falsehood—false in its accessories, but true in its main facts—as one would resent an insult. Fortune favoured me, however, far more than I had any right to expect.

There is a singular disposition in the American character
to believe every well-mannered European at least a count.
I do not mean that those who have seen the world are not
like other persons in this respect; but a very great proportion of the country never has seen any other world than a
world of " business." The credulity on this subject sur-
passeth belief; and, were I to relate facts of this nature that
might be established in a court of justice, the very parties
connected with them would be ready to swear that they are
caricatures. Now, well-mannered I trust I am, and, though
plainly dressed and thoroughly disguised, neither my air
nor attire was absolutely mean. As my clothes were new,
I was neat in my appearance; and there were possibly
some incongruities about the last, that might have struck
eyes more penetrating than those of my companions. I
could see that both father and daughter felt a lively interest
in me, the instant I gave them reason to believe I was one
of better fortunes. So many crude notions exist among us
on the subject of convulsions and revolutions in Europe, that
I dare say, had I told any improbable tale of the political
condition of Prussia, it would have gone down; for nothing
so much resembles the ignorance that prevails in America,
generally, concerning the true state of things in Europe, as
the ignorance that prevails in Europe, generally, concerning
the true state of things in America. As for Mary, her soft
eyes seemed to me to be imbued with thrice their customary
gentleness and compassion, as she recoiled a step in native
modesty, and gazed at me, when I had made my revelation.

" If such is the case, my young friend," returned the clergyman, with benevolent interest, " you ought, and _might_
easily be placed in a better position than this you are now
in. Have you any knowledge of Greek?"

" Certainly—Greek is moch study in Charmany."

' In for a penny, in for a pound,' I thought.

"And the modern languages—do you understand any of
them?"

"I speaks de five great tongues of Europe, more ast less
well; and I read dem all, easily."

" The _five_ tongues!" said the clergyman, counting on his
fingers; " what can they be, Mary?"

"French, and German, and Spanish, and Italian, I suppose, sir."

"These make but four. What can be the fifth, my dear?"

"De yoong laty forgets de Englisch. De Englisch is das funf."

"Oh! yes, the English!" exclaimed the pretty creature, pressing her lips together to prevent laughing in my face.

"True—I had forgotten the English, not being accustomed to think of it as a mere European tongue. I suppose, young man, you naturally speak the English less fluently than any other of your five languages?"

"Ya!"

Again the smile struggled to the lips of Mary.

"I feel a deep interest in you as a stranger, and am sorry we have only met to part so soon. Which way shall you be likely to direct your steps, my Prussian young friend?"

"I go to a place which is callet Ravensnest—goot place to sell vatch, dey tells me."

"Ravensnest!" exclaimed the father.

"Ravensnest!" repeated the daughter, and that in tones which put the hurdy-gurdy to shame.

"Why, Ravensnest is the place where I live, and the parish of which I am the clergyman—the Protestant Episcopal clergyman, I mean."

This, then, was the Rev. Mr. Warren, the divine who had been called to our church the very summer I left home, and who had been there ever since! My sister Martha had written me much concerning these people, and I felt as if I had known them for years. Mr. Warren was a man of good connexions, and some education, but of no fortune whatever, who had gone into *the* Church—it was the church of his ancestors, one of whom had actually been an English bishop, a century or two ago—from choice, and contrary to the wishes of his friends. As a preacher, his success had never been great; but for the discharge of his duties no man stood higher, and no man was more respected. The living of St. Andrew's, Ravensnest, would have been poor enough, had it depended on the contributions of the parishioners. These last gave about one hundred and fifty dollars a-year, for their share of the support of a priest. I gave another hundred, as regularly as clock-work, and had been made to. do so throughout a long minority ; and my grand-mother and sister made up another fifty between them. But there was a glebe of fifty acres of capital land, a wood-lot, and a fund of two thousand dollars at interest ; the whole proceeding from endowments made by my grandfa-ther, during his lifetime. Altogether, the living may have been worth a clear five hundred dollars a-year, in addition to a comfortable house, hay, wood, vegetables, pasture, and some advantages in the way of small crops. Few country clergymen were better off than the rector of St. Andrew's, Ravensnest, and all as a consequence of the feudal and aristocratic habits of the Littlepages, though I say it, per-haps, who might better not, in times like these.

.My letters had told me that the Rev. Mr. Warren was a widower ; that Mary was his only child ; that he was a *truly* pious, not a *sham*-pious, and a really zealous clergy-man ; a man of purest truth, whose word was gospel—of great simplicity and integrity of mind and character ; that he never spoke evil of others, and that a complaint of this world and its hardships seldom crossed his lips. He loved his fellow-creatures, both naturally and · on principle ; mourned over the state of the diocese, and greatly pre-ferred piety even to high-churchism. High-churchman he was, nevertheless ; though it was not a high-churchmanship that outweighed the loftier considerations of· his christian duties, and left him equally without opinions of his own in matters of morals, and without a proper respect, in practice, for those that he had solemnly vowed to maintain.

His daughter was described as a sweet-tempered, arch, modest, sensible, and well-bred girl, that had received a far better education than her father's means would have per-mitted him to bestow, through the liberality and affection of a widowed sister of her mother's, who was affluent, and had caused her to attend the same school as that to which she.had sent her own daughters. In a word, she was a most charming neighbour ; and her presence at Ravensnest had rendered Martha's annual visits to the "old house" (built in 1785) not only less irksome, but actually pleasant. Such had been my sister's account of the Warrens and their qualities, throughout a correspondence of five years.

I have even fancied that she loved this Mary Warren better
than she loved any of her uncle's wards, herself of course
excepted.

The foregoing flashed through my mind, the instant the
clergyman announced himself; but the coincidence of our
being on the way to the same part of the country, seemed
to strike him as forcibly as it did myself. What Mary
thought of the matter, I had no means of ascertaining.

"This is singular enough," resumed Mr. Warren. "What
has directed your steps towards Ravensnest?"

"Dey tell mine ooncle 'tis goot place to sell moch vatch."

"You have an uncle, then? Ah! I see him there in the
street, showing a watch at this moment to a gentleman. Is
your uncle a linguist, too, and has he been as well educated
as you seem to be yourself?"

"Certain—he moch more of a shentleman dan ast de
shentleman to whom he now sell vatch."

"These must be the very persons," put in Mary, a little
eagerly, "of whom Mr. Newcome spoke, as the"—the dear
girl did not like to say pedlars, after what I had told them
of my origin; so she added—"dealers in watches and
trinkets, who intended to visit our part of the country."

"You are right, my dear, and the whole matter is now
clear. Mr. Newcome said he expected them to join us at
Troy, when we should proceed in the train together, as far
as Saratoga. But here comes Opportunity herself, and her
brother cannot be far off."

At that moment, sure enough, my old acquaintance, Opportunity Newcome, came into the room, a public parlour,
with an air of great self-satisfaction, and a *nonchalance* of
manner that was not a little more peculiar to herself than it
is to most of her caste. I trembled for my disguise, since,
to be quite frank on a very delicate subject, Opportunity had
made so very dead a set at me—"setting a cap" is but a
pitiful phrase to express the assault I had to withstand—as
scarcely to leave a hope that her feminine instinct, increased
and stimulated with the wish to be mistress of the Nest
house, could possibly overlook the thousand and one personal peculiarities that must still remain about one, whose
personal peculiarities she had made her particular study.

8

CHAPTER VI.

" O, sic a geek she gave her head,
 And sic a toss she gave her feather ;
Man, saw ye ne'er a-bonnier lass
Before, among the blooming heather ?"

ALLAN CUNNINGHAM.

"AH ! here are some charming French *vignettes !*" cried
Opportunity, running up to a table where lay some inferior
coloured engravings, that were intended to represent the
cardinal virtues, under the forms of tawdry female beauties.
The workmanship was French, as were the inscriptions.
Now, Opportunity knew just enough French to translate
these inscriptions, simple and school-girl as they were, as
wrong as they could possibly be translated, under the circumstances.

" *La Vertue*," cried Opportunity, in a high, decided way,
as if to make sure of an audience, " *The* Virtue ; *La Solitude*," pronouncing the last word in a desperately English
accent, " *The* Solitude ; La Charité, *The* Charity. It is
really delightful, Mary, as ' Sarah Soothings' would say, to
meet with these glimmerings of taste in this wilderness of
the world."

I wondered who the deuce "Sarah Soothings" could be,
but afterwards learned this was the nom-de-guerre of a
female contributor to the magazines, who, I dare say, silly
as she might be, was never silly enough to record the sentiments Opportunity had just professed to repeat. As for
The-la Charité, and *The la Vertue*, they did not in the
least surprise me ; for Martha, the hussy, often made herself merry by recording that young lady's *tours de force* in
French. On one occasion I remember she wrote me, that
when Opportunity wished to say *On est venu me chercher*,
instead of saying "I am come for," in homely English,
which would have been the best of all, she had flown off in
the high flight of " Je suis venue pour."

Mary smiled, for she comprehended perfectly the difference between *la Solitude* and *the* Solitude; but she said nothing. I must acknowledge that I was so indiscreet as to smile also, though, Opportunity's back being turned towards us, these mutual signs of intelligence that escaped us both through the eyes, opened a species of communication that, to me at least, was infinitely agreeable.

Opportunity, having shown the owner of the strange figure at which she had just glanced on entering the room, that she had studied French, now turned to take a better look at him. I have reason to think my appearance did not make a very happy impression on her; for she tossed her head, drew a chair, seated herself in the manner most opposed to the descent of down, and opened her budget of news, without the least regard to my presence, and apparently with as little attention to the wishes and tastes of her companions. Her accent, and jumping, hitching mode of speaking, with the high key in which she uttered her sentiments, too, all grated on my ears, which had become a little accustomed to different habits, in young ladies in particular, in the other hemisphere. I confess myself to be one of those who regard an even, quiet, graceful mode of utterance, as even a greater charm in a woman than beauty. Its effect is more lasting, and seems to be directly connected with the character. Mary Warren not only pronounced like one accustomed to good society; but the modulations of her voice, which was singularly sweet by nature, were even and agreeable, as is usual with well-bred women, and as far as possible from the jerking, fluttering, now rapid, now drawling manner of Opportunity. Perhaps, in this age of " loose attire," loose habits, and free and easy deportment, the speech denotes the gentleman, or the lady, more accurately than any other off-hand test.

"Sen is enough to wear out anybody's patience !" exclaimed Opportunity. "We must quit Troy in half an hour; and I have visits that I ought to pay to Miss Jones, and Miss White, and Miss Black, and Miss Green, and Miss Brown, and three or four others; and I can't get him to come near me."

"Why not go alone ?" asked Mary, quietly. "It is but a step to two or three of the houses, and you cannot possibly lose your way. I will go with you, if you desire it."

"Oh! lose my way? no, indeed! I know it too well for that. I wasn't educated in Troy, not to know something of the streets. But it looks so, to see a young lady walking in the streets without a beau! I never wish to cross a room in company without a beau; much less to cross a street. No; if Sen don't come in soon, I shall miss seeing every one of my friends, and that will be a desperate disappointment to us all; but it can't be helped: walk without a beau I *will not*, if I never see one of them again."

"Will you accept of me, Miss Opportunity?" asked Mr. Warren. "It will afford me pleasure to be of service to you."

"Lord! Mr. Warren, you don't think of setting up for a beau at your time of life, do you? Everybody would see that you're a clergyman, and I might just as well go alone. No, if Sen don't come in at once, I must lose my visits; and the young ladies will be *so* put out about it, I know! Araminta Maria wrote me, in the most particular manner, never to go through Troy without stopping to see *her*, if I didn't see another mortal; and Katherine Clotilda has as much as said she would never forgive me if I passed her door. But Seneca cares no more for the friendships of young ladies, than he does"—Miss Newcome pronounced this word "doos," notwithstanding her education, as she did "been," "ben," and fifty others just as much out of the common way—"But Seneca cares no more for the friendships of young ladies, than he does for the young patroon. I declare, Mr. Warren, I believe Sen will go crazy unless the anti-renters soon get the best of it; he does nothing but think and talk of ' rents,' and ' aristocracy,' and ' poodle usages,' from morning till night."

We all smiled at the little mistake of Miss Opportunity, but it was of no great consequence; and I dare say she knew what she meant as well as most others who use the same term, though they spell it more accurately. "Poodle usages" are quite as applicable to anything now existing in America, as "feudal usages."

"Your brother is then occupied with a matter of the last importance to the community of which he is a member," answered the clergyman, gravely. "On the termination of this anti-rent question hangs, in my judgment a vast amount of the future character, and much of the future destiny, of New York."

"I wonder, now! I'm surprised to hear you say this Mr. Warren, for generally you're thought to be unfriendly to the movement. Sen says, however, that everything looks well, and that *he* believes the tenants will get their lands throughout the State before they've done with it. He tells me we shall have Injins enough this summer at Ravensnest. The visit of old Mrs. Littlepage has raised a spirit that will not easily be put down, he says."

"And why should the visit of Mrs. Littlepage to the house of her grandson, and to the house built by her own husband, and in which she passed the happiest days of her life, 'raise a spirit,' as you call it, in any one in that part of the country?"

"Oh! you're episcopal, Mr. Warren; and we all know how the Episcopals feel about such matters. But, for my part, I don't think the Littlepages are a bit better than the Newcomes, though I won't liken them to some I could name at Ravensnest; but I don't think they are any better than you, yourself; and why should they ask so much more of the law than other folks?"

"I am not aware that they do ask more of the law than others; and, if they do, I'm sure they obtain less. The law in this country is virtually administered by jurors, who take good care to graduate justice, so far as they can, by a scale suited to their own opinions, and, quite often, to their prejudices. As the last are so universally opposed to persons in Mrs. Littlepage's class in life, if there be a chance to make her suffer, it is pretty certain it will be improved."

"Sen says he can't see why he should pay rent to a Littlepage, any more than a Littlepage should pay rent to him."

"I am sorry to hear it, since there is a very sufficient reason for the former, and no reason at all for the latter. Your brother uses the land of Mr. Littlepage, and that is a reason why he should pay him rent. If the case were reversed, then, indeed, Mr. Littlepage should pay rent to your brother."

"But what reason is there that these Littlepages should go on from father to son, from generation to generation, as

8 *

our landlords, when we're just as good as they. It's time
there was some change. Besides, only think, we've been
at the mills, now, hard upon eighty years, grandpa having
first settled there ; and we have had them very mills, now,
for three generations among us."

" High time, therefore, Opportunity, that there should be
some change," put in Mary, with a demure smile.

" Oh ! you 're so intimate with Marthy Littlepage, I 'm
not surprised at anything *you* think or say. But reason is
reason, for all that. I haven't the least grudge in the world
against young Hugh Littlepage; if foreign lands haven't
spoilt him, as they say they 're desperate apt to do, he 's an
agreeable young gentleman, and I can't say that *he* used to
think himself any better than other folks."

" I should say none of the family are justly liable to the
charge of so doing," returned Mary.

", Well, I 'm amazed to hear you say *that*, Mary Warren.
To my taste, Marthy Littlepage is as disagreeable as she
can be. If the anti-rent cause had nobody better than she
is to oppose it, it would soon triumph."

· " May I ask, Miss Newcome, what particular reason you
have for so thinking ?" asked Mr. Warren, who had kept his
eye on the young lady the whole time she had been thus
running on, with an interest that struck me as somewhat
exaggerated, when one remembered the character of the
speaker, and the value of her remarks.

" I think so, Mr. Warren, because everybody says so,"
was the answer. " If Marthy Littlepage don't think herself
better than other folks, why don't she *act* like other folks.
Nothing is good enough for her in her own conceit."

Poor little Patt, who was the very *beau idéal* of nature
and simplicity, as nature and simplicity manifest themselves
under the influence of refinement and good-breeding, was
here accused of fancying herself better than this ambitious
young lady, for no other reason than the fact of the little
distinctive peculiarities of her air and deportment, which
Opportunity had found utterly unattainable, after one or two
efforts to compass them. In this very fact is the secret
of a thousand of the absurdities and vices that are going up
and down the land at this moment, like raging lions, seeking
whom they may devour. Men often turn to their statute-

books and constitution to find the sources of obvious evils, that, in truth, have their origin in some of the lowest passions of human nature. The entrance of Seneca at that moment, however, gave a new turn to the discourse, though it continued substantially the same. I remarked that Seneca entered with his hat on, and that he kept his head covered during most of the interview that succeeded, notwithstanding the presence of the two young ladies and the divine. As for myself, I had been so free as to remove my cap, though many might suppose it was giving myself airs, while others would have imagined it was manifesting a degree of respect to human beings that was altogether unworthy of freemen. It is getting to be a thing so particular and aristocratic to take off the hat on entering a house, that few of the humbler democrats of America now ever think of it!

As a matter of course, Opportunity upbraided her delinquent brother for not appearing sooner to act as her beau; after which, she permitted him to say a word for himself. That Seneca was in high good-humour, was easily enough to be seen; he even rubbed his hands together in the excess of his delight.

"Something has happened to please Sen," cried the sister, her own mouth on a broad grin, in her expectation of coming in for a share of the gratification. "I wish you would get him to tell us what it is, Mary; he'll tell *you* anything."

I cannot describe how harshly this remark grated on my nerves. The thought that Mary Warren could consent to exercise even the most distant influence over such a man as Seneca Newcome, was to the last degree unpleasant to me, and I could have wished that she would openly and indignantly repel the notion. But Mary Warren treated the whole matter very much as a person who was accustomed to such remarks would be apt to do. I cannot say that she manifested either pleasure or displeasure; but a cold indifference was, if anything, uppermost in her manner. Possibly, I should have been content with this; but I found it very difficult to be so. Seneca, however, did not wait for Miss Warren to exert her influence to induce him to talk, but appeared well enough disposed to do it of his own accord.

" Something *has* happened to please me, I must own," he answered; " and I would as lief Mr. Warren should know what it is, as not.   Things go ahead finely among us anti-renters, and we shall carry all our p'ints before long!"

" I wish I were certain no points would be carried but those that ought to be carried, Mr. Newcome," was the answer.   " But what has happened, lately, to give a new aspect to the affair?"

" We 're gaining strength among the politicians.   Both sides are beginning to court us, and the 'spirit of the insti-tutions' will shortly make themselves respected."

" I am delighted to hear that!   It is in the intention of the institutions to repress covetousness, and uncharitable-ness, and all frauds, and to do nothing but what is right," observed Mr. Warren. -

"Ah! here comes my friend the travelling jeweller," said Seneca, interrupting the clergyman, in order to salute my uncle, who at that instant showed himself in the door of the room, cap in hand.   " Walk in, Mr. Dafidson, since that is your name: Rev. Mr. Warren—Miss Mary Warren—Miss Opportunity Newcome, my sister, who will be glad to look at your wares.   The cars will be detained on some special business, and we have plenty of time before us."

All this was done with a coolness and indifference of manner which went to show that Seneca had no scruples whatever on the subject of whom he introduced to any one. As for my uncle, accustomed to these free and easy man-ners, and probably not absolutely conscious of the figure he cut in his disguise, he bowed rather too much like a gentle-man for one of his present calling, though my previous explanation of our own connexion and fallen fortunes had luckily prepared the way for this deportment.

" Come in, Mr. Dafidson, and open your box—my sister may fancy some of your trinkets; I never knew a girl that didn't."

The imaginary pedlar entered, and placed his box on a table near which I was standing, the whole party imme-diately gathering around it.   My presence had attracted no particular attention from either Seneca or his sister, the room being public, and my connexion with the vender of trinkets known.   In the mean time, Seneca was too full of his good news to let the subject drop; while the watches, rings, chains, brooches, bracelets, &c. &c., were passed under examination.

"Yes, Mr. Warren, I trust we are about to have a complete development of the spirit of our institutions, and that in futur' there will be no privileged classes in New York, at least."

"The last will certainly be a great gain, sir," the divine coldly answered. "Hitherto, those who have most suppressed the truth, and who have most contributed to the circulation of flattering falsehoods, have had undue advantages in America."

Seneca, obviously enough, did not like this sentiment; but I thought, by his manner, that he was somewhat accustomed to meeting with such rebuffs from Mr. Warren.

"I suppose you will admit there *are* privileged classes now among us, Mr. Warren?"

"I am ready enough to allow that, sir; it is too plain to be denied."

"Wa-all, I should like to hear *you* p'int 'em out; that I might see if we agree in our sentiments."

"Demagogues are a highly privileged class. The editors of newspapers are another highly privileged class; doing things, daily and hourly, which set all law and justice at defiance, and invading, with perfect impunity, the most precious rights of their fellow-citizens. The power of both is enormous; and, as in all cases of great and irresponsible power, both enormously abuse it."

"Wa-all, that's not my way of thinking at all. In my judgment, the privileged classes in this country are your patroons and your landlords; men that's not satisfied with a reasonable quantity of land, but who wish to hold more than the rest of their fellow-creatur's."

"I am not aware of a single privilege that any patroon— of whom, by the way, there no longer exists one, except in name—or any landlord, possesses over any one of his fellow-citizens."

"Do you call it no privilege for a man to hold all the land there may happen to be in a township? I call that a great privilege; and such as no man should have in a free country. Other people want land as well as your Van

Renssalaers and Littlepages; and other people mean to have it, too."

"On that principle, every man who owns more of any one thing than his neighbour is privileged. Even I, poor as I am, and am believed to be, am privileged over you, Mr. Newcome. I own a cassock, and have two gowns, one old and one new, and various other things of the sort, of which you have not one. What is more, I am privileged in another sense; since I can *wear* my cassock and gown, and bands, and *do* wear them often; whereas you cannot wear one of them all without making yourself laughed at."

"Oh! but them are not privileges I care anything about; if I did I would put on the things, as the law does not prohibit it."

"I beg your pardon, Mr. Newcome; the law does prohibit you from wearing *my* cassock and gown contrary to my wishes."

"Wa-all, wa-all, Mr. Warren; we never shall quarrel about that; I don't desire to wear your cassack and gown."

"I understand you, then; it is only the things that you *desire* to use that you deem it a privilege for the law to leave me."

"I am afraid we shall never agree, Mr. Warren, about this anti-rent business; and I'm very sorry for it, as I wish particularly to think as you do," glancing his eye most profanely towards Mary as he spoke. "I am for the movement-principle, while you are too much for the stand-still doctrine."

"I am certainly for remaining stationary, Mr. Newcome, if progress mean taking away the property of old and long established families in the country, to give it to those whose names are not to be found in our history; or, indeed, to give it to any but those to whom it rightfully belongs."

"We shall never agree, my dear sir, we shall never agree;" then, turning towards my uncle with the air of superiority that the vulgar so easily assume—"What do *you* say to all this, friend Dafidson—are you up-rent or down-rent?"

"Ja, mynheer," was the quiet answer;" "I always downs mit der rent vens I leave a house or a garten. It is goot to pay de debts; ja, it ist herr goot."

This answer caused the clergyman and his daughter to smile, while Opportunity laughed outright.

"You won't make much of your Dutch friend, Sen," cried this buoyant young lady; "he says you ought to keep on paying rent!"

"I apprehend Mr. Dafidson does not exactly understand the case," answered Seneca, who was a good deal disconcerted, but was bent on maintaining his point. "I have understood you to say that you are a man of liberal principles, Mr. Dafidson, and that you 've come to America to enjoy the light of intelligence and the benefits of a free government."

"Ja; ven I might coome to America, I say, vell, dat 'tis a goot coontry, vhere an honest man might haf vhat he 'arns, ant keep it, too. Ja, ja! dat ist vhat I say, ant vhat I dinks."

"I understand you, sir; you come from a part of the world where the nobles eat up the fat of the land, taking the poor man's share as well as his own, to live in a coun try where the law is, or soon will be, so equal that no citizen will dare to talk about his *estates*, and hurt the feelin's of such as haven't got any."

My uncle so well affected an innocent perplexity at the drift of this remark as to make me smile, in spite of an effort to conceal it. Mary Warren saw that smile, and another glance of intelligence was exchanged between us; though the young lady immediately withdrew her look, a little consciously and with a slight blush.

"I say that you like equal laws and equal privileges, friend Dafidson," continued Seneca, with emphasis; "and that you have seen too much of the evils of nobility and of feudal oppression in the old world, to wish to fall in with them in the new."

"Der noples ant der feudal privileges ist no goot," answered the trinket-pedlar, shaking his head with an appearance of great distaste.

"Ay, I knew it would be so; you see, Mr. Warren, no man who has ever lived under a feudal system can ever feel otherwise."

"But what have we to do with feudal systems, Mr. Newcome? and what is there in common between the landlords of New York and the nobles of Europe, and between their leases and feudal tenures?"

"What is there? A vast deal too much, sir, take my word for it. Do not our very governors, even while ruthlessly calling on one citizen to murder another——"

"Nay, nay, Mr. Newcome," interrupted Mary Warren, laughing, "the governors call on the citizens *not* to murder each other."

"I understand you, Miss Mary; but we shall make anti-renters of you both before we are done. Surely, sir, there is a great deal too much resemblance between the nobles of Europe and our landlords, when the honest and free-born tenants of the last are obliged to pay tribute for permission to live on the very land that they till, and which they cause to bring forth its increase."

"But men who are not noble let their lands in Europe; nay, the very serfs, as they become free and obtain riches, buy lands and let them, in some parts of the old world, as I have heard and read."

"All feudal, sir. The whole system is pernicious and feudal, serf or no serf."

"But, Mr. Newcome," said Mary Warren, quietly, though with a sort of demure irony in her manner that said she was not without humour, and understood herself very well, "even you let your land—land that you lease, too, and which you do not own, except as you hire it from Mr. Littlepage."

Seneca gave a hem, and was evidently disconcerted; but he had too much of the game of the true progressive movement—which merely means to *lead* in changes, though they may lead to the devil—to give the matter up. Repeating the hem, more to clear his brain than to clear his throat, he hit upon his answer, and brought it out with something very like triumph.

"That is one of the evils of the present system, Miss Mary. Did I own the two or three fields you mean, and to attend to which I have no leisure, I might *sell* them; but now it is impossible, since I can give no deed. The instant my poor uncle dies—and he can't survive a week, being, as you must know, nearly gone—the whole property, mills, tavern, farms, timber-lot and all, fall in to young Hugh Littlepage, who is off frolicking in Europe, doing no good to himself or others, I'll venture to say, if the truth were known. That is another of the hardships of the feudal system; it enables one man to travel in idleness, wasting his substance in foreign lands, while it keeps another at home, at the plough-handles and the cart-tail."

"And why do you suppose Mr. Hugh Littlepage wastes his substance, and is doing himself and country no good in foreign lands, Mr. Newcome? That is not at all the character I hear of him, nor is it the result that I expect to see from his travels."

"The money he spends in Europe might do a vast deal of good at Ravensnest, sir."

"For my part, my dear sir," put in Mary again, in her quiet but pungent way, "I think it remarkable that neither of our late governors has seen fit to enumerate the facts just mentioned by Mr. Newcome among those that are opposed to the spirit of the institutions. It is, indeed, a great hardship that Mr. Seneca Newcome cannot sell Mr. Hugh Littlepage's land."

"I complain less of that," cried Seneca, a little hastily "than of the circumstance that all my rights in the property must go with the death of my uncle. *That*, at least, even you, Miss Mary, must admit is a great hardship."

"If your uncle were unexpectedly to revive, and live twenty years, Mr. Newcome——"

"No, no, Miss Mary," answered Seneca, shaking his head in a melancholy manner; "*that* is absolutely impossible. It would not surprise me to find him dead and buried on our return."

"But, admit that you may be mistaken, and that your lease should continue—you would still have a rent to pay?"

"Of that I wouldn't complain in the least. If Mr. Dunning, Littlepage's agent, will just promise, in as much as half a sentence, that we can get a new lease on the old terms, I'd not say a syllable about it."

"Well, here is one proof that the system has its advantages!" exclaimed Mr. Warren, cheerfully. "I'm delighted to hear you say this; for it is something to have a class of men among us whose simple promises, in a matter of money, have so much value! It is to be hoped that their example will not be lost."

9

" Mr. Newcome has made an admission I am also glad to hear," added Mary, as soon as her father had done speaking. " His willingness to accept a new lease on the old terms is a proof that he has been living under a good bargain for himself hitherto, and that down to the present moment he has been the obliged party."

This was very simply said, but it bothered Seneca amazingly. As for myself, I was delighted with it, and could have kissed the pretty, arch creature who had just uttered the remark; though I will own that as much might have been done without any great reluctance, had she even held her tongue. As for Seneca, he did what most men are apt to do when they have the consciousness of not appearing particularly well in a given point of view; he endeavoured to present himself to the eyes of his companions in another.

" There is one thing, Mr. Warren, that I think you will admit ought not to be," he cried, exultingly, " whatever Miss Mary thinks about it ; and that is, that the Littlepage pew in your church ought to come down."

" I will not say that much, Mr. Newcome, though I rather think my daughter will. I believe, my dear, you are of Mr. Newcome's way of thinking in respect to this canopied pew, and also in respect to the old hatchments?"

— " I wish neither was in the church," answered Mary, in a low voice.

From that moment I was fully resolved neither should be, as soon as I got into a situation to control the matter.

" In that I agree with you entirely, my child," resumed the clergyman ; " and were it not for this movement connected with the rents, and the false principles that have been so boldly announced of late years, I might have taken on myself the authority, as rector, to remove the hatchments. Even according to the laws connected with the use of such things, they should have been taken away a generation or two back. As to the pew, it is a different matter. It is private property ; was constructed with the church, which was built itself by the joint liberality of the Littlepages and mother Trinity ; and it would be a most ungracious act to undertake to destroy it under such circumstances, and more especially in the absence of its owner."

"You agree, however, that it ought not to be there?" asked Seneca, with exultation.

"I wish with all my heart it were not. I dislike every thing like worldly distinction in the house of God; and heraldic emblems, in particular, seem to me very much out of place where the cross is seen to be in its proper place."

"Wa-all, now, Mr. Warren, I can't say I much fancy crosses about churches either. What's the use in raising vain distinctions of any sort. A church is but a house, after all, and ought so to be regarded."

"True," said Mary, firmly; "but the house of God."

"Yes, yes, we all know, Miss Mary, that you Episcopalians look more at outward things, and more respect outward things, than most of the other denominations of the country."

"Do you call leases 'outward things,' Mr. Newcome?" asked Mary, archly; "and contracts, and bargains, and promises, and the rights of property, and the obligation to 'do as you would be done by?'"

"Law! good folks," cried Opportunity, who had been all this time tumbling over the trinkets, "I wish it was 'down with the rent' for ever, with all my heart; and that not another word might ever be said on the subject. Here is one of the prettiest pencils, Mary, I ever did see; and its price is only four dollars. I wish, Sen, you'd let the rent alone, and make me a present of this very pencil."

As this was an act of which Seneca had not the least intention of being guilty, he merely shifted his hat from one side of his head to the other, began to whistle, and then he coolly left the room. My uncle Ro profited by the occasion to beg Miss Opportunity would do him the honour to accept the pencil as an offering from himself.

"You an't surely in earnest!" exclaimed Opportunity flushing up with surprise and pleasure. "Why, you told me the price was four dollars; and even that seems to me desperate little!"

"Dat ist de price to anudder," said the gallant trinket-dealer; "but dat ist not de price to you, Miss Opportunity. Ve shall trafel togedder; ant vhen ve gets to your coontry you vill dell me de best houses vhere I might go mit my vatches ant drinkets."

" That I will ; and get you in at the Nest Ho.ise, in the
bargain," cried Opportunity, pocketing the pencil without
further parley.

In the mean time my uncle selected a very neat seal, the
handsomest he had, being of pure metal, and having a real
topaz in it, and offered it to Mary Warren, with his best
bow. I watched the clergyman's daughter with anxiety,
as I witnessed the progress of this *galantérie*, doubting and
hoping at each change of the ingenuous and beautiful countenance of her to whom the offering was made. Mary coloured, smiled, seemed embarrassed, and, as I feared, for a
single moment doubting; but I must have been mistaken,
as she drew back, and, in the sweetest manner possible,
declined to accept the present. I saw that Opportunity's
having just adopted a different course added very much to
her embarrassment, as otherwise she might have said something to lessen the seeming ungraciousness of the refusal.
Luckily for herself, however, she had a gentleman to deal
with, instead of one in the station that my uncle Ro had vo-
luntarily assumed. When this offering was made, the pretended pedlar was ignorant altogether of the true characters
of the clergyman and his daughter, not even knowing that
he saw the rector of St. Andrew's, Ravensnest. But the
manner of Mary at once disabused him of an error into
which he had fallen through her association with Opportunity, and he now drew back himself with perfect tact, bowing and apologizing in a way that I thought must certainly
betray his disguise. It did not, however; for Mr. Warren,
with a smile that denoted equally satisfaction at his daughter's conduct, and a grateful sense of the other's intended
liberality, but with a simplicity that was of proof, turned to
me and begged a tune on the flute which I had drawn from
my pocket and was holding in my hand, as expecting some
such invitation.

If I have any accomplishment, it is connected with music;
and particularly with the management of the flute. On this
occasion I was not at all backward about showing off, and
I executed two or three airs, from the best masters, with as
much care as if I had been playing to a salon in one of the
best quarters of Paris. I could see that Mary and her father
were both surprised at the execution, and that the first was

delighted. We had a most agreeable quarter of an hour together; and might have had two, had not Opportunity— who was certainly well named, being apropos of every- thing—began of her own accord to sing, though not with- out inviting Mary to join her. As the latter declined this public exhibition, as well as my uncle Ro's offering, Sene- ca's sister had it all to herself; and she sang no less than three songs, in quick succession, and altogether unasked. I shall not stop to characterize the music or the words of these songs, any further than to say they were all, more or less, of the Jim Crow school, and executed in a way that did them ample justice.

As it was understood that we were all to travel in the same train, the interview lasted until we were ready to pro- ceed; nor did it absolutely terminate then. As Mary and Opportunity sat together, Mr. Warren asked me to share his seat, regardless of the hurdy-gurdy; though my attire, in addition to its being perfectly new and neat, was by no means of the mean character that it is usual to see adorning street-music in general. On the whole, so long as the in strument was not *en evidence*, I might not have seemed very much out of place seated at Mr. Warren's side. In this manner we proceeded to Saratoga, my uncle keeping up a private discourse the whole way with Seneca, on mat- ters connected with the rent movement.

As for the divine and myself, we had also much interest- ing talk together. I was questioned about Europe in gene- ral, and Germany in particular; and had reason to think my answers gave surprise as well as satisfaction. It was not an easy matter to preserve the Doric of my assumed dialect, though practice and fear contributed their share to render me content to resort to it. I made many mistakes, of course, but my listeners were not the persons to discover them. I say my listeners, for I soon ascertained that Mary Warren, who sat on the seat directly before us, was a pro- foundly attentive listener to all that passed. This circum- stance did not render me the less communicative, though it did increase the desire I felt to render what I said worthy of such a listener. As for Opportunity, she read a news- paper a little while, munched an apple a very little while,

9 *

and slept the rest of the way. But the journey between
modern Troy and Saratoga is not a long one, and was soon
accomplished.

CHAPTER VII.

"I will tell you ;
If you' ll bestow a small (of what you have little),
Patience, a while, you 'll hear the belly's answer."
MENENIUS AGRIPPA.

AT the springs we parted, Mr. Warren and his friends
finding a conveyance, with their own horses, in readiness to
carry them the remainder of the distance. As for my uncle
and myself, it was understood that we were to get on in the
best manner we could, it being .expected that we should
reach Ravensnest in the course of a day or two. According to the theory of our new business, we ought to travel on
foot, but we had a reservation *in petto* that promised us also
the relief of a comfortable wagon of some sort or other.

" Well," said my uncle, the moment we had got far
enough from our new acquaintances to be out of ear-shot,
" I must say one thing in behalf of Mr. Seneky, as he calls
himself, or Sen, as his elegant sister calls him; and that is,
that I believe him to be one of the biggest scoundrels the
state holds."

" This is not drawing his character *en beau*," I answered,
laughing. " But why do you come out so decidedly upon
him at this particular moment?"

" Because this particular moment happens to be the first
in which I have had an opportunity to, say anything since
I have known the rascal. You must have remarked that
the fellow held me in discourse from the time we left Troy
until we stopped here."

" Certainly ; I could see that his tongue was in motion
unceasingly : what he said, I have to conjecture."

" He said enough to lay bare his whole character. Our subject was anti-rent, which he commenced with a view to explain it to a foreigner; but I managed to lead him on, step by step, until he let me into all his notions and expectations on the subject. Why, Hugh, the villain actually proposed that you and I should enlist, and turn ourselves into two of the rascally mock redskins."·

" Enlist! Do they still persevere so far as to keep up that organization, in the very teeth of the late law?"

" The law! What do two or three thousand voters care for any penal law, in a country like this? Who is to enforce the law against them? Did they commit murder, and were they even convicted, as *might* happen under the excitement of such a crime, they very well know nobody would be hanged. Honesty is always too passive in matters that do not immediately press on its direct interests. It is for the interest of every honest man in the State to set his face against this anti-rent movement, and to do all he can, by his vote and influence, to put it down into the dirt, out of which it sprang, and into which it should be crushed; but not one in a hundred, even of those who condemn it *totu cœlo*, will go a foot out of their way even to impede its pro gress. All depends on those who have the power; and they will exert that power so as to conciliate the active rogue, rather than protect the honest man. You are to remember that the laws are executed here on the principle that ' what is everybody's business is nobody's business.' " ·

" You surely do not believe that the authorities will wink at an open violation of the laws!"

" That will depend on the characters of individuals; most will, but some will not. You and I would be punished soon enough, were there a chance, but the mass would escape. Oh! we have had some precious disclosures in our corner of the car! The two or three men who joined Newcome are from anti-rent districts, and seeing me with their friend, little reserve has been practised. One of those men is an anti-rent lecturer; and, being somewhat didactic, he favoured me with some of his arguments, *seriatim*."

" How! Have they got to lectures? I should have supposed the newspapers would have been the means of circulating their ideas."

"Oh, the newspapers, like hogs swimming too freely, have cut their own throats; and it seems to be fashionable, just at this moment, not to believe them. Lecturing is the great moral lever of the nation at present."

"But a man can lie in a lecture, as well as in a newspaper."

"Out of all question; and if many of the lecturers are of the school of this Mr. Holmes—'Lecturer Holmes,' as Seneca called him—but, if many are of *his* school, a pretty set of liberty-takers with the truth must they be."

"You detected him, then, in some of these liberties?"

"In a hundred: nothing was easier than for a man in my situation to do that; knowing, as I did, so much of the history of the land-titles of the State. One of his arguments partakes so largely of the weak side of our system, that I must give it to you. He spoke of the gravity of the disturbances—of the importance to the peace and character of the State of putting an end to them; and then, by way of corollary to his proposition, produced a scheme for changing the titles, IN ORDER TO SATISFY THE PEOPLE!"

"The people, of course, meaning the tenants; the landlords and *their* rights passing for nothing."

"That is one beautiful feature of the morality—an eye, or a cheek, if you will—but here is the *nose*, and highly Roman it is. A certain portion of the community wish to get rid of the obligations of their contracts; and finding it cannot be done by law, they resort to means that are opposed to all law, in order to effect their purposes. Public lawbreakers, violators of the public peace, they make use of their own wrong as an argument for perpetuating another that can be perpetuated in no other way. I have been looking over some of the papers containing proclamations, &c., and find that both law-makers and law-breakers are of one mind as to this charming policy. Without a single manly effort to put down the atrocious wrong that is meditated, the existence of the wrong itself is made an argument for meeting it with concessions, and thus sustaining it. Instead of using the means the institutions have provided for putting down all such unjust and illegal combinations, the combinations are a sufficient reason of themselves why the laws should be altered, and wrong be done to a few, in order that many may be propitiated, and their votes secured."

"This is reasoning that can be used only' where real grievances exist. But there are no real grievances in the case of the tenants. They may mystify weak heads in the instance of the Manor leases, with their quarter sales, fat hens, loads of wood and days' works; but my leases are all on three lives, with rent payable in money, and with none of the conditions that are called feudal, though no more feudal than any other bargain to pay articles in kind. One might just as well call a bargain made by a butcher to deliver pork, for a series of years feudal. However, feudal or not, my leases, and those of most other landlords, are running on lives; and yet, by what I can learn, the discontent is general; and the men who have solemnly bargained to give up their farms at the expiration of the lives are just as warm for the 'down-rent' and titles in fee, as the Manor tenants themselves! They say that the obligations given for actual purchases are beginning to be discredited."

"You are quite right; and there is one of the frauds practised on the world at large. In the public documents, only the Manor leases, with their pretended feudal covenants and their perpetuity, are kept in view, while the combination goes to *all* leases, or nearly all, and certainly to all *sorts* of leases, where the estates are of sufficient extent to allow of the tenants to make head against the landlords. I dare say there are hundreds of tenants, even on the property of the Rensselaers, who are honest enough to be willing to comply with their contracts if the conspirators would let them; but the rapacious spirit is abroad among the occupants of other lands, as well as among the occupants of theirs, and the government considers its existence a proof that concessions should be made. The discontented must be appeased, right or not!"

"Did Seneca say anything on the subject of his own interests?"

"He did; not so much in conversation with me, as in the discourse he held with 'Lecturer Holmes.' I listened attentively, happening to be familiar, through tradition and through personal knowledge, with all the leading facts of the case. As you will soon be called on to act in that matter for yourself, I may as well relate them to you. They will serve, also, as guides to the moral merits of the occu pation of half the farms on your estate. These are things, moreover, you would never know by public statements, since all the good bargains are smothered in silence, while those that may possibly have been a little unfavourable to the tenant are proclaimed far and near. It is quite possible that, among the many thousands of leased farms that are to be found in the State, some bad bargains may have been made by the tenants ; but what sort of a government is that which should undertake to redress evils of this nature? If either of the Renssalaers, or you yourself, were to venture to send a memorial to the Legislature setting forth the grievances *you* labour under in connection with this very ' mill lot'——and serious losses do they bring to you, let me tell you, though grievances, in the proper sense of the term, they are not——you and your memorial would be met with a general and merited shout of ridicule and derision. *One* man has no rights, as opposed to a dozen."

" So much difference is there between ' *de la Rochefoucauld et de la Rochefoucauld.*"

" All the difference in the world : but let me give you the facts, for they will serve as a rule by which to judge of many others. In the first place, my great-grandfather Mordaunt, the ' patentee,' as he was called, first let the mill lot to the grandfather of this Seneca, the tenant then being quite a young man. In order to obtain settlers, in that early day, it was necessary to give them great advantages, for there was vastly more land than there were people to work it. The first lease, therefore, was granted on highly advantageous terms to that Jason Newcome, whom I can just remember. He had two characters ; the one, and the true, which set him down as a covetous, envious, narrow-minded provincial, who was full of cant and roguery. Some traditions exist among us of his having been detected in stealing timber, and in various other frauds. In public he is one of those virtuous and hard-working pioneers who have transmitted to their descendants all their claims, those that are supposed to be moral, as well as those that are known to be legal. This flummery may do for elderly ladies, who affect snuff and bohea, and for some men who have minds of the same calibre, but they are not circumstances to influence such legislators and executives as are fit to be legislators and executives. Not a great while before my father's marriage, the said Jason still living and in possession, the lease expired, and a new one was granted for three lives, or twenty-one years certain, of which one of the lives is still running. That lease was granted, on terms highly favourable to the tenant, sixty years since, old Newcome, luckily for himself and his posterity, having named this long-lived son as one of his three lives. Now Seneky, God bless him! is known to lease a few of the lots that have fallen to his share of the property for more money than is required to meet all your rent on the whole. Such, in effect, has been the fact with that mill-lot for the last thirty years, or even longer; and the circumstance of the great length of time so excellent a bargain has existed, is used as an argument why the Newcomes ought to have a deed of the property for a nominal price; or, indeed, for no price at all, if the tenants could have their wishes."

"I am afraid there is nothing unnatural in thus perverting principles; half mankind appear to me really to get a great many of their notions *dessus dessous*."

"Half is a small proportion; as you will find, my boy, when you grow older. But was it not an impudent proposal of Seneca, when he wished you and me to join the corps of 'Injins?'"

"What answer did you make? Though I suppose it would hardly do for us to go disguised and armed, now that the law makes it a felony, even while our motive, at the bottom, might be to aid the law."

"Catch me at that act of folly! Why, Hugh, could they prove such a crime on either of *us*, or any one connected with an old landed family, we should be the certain victims. No governor would dare pardon *us*. No, no; clemency is a word reserved for the obvious and confirmed rogues."

"We might get a little favour on the score of belonging to a very powerful body of offenders."

"True; I forgot that circumstance. The more numerous the crimes and the criminals, the greater the probability of impunity; and this, too, not on the general principle that power cannot be resisted, but on the particular principle that a thousand or two votes are of vast importance,

where three thousand can turn an election. God only knows
where this thing is to end !"

We now approached one of the humbler taverns of the
place, where it was necessary for those of our apparent pretensions to seek lodgings, and the discourse was dropped.
It was several weeks too early in the season for the Springs
to be frequented, and we found only a few of those in the
place who drank the waters because they really required
them. My uncle had been an old stager at Saratoga—a
beau of the " purest water," as he laughingly described himself—and he was enabled to explain all that it was necessary for me to know. An American watering-place, however, is so very much inferior to most of those in Europe,
as to furnish very little, in their best moments, beyond the
human beings they contain, to attract the attention of the
traveller.

In the course of the afternoon we availed ourselves of the
opportunity of a return vehicle to go as far as Sandy Hill,
where we passed the night. The next morning, bright and
early, we got into a hired wagon and drove across the country until near night, when we paid for our passage, sent the
vehicle back, and sought a tavern. At this house, where
we passed the night, we heard a good deal of the " Injins" having made their appearance on the Littlepage lands, and many
conjectures as to the probable result. We were in a township, or rather on a property that was called Mooseridge,
and which had once belonged to us, but which, having been
sold, and in a great measure paid for by the occupants, no
one thought of impairing the force of the covenants under
which the parties held. The most trivial observer will soon
discover that it is only when something is to be gained that
the aggrieved citizen wishes to disturb a covenant. Now,
I never heard any one say a syllable against either of the
covenants of his lease under which he held his farm, let him
be ever so loud against those which would shortly compel
him to give it up ! Had I complained of the fact—and such
facts abounded—that my predecessors had incautiously let
farms at such low prices that the lessees had been enabled
to pay the rents for half a century by subletting small portions of them, as my uncle Ro had intimated, I should be

pointed at as a fool. " Stick to your bond" would have been the cry, and " Shylock" would have been forgotten. I do not say that there is not a vast difference between the means of acquiring intelligence, the cultivation, the manners, the social conditions, and, in some senses, the social obligations of an affluent landlord and a really hard-working, honest, well-intentioned husbandman, his tenant—differences that should dispose the liberal and cultivated gentleman to bear in mind the advantages he has perhaps inherited, and not acquired by his own means, in such a way as to render him, in a certain degree, the repository of the interests of those who hold under him ; but, while I admit all this, and say that the community which does not possess such a class of men is to be pitied, as it loses one of the most certain means of liberalizing and enlarging its notions, and of improving its civilization, I am far from thinking that the men of this class are to have their real superiority of position, with its consequences, thrown into their faces only when they are expected to give, while they are grudgingly denied it on all other occasions ! There is nothing so likely to advance the habits, opinions, and true interests of a rural population, as to have them all directed by the intelligence and combined interests that ought to mark the connection between landlord and tenant. It may do for one class of political economists to prate about a state of things which supposes every husbandman a freeholder, and rich enough to maintain his level among the other freeholders of the State. But we all know that as many minute gradations in means must and do exist in a community, as there exists gradations in characters. A majority soon will, in the nature of things, be below the level of the freeholder, and by destroying the system of having landlords and tenants, two great evils are created—the one preventing men of large fortunes from investing in lands, as no man will place his money where it will be insecure or profitless, thereby cutting off real estate generally from the benefits that might be and would be conferred by their capital, as well as cutting it off from the benefits of the increased price which arise from having such buyers in the market ; and the other is, to prevent any man from being a husbandman who has not the money necessary to purchase a farm. But they who want

10

farms *now*, and they who will want votes next November do not look quite so far ahead as that, while shouting " equal rights, ' they are, in fact, for preventing the poor husband-man from being anything but a day-labourer.

We obtained tolerably decent lodgings at our inn, though the profoundest patriot America possesses, if he know any-thing of other countries, or of the best materials of his own, cannot say much in favour of the sleeping arrangements of an ordinary country inn. The same money and the same trouble would render that which is now the very *beau idéal* of discomfort, at least tolerable, and in many instances good. But who is to produce this reform? According to the opi-nions circulated among us, the humblest hamlet we have has already attained the highest point of civilization.; and as for the people, without distinction of classes, it is universally admitted that they are the best educated, the acutest, and the most intelligent in Christendom ;—no, I must correct myself; they are all this, except when they are in the act of leasing lands, and then the innocent and illiterate husbandmen are the victims of the arts of designing landlords, the wretches !*

---

* Mr. Hugh Littlepage writes a little sharply, but there is truth in all he says, at the bottom. His tone is probably produced by the fact that there is so serious an attempt to deprive him of his old paternal estate, an attempt which is receiving support in high quarters. In addition to this provocation, the Littlepages, as the manuscript shows farther on, are traduced, as one means of effecting the objects of the anti-renters; no man, in any community in which it is necessary to work on public sentiment in order to accomplish such a purpose, ever being wronged without being calumniated. As respects the inns, truth compels me, as an old traveller, to say that Mr. Littlepage has much reason for what he says. I have met with a better bed in the lowest French tavern I ever was compelled to use, and in one instance I slept in an inn frequented by carters, than in the best purely country inn in America. In the way of neatness, however, more is usually to be found in our New York village taverns than in the public hotels of Paris itself. As for the hit touching the intelligence of the people, it is merited; for I have myself heard subtle distinctions drawn to show that the " people" of a former generation were not as knowing as the " people" of this, and imputing the covenants of the older leases to that circumstance, instead of imputing them to their true cause, the opinions and practices of the times. Half a century's experience would induce me to say that the " people" were never particularly dull in making a bargain.—EDITOR.

We passed an hour on the piazza, after eating our supper, and there being a collection of men assembled there,
inhabitants of the hamlet, we had an opportunity to get into
communication with them. My uncle sold a watch, and I
played on the hurdy-gurdy, by way of making myself popular. After this beginning, the discourse turned on the en-
grossing subject of the day, anti-rentism. The principal
speaker was a young man of about six-and-twenty, of a
sort of shabby genteel air and appearance, whom I soon
discovered to be the attorney of the neighbourhood. His
name was Hubbard, while that of the other principal speaker
was Hall. The last was a mechanic, as I ascertained, and
was a plain-looking working-man of middle age. Each of
these persons seated himself on a common " kitchen chair,"
leaning back against the side of the house, and, of course,
resting on the two hind legs of the rickety support, while
he placed his own feet on the rounds in front. The atti-
tudes were neither graceful nor picturesque, but they were
so entirely common as to excite no surprise. As for Hall,
he appeared perfectly contented with his situation, after
fidgeting a little to get the two supporting legs of his chair
just where he wanted them ; but Hubbard's eye was restless,
uneasy, and even menacing, for more than a minute. He
drew a knife from his pocket—a small, neat pen-knife only, it
is true—gazed a little wildly about him, and just as I thought
he intended to abandon his nicely poised chair, and to make
an assault on one of the pillars that upheld the roof of the
piazza, the innkeeper advanced, holding in his hand several
narrow slips of pine board, one of which he offered at once
to 'Squire Hubbard. This relieved the attorney, who took
the wood, and was soon deeply plunged in, to me, the unknown delights of whittling. I cannot explain the mysterious pleasure that so many find in whittling, though the
prevalence of the custom is so well known. But I cannot
explain the pleasure so many find in chewing tobacco, or in
smoking. The precaution of the landlord was far from
being unnecessary, and appeared to be taken in good part
by all to whom he offered " whittling-pieces," some six or
eight in the whole. The state of the piazza, indeed, proved
that the precaution was absolutely indispensable, if he did
not wish to see the house come tumbling down about his

head. In order that those who have never seen such things
may understand their use, I will go a little out of the way
to explain.

The inn was of wood, a hemlock frame with a " siding"
of clap-boards. In this there was nothing remarkable, many
countries of Europe, even, still building principally of wood.
Houses of lath and plaster were quite common, until within
a few years, even in large towns. I remember to have seen
some of these constructions, while in London, in close connection with the justly celebrated Westminster Hall; and of
such materials is the much-talked-of miniature castle of
Horace Walpole, at Strawberry Hill. But the inn of Mooseridge had some pretensions to architecture, besides being
three or four times larger than any other house in the place.
A piazza it enjoyed, of course; it must be a pitiful village
inn that does not: and building, accessaries and all, rejoiced
in several coats of a spurious white lead. The columns of
this piazza, as well as the clap-boards of the house itself,
however, exhibited the proofs of the danger of abandoning
your true whittler to his own instincts. Spread-eagles, five-
points, American flags, huzzahs for Polk! the initials of
names, and names at full length, with various other similar
conceits, records, and ebullitions of patriotic or party-otic
feelings, were scattered up and down with an affluence that
said volumes in favour of the mint in which they had been
coined. But the most remarkable memorial of the industry
of the guests was to be found on one of the columns; and
it was one at a corner, too, and consequently of double importance to the superstructure—unless, indeed, the house
were built on that well-known principle of American architecture of the last century, which made the architrave uphold the pillar, instead of the pillar the architrave. The
column in question was of white pine, as usual—though latterly, in brick edifices, bricks and stucco are much resorted
to—and, at a convenient height for the whittlers, it was literally cut two-thirds in two. The gash was very neatly
made—that much must be said-for it—indicating skill and
attention; and the surfaces of the wound were smoothed in
a manner to prove that appearances were not neglected.

" Vat do das?". I asked of the landlord, pointing to this
gaping wound in the main column of his piazza.

"That! Oh! That's only the whittlers," answered the host, with a good-natural smile.

Assuredly the Americans *are* the best-natured people on earth! Here was a man whose house was nearly tumbling down about his ears—always bating the principle in architecture just named—and he could smile as Nero may be supposed to have done when fiddling over the conflagration of Rome.

"But vhy might de vhittler vhittle down your house?"

"Oh! this is a free country, you know, and folks do pretty much as they like in it," returned the still smiling host. "I let 'em cut away as long as I dared, but it was high time to get out 'whittling-pieces' I believe you must own. It's best always to keep a ruff (roof) over a man's head, to be ready for bad weather. A week longer would have had the column in two."

"Vell, I dinks I might not bear dat! Vhat ist mein house ist mein house, ant dey shall not so moch vittles."

"By letting 'em so much vittles there, they so much vittles in the kitchen; so you see there is policy in having your under-pinnin' knocked away sometimes, if it's done by the right sort of folks."

"You're a stranger in these parts, friend?" observed Hubbard, complacently, for by this time his "whittling-piece" was reduced to a shape, and he could go on reducing it, according to some law of the art of whittling, with which I am not acquainted. "We are not so particular in such matters as in some of your countries in the old world."

"Ja—das I can see. But does not woot ant column cost money in America, someding?"

"To be sure it does. There is not a man in the country who would undertake to replace that pillar with a new one, paint and all, for less than ten dollars."

This was an opening for a discussion on the probable cost of putting a new pillar into the place of the one that was injured. Opinions differed, and quite a dozen spoke on the subject; some placing the expense as high as fifteen dollars, and others bringing it down as low as five. I was struck with the quiet and self-possession with which each man delivered his opinion, as well as with the language used. The accent was uniformly provincial, that of Hubbard included,

10 *

having a strong and unpleasant taint of the dialect of New
England in it; and some of the expressions savoured a little
of the stilts of the newspapers; but, on the whole, the language was sufficiently accurate and surprisingly good, considering the class in life of the speakers.   The conjectures,
too, manifested great shrewdness and familiarity with practical things, as well as, in a few instances, some reading.
Hall, however, actually surprised me.   He spoke with a
precision and knowledge of mechanics that would have done
credit to a scholar, and with a simplicity that added to the
influence of what he said.   Some casual remark induced me
to put in—" Vell, I might s'pose an Injin voult cut so das
column, but I might not s'pose a vhite man could."   This
opinion gave the discourse a direction towards anti-rentism,
and in a few minutes it caught all the attention of my uncle
Ro and myself.

"This business is going ahead after all!" observed Hubbard, evasively, after others had had their say.

"More's the pity," put in Hall.   "It might have been
put an end to in a month, at any time, and ought to be put
an end to in a civilized land."

"You will own, neighbour Hall, notwithstanding, it would
be a great improvement in the condition of the tenants all
over the State, could they change their tenures into freeholds."

"No doubt 't would; and so it would be a great improvement in the condition of any journeyman in my shop if he
could get to be the boss.   But that is not the question here,
the question is, what right has the State to say any man
shall sell his property unless he wishes to sell it?   A pretty
sort of liberty we should have if we all held our houses and
gardens under such laws as that supposes!"

"But do we not all hold our houses and gardens, and
farms, too, by some such law?" rejoined the attorney, who
evidently respected his antagonist, and advanced his own
opinions cautiously.   "If the public wants land to use, it
can take it by paying for it."

"Yes, to *use;* but use is everything.   I've read that old
report of the committee of the House, and don't subscribe to
its doctrines at all.   Public 'policy,' in that sense, doesn't
at all mean public 'use.'   If land is wanted for a road, or a

fort, or a canal, it must be taken, under a law, by appraise-
ment, or the thing could not be had at all; but to pretend,
because one side to a contract wishes to alter it, that the State
has a right to interfere, on the ground that the discontented
can be bought off in this way easier and cheaper than they
can be made to obey the laws, is but a poor way of supporting the right. The same principle, carried out, might prove
it would be easier to buy off pickpockets by compromising
than to punish them. Or it would be easy to get round all
sorts of contracts in this way."

"But all governments use this power when it becomes
necessary, neighbour Hall."

"That word *necessary* covers a great deal of ground,
'Squire Hubbard. The most that can be made of the necessity here is to say it is cheaper, and may help along parties to their objects better. No man doubts that the State
of New York can put down these anti-renters; and, I trust,
will put them down, so far as force is concerned. There is,
then, no other necessity in the case, to begin with, than the
necessity which demagogues always feel, of getting as many
votes as they can."

"After all, neighbour Hall, these votes are pretty powerful weapons in a popular government."

"I'll not deny that; and now they talk of a convention
to alter the constitution, it is a favourable moment to teach
such managers they shall not abuse the right of suffrage in
this way."

"How is it to be prevented? You are an universal suffrage man, I know?"

"Yes, I'm for universal suffrage among honest folks;
but do not wish to have my rulers chosen by them that are
never satisfied without having their hands in their neighbours' pockets. Let 'em put a clause into the constitution
providing that no town, or village, or county shall hold a
poll within a given time after the execution of process has
been openly resisted in it. That would take the conceit out
of all such law-breakers, in very short order."

It was plain that this idea struck the listeners, and several
even avowed their approbation of the scheme aloud. Hubbard received it as a new thought, but was more reluctant

to admit its practicability. As might be expected from a lawyer accustomed to practise in a small way, his objections savoured more of narrow views than of the notions of a statesman.

" How would you determine the extent of the district to be disfranchised?" he asked.

" Take the legal limits as they stand. If process be resisted openly by a combination strong enough to look down the agents of the law in a town, disfranchise that town for a given period; if in more than one town, disfranchise the offending towns; if a county, disfranchise the whole county."

" But, in that way you would punish the innocent with the guilty."

" It would be for the good of all; besides, you punish the innocent for the guilty, or *with* the guilty rather, in a thousand ways. You and I are taxed to keep drunkards from starving, because it is better to do that than to offend humanity by seeing men die of hunger, or tempting them to steal. When you declare martial law you punish the innocent with the guilty, in one sense; and so you do in a hundred cases. All we have to ask is, if it be not wiser and better to disarm demagogues, and those disturbers of the public peace who wish to pervert their right of suffrage to so wicked an end, by so simple a process, than to suffer them to effect their purposes by the most flagrant abuse of their political privileges?"

" How would you determine *when* a town should lose the right of voting?"

" By evidence given in open court. The judges would be the proper authority to decide in such a case; and they would decide, beyond all question, nineteen times in twenty, right. It is the interest of every man who is desirous of exercising the suffrage on right principles, to give him some such protection against them that wish to exercise the suffrage on wrong. A peace-officer can call on the *posse comitatus* or on the people to aid him; if enough appear to put down the rebels, well and good; but if enough do not appear, let it be taken as proof that the district is not worthy of giving the votes of freemen. They who abuse such a liberty as man enjoys in this country are the least entitled to our sympathies.. As for the mode, that could easily be determined, as soon as you settled the principle."

The discourse went on for an hour, neighbour Hall giving his opinions still more at large. I listened equally with pleasure and surprise. " These, then, after all," I said to myself, " are the real bone and sinew of the country. There are tens of thousands of this sort of men in the State, and why should they be domineered over, and made to submit to a legislation and to practices that are so often without principle, by the agents of the worst part of the community? Will the honest for ever be so passive, while the corrupt and dishonest continue so active?" On my mentioning these notions to my uncle, he answered:—

" Yes; it ever has been so, and, I fear, ever will be so. *There* is the curse of this country," pointing to a table covered with newspapers, the invariable companion of an American inn of any size. " So long as men believe what they find *there*, they can be nothing but dupes or knaves."

- " But there is good in newspapers."

" That adds to the curse. If they were nothing but lies, the world would soon reject them; but how few are able to separate the true from the false! Now, how few of these papers speak the truth about this very anti rentism! Occasionally an honest man in the corps does come out; but where one does this, ten affect to think what they do not believe, in order to secure votes;—votes, votes, votes. In that simple word lies all the mystery of the matter."

. " Jefferson said, if he were to choose between a government without newspapers, or newspapers without a government, he would take the last."

" Ay, Jefferson did not mean newspapers as they are now. I am old enough to see the change that has taken place. In his day, three or four fairly convicted lies would damn any editor; now, there are men that stand up under a thousand. I 'll tell you what, Hugh, this country is jogging on under two of the most antagonist systems possible — Christianity and the newspapers. The first is daily hammering into every man that he is a miserable, frail, good-for-nothing being, while the last is eternally proclaiming the perfection of the people and the virtues of self-government."

"Perhaps too much stress ought not to be laid on either."
"The first is certainly true, under limitations that we all understand; but as to the last, I will own I want more evidence than a newspaper eulogy to believe it."

After all, my uncle Ro is sometimes mistaken; though candour compels me to acknowledge that he is very often right.

CHAPTER VIII.

"I see thee still;
Remembrance, faithful to her trust,
Calls thee in beauty from the dust;
Thou comest in the morning light,
Thou 'rt with me through the gloomy night;
In dreams I meet thee as of old:
Then thy soft arms my neck enfold,
And thy sweet voice is in my ear :
In every sense to memory dear
    I see thee still."
                              SPRAGUE.

It was just ten in the morning of the succeeding day when my uncle Ro and myself came in sight of the old house at the Nest. I call it *old*, for a dwelling that has stood more than half a century acquires a touch of the venerable, in a country like America. To me it was truly old, the building having stood there, where I then saw it, for a period more than twice as long as that of my own existence, and was associated with all my early ideas. From childhood I had regarded that place as my future home, as it had been the home of my parents and grand-parents, and, in one sense, of those who had gone before them for two generations more. The whole of the land in sight—the rich bottoms, then waving with grass—the side-hills, the woods, the distant mountains—the orchards, dwellings, barns, and all the other accessaries of rural life that appertained to the soil, were mine, and had thus become without a single act of injustice to any human being, so far as I knew and believed. Even the red man had been fairly bought off by Herman Mordaunt, the patentee, and so Susquesus, the Redskin of Ravensnest, as our old Onondago was often called, had ever admitted the fact to be. It was natural that I should love an estate thus inherited and thus situated. No CIVILIZED MAN, NO MAN, INDEED, SAVAGE OR NOT, HAD EVER BEEN THE OWNER OF THOSE BROAD ACRES, BUT THOSE WHO WERE OF MY OWN BLOOD. This is what few besides Americans *can* say; and when it can be said truly, in parts of the country where the arts of life have spread, and amid the blessings of civilization, it becomes the foundation of a sentiment so profound, that I do not wonder those adventurers-errant who are flying about the face of the country, thrusting their hands into every man's mess, have not been able to find it among their other superficial discoveries. Nothing can be less like the ordinary cravings of avarice than the feeling that is thus engendered; and I am certain that the general tendency of such an influence is to elevate the feelings of him who experiences it.

And there were men among us, high in political station— high as such men ever can get, for the consequence of having such men in power is to draw down station itself nearer to their own natural level—but men in power had actually laid down propositions in political economy which, if carried out, would cause me to sell all that estate, reserving, perhaps, a single farm for my own use, and reinvest the money in such a way as that the interest I obtained might equal my present income! It is true, this theory was not directly applied to me, as my farms were to fall in by the covenants of their leases, but it had been directly applied to Stephen and William Van Rensselaer, and, by implication, to others; and my turn might come next. What business had the Rensselaers, or the Livingstons, or the Hunters, or the Littlepages, or the Verplancks, or the Morgans, or the Wadsworths, or five hundred others similarly placed, to entertain " sentiments" that interfered with " business," or that interfered with the wishes of any straggling Yankee who had found his way out of New England, and wanted a par ticular farm on his own terms? It is aristocratic to put sentiment in opposition to trade; and TRADE ITSELF IS NOT TO

BE TRADE ANY LONGER THAN ALL THE PROFIT IS TO BE
FOUND ON THE SIDE OF NUMBERS. Even the principles of
noly trade are to be governed by majorities!

Even my uncle Ro, who never owned a foot of the property,
could not look at it without emotion. He too had
been born there—had passed his childhood there—and loved
the spot without a particle of the grovelling feeling of avarice. He took pleasure in remembering that our race had
been the only owners of the soil on which he stood, and had
that very justifiable pride which belongs to enduring respectability and social station.

"Well, Hugh," he cried, after both of us had stood gazing
at the grey walls of the good and substantial, but certainly
not very beautiful dwelling, "here we are, and we now may
determine on what is next to be done. Shall we march
down to the village, which is four miles distant, you will
remember, and get our breakfasts there?—shall we try one
of your tenants?—or shall we plunge at once in medias res,
and ask hospitality of my mother and your sister?"

"The last might excite suspicion, I fear, sir. Tar and
feathers would be our mildest fate did we fall into the hands
of the Injins."

"Injins! Why not go at once to the wigwam of Susquesus, and get out of him and Yop the history of the state
of things. I heard them speaking of the Onondago at our
tavern last night, and while they said he was generally
thought to be much more than a hundred, that he was still
like a man of eighty. That Indian is full of observation,
and may let us into some of the secrets of his brethren."

"They can at least give us the news from the family;
and though it might seem in the course of things for pedlars
to visit the Nest House, it will be just as much so for them
to halt at the wigwam."

This consideration decided the matter, and away we went
towards the ravine or glen, on the side of which stood the
primitive-looking hut that went by the name of the "wigwam." The house was a small cabin of logs, neat and
warm, or cool, as the season demanded. As it was kept
up, and was whitewashed, and occasionally furnished anew
by the landlord—the odious creature! he who paid for so
many similar things in the neighbourhood—it was never

unfit to be seen, though never of a very alluring, cottage-
like character. There was a garden, and it had been properly made that very season, the negro picking and pecking
about it, during the summer, in a way to coax the vegetables and fruits on a little, though I well knew that the regular weedings came from an assistant at the Nest, who was
ordered to give it an eye and an occasional half-day. On
one side of the hut there was a hog-pen and a small stable
for a cow; but on the other the trees of the virgin forest,
which had never been disturbed in that glen, overshadowed
the roof. This somewhat poetical arrangement was actually
the consequence of a compromise between the tenants of the
cabin, the negro insisting on the accessories of his rude civilization, while the Indian required the shades of the woods
to reconcile him to his position. Here had these two singularly associated beings—the one deriving his descent from
the debased races of Africa, and the other from the fierce
but lofty-minded aboriginal inhabitant of this continent —
dwelt nearly for the whole period of an ordinary human
life. The cabin itself began to look really ancient, while
those who dwelt in it had little altered within the memory
of man! Such instances of longevity, whatever theorists
may say on the subject, are not unfrequent among either
the blacks or the " natives," though probably less so among
the last than among the first, and still less so among the
first of the northern than of the southern sections of the re
public. It is common to say that the great age so often
attributed to the people of these two races is owing to ignorance of the periods of their births, and that they do not
live longer than the whites. This may be true, in the main,
for a white man is known to have died at no great distance
from Ravensnest, within the last five-and-twenty years, who
numbered more than his six score of years; but aged negroes and aged Indians are nevertheless so common, when
the smallness of their whole numbers is remembered, as to
render the fact apparent to most of those who have seen
much of their respective people.

There was no highway in the vicinity of the wigwam, for
so the cabin was generally called, though wigwam, in the
strict meaning of the word, it was not. As the little building stood in the grounds of the Nest House, which contain

11

two hundred acres, a bit of virgin forest included, and exclusively of the fields that belonged to the adjacent farm, it
was approached only by foot-paths, of which several led to
and from it, and by one narrow, winding carriage-road,
which, in passing for miles through the grounds, had been
.ed near the hut, in order to enable my grandmother and
sister, and, I dare say, my dear departed mother, while she
lived, to make their calls in their frequent airings. By this
sweeping road we approached the cabin.

. "There are the two old fellows, sunning themselves this
fine day!" exclaimed my uncle, with something like tremor
in his voice, as we drew near enough to the hut to distinguish objects. "Hugh, I never see these men without a
feeling of awe, as well as of affection. They were the
friends, and one was the slave of my grandfather; and as
long as I can remember, have they been aged men! They
seem to be set up here as monuments of the past, to connect
the generations that are gone with those that are to come."

"If so, sir, they will soon be all there is of their sort. . It
really seems to me that, if things continue much longer in
their present direction, men will begin to grow jealous and
envious of history itself, because its actors have left descendants to participate in any little credit they may have
gained."

. "Beyond all contradiction, boy, tnere is a strange per-
version of the old and natural sentiments on this head among
us. But you must bear in mind the fact, that of the two
millions and a half the State contains, not half a million,
probably, possess any of the true York blood, and can consequently feel any of the sentiments connected with the
birth-place and the older traditions of the very society in
which they live. A great deal must be attributed to the
facts of our condition; though I admit those facts need not,
and ought not to unsettle principles. But look at those two
old fellows! There they are, true to the feelings and habits
of their races, even after passing so long a time together in
this hut. There squats Susquesus on a stone, idle and disdaining work, with his rifle leaning against the apple-tree;
while Jaaf—or Yop, as I believe it is better to call him—is
pecking about in the garden, still a slave at his work, in
fancy at least."

" And which is the happiest, sir—the industrious old man or the idler?"

." Probably each finds most happiness in indulging his own early habits. The Onondago never *would* work, however, and I have heard my father say, great was his happiness when he found he was to pass the remainder of his days in *otium cum dignitate,* and without the necessity of making baskets."

" Yop is looking at us; had we not better go up at once and speak to them?"

" Yop may stare the most openly, but my life on it the Indian *sees* twice as much. His faculties are the best, to begin with; and he is a man of extraordinary and characteristic observation. In his best days nothing ever escaped him. As you say, we will approach."

My uncle and myself then consulted on the expediency of using broken English with these two old men, of which, at first, we saw no necessity; but when we remembered that others might join us, and that our communications with the two might be frequent for the next few days, we changed our minds, and determined rigidly to observe our incognitos.

As we came up to the door of the hut, Jaaf slowly left his little garden and joined the Indian, who remained immoveable and unmoved on the stone which served him for a seat. We could see but little change in either during the five years of our absence, each being a perfect picture, in his way, of extreme but not decrepit old age in the men of his race. Of the two, the black—if black he could now be called, his colour being a muddy grey—was the most altered, though that seemed scarcely possible when I saw him last. As for the Trackless, or Susquesus, as he was commonly called, his temperance throughout a long life did him good service, and his half-naked limbs and skeleton-like body, for he wore the summer dress of his people, appeared to be made of a leather long steeped in a tannin of the purest quality. His sinews, too, though much stiffened, seemed yet to be of whip-cord, and his whole frame a species of indurated mummy that retained its vitality. The colour of the skin was less red than formerly, and more closely approached to that

of the negro, as the latter now was, though perceptibly dif.
ferent.

" Sago—sago," cried my uncle, as we came quite near,
seeing no risk in using that familiar semi-Indian salutation.*
" Sago, sago, dis charmin' mornin ; in my tongue, dat mighi
be *guten tag.*"

" Sago," returned the Trackless, in his deep, guttural
voice, while old Yop brought two lips together that resem-
bled thick pieces of overdone beef-steak, fastened his red-
encircled gummy eyes on each of us in turn, pouted once
more, working his jaws as if proud of the excellent teeth they
still held, and said nothing. As the slave of a Littlepage, h
held pedlars as inferior beings ; for the ancient negroes ot
New York ever identified themselves, more or less, with the
families to which they belonged, and in which they so often
were born. " Sago," repeated the Indian, slowly, courteously, and with emphasis, after he had looked a moment longer
at my uncle, as if he saw something about him to command
respect.

" Dis ist charmin' day, frients," said uncle Ro, placing
himself coolly on a log of wood that had been hauled for
the stove, and wiping his brow. " Vat might you calls dis
coontry ?"

" Dis here ?" answered Yop, not without a little contempt.
" Dis is York Colony ; where you come from to ask sich a
question ?"

" Charmany. Dat ist far off, but a goot coontry ; ant
dis ist goot coontry too."

---

* The editor has often had occasion to explain the meaning of terms
of this nature. The colonists caught a great many words from the
Indians they first knew, and used them to all other Indians, though
not belonging to their languages ; and these other tribes using them
as English, a sort of limited *lingua frança* has grown up in the
country that everybody understands. It is believed that " moccasin,"
" squaw," " pappoose," " sago," " tomahawk," " wigwam," &c. &c.,
all belong to this class of words. There can be little doubt that the
sobriquet of " Yankees" is derived from " Yengeese," the manner in
which the tribes nearest to New England pronounced the word " English." It is to this hour a provincialism of that part of the country to
pronounce this word " *Eng*-lish" instead of " *Ing*-lish," its conventional sound. The change from " *Eng*-lish" to " *Yen*-geese" is very
trifling.— EDITOR.

" Why you leab him, den, if he be good country, eh ?"

" Vhy you leaf Africa, canst you dell me dat ?" retorted uncle Ro, somewhat coolly.

" Nebber was dere," growled old Yop, bringing his blubber lips together somewhat in the manner the boar works his jaws when it is prudent to get out of his way. " I 'm York-nigger born, and nebber seen no Africa ; and nebber want to see him, nudder."

It is scarcely necessary to say that Jaaf belonged to a school by which the term of " coloured gentleman" was never used. The men of his time, and stamp called themselves " niggers ;" and ladies and gentlemen of that age took them at their word, and called them " niggers" too ; a term that no one of the race ever uses now, except in the way of reproach, and which, by one of the singular workings of our very wayward and common nature, he is' more apt to use than any other, when reproach is intended.

My uncle paused a moment to reflect before he continued a discourse that had not appeared to commence under very flattering auspices.

" Who might lif in dat big stone house ?" asked uncle Ro, as soon as he thought the negro had had time to cool a little.

" Anybody can see you no Yorker, by dat werry speech,' answered Yop, not at all mollified by such a question. " Who *should* lib dere but Gin'ral Littlepage ?"

" Vell, I dought he wast dead, long ago."

" What if he be ? It 's his house, and he lib in it ; ano ole *young* missus lib dere too."

Now, there had been three generations of generals among the Littlepages, counting from father to son. First, there had been Brigadier General Evans Littlepage, who held that rank in the militia, and died in service during the revolution. The next was Brigadier General Cornelius Littlepage, who got his rank by brevet, at the close of the same war, in which he had actually figured as a colonel of the New York line. Third, and last, was my own grandfather, Major General Mordaunt Littlepage : he had been a captain in his father's regiment at the close of the same struggle, got the brevet of major at its termination, and rose to be a Major General of the militia, the station he held for

11 *

many years before he died. As soon as the privates had
the power to elect their own officers, the position of a Major
General in the militia ceased to be respectable, and few gentlemen could be induced to serve. As might have been
foreseen, the militia itself fell into general contempt, where
it now is, and where it will ever remain until a different
class of officers shall be chosen. The people can do a great
deal, no doubt, but they cannot make a " silk purse out of
a sow's ear." . As soon as officers from the old classes shall
be appointed, the militia will come up; for in no interest in
life is it so material to have men of certain habits, and notions, and education, in authority, as in those connected with
the military service. A great many fine speeches may be
made, and much patriotic eulogy expended on the intrinsic
virtue and intelligence of the people, and divers projects entertained to make " citizen-soldiers," as they are called; but
citizens never can be, and never will be turned into soldiers
at all, good or bad, until proper officers are placed over
them. To return to Yop— .

" Bray vhat might be der age of das laty dat you callet
olt young missus?" asked my uncle.

" Gosh! she nutten but gal—born sometime just a'ter ole
French war. Remember her well 'nough when she Miss
Dus Malbone. Young masser Mordaunt take fancy to her,
and make her he wife."

" Vell, I hopes you hafn't any objection to der match?"

" Not I; she clebber young lady den, and she werry
clebber young lady now."

And this of my venerable grandmother, who had fairly
seen her four-score years!

" Who might be der master of das big house now?"

" Gin'ral Littlepage, does n't I tell ye! Masser Mordaunt's name, *my* young master. Sus, dere, only Injin; he
nebber so lucky as hab a good master. Niggers gettin'
scarce, dey tells me, now-a-days, in dis world!"

" Injins, too, I dinks; dere ist no more redskins might be
blenty."

The manner in which the Onondago raised his figure, and
the look he fastened on my uncle, were both fine and startling. As yet he had said nothing beyond the salutation;
but I could see he now intended to speak.

" New tribe," he said, after regarding us for half a mi-
nute intently ; " what you call him—where he come from ?"
" Ja, ja—das ist der anti-rent redskins. Haf you seen
'em, Trackless ?"
" Sartain ; come to see me—face in bag—behave like
squaw ; poor Injin—poor warrior !"
" Yees, I believes dat ist true enough. I can't bear soch
Injin ! — might not be soch Injin in world. Vhat you call
'em, eh ?"
Susquesus shook his head slowly, and with dignity.
Then he gazed intently at my uncle ; after which he fastened his eyes, in a similar manner on me. In this manner
his looks turned from one to the other for some little time,
when he again dropped them to the earth, calmly and in
silence. I took out the hurdy-gurdy, and began to play a
lively air—one that was very popular among the American
blacks, and which, I am sorry to say, is getting to be not
less so among the whites. No visible effect was produced
on Susquesus, unless a slight shade of contempt was visible
on his dark features. With Jaaf, however, it was very different. Old as he was, I could see a certain nervous twitch-
ing of the lower limbs, which indicated that the old fellow
actually felt some disposition to dance. It soon passed
away, though his grim, hard, wrinkled, dusky, grey countenance continued to gleam with a sort of dull pleasure for
some time. There was nothing surprising in this, the indifference of the Indian to melody being almost as marked as
the negro's sensitiveness to its power.
It was not to be expected that men so aged would be disposed to talk much. The Onondago had ever been a silent
man ; dignity and gravity of character uniting with prudence to render him so. But Jaaf was constitutionally gar-
rulous, though length of days had necessarily much diminished the propensity. At that moment a fit of thoughtful
and melancholy silence came over my uncle, too, and all
four of us continued brooding on our own reflections for two
or three minutes after I had ceased to play. Presently the
even, smooth approach of carriage-wheels was heard, and
a light, summer vehicle that was an old acquaintance, came
whirling round the stable, and drew up within ten feet of
the spot where we were all seated.

My heart was in my mouth, at this unexpected interruption, and I could perceive that my uncle was scarcely less
affected. Amid the flowing and pretty drapery of summer
shawls, and the other ornaments of the female toilet, were
four youthful and sunny faces, and one venerable with
years. In a word, my grandmother, my sister, and my
uncle's two other wards, and Mary Warren, were in the
carriage; yes, the pretty, gentle, timid, yet spirited and
intelligent daughter of the rector was of the party, and
seemingly quite at home and at her ease, as one among
friends. She was the first to speak even, though it was in
a low, quiet voice, addressed to my sister, and in words that
appeared extorted by surprise.

" There are the very two pedlars of whom I told you,
Martha," she said, " and now you may hear the flute well
played."

" I doubt if he can play better than Hugh," was my dear
sister's answer. " But we 'll have some of his music, if it
be only to remind us of him who is so far away."

" The music we can and will have, my child," cried my
grandmother, cheerfully; " though _that_ is not wanted to
remind us of our absent boy. Good morrow, Susquesus;
I hope this fine day agrees with you."

" Sago," returned the Indian, making a dignified and
even graceful forward gesture with one arm, though he did
not rise. " Weadder good—Great Spirit good, dat reason.
How squaws do?"

" We are all well, I thank you, Trackless. Good morrow, Jaaf; how do _you_ do, this fine morning?"

Yop, or Jaap, or Jaaf, rose tottering, made a low obei-
sance, and then answered in the semi-respectful, semi-fami-
liar manner of an old, confidential family servant, as the
last existed among our fathers:

" T'ank 'ee, Miss Dus, wid all my heart," he answered.
" Pretty well to-day; but ole Sus, he fail, and grow ol'er
and ol'er desp'ate fast!"

Now, of the two, the Indian was much the finest relic of
human powers, though he was less uneasy and more stationary than the black. But the propensity to see the mote
in the eye of his friend, while he forgot the beam in his
own, was a long-established and well-known weakness of

Jaaf, and its present exhibition caused everybody to smile. I was delighted with the beaming, laughing eyes of Mary Warren in particular, though she said nothing.

"I cannot say I agree with you, Jaaf," returned my smiling grandmother. "The Trackless bears his years surprisingly; and I think I have not seen him look better this many a day than he is looking this morning. We are none of us as young as we were when we first became acquainted, Jaaf — which is now near, if not quite, three-score years ago."

"You nuttin' but gal, nudder," growled the negro. "Ole Sus be raal ole fellow; but Miss Dus and Masser Mordaunt, dey get married only tudder day. Why *dat* was a'ter de revylooshen!"

"It was, indeed," replied the venerable woman, with a touch of melancholy in her tones; "but the revolution took place many, many a long year since!"

"Well, now, I be surprise, Miss Dus! How you call *dat* so long, when he only be tudder day?" retorted the pertinacious negro, who began to grow crusty, and to speak in a short, spiteful way, as if displeased by hearing that to which he could not assent. "Masser Corny was little ole, p'r'aps, if he lib, but all de rest ob you nuttin' but children. Tell me one t'ing, Miss Dus, be it true dey's got a town at Satanstoe?"

"An attempt was made, a few years since, to turn the whole country into towns, and, among other places, the Neck; but I believe it will never be anything more than a capital farm."

"So besser. *Dat* good land, I tell you! One acre down dere wort' more dan twenty acre up here."

"My grandson would not be pleased to hear you say that, Jaaf."

"Who your grandson, Miss Dus. Remember you hab little baby tudder day; but baby can't hab baby."

"Ah, Jaaf, my old friend, my babies have long since been men and women, and are drawing on to old age. One, and he was my first born, is gone before us to a better world, and *his* boy is now your young master. This young lady, that is seated opposite to me, is the sister of that young

master, and she would be grieved to think you have forgotten her."

Jaaf laboured under the difficulty so common to old age ·
he was forgetful of things of more recent date, while he remembered those which had occurred a century ago! The
memory is a tablet that partakes of the peculiarity of all
our opinions and habits. In youth it is easily impressed,
and the images then engraved on it are distinct, deep and
lasting, while those that succeed become crowded, and take
less root, from the circumstance of finding the ground
already occupied. In the present instance, the age was so
great that the change was really startling, the old negro's
recollections occasionally coming on the mind like a voice
from the grave. As for the Indian, as I afterwards ascertained, he was better preserved in all respects than the
black ; his great temperance in youth, freedom from labour,
exercise in the open air, united to the comforts and abundance of semi-civilized habits, that had now lasted for near
a century, contributing to preserve both mind and body.
As I now looked at him, I remembered what I had heard in
boyhood of his history.

There had ever been a mystery about the life of the Onondago. If any one of our set had ever been acquainted with
the facts, it was Andries Coejemans, a half-uncle of my dear
grandmother, a person who has been known among us by
the *sobriquet* of the Chainbearer. My grandmother had
told me that " uncle Chainbearer," as we all called the old
relative, *did* know all about Susquesus, in his time—the
reason why he had left his tribe, and become a hunter, and
warrior, and runner among the pale-faces—and that he had
always said the particulars did his red friend great credit,
but that he would reveal it no further. So great, however,
was uncle Chainbearer's reputation for integrity, that such
an opinion was sufficient to procure for the Onondago the
fullest confidence of the whole connection, and the experience of four-score years and ten had proved that this confidence was well placed. Some imputed the sort of exile in
which the old man had so long lived to love ; others to war,
and others, again, to the consequences of those fierce personal feuds that are known to occur among men in the sa-

vage state. But all was just as much a mystery and matter of conjecture, now we were drawing near to the middle of the nineteenth century, as it had been when our forefathers were receding from the middle of the eighteenth! To return to the negro.

Although Jaaf had momentarily forgotten me, and quite forgotten my parents, he remembered my sister, who was in the habit of seeing him so often. In what manner he connected her with the family, it is not easy to say; but he knew her not only by sight, but by name, and, as one might say, by blood.

"Yes, yes," cried the old fellow, a little eagerly, ' champ. ing' his thick lips together, somewhat as an alligator snaps his jaws, "yes, I knows Miss Patty, of course. Miss Patty is werry han'some, and grows han'somer and han'somer ebbery time I sees her—yah, yah, yah !" The laugh of that old negro sounded startling and unnatural, yet there was something of the joyous in it, after all, like every negro's laugh. "Yah, yah, yah ! Yes, Miss Patty won'erful han'some, and werry like Miss Dus. I s'pose, now, Miss Patty wast born about 'e time dat Gin'ral Washington die."

As this was a good deal more than doubling my sister's age, it produced a common laugh among the light-hearted girls in the carriage. A gleam of intelligence that almost amounted to a smile also shot athwart the countenance of the Onondago, while the muscles of his face worked, but he said nothing. I had reason to know afterwards that the tablet of his memory retained its records better.

"What friends have you with you to-day, Jaaf," inquired my grandmother, inclining her head towards us pedlars graciously, at the same time; a salutation that my uncle Ro and myself rose hastily to acknowledge.

As for myself, I own honestly that I could have jumped into the vehicle and kissed my dear grandmother's still good-looking but colourless cheeks, and hugged Patt, and possibly some of the others, to my heart. Uncle Ro had more command of himself; though I could see that the sound of his venerable parent's voice, in which the tremour was barely perceptible, was near overcoming him.

"Dese be pedlar, ma'am, I do s'pose," answered the black. "Dey's got box wid somet'in' in him, and dey's got new

kind of fiddle. Come, young man, gib Miss Dus a tune—
a libely one ; sich as make an ole nigger dance."

I - drew · round the hurdy-gurdy,, and was beginning to
flourish away, when a gentle, sweet voice, raised a little
louder than usual by eagerness, interrupted me.

" Oh ! not that thing, not that ; the flute, the flute !" exclaimed Mary Warren, blushing to the eyes at her own bold
ness, the instant she saw that she was heard, and that I was
about to comply.

It is hardly necessary to say that I bowed respectfully,
laid down the hurdy-gurdy, drew the flute from my pocket,
and, after a few flourishes, commenced playing one of the
newest airs, or melodies, from a favourite opera. I saw the
colour rush into Martha's cheeks the moment I had got
through a bar or two, and the start she gave satisfied me
that the dear girl remembered her brother's flute. I had
played on that very instrument ever since I was sixteen, but
I had made an immense progress in the art during the five
years just passed in Europe. Masters at Naples, Paris, Vienna and London had done a great deal for me ; and I trust
I shall not be thought vain if I add, that nature had done
something, too. My excellent grandmother listened in profound attention, and all four of the girls were enchanted.

" That music is worthy of being heard in a room," ob
served the former, as soon as I concluded the air ; " and
we shall hope to hear it this evening, at the Nest House, if
you remain anywhere near us. In the mean time, we must
pursue our airing."

As my grandmother spoke she leaned forward, and extended her hand to me, with a benevolent smile. I advanced, received the dollar that was offered, and, unable to
command my feelings, raised the hand to my lips, respectfully but with fervour. Had Martha's face been near me,
it would have suffered also. · I suppose there was nothing
in this respectful salutation that struck the spectators as very
much out of the way, foreigners having foreign customs,
but I saw a flush in my venerable grandmother's cheek, as
the carriage moved off. *She* had noted the warmth of the
manner. My uncle had turned away, I dare say to conceal
the tears that started to his eyes, and Jaaf followed towards
the door of the hut, whither my uncle moved, in order to

do the honours of the place. This left me quite alone with the Indian.

"Why no kiss *face* of grandmodder?" asked the Onondago, coolly and quietly.

Had a clap of thunder broken over my head, I could not have been more astonished! The disguise that had deceived my nearest relations — that had baffled Seneca Newcome, and had set at naught even his sister Opportunity — had failed to conceal me from that Indian, whose faculties might be supposed to have been numbed with age!

"Is it possible that you know me, Susquesus!" I exclaimed, signing towards the negro at the same time, by way of caution; "that you remember me, at all! I should have thought this wig, these clothes, would have concealed me."

"Sartain," answered the aged Indian, calmly. "Know young chief soon as see him; know fader—know mudder; know gran'fader; gran'mudder—great-gran'fader; *his* fader, too; know all. Why forget young chief?"

"Did you know me before I kissed my grandmother's hand, or only by that act?

"Know as soon as see him. What eyes good for, if don't know? Know uncle, dere, sartain; welcome home!"

"But you will not let others know us, too, Trackless? We have always been friends, I hope?"

"Be sure, friends. Why ole eagle, wid white head, strike young pigeon? Nebber hatchet in 'e path between Susquesus and any of de tribe of Ravensnest. Too ole to dig him up now."

"There are good reasons why my uncle and myself should not be known for a few days. Perhaps you have heard something of the trouble that has grown up between the landlords and the tenants, in the land?"

"What dat trouble?"

"The tenants are tired of paying rent, and wish to make a new bargain, by which they can become owners of the farms on which they live."

A grim light played upon the swarthy countenance of the Indian: his lips moved, but he uttered nothing aloud.

"Have you heard anything of this, Susquesus?"

12

" Little bird sing sich song in my ear—didn't like to hear it."

" And of Indians who are moving up and down the country, armed with rifles and dressed in calico ?"

" What tribe, dem Injin," asked the Trackless, with a quickness and a fire I did not think it possible for him to retain. " What 'ey do, marchin' 'bout ? — on war-path, eh ?"

" In one sense they may be said to be so. They belong to the anti-rent tribe ; do you know such a nation ?",

" Poor Injin dat, b'lieve. Why come so late ? — why no come when 'e foot of Susquesus light as feather of bird ? — why stay away till pale-faces plentier dan leaf on tree, or snow in air ? Hundred year ago, when dat oak little, sich Injin might be good ; now, he good for nuttin'."

" But you will keep our secret, Sus ? — will not even tell the negro who we are ?"

The Trackless simply nodded his head in assent. After this he seemed to me to sink back in a sort of brooding lethargy, as if indisposed to pursue the subject. I left him to go to my uncle, in order to relate what had just passed. Mr. Roger Littlepage was as much astonished as I had been myself, at hearing that one so aged should have detected us through disguises that had deceived our nearest of kin. But the quiet penetration and close observation of the man had long been remarkable. As his good faith was of proof, however, neither felt any serious apprehension of being betrayed, as soon as he had a moment for reflection.

CHAPTER IX.

" He saw a cottage with a double coach-house,
A cottage of gentility ;
And the devil did grin, for his darling sin
Is the pride that apes humility."

Devil's Thoughts.

It was now necessary to determine what course we ought next to pursue. It might appear presuming in men of our pursuits to go to the Nest before the appointed time; and did we proceed on, to the village, we should have the distance between the two places to walk over twice, carrying our instruments and jewel-box. After a short consultation, it was decided to visit the nearest dwellings, and to remain as near my own house as was practicable, making an arrangement to sleep somewhere in its immediate vicinity. Could we trust any one with our secret, our fare would probably be all the better; but my uncle thought it most prudent to maintain a strict incognito until he had ascertained the true state of things in the town.

We took leave of the Indian and the negro, therefore, promising to visit them again in the course of that or the succeeding day, and followed the path that led to the farmhouse. It was our opinion that we might, at least, expect to meet with friends in the occupants of the home farm. The same family had been retained in possession there for three generations, and being hired to manage the husbandry and to take care of the dairy, there was not the same reason for the disaffection, that was said so generally to exist among the tenantry, prevailing among them. The name of this family was Miller, and it consisted of the two heads and some six or seven children, most of the latter being still quite young.

" Tom Miller was a trusty lad, when I knew much of him," said my uncle, as we drew near to the barn, in which we saw the party mentioned, at work; " and he is said to have behaved well in one or two alarms they have had at the Nest, this summer; still, it may be wiser not to let even him into our secret as yet."

"I am quite of your mind, sir," I answered; "for who knows that he has not just as strong a desire as any of them to own the farm on which he lives? He is the grandson of the man who cleared it from the forest, and has much the same title as the rest of them."

"Very true; and why should not that give him just as good a right to claim an interest in the farm, beyond that he has got under his contract to work it, as if he held a lease? He who holds a lease gets no right beyond his bargain; nor does this man. The one is paid for his labour by the excess of his receipts over the amount of his annual rent, while the other is paid partly in what he raises, and partly in wages. In principle there is no difference whatever, not a particle; yet I question if the veriest demagogue in the State would venture to say that the man, or the family, which works a farm for hire, even for a hundred years, gets the smallest right to say he shall not quit it, if its owner please, as soon as his term of service is up!"

"'The love of money is the root of all evil;' and when that feeling is uppermost, one can never tell what a man will do. The bribe of a good farm, obtained for nothing, or for an insignificant price, is sufficient to upset the morality of even Tom Miller."

"You are right, Hugh; and here is one of the points in which our political men betray the cloven foot. They write, and proclaim, and make speeches, as if the anti-rent troubles grew out of the durable lease system solely, whereas we all know that it is extended to all descriptions of obligations given for the occupancy of land—life leases, leases for a term of years, articles for deeds, and bonds and mortgages. It is a wide-spread, though not yet universal attempt of those who have the least claim to the possession of real estate, to obtain the entire right, and that by agencies that neither the law nor good morals will justify. It is no new expedient for partizans to place *en evidence* no more of their principles and intentions than suits their purposes. But, here we are within ear-shot, and must resor. to the High Dutch. *Guten tag, guten tag*," continued uncle Ro, dropping easily into the broken English of our masquerade, as we walked into the barn, where Miller, two of his older boys, and a couple of hired men were at work, grinding scythes and preparing for the approaching hay-harvest. " It might be warm day, dis fine mornin'."

" Good day, good day," cried Miller, hastily, and glancing his eye a little curiously at our equipments. " What have you got in your box—essences?"

" Nein ; vatches and drinkets ;" setting down the box and opening it at once, for the inspection of all present. " Von't you burchase a goot vatch, dis bleasant mornin'?"

" Be they ra-al gold ?" asked Miller, a little doubtingly. " And all them chains and rings, be they gold too?"

" Not true golt ; nein, nein, I might not say dat. But goot enough golt for blain folks, like you and me."

" Them things would never do for the grand quality over at the big house !" cried one of the labourers who was un-known to me, but whose name I soon ascertained was Joshua Brigham, and who spoke with a sort of malicious sneer that at once betrayed *he* was no friend. " You mean 'em for poor folks, I s'pose?"

" I means dem for any bodies dat will pay deir money for 'em," answered my uncle. " Vould you like a vatch?"

" That would I ; and a farm, too, if I could get 'em cheap," answered Brigham, with a sneer he did not attempt to conceal. " How do you sell farms to-day?"

" I haf got no farms ; I sells drinkets and vatches, but I doesn't sell farms. Vhat I haf got I vill sell, but I cannot sells vhat I haf not got."

" Oh ! you 'll get all you want if you 'll stay long enough in this country ! This is a free land, and just the place for a poor man ; or it will be, as soon as we get all the lords and aristocrats out of it."

This was the first time I had ever heard this political blarney with my own ears, though I had understood it was often used by those who wish to give to their own particular envy and covetousness a grand and sounding air.

" Vell, I haf heards dat in America dere might not be any noples ant aristocrats," put in my uncle, with an appear-ance of beautiful simplicity ; " and dat dere ist not ein graaf 'n der whole coontry."

12 *

"Oh! there's all sorts of folks here, just as they are to
be found elsewhere,".cried Miller, seating himself coolly on
the end of the grindstone-frame, to open and look into the
mysteries of one of the watches. "Now, Josh Brigham,
here, calls all that's above him in the world aristocrats, but
he doesn't call all that's below him his equals."

I liked that speech; and I liked the cool, decided way
in which it was uttered. It denoted, in its spirit, a man who
saw things as they are, and who was not afraid to say what
he thought about them. My uncle Ro was surprised, and
that agreeably, too, and he turned to Miller to pursue the
discourse.

"Den dere might not be any nopility in America, after
all?" he asked, inquiringly.

"Yes, there's plenty of such lords as Josh here, who
want to be uppermost so plaguily that they don't stop to
touch all the rounds of the ladder. I tell him, friend, he
wants to get on too fast, and that he mustn't set up for a
gentleman before he knows how to behave himself."

Josh looked a little abashed at a rebuke that came from
one of his own class, and which he must have felt, in secret, was merited. But the demon was at work in him, and
he had persuaded himself that he was the champion of a
quality as sacred as liberty, when, in fact, he was simply
and obviously doing neither more nor less than breaking
the tenth commandment. He did not like to give up, while
he skirmished with Miller, as the dog that has been beaten
already two or three times growls over a bone at the approach of his conqueror.

"Well, thank heaven," he cried, "*I* have got some spirit
in my body."

"That's very true, Joshua," answered Miller, laying
down one watch and taking up another; "but it happens to
be an evil spirit."

"Now, here's them Littlepages; what makes them better than other folks?"

"You had better let the Littlepages alone, Joshua, seein'
they're a family that you know nothing at all about."

"I don't want to know them; though I *do* happen to
know all I want to know. I despise 'em."

" No you don't, Joshy, my boy ; nobody despises folks they talk so spitefully about. What's the price of this here watch, friend ?"

" Four dollars," said my uncle, eagerly, falling lower than was prudent, in his desire to reward Miller for his good feeling and sound sentiments. " Ja, ja—you might haf das vatch for four dollars."

" I'm afraid it isn't good for anything," returned Miller, feeling the distrust that was natural at hearing a price so low. " Let's have another look at its inside."

No man probably, ever bought a watch without looking into its works with an air of great intelligence, though none but a mechanician is any wiser for his survey. Tom Miller acted on this principle, for the good looks of the machine he held in his hand, and the four dollars, tempted him sorely It had its effect, too, on the turbulent and envious Joshua, who seemed to understand himself very well in a bargain. Neither of the men had supposed the watches to be of gold, for though the metal that is in a watch does not amount to a great deal, it is usually of more value than all that was asked for the " article", now under examination. In point of fact, my uncle had this very watch " invoiced to him" at twice the price he now put it at.

" And what do you ask for this ?" demanded Joshua, taking up another watch of very similar looks and of equal value to the one that Miller still retained open in his hand. " Won't you let this go for three dollars ?"

" No ; der brice of dat is effery cent of forty dollars," answered uncle Ro, stubbornly.

" The two men now looked at the pedlar in surprise. Miller took the watch from his hired man, examined it attentively, compared it with the other, and then demanded its price anew.

" .You might haf eider of dem vatches for four dollars," returned my uncle, as I thought, incautiously.

This occasioned a new surprise, though Brigham fortunately referred the difference to a mistake.

" Oh !" he said, " I understood you to say *forty* dollars. Four dollars is a different matter."

" Josh," interrupted the more observant and cooler-headed Miller, " it is high time, now, you and Peter go and look

a'ter them sheep. The conch will soon be blowing for dinner. If you want a trade, you can have one when you get
back."   -

Notwithstanding the plainness of his appearance and language, Tom Miller was captain of his own company. He
gave this order quietly, and in his usual familiar way, but
it was obviously to be obeyed without a remonstrance. In
a minute the two hired men were off in company, leaving
no one behind in the barn but Miller, his sons, and us two.
I could see there was a motive for all this, but did not understand it.

" Now *he's* gone," continued Tom quietly, but laying an
emphasis that sufficiently explained his meaning, " perhaps
you 'll let me know the true price of this watch. I 've a
mind for it, and may be we can agree."

" Four dollars," answered my uncle, distinctly. , " I haf
said you might haf it for dat money, and vhat I haf said
once might always be." '

" I will take it, then. I almost wish you had asked eight,
though four dollars saved is suthin' for a poor man. It 's
so plaguy cheap I 'm a little afraid on 't ; but I 'll ventur'.
There ; there 's your money, and in hard cash."

" Dank, you, sir. Won't das ladies choose to look at my
drinkets ?"   ' \

" Oh ! if you want to deal with ladies who buy chains
and rings, the Nest House is the place. My woman wouldn't
know what to do with sich things, and don't set herself up
for a fine lady at all. That chap who has just gone for the
sheep is the only great man we have about this farm."

" Ja, ja ; he ist a nople in a dirty shirt : ja, ja ; why hast
he dem pig feelin's ?"   -   .

" I believe you have named them just as they ought to
be, *pig's* feelin's. It 's because he wishes to thrust his own
snout all over the trough, and is mad when he finds anybody else's in the way. We 're getting to have plenty of
such fellows up and down the country, and an uncomfortable time they give us. Boys, I *do* believe it will turn out
a'ter all, that Josh is an Injin !" ·

" I *know* he is," answered the oldest of the two sons, a
lad of nineteen ; " where else should he be so much of
nights and Sundays, but at their trainin's ?—and what was

the meanin' of the calico bundle I saw under his arm a month ago, as I told you on at the time?"

"If I find it out to be as you say, Harry, he shall tramp off of this farm. I'll have no Injins here!"

"Vell I dought I dit see an olt Injin in a hut up yonder ast by der woots!" put in my uncle, innocently.

"Oh! that is Susquesus, an Onondago; he is a true Injin, and a gentleman; but we have a parcel of the mock gentry about, who are a pest and an eye-sore to every honest man in the country. Half on 'em are nothing but thieves in mock Injin dresses. The law is ag'in 'em, right is ag'in 'em, and every true friend of liberty in the country ought to be ag'in 'em."

"Vhat ist der matter in dis coontry? I hear in Europe how America ist a free lant, ant how efery man hast his rights; but since I got here dey do nothin' but talk of barons, and noples, and tenants, and arisdograts, and all der bat dings I might leaf behint me, in der olt worlt."

"The plain matter is, friend, that they who have got little, envy them that's got much; and the struggle is to see which is the strongest. On the one side is the law, and right, and bargains, and contracts; and on the other thousands—not of dollars, but of men. Thousands of voters; d' ye understand?"

"Ja, ja—I oonderstands; dat ist easy enough. But vhy do dey dalk so much of noples and arisdograts?—ist der noples and arisdograts in America?"

"Well, I don't much understand the natur' of sich things, there sartainly is a difference in men, and a difference in their fortun's, and edications, and such sort of things."

"Und der law, den, favours der rich man at der cost of der poor, in America, too, does it? Und you haf arisdograts who might not pay taxes, and who holt all der offices, and get all der pooblic money, and who ist petter pefore de law, in all dings, dan ast dem dat be not arisdograts? Is it so?"

Miller laughed outright, and shook his head at this question, continuing to examine the trinkets the whole time.

"No, no, my friend, we've not much of *that*, in this part of the world, either. Rich men get very few offices, to begin with; for it's an argooment in favour of a man for an

office, that he's poor, and *wants* it. Folks don't so much
ask who the office wants, as who wants the office. Then,
as for taxes, there isn't much respect paid to the rich, on
that score. Young 'Squire Littlepage pays the tax on this
farm directly himself, and it's assessed half as high ag'in,
all things considered, as any other farm on his estate."

"But dat ist not right."

"Right! Who says it is?—or who thinks there is anything right about assessments, anywhere? I have heard
assessors, with my own ears, use such words as these :—
'Sich a man is rich, and can afford to pay,' and 'sich a
man is poor, and it will come hard on him.' Oh! they
kiver up dishonesty, now-a-days, under all sorts of argoo-
ments."

"But der law; der rich might haf der law on deir side,
surely?"

"In what way, I should like to know? Juries be everything, and juries will go accordin' to their feelin's, as well
as other men. I've seen the things with my own eyes.
The county pays just enough a-day to make poor men like to
be on juries, and they never fail to attend, while them that
can pay their fines stay away, and so leave the law pretty
much in the hands of one party. No rich man gains his
cause, unless his case is so strong it can't be helped."

I had heard this before, there being a very general complaint throughout the country of the practical abuses connected with the jury system. I have heard intelligent lawyers complain, that whenever a cause of any interest is
to be tried, the first question asked is not "what are the
merits?" "which has the law and the facts on his side?"
but "who is likely to be on the jury?"—thus obviously
placing the composition of the jury before either law or evidence. Systems may have a very fair appearance on paper
and as theories, that are execrable in practice. As for juries, I believe the better opinion of the intelligent of all countries is, that while they are a capital contrivance to resist
the abuse of power in narrow governments, in governments
of a broad constituency they have the effect, which might
easily be seen, of placing the control of the law in the
hands of those who would be most apt to abuse it; since it
is adding to, instead of withstanding and resisting the con-

trolling authority of the State, from which, in a popular government, most of the abuses must unavoidably proceed.

As for my uncle Ro, he was disposed to pursue the subject with Miller, who turned out to be a discreet and conscientious man. After a very short pause, as if to reflect on what had been said, he resumed the discourse.

"Vhat, den, makes arisdograts in dis coontry?" asked my uncle.

"Wa-a-l"—no man but an American of New England descent, as was the case with Miller, can give this word its attic sound—"Wa-a-l, it's hard to say. I hear a great deal about aristocrats, and I read a great deal about aristocrats, in this country, and I know that most folks look upon them as hateful, but I'm by no means sartain I know what an aristocrat is. Do you happen to know anything about it, friend?"

"Ja, ja; an arisdograt ist one of a few men dat hast all de power of de government in deir own hands."

"King! That isn't what we think an aristocrat in this part of the world. Why, we call them critturs here DIMIGOGUES! Now, young 'Squire Littlepage, who owns the Nest House, over yonder, and who is owner of all this estate, far and near, is what we call an aristocrat, and he hasn't power enough to be named town clerk, much less to anything considerable, or what is worth having."

"How can he be an aristodograt, den?"

"How, sure enough, if your account be true! I tell you 'tis the dimigogues that be the aristocrats of America. Why, Josh Brigham, who has just gone for the sheep, can get more votes for any office in the country than young Littlepage!"

"Berhaps dis young Littlebage ist a pat yoong man?"

"Not he; he's as good as any on 'em, and better than most. Besides, if he was as wicked as Lucifer, the folks of the country don't know anything about it, sin' he's be'n away ever sin' he has be'n a man."

"Vhy, den, gan't he haf as many votes as dat poor, ignorant fellow might haf? — das ist ott."

"It is odd, but it's true as gospel. Why, it may not be so easy to tell. Many men, many minds, you know. Some folks don't like him because he lives in a big house; some

hate him because they think he is better off than they are
themselves; others mistrust him because he wears a fine
coat; and some pretend to laugh at him because he got his
property from his father, and grand'ther, and so on, and
didn't make it himself. Accordin' to some folks' notions,
now-a-days, a man ought to enj'y only the property he
heaps together himself."

"If dis be so, your Herr Littlebage ist no arisdograt."

"Wa-a-l, that isn't the idee, hereaway. We have had a
great many meetin's, latterly, about the right of the people
to their farms; and there has been a good deal of talk at
them meetin's consarnin' aristocracy and feudal tenors; do
you know what a feudal tenor is, too?"

"Ja; dere ist moch of dat in Teutchland—in mine coontry. It ist not ferry easy to explain it in a few vords, but
der brincipal ding ist dat der vassal owes a serfice to hist
lort. . In de olten dimes dis serfice vast military, und dere
ist someding of dat now. It ist de noples who owe der feu
dal serfice, brincipally, in mine coontry, and dey owes it tc
de kings und brinces."

"And don't you call giving a chicken for rent feudal ser
vice, in Germany?"

Uncle Ro and I laughed, in spite of our efforts to the con
trary, there being a bathos in this question that was su
premely ridiculous. Curbing his merriment, however, as
soon as he could, my uncle answered the question.

"If der landlordt hast a right to coome and dake as many
cnickens as he bleases, und ast often ast he bleases, den dat
wouldt look like a feudal right; but if de lease says dat sc
many chickens moost be paid a-year, for der rent, vhy dat
ist all der same as baying so much moneys; und it might
be easier for der tenant to bay in chicken ast it might be to
bay in der silver. Vhen a man canst bay his debts in vhat
he makes himself, he ist ferry interpentent."

"It does seem so, I vow! Yet there's folks about here
and some at Albany, that call it feudal for a man to have
to carry a pair of fowls to the landlord's office, and the landlord an aristocrat for asking it!"

"But der man canst sent a poy, or a gal, or a nigger
wid his fowls, if he bleases?"

"Sartain; all that is asked is that the fowls should come.

"Und vhen der batroon might owe hist tailor, or hist snoemaker, must he not go to hist shop, or find him and bay him vhat he owes, or be suet for der debt?"

"That's true, too; boys, put me in mind of telling that to Josh, this evening. Yes, the greatest landlord in the land must hunt up his creditor, or be sued, all the same as the lowest tenant."

"Und he most bay in a partic'lar ding; he most bay in golt or silver?"

"True; lawful tender is as good for one as 'tis for t' other."

"Und if your Herr Littlebage signs a baper agreein' to gif der apples from dat orchart to somebody on his landts, most he send or carry der apples, too?"

"To be sure; that would be the bargain."

"Und he most carry der ferry apples dat grows on dem ferry drees, might it not be so?"

"All true as gospel. If a man contracts to sell the apples of one orchard, he can't put off the purchaser with the apples of another."

"Und der law ist der same for one ast for anudder, in dese t'ings?"

"There is no difference; and there should be none."

"Und der batroons und der landlordts wants to haf der law changet, so dat dey may be excuset from baying der debts accordin' to der bargains, und to gif dem atfantages over der poor tenants?"

"I never heard anything of the sort, and don't believe they want any such change."

"Of vhat, den, dost der beople complain?"

"Of having to pay rent at all; they think the landlords ought to be made to sell their farms, or give them away. Some stand out for the last."

"But der landlordts don't vant to sell deir farms; und dey might not be made to sell vhat ist deir own, and vhat dey don't vant to sell, any more dan der tenants might be made to sell deir hogs and deir sheep, vhen dey don't vant to sell dem."

"It does seem so, boys, as I've told the neighbours, all along. But I'll tell this Dutchman all about it. Some folks

13

want the State to look a'ter the title of young Littlepage, pretending he has no title."

"But der State wilt do dat widout asking for it particularly, vill it not?"

"I never heard that it would."·

"If anybody hast a claim to der broperty, vilt not der courts iry it?"

"Yes, yes—in that way; but a tenant can't set up a title ag'in his landlord."

"Vhy should he? He canst haf no title but his landlort's, and it vould be roguery and cheatery to let a man get into der bossession of a farm under der pretence of hiring it, und den coome out und claim it as owner. If any tenant dinks he hast a better right dan his landlort, he can put der farm vhere it vast before he might be a tenant, und den der State wilt examine into der title, I fancys."

"Yes, yes—in that way; but these men want it another way. What they want is for the State to set up a legal examination, and turn the landlords off altogether, if they can, and then let themselves have the farms in their stead."

"But dat would not be honest to dem dat hafen't nothing to do wid der farms. If der State owns der farms, it ought to get as moch as it can for dem, and so safe all der people from baying taxes. It looks like roguery, all roundt.'

"I believe it is that, and nothing else! As you say, the State will examine into the title as it is, and there is no need of any laws about it."

"Would der State, dink you, pass a law dat might inquire into de demandts dat are made against der batroons, vhen der tratesmen sent in deir bills?"

"I should like to see any patroon ask sich a thing! He would be laughed at, from York to Buffalo."

"Und he would desarf it. By vhat I see, frient, your denants be der arisdograts, und der landlordts der vassals."

"Why you see — what may your name be? — as we're likely to become acquainted, I should like to know your name.

"My name is Greisenbach, und I comes from Preussen."

"Well, Mr. Greisenbach, the difficulty about aristocracy is this. Hugh Littlepage is rich, and his money gives him

advantages that other men can't enj'y. Now, that sticks
in some folks' crops."

"Oh! den it ist meant to divite broperty in dis coontry;
und to say no man might haf more ast anudder?"

"Folks don't go quite as far as that, yet; though some
of their talk does squint that-a-way, I must own. Now,
there are folks about here that complain that old Madam
Littlepage and her young ladies don't visit the poor."

"Vell, if deys be hard-hearted, und hast no feelin's for
der poor and miseraple———"

"No, no; that is not what I mean, neither. As for that
sort of poor, everybody allows they do more for *them* than
anybody else about here. But they don't visit the poor that
isn't in want."

"Vell, it ist a ferry coomfortable sort of poor dat ist not
in any vant. Berhaps you mean dey don't associate wid
'em, as equals?"

"That's it. Now, on that head, I must say there is
some truth in the charge, for the gals over at the Nest never
come here to visit my gal, and Kitty is as nice a young
thing as there is about."

"Und Gitty goes to visit the gal of the man who lives
over yonter, in de house on der hill?" pointing to a residence of a man of the very humblest class in the town.

"Hardly! Kitty's by no means proud, but I shouldn't
like her to be too thick there."

"Oh! you're an arisdograt, den, after all; else might
your daughter visit dat man's daughter."

"I tell you, Grunzebach, or whatever your name may
be," returned Miller, a little angrily, though a particularly
good-natured man in the main, "that *my* gal shall *not* visit
old Steven's da'ghters."

"Vell, I'm sure she might do as she bleases; but I dinks
der Mademoiselles Littlepage might do ast dey pleases, too."

"There is but one Littlepage gal; if you saw them out
this morning in the carriage, you saw two York gals and
parson Warren's da'ghter with her."

"Und dis parson Warren might be rich, too?"

"Not he; he hasn't a sixpence on 'arth but what he gets
from the parish. Why he is so poor his friends had to edi-
cate his da'ghter, I have heern say, over and over!"

"Und das Littlepage gal und de Warren gal might bo goot friends?"

"They are the thickest together of any two young women in this part of the world. I 've never seen two gals more intimate. Now, there's a young lady in the town, one Opportunity Newcome, who, one might think, would stand before Mary Warren at the big house, any day in the week, but she doesn't! Mary takes all the shine out on her."

"Which ist der richest, Obbordunity or Mary?"

"By all accounts Mary Warren has nothing, while Opportunity is thought to come next to Matty herself, as to property, of all the young gals about here. But Opportunity is no favourite at the Nest."

"Den it would seem, after all, dat dis Miss Littlebage does not choose her friends on account of riches. She likes Mary Warren, who ist boor, und she does not like Obbordunity, who ist vell to do in de vorlt. Berhaps der Littlepages be rot as big arisdograts as you supposes."

Miller was bothered, while I felt a disposition to laugh. One of the commonest errors of those who, from position and habits, are unable to appreciate the links which connect cultivated society together, is to refer everything to riches. Riches, in a certain sense, as a means and through their consequences, may be a principal agent in dividing society into classes; but, long after riches have taken wings, their fruits remain, when good use has been made of their presence. So untrue is the vulgar opinion—or it might be better to say the opinion of the vulgar—that money is the one tie which unites polished society, that it is a fact which all must know who have access to the better circles of even our own commercial towns, that those circles, loosely and accidentally constructed as they are, receive with reluctance, nay, often sternly exclude, vulgar wealth from their associations, while the door is open to the cultivated who have nothing. The young, in particular, seldom think much of money, while family connections, early communications, similarity of opinions, and, most of all, of tastes, bring sets together, and often keep them together long after the golden band has been broken.

But men have great difficulty in comprehending things

that lie beyond their reach; and money being apparent to the senses, while refinement, through its infinite gradations, is visible principally, and, in some cases, exclusively to its possessors, it is not surprising that common minds should refer a tie that, to them, would otherwise be mysterious, to the more glittering influence, and not to the less obvious. Infinite, indeed, are the gradations of cultivated habits; nor are as many of them the fruits of caprice and self-indulgence as men usually suppose. There is a common sense, nay, a certain degree of wisdom, in the laws of even etiquette, while they are confined to equals, that bespeak the respect of those who understand them. As for the influence of associations on men's manners, on their exteriors, and even on their opinions, my uncle Ro has long maintained that it is so apparent that one of his time of life could detect the man of the world, at such a place as Saratoga even, by an intercourse of five minutes; and what is more, that he could tell the class in life from which he originally emerged. He tried it, the last summer, on our return from Ravensnest, and I was amused with his success, though he made a few mistakes, it must be admitted.

"That young man comes from the better circles, but he has never travelled," he said, alluding to one of a group which still remained at table; "while he who is next him *has* travelled, but commenced badly." This may seem a very nice distinction, but I think it is easily made. "There are two brothers, of an excellent family in Pennsylvania," he continued, "as one might know from the name; the eldest has travelled, the youngest has not." This was a still harder distinction to make, but one who knew the world as well as my uncle Ro could do it. He went on amusing me by his decisions—all of which were respectable, and some surprisingly accurate—in this way for several minutes. Now, like has an affinity to like, and in this natural attraction is to be found the secret of the ordinary construction of society. You shall put two men of superior minds in a room full of company, and they will find each other out directly, and enjoy the accident. The same is true as to the mere modes of thinking that characterize social castes; and it is truer in this country, perhaps, than most others, from the mixed character of our associations. Of the two, I am really of opinion that the man of high intellect, who meets with one of moderate capacity, but of manners and social opinions on a level with his own, has more pleasure in the communication than with one of equal mind, but of inferior habits.

That Patt should cling to one like Mary Warren seemed to me quite as natural as that she should be averse to much association with Opportunity Newcome. The money of the latter, had my sister been in the least liable to such an influence, was so much below what she had been accustomed, all her life, to consider affluence, that it would have had no effect, even had she been subject to so low a consideration in regulating her intercourse with others. But this poor Tom Miller could not understand. He could "only reason from what he knew," and he knew little of the comparative notions of wealth, and less of the powers of cultivation on the mind and manners. He was struck, however, with a fact that did come completely within the circle of his own knowledge, and that was the circumstance that Mary Warren, while admitted to be poor, was the bosom friend of her whom he was pleased to call, sometimes, the "Littlepage gal." It was easy to see he felt the force of this circumstance; and it is to be hoped that, as he was certainly a wiser, he also became a better man, on one of the most common of the weaknesses of human frailty.

"Wa-a-l," he replied to my uncle's last remark, after fully a minute of silent reflection, "I don't know! It would seem so, I vow; and yet it hasn't been my wife's notion, nor is it Kitty's. You're quite upsetting my idees about aristocrats; for though I like the Littlepages, I've always set 'em down as desp'rate aristocrats."

"Nein, nein; dem as vat you calls dimigogues be 'der American arisdograts. Dey gets all der money of der pooblic, und haf all der power, but dey gets a little mads because dey might not force demselves on der gentlemen and laties of der coontry, as vell as on der lands und der offices!"

"I swan! I don't know but this may be true! A'ter all, I don't know what right anybody has to complain of the Littlepages."

"Does dey dreat beoples vell, as might coome to see dem?"

"Yes, indeed! if folks treat *them* well, as sometimes

doesn't happen. I've seen hogs here"—Tom was a little
Saxon in his figures, but their nature will prove their justi-
fication—" I've seen hogs about here, bolt right in before
old Madam Littlepage, and draw their chairs up to her fire,
and squirt about the tobacco, and never think of even taking
off their hats. Them folks be always huffy about their own
importance, though they never think of other people's
feelin's."

We were interrupted by the sound of wheels, and looking round, we perceived that the carriage of my grandmother had driven up to the farm-house door, on its return
home. Miller conceived it to be no more than proper to go
and see if he were wanted, and we followed him slowly, it
being the intention of my uncle to offer his mother a watch,
by way of ascertaining if she could penetrate his disguise.

CHAPTER X.

" Will you buy any tape,
Or lace for your cape ? —
Come to the pedlar,
Money's a medler
That doth utter all men's ware-a."
Winter's Tale.

THERE they sat, those four young creatures, a perfect
galaxy of bright and beaming eyes. There was not a plain
face among them ; and I was struck with the circumstance
of how rare it was to meet with a youthful and positively
ugly American female. Kitty, too, was at the door by the
time we reached the carriage, and she also was a blooming
and attractive-looking girl. It was a thousand pities that
she spoke, however ; the vulgarity of her utterance, tone
of voice, cadences, and accent, the latter a sort of singing
whine, being in striking contrast to a sort of healthful and
vigorous delicacy that marked her appearance. All the

bright eyes grew brighter as I drew nearer, carrying the
flute in my hand; but neither of the young ladies spoke.

"Buy a vatch, ma'ams," said uncle Ro, approaching his
mother, cap in hand, with his box open.

"I thank you, friend; but I believe all here are provided
with watches already."

"Mine ist ferry sheaps."

"I dare say they may be," returned dear grandmother,
smiling; "though cheap watches are not usually the best.
Is that very pretty pencil gold?"

"Yes, ma'ams; it ist of *goot* gold. If it might not be, I
might not say so."

I saw suppressed smiles among the girls; all of whom,
however, were too well-bred to betray to common observers
the sense of the ridiculous that each felt at the equivoque
that suggested itself in my uncle's words.

"What is the price of this pencil," asked my grandmother.

Uncle Roger had too much tact to think of inducing his
mother to make a purchase as he had influenced Miller, and
he mentioned something near the true value of the "article,"
which was fifteen dollars.

"I will take it," returned my grandmother, dropping
three half eagles into the box; when, turning to Mary Warren, she begged her acceptance of the pencil, with as much
respect in her manner as if she solicited instead of conferred
a favour.

Mary Warren's handsome face was covered with blushes;
she looked pleased, and she accepted the offering, though I
thought she hesitated one moment about the propriety of so
doing, most probably on account of its value. My sister
asked to look at this little present; and after admiring it, it
passed from hand to hand, each praising its shape and ornaments. All my uncle's wares, indeed, were in perfect good
taste, the purchase having been made of an importer of character, and paid for at some cost. The watches, it is true,
were, with one or two exceptions, cheap, as were most of
the trinkets; but my uncle had about his person a watch,
or two, and some fine jewelry, that he had brought from
Europe himself, expressly to bestow in presents, among

which had been the pencil in question, and which he had
dropped into the box but a moment before it was sold.

"Wa-a-l, Madam Littlepage," cried Miller, who used the
familiarity of one born on the estate, "this is the queerest
watch-pedlar I've met with, yet. He asks fifteen dollars
for that pencil, and only four for this watch!" showing his
own purchase as he concluded.

My grandmother took the watch in her hand, and examined it attentively.

"It strikes me as singularly cheap!" she remarked,
glancing a little distrustfully, as I fancied, at her son, as if
she thought he might be selling his brushes cheaper than
those who only stole the materials, because he stole them
ready made. "I know that these watches are made for
very little in the cheap countries of Europe, but one can
hardly see how this machinery was put together for so small
a sum."

"I has 'em, matam, at all brices," put in my uncle.

"I have a strong desire to purchase a *good* lady's watch,
but should a little fear buying of any but a known and regular dealer."

"You needn't fear us, ma'am," I ventured to say. "If
we might sheat anypodies, we shouldn't sheat so goot a
laty."

I do not know whether my voice struck Patt's ear pleasantly, or a wish to see the project of her grandmother car
ried out at once, induced my sister to interfere; but interfere she did, and that by urging her aged parent to put
confidence in us. Years had taught my grandmother caution, and she hesitated.

"But all these watches are of base metal, and I want one
of good gold and handsome finish," observed my grand
mother.

My uncle immediately produced a watch that he had
bought of Blondel, in Paris, for five hundred francs, and
which was a beautiful little ornament for a lady's belt. He
gave it to my grandmother, who read the name of the manu-
facturer with some little surprise. The watch itself was
then examined attentively, and was applauded by all.

"And what may be the price of this?" demanded my
grandmother.

"One, hoondred dollars, matam; and sheaps at dat." :

Tom Miller looked at the bit of tinsel in his own hand, and at the smaller, but exquisitely-shaped "article" that my grandmother held up to look at, suspended by its bit of ribbon, and was quite as much puzzled as he had evidently been a little while before, in his distinctions between the rich and the poor. Tom was not able to distinguish the base from the true; that was all.

My grandmother did not appear at all alarmed at the price, though she cast another distrustful glance or two, over, her spectacles, at the imaginary pedlar. At length the beauty of the watch overcame her.

"If you will bring this watch to yonder large dwelling, I will pay you the hundred dollars for it," she said; "I have not as much money with me here."

"Ja, ja—ferry goot; you might keep das vatch, laty, und I will coome for der money after I haf got some dinners of somebodys."

My grandmother had no scruple about accepting of the credit, of course, and she was about to put the watch in her pocket, when Patt laid her little gloved hand on it, and cried—

"Now, dearest grandmother, let it be done at once — there is no one but us three present, you know!"

"Such is the impatience of a child!" exclaimed the elder lady, laughing. "Well, you shall be indulged. I gave you that pencil for a keep-sake, Mary, only *en attendant,* it having been my intention to offer a watch, as soon as a suitable one could be found, as a memorial of the sense I entertain of the spirit you showed during that dark week in which the anti-renters were so menacing. Here, then, is such a watch as I might presume to ask you to have the goodness to accept."

Mary Warren seemed astounded! The colour mounted to her temples; then she became suddenly pale. I had never seen so pretty a picture of gentle female distress — a distress that arose from conflicting, but creditable feelings.

"Oh! Mrs. Littlepage!" she exclaimed, after looking in astonishment at the offering for a moment, and in silence. "You cannot have intended that beautiful watch for me!"

"For you, my dear; the beautiful watch is not a whit too good for my beautiful Mary."

" But, dear, *dear* Mrs. Littlepage, it is altogether too handsome for my station — for my means."

" A lady can very well wear such a watch ; and you are a lady in every sense of the word, and so you need have no scruples on that account. As for the means, you will not misunderstand me if I remind you that it will be bought with my means, and there can be no extravagance in the purchase."

" But we are so poor, and that watch has so rich an appearance ! It scarcely seems right."

" I respect your feelings and sentiments, my dear girl, and can appreciate them. I suppose you know I was once as poor, nay, much poorer than you are, yourself."

" You, Mrs. Littlepage ! No, that can hardly be. You are of an affluent and very respectable family, I know."

" It is quite true, nevertheless, my dear. I shall not affect extreme humility, and deny that the Malbones did and do belong to the gentry of the land, but my brother and myself were once so much reduced as to toil with the surveyors, in the woods, quite near this property. We had then no claim superior to yours, and in many respects were reduced much lower. Besides, the daughter of an educated and well-connected clergyman has claims that, in a worldly point of view alone, entitle her to a certain consideration. You will do me the favour to accept my offering ?"

" Dear Mrs. Littlepage ! I do not know how to refuse *you*, or how to accept so rich a gift ! You will let me consult my father, first ?"

" That will be no more than proper, my dear," returned my beloved grandmother, quietly putting the watch into her own pocket; " Mr. Warren, luckily, dines with us, and the matter can be settled before we sit down to table."

This ended the discussion, which had commenced under an impulse of feeling that left us all its auditors. As for my uncle and myself, it is scarcely necessary to say we were delighted with the little scene. The benevolent wish to gratify, on the one side, with the natural scruples on the other, about receiving, made a perfect picture for our contemplation. The three girls, who were witnesses of what passed, too much respected Mary's feelings to interfere, though Patt restrained herself with difficulty. As to Tom

Miller and Kitty, they doubtless wondered why " Warren's gal" was such a fool as to hesitate about accepting a watch that was worth a hundred dollars. This was another point they did not understand. -   ·   ·   ⌐

" You spoke of dinner," continued my grandmother, look‐ ing at my uncle. " If you and your companion will follow as to the house, I will pay you for the watch, and order you a dinner in the bargain."

We were right down glad to accept this offer, making our bows, and expressing our thanks, as the carriage whirled off. We remained a moment, to take our leave of Miller.

" When you 've got through at the Nest," said that semi‐ worthy fellow, " give us another call here. I should like my woman and Kitty to have a look at your finery, before you go down to the village with it."

- With a promise to return to the farm-house, we proceeded on our way to the building which, in the familiar parlance of the country, was called the Nest, or the Nest House, from Ravensnest, its true name, and which Tom Miller, in his country dialect, called the " Neest." The distance be‐ tween the two buildings was less than half a mile, the grounds of the family residence lying partly between them. Many persons would have called the extensive lawns which surrounded my paternal abode a park, but it never bore that name with us. They were too large for a paddock, and might very well have come under the former appellation; but, as deer, or animals of any sort, except those that are domestic, had never been kept within it, the name had not been used. We called them the grounds — a term which applies equally to large and small enclosures of this nature — while the broad expanse of verdure which lies directly under the windows goes by the name of the lawn. Not‐ withstanding the cheapness of land among us, there has been very little progress made in the art of landscape gar‐ dening; and if we have anything like park scenery, it is far more owing to the gifts of a bountiful nature than to any of the suggestions of art. Thanks to the cultivated taste of Downing, as well as to his well-directed labours, this re‐ proach is likely to be soon removed, and country life will acquire this pleasure, among the many others that are so peculiarly its own. After lying for more than twenty years

— a stigma on the national taste — disfigured by, ravines or gullies, and otherwise in a rude and discreditable condition, the grounds of the White House have been brought into a condition to denote that they are the property of a civilized country. The Americans are as apt at imitation as the Chinese, with a far greater disposition to admit of change; and little beyond good models are required to set them on the right track. But it is certain that, as a nation, we have yet to acquire nearly all that belongs to the art I have mentioned that lies beyond avenues of trees, with an occasional tuft of shrubbery. The abundance of the latter, that forms the wilderness of sweets, the *masses* of flowers that spot the surface of Europe, the beauty of curved lines, and the whole finesse of surprises, reliefs, back-grounds and vistas, are things so little known among us as to be almost " arisdogratic," as my uncle Ro would call the word.

· Little else had been done at Ravensnest than to profit by the native growth of the trees, and to take advantage of the favourable circumstances in the formation of the grounds. Most travellers imagine that it might be an easy thing to lay out a park in the virgin forest, as the axe might spare the thickets, and copses, and woods, that elsewhere are the fruits of time and planting. This is all a mistake, however, as the rule; though modified exceptions may and do exist. The tree of the American forest shoots upward toward the light, growing so tall and slender as to be unsightly; and even when time has given its trunk a due size, the top is rarely of a breadth to ornament a park or a lawn, while its roots, seeking their nourishment in the rich alluvium formed by the decayed leaves of a thousand years, lie too near the surface to afford sufficient support after losing the shelter of its neighbours. It is owing to reasons like these that the ornamental grounds of an American country-house have usually to be commenced *ab origine*, and that natural causes so little aid in finishing them.

My predecessors had done a little towards assisting nature, at the Nest, and what was of almost equal importance, in the state of knowledge on this subject as it existed in the country sixty years since, they had done little to mar her efforts. The results were, that the grounds of Ravensnest possess a breadth that is the fruit of the breadth of our lands,

14

and a rural beauty which, without being much aided by art,
was still attractive. The herbage was kept short by sheep,
of which one thousand, of the fine wool, were feeding on
the lawns, along the slopes, and particularly on the distant
heights, as we crossed the grounds on our way to the doors.

The Nest House was a respectable New York country
dwelling, as such buildings were constructed among us in
the last quarter of the past century, a little improved and
enlarged by the second and third generations of its owners.
The material was of stone, the low cliff on which it stood
supplying enough of an excellent quality; and the shape of
the main *corps de batiment* as near a square as might be.
Each face of this part of the constructions offered five windows
to view, this being almost the prescribed number for
a country residence in that day, as three have since got to
be in towns. These windows, however, had some size, the
main building being just sixty feet square, which was about
ten feet in each direction larger than was common so soon
after the revolution. But wings had been added to the original
building, and that on a plan which conformed to the
shape of a structure in square logs, that had been its predecessor
on its immediate site. These wings were only of a
story and a half each, and doubling on each side of the main
edifice just far enough to form a sufficient communication,
they ran back to the very verge of a cliff some forty feet in
height, overlooking, at their respective ends, a meandering
rivulet, and a wide expanse of very productive flats, that
annually filled my barns with hay and my cribs with corn.
Of this level and fertile bottom-land there was near a thousand
acres, stretching in three directions, of which two hundred
belonged to what was called the Nest Farm. The
remainder was divided among the farms of the adjacent tenantry.
This little circumstance, among the thousand-and-one
other atrocities that were charged upon me, had been
made a ground of accusation, to which I shall presently have
occasion to advert. I shall do this the more readily, because
the fact has not yet reached the ears and set in motion the
tongues of legislators — Heaven bless us, how words do get
corrupted by too much use! — in their enumeration of the
griefs of the tenants of the State.

Everything about the Nest was kept in perfect order, and

n a condition to do credit to the energy and taste of my
grandmother, who had ordered all these things for the last
few years, or since the death of my grandfather. This circumstance, connected with the fact that the building was
larger and more costly than those of most of the other citizens of the country, had, of late years, caused Ravensnest
to be termed an "aristocratic residence." This word "aristocratic," I find since my return home, has got to be a term
of expansive signification, its meaning depending on the
particular habits and opinions of the person who happens to
use it. Thus, he who chews tobacco thinks it aristocratic
in him who deems the practice nasty not to do the same;
the man who stoops accuses him who is straight in the back
of having aristocratic shoulders; and I have actually met
with one individual who maintained that it was excessively
aristocratic to pretend not to blow one's nose with his fingers. It will soon be aristocratic to maintain the truth of
the familiar Latin axiom of "*de gustibus non disputandum
est.*"

As we approached the door of the Nest House, which
opened on the piazza that stretched along three sides of the
main building, and the outer ends of both wings, the coachman was walking his horses away from it, on the road that
led to the stables. The party of ladies had made a considerable circuit after quitting the farm, and had arrived but
a minute before us. All the girls but Mary Warren had
entered the house, careless on the subject of the approach
of two pedlars; she remained, however, at the side of my
grandmother, to receive us.

"I believe in my soul," whispered uncle Ro, "that my
dear old mother has a secret presentiment who we are, by
her manifesting so much respect.—T'ousand t'anks, matam,
t'ousand t'anks," he continued, dropping into his half-accu-
rate half-blundering broken English, "for dis great honour,
such as we might not expect das laty of das house to wait
for us at her door."

"This young lady tells me that she has seen you before,
and that she understands you are both persons of education
and good manners, who have been driven from your native
country by political troubles. Such being the case, I cannot regard you as common pedlars. I have known what it

was to be reduced in fortune," — my dear grandmother's voice trembled a little — "and can feel for those who thus suffer."

"Matam, dere might be moch trut' in some of dis," answered my uncle, taking off his cap, and bowing very much like a gentleman, an act in which I imitated him immediately. "We *haf* seen petter tays; und my son, dere, hast peen edicatet at an university. But we are now poor pedlars of vatches, und dem dat might make moosic in der streets."

My grandmother looked as a lady would look under such circumstances, neither too free to forget present appearances, nor coldly neglectful of the past. She knew that something was due to her own household, and to the example she ought to set it, while she felt that far more was due to the sentiment that unites the cultivated. We were asked into the house, were told a table was preparing for us, and were treated with a generous and considerate hospitality that involved no descent from her own character, or that of the sex; the last being committed to the keeping of every lady.

In the mean time, business proceeded with my uncle. He was paid his hundred dollars; and all his stores of value, including rings, brooches, ear-rings, chains, bracelets, and other trinkets that he had intended as presents to his wards, were produced from his pockets, and laid before the bright eyes of the three girls — Mary Warren keeping in the back ground, as one who ought not to look on things unsuited to her fortune. Her father had arrived, however, had been consulted, and the pretty watch was already attached to the girdle of the prettier waist. I fancied the tear of gratitude that still floated in her serene eyes was a jewel of far higher price than any my uncle could exhibit.

We had been shown into the library, a room that was in the front of the house, and of which the windows all opened on the piazza. I was at first a little overcome, at thus finding myself, and unrecognized, under the paternal roof, and in a dwelling that was my own, after so many years of absence. Shall I confess it! Everything appeared diminutive and mean, after the buildings to which I had been accustomed in the old world. I am not now drawing comparisons with the palaces of princes, and the abodes of the

great, as the American is apt to fancy, whenever anything
is named that is superior to the things to which he is accustomed; but to the style, dwellings, and appliances of domestic life that pertain to those of other countries who have not
a claim in anything to be accounted my superiors—scarcely
my equals. In a word, American aristocracy, or that which
it is getting to be the fashion to stigmatize as aristocratic,
would be deemed very democratic in most of the nations of
Europe. Our Swiss brethren have their chateaux and their
habits that are a hundred times more aristocratic than anything about Ravensnest, without giving offence to liberty;
and I feel persuaded, were the proudest establishment in all
America pointed out to a European as an aristocratic abode,
he would be very apt to laugh at it, in his sleeve. The secret of this charge among ourselves is the innate dislike
which is growing up in the country to see any man distinguished from the mass around him in anything, even though
it should be in merit. It is nothing but the expansion of
the principle which gave rise to the traditionary feud between the "plebeians and patricians" of Albany, at the
commencement of this century, and which has now descended so much farther than was then contemplated by the
soi-disant "plebeians" of that day, as to become quite disagreeable to their own descendants. But to return to myself—

I will own that, so far from finding any grounds of exultation in my own aristocratical splendour, when I came
to view my possessions at home, I felt mortified and disappointed. The things that I had fancied really respectable,
and even fine, from recollection, now appeared very common-place, and in many particulars mean. "Really," I
found myself saying *sotto voce*, "all this is scarcely worthy
of being the cause of deserting the right, setting sound principles at defiance, and of forgetting God and his commandments!" Perhaps I was too inexperienced to comprehend
how capacious is the maw of the covetous man, and how
microscopic the eye of envy.

"You are welcome to Ravensnest," said Mr. Warren,
approaching and offering his hand in a friendly way, much
as he would address any other young friend; "we arrived
a little before you, and I have had my ears and eyes open

14 *

ever since, in the hope of hearing your flute, and of seeing
your form in the highway, near the parsonage, where you
promised to visit me."

Mary was standing at her father's elbow, as when I first
saw her, and she gazed wistfully at my flute, as she would
not have done had she seen me in my proper attire, assuming
my proper character.

"I danks you, sir," was my answer. "We might haf
plenty of times for a little moosic, vhen das laties shall be
pleaset to say so. I canst blay Yankee Doodle, Hail Co-
loombias, and der 'Star Spangled Banner,' und all dem airs,
as dey so moch likes at der taverns and on der road."

Mr. Warren laughed, and he took the flute from my hand,
and began to examine it. I now trembled for the incognito!
The instrument had been mine for many years, and was a
very capital one, with silver keys, stops, and ornaments.
What if Patt — what if my dear grandmother should recognise it! I would have given the handsomest trinket in my
uncle's collection to get the flute back again into my own
hands; but, before an opportunity offered for that, it went
from hand to hand, as the instrument that had produced the
charming sounds heard that morning, until it reached those
of Martha. The dear girl was thinking of the jewelry,
which, it will be remembered, was rich, and intended in
part for herself; and she passed the instrument on, saying,
hurriedly,—

"See, dear grandmother, this is the flute which you pronounced the sweetest toned of any you had ever heard!"

My grandmother took the flute, started, put her spectacles
closer to her eyes, examined the instrument, turned pale —
for her cheeks still retained a little of the colour of their
youth — and then cast a glance hurriedly and anxiously at
me. I could see that she was pondering on something profoundly in her most secret mind, for a minute or two.
Luckily the others were too much occupied with the box of
the pedlar to heed her movements. She walked slowly out
of the door, almost brushing me as she passed, and went
into the hall. Here she turned, and, catching my eye, she
signed for me to join her. Obeying this signal, I followed,
until I was led into a little room, in one of the wings, that I
well remembered as a sort of private parlour attached to my

grandmother's own bed-room. To call it a *boudoir* would
be to caricature things, its furniture being just that of the
sort of room I have mentioned, or of a plain, neat, comfortable, country parlour. Here my grandmother took her seat
on a sofa, for she trembled so she could not stand, and then
she turned to gaze at me wistfully, and with an anxiety it
would be difficult for me to describe.

. " Do not keep me in suspense !" she said, almost awfully
in tone and manner, " am I right in my conjecture ?"

. " Dearest grandmother, you are !" I answered, in my natural voice.

No more was needed : we hung on each other's necks, as
had been my wont in boyhood. .

" But who is that pedlar, Hugh ?" demanded my grandmother, after a time. " Can it possibly be Roger, my son ?"

" It is no other ; we have come to visit you, incog."

" And why this disguise ? — Is it connected with the troubles ?"

" Certainly ; we have wished to take a near view with
our own eyes, and supposed it might be unwise to come
openly, in our proper characters."

" In this you have done well ; yet I hardly know how to
welcome you, in your present characters. On no account
must your real names be revealed. The demons of tar and
feathers, the sons of liberty and equality, who illustrate their
principles as they do their courage, by attacking the few
with the many, would be stirring, fancying themselves heroes and martyrs in the cause of justice, did they learn you
were here. Ten armed and resolute men might drive a
hundred of them, I do believe ; for they have all the cowardice of thieves, but they are heroes with the unarmed and
feeble. Are you safe, yourselves, appearing thus disguised,
under the new law ?" .

" We are not armed, not having so much as a pistol ; and
that will protect us."

" I am sorry to say, Hugh, that this country is no longer
what I once knew it. Its justice, if not wholly departed, is
taking to itself wings, and its blindness, not in a disregard
of persons, but in a faculty of seeing only the stronger side.
A landlord, in my opinion, would have but little hope, with
jury, judge, or executive, for doing that which thousands

of the tenants have done, still do, and will contir ue to do,
with perfect impunity, unless some dire catastrophe stimu-
lates the public functionaries to their duties, by awakening
public indignation."

" This is a miserable state of things, dearest grandmother;
and what makes it worse, is the cool indifference with which
most persons regard it. A better illustration of the utter
selfishness of human nature cannot be given, than in the
manner in which the body of the people look on, and see
wrong thus done to a few of their number." --

"Such persons as Mr. Seneca Newcome would answer,
that the public sympathises with the poor, who are oppressed
by the rich, because the last do not wish to let the first rob
them of their estates! We hear a great deal of the strong
robbing the weak, all over the world, but few among ourselves, I am afraid, are sufficiently clear-sighted to see how
vivid an instance of the truth now exists among ourselves."

" Calling the tenants the strong, and the landlords the
weak?"

" Certainly; numbers make strength, in this country in
which all power in practice, and most of it in theory, rests
with the majority. Were there as many landlords as there
are tenants, my life on it, no one would see the least injustice in the present state of things."

" So says my uncle: but I hear the light steps of the
girls — we must be on our guard."

At that instant Martha entered, followed by all three of
the girls, holding in her hand a very beautiful Manilla chain
that my uncle had picked up in his travels, and had purchased as a present to my future wife, whomsoever she
might turn out to be, and which he had had the indiscretion
to show to his ward. A look of surprise was cast by each
girl in succession, as she entered the room, on me, but neither said, and I fancy neither thought much of my being
shut up there with an old lady of eighty, after the first moment. Other thoughts were uppermost at the moment.

" Look at this, dearest grandmamma!" cried Patt, holding
up the chain as she entered the room. " Here is just the
most exquisite chain that was ever wrought, and of the
purest gold; but the pedlar refuses to part with it!"

" Perhaps you do not offer enough, my child; it is, indeed, very, very beautiful; pray what does he say is its value?"

"One hundred dollars, he says; and I can readily believe it, for its weight is near half the money. I do wish Hugh were at home; I am certain he would contrive to get it, and make it a present to me!"

"Nein, nein, young lady," put in the pedlar, who, a little unceremoniously, had followed the girls into the room, though he knew, of course, precisely where he was coming; "dat might not be. Dat chain is der broperty of my son, t'ere, und I haf sworn it shalt only be gifen to his wife."

Patt coloured a little, and she pouted a good deal; then she laughed outright.

"If it is only to be had on those conditions, I am afraid I shall never own it," she said, saucily, though it was intended to be uttered so low as not to reach my ears. "I will pay the hundred dollars out of my own pocket-money, however, if that will buy it. Do say a good word for me, grandmamma!"

How prettily the hussy uttered that word of endearment, so different from the "paw" and "maw" one hears among the dirty-noses that are to be found in the mud-puddles! But our grand-parent was puzzled, for she knew with whom she had to deal, and of course saw that money would do nothing. Nevertheless, the state of the game rendered it necessary to say and do something that might have an appearance of complying with Patty's request.

"Can I have more success in persuading you to change your mind, sir?" she said, looking at her son in a way that let him know at once, or at least made him suspect at once, that she was in his secret. "It would give me great pleasure to be able to gratify my grand-daughter, by making her a present of so beautiful a chain."

My uncle Ro advanced to his mother, took the hand she had extended with the chain in it, in order the better to admire the trinket, and he kissed it with a profound respect, but in such a manner as to make it seem to the lookers-on an act of European usage, rather than what it was, the tempered salute of a child to his parent.

"Laty," he then said, with emphasis, "if anyboty might make me change a resolution long since made, it would be

one as fenerable, und gracious, und goot as I am sartain
you most be. But I haf vowet to gif dat chain to das wife
of mine son, vhen he might marry, one day, some bretty
young American; und it might not be."

Dear grandmother smiled; but now she understood that
it was really intended the chain was to be an offering to my
wife, she no longer wished to change its destination. She
examined the bauble a few moments, and said to me —

"Do you wish this, as well as your un — father, I should
say? It is a rich present for a poor man to make."

"Ja, ja, laty, it ist so; but vhen der heart goes, golt
might be t'ought sheap to go wid it."

The old lady was half ready to laugh in my face, at hearing this attempt at Germanic English; but the kindness, and
delight, and benevolent tenderness of her still fine eyes, made
me wish to throw myself in her arms again, and kiss her.
Patt continued to *bouder* for a moment or two longer, but
her excellent nature soon gave in, and the smiles returned
to her countenance, as the sun issues from behind a cloud
in May.

"Well, the disappointment may and must be borne," she
said, good-naturedly; "though it is much the most lovely
chain I have ever seen."

"I dare say the right person will one day find one quite
as lovely to present to you!" said Henrietta Coldbrook, a
little pointedly.

I did not like this speech. It was an allusion that a well-
bred young woman ought not to have made, at least before
others, even pedlars; and it was one that a young woman
of a proper tone of feeling would not be apt to make. I determined from that instant the chain should never belong to
Miss Henrietta, though she was a fine, showy girl, and
though such a decision would disappoint my uncle sadly. I
was a little surprised to see a slight blush on Patt's cheek,
and then I remembered something of the name of the traveller, Beekman. Turning towards Mary Warren, I saw
plain enough that she was disappointed because my sister
was disappointed, and for no other reason in the world.

"Your grandmother will meet with another chain, when
she goes to town, that will make you forget this," she whispered, affectionately, close at my sister's ear.

Patt smiled, and kissed her friend with a warmth of manner that satisfied me these two charming young creatures
loved each other sincerely. But my dear old grandmother's
curiosity had been awakened, and she felt a necessity for
having it appeased. She still held the chain, and as she
returned it to me, who happened to be nearest to her, she
said —

"And so, sir, your mind is sincerely made up to offer
this chain to your future wife?"

"Yes, laty; or what might be better, to das yoong frau,
before we might be marriet."

"And is your choice made?" glancing round at the girls,
who were grouped together, looking at some other trinkets
of my uncle's. "Have you chosen the young woman who
is to possess so handsome a chain?"

"Nein, nein," I answered, returning the smile, and glancing also at the group; "dere ist so many peautiful laties in
America, one needn't be in a hurry. In goot time I shalt
find her dat ist intended for me."

"Well, grandmamma," interrupted Patt, "since nobody
can have the chain, unless on certain conditions, here are
the three other things that we have chosen for Ann, Henrietta, and myself, and they are a ring, a pair of bracelets
and a pair of ear-rings. The cost, altogether, will be two
hundred dollars; can you approve of that?"

My grandmother, now she knew who was the pedlar, understood the whole matter, and had no scruples. The bar
gain was soon made, when she sent us all out of the room,
under the pretence we should disturb her while settling with
the watch-seller. Her real object, however, was to be alone
with her son, not a dollar passing between them, of course.

CHAPTER XI.

" Our life was changed.   Another love
 In its lone woof began to twine ;
But oh! the golden thread was wove
Between my-sister's heart and mine."
                                        WILLIS.

HALF an hour later, uncle Ro and myself were seated at
table, eating our dinners as quietly as if we were in an inn.
The footman who had set the table was an old family servant, one who had performed the same sort of duty in that
very house for a quarter of a century.   Of course he was
not an American, no *man* of American birth ever remaining so long a time in an inferior station, or in any station
so low as that of a house-servant.   If he has good qualities
enough to render it desirable to keep him, he is almost certain to go up in the world ; if not, one does not care particularly about having him.   But Europeans are less elastic
and less ambitious, and it is no uncommon thing to find one
of such an origin remaining a long time in the same service.
Such had been the fact with this man, who had followed
my own parents from Europe, when they returned from
their marriage tour, and had been in the house on the occasion of my birth.   From that time he had continued at the
Nest, never marrying, nor ever manifesting the smallest
wish for any change.   He was an Englishman by birth ;
and what is very unusual in a servant of that country, when
transferred to America, the " letting-up," which is certain
to attend such a change from the depression of the original
condition to that in which he is so suddenly placed, had not
made him saucy.   An American is seldom what is called
impudent, under any circumstances ; he is careless, nay ig
norant of forms ; pays little or no purely conventional respect ; does not understand half the social distinctions which
exist among the higher classes of even his own countrymen,
and fancies there are equalities in things about which, in
truth, there is great inequality between himself and others

merely because he has been taught that all men are equal
in rights; but he is so unconscious of any pressure as
seldom to feel a disposition to revenge himself by impudence.

But, while John was not impudent either, he had a footman's feeling towards those whom he fancied no better than
himself. He had set the table with his customary neatness
and method, and he served the soup with as much regularity as he would have done had we sat there in our proper characters, but then he withdrew. He probably remembered that the landlord, or upper servant of an English hotel,
is apt to make his appearance with the soup, and to disappear as that disappears. So it was with John; after removing the soup, he put a dumb-waiter near my uncle,
touched a carving-knife or two, as much as to say "help
yourselves," and quitted the room. As a matter of course,
our dinner was not a very elaborate one, it wanting two or
three hours to the regular time of dining, though my grandmother had ordered, in my hearing, one or two delicacies
to be placed on the table, that had surprised Patt. Among
the extraordinary things for such guests was wine. The
singularity, however, was a little explained by the quality
commanded, which was Rhenish.

My uncle Ro was a little surprised at the disappearance
of John; for, seated in that room, he was so accustomed to
his face, that it appeared as if he were not half at home
without him.

"Let the fellow go," he said, withdrawing his hand from
the bell-cord, which he had already touched to order him back
again; "we can talk more freely without him. Well, Hugh,
here you are, under your own roof, eating a charitable dinner, and treated as hospitably as if you did not own all you
can see for a circle of five miles around you. It was a
lucky idea of the old-lady's, by the way, to think of ordering this Rudesheimer, in our character of Dutchmen! How
amazingly well she is looking, boy!"

"Indeed she is; and I am delighted to see it. I do not
know why my grandmother may not live these twenty
years; for even that would not make her near as old as
Sus, who, I have often heard her say, was a middle-aged
man when she was born."

15

"True; she seems like an elder sister to me, rather than as a mother, and is altogether a most delightful old woman. But, if we had so charming an old woman to receive us, so are there also some very charming *young* women — hey, Hugh?"

"I am quite of your way of thinking, sir; and must say I have not, in many a day, seen two as charming creatures as I have met with here."

" *Two!* — umph; a body would think *one* might suffice Pray, which may be the two, Master Padishah?"

"Patt and Mary Warren, of course. The other two are well enough, but these two are excellent."

My uncle Ro looked grum, but he said nothing for some time. Eating is always an excuse for a broken conversation, and he ate away as if resolute not to betray his disappointment. But it is a hard matter for a gentleman to do nothing but eat at table, and so was obliged to talk.

"Everything looks well here, after all, Hugh," observed my uncle. "These anti-renters may have done an infinite deal of harm in the way of abusing principles, but they do not seem to have yet destroyed any material things."

"It is not their cue, sir. The crops are their own; and as they hope to own the farms, it would be scarcely wise to injure what, no doubt, they begin to look on as their own property, too. As for the Nest House, grounds, farm, &c., I dare say they will be very willing to leave me them for a while longer, provided they can get everything else away from me."

"For a time longer, at least; though that is the folly of those who expect to get along by concessions; as if men were ever satisfied with the yielding of a part, when they ask that which is wrong in itself, without sooner or later expecting to get the whole. As well might one expect the pickpocket who had abstracted a dollar, to put back two-and-sixpence change. But things really look well, around the place."

"So much the better for us. Though, to my judgment and taste, Miss Mary Warren looks better than anything else I have yet seen in America."

Another "umph" expressed my uncle's dissatisfaction —

displeasure would be too strong a word — and he continued eating.

"You have really some good Rhenish in your cellar, Hugh," resumed uncle Ro, after tossing off one of the knowing green glasses full—though I never could understand why any man should wish to drink his wine out of green, when he might do it out of crystal. "It must have been a purchase of mine, made when we were last in Germany, and for the use of my mother."

"As you please, sir; it neither adds nor subtracts from the beauty of Martha and her friend."

"Since you are disposed to make these boyish allusions, be frank with me, and say, at once, how you like my wards."

"Meaning, of course, sir, my own sister exclusively. I will be as sincere as possible, and say that, as to Miss Marston, I have no opinion at all; and as to Miss Coldbrook, she is what, in Europe, would be called a 'fine' woman."

"You can say nothing as to her mind, Hugh, for you have had no opportunity for forming an opinion."

"Not much of a one, I will own. Nevertheless, I should have liked her better had she spared the allusion to the 'proper person' who is one day to forge a chain for my sister, to begin with."

"Poh, poh; that is the mere squeamishness of a boy. I do not think her in the least pert or forward, and your construction would be *tant soit peu* vulgar."

"Put your own construction on it, *mon oncle; I* do not like it."

"I do not wonder young men remain unmarried; they are getting to be so ultra in their tastes and notions."

A stranger might have retorted on an old bachelor, for such a speech, by some allusion to his own example; but I well knew that my uncle Ro had once been engaged, and that he lost the object of his passion by death, and too much respected his constancy and true sentiments ever to joke on such subjects.' I believe he felt the delicacy of my forbearance rather more than common, for he immediately manifested a disposition to relent, and to prove it by changing the subject.

"We can never stay here to-night," he said. "It would be at once to proclaim our names—our name, I might say—a name that was once so honoured and beloved in this town, and which is now so hated!"

"No, no; not as bad as that. We have done nothing to merit hatred."

"*Raison de plus* for hating us so much the more heartily. When men are wronged, who have done nothing to deserve it, the evil-doer seeks to justify his wickedness to himself by striving all he can to calumniate the injured party; and the more difficulty he finds in doing that to his mind, the more profound is his hatred. Rely on it, we are most sincerely disliked here, on the spot where we were once both much beloved. Such is human nature."

At that moment John returned to the room, to see how we were getting on, and to count his forks and spoons, for I saw the fellow actually doing it. My uncle, somewhat indiscreetly, I fancied, but by merely following the chain of thought then uppermost in his mind, detained him in conversation.

"Dis broperty," he said, inquiringly, "is de broperty of one Yeneral Littlepage, I hears say?"

"Not of the General, who was Madam Littlepage's husband; and who has long been dead, but of his grandson, Mr. Hugh."

"Und vhere might he be, dis Mr. Hugh?—might he be at hand, or might he not?"

"No; he's in Europe; that is to say, in Hengland." John thought England covered most of Europe, though he had long gotten over his wish to return. "Mr. Hugh and Mr. Roger be both habsent from the country, just now."

"Dat ist unfortunate, for dey dells me dere might be moch troobles here abouts, and Injin-acting."

"There is, indeed; and a wicked thing it is, that there should be anything of the sort."

"Und vhat might be der reason of so moch troobles?—and vhere ist der blame?"

"Well, that is pretty plain, I fancy," returned John, who, in consequence of being a favoured servant at head-quarters, fancied himself a sort of cabinet minister, and had much pleasure in letting his knowledge be seen. "The tenants on this estate wants to be landlords; and as they can't be so, so long as Mr. Hugh lives and won't let 'em, why they just tries all sorts of schemes and plans to frighten people out of their property. I never go down to the village but I nas a talk with some of them, and that in a way that might do them some good, if anything can."

"Und vhat dost you say?—und vid whom dost you talk, as might do dem moch goot?"

"Why, you see, I. talks more with one 'Squire Newcome, as they calls him, though he's no more of a real 'squire than you be—only a sort of an attorney, like, such as they has in this country. You come from the old countries, I believe?"

"Ja, ja—dat ist, yes—we comes from Charmany; so you can say vhat you bleases."

"They has queer 'squires in this part of the world, if truth must be said. But that's neither here nor there, though I give this Mr. Seneca Newcome as good as he sends. What is it you wants, I says to him?—you can't all be landlords—somebody must be tenants; and if you didn't want to be tenants, how come you to be so? Land is plenty in this country, and cheap too; and why didn't you buy your land at first, instead of coming to rent of Mr. Hugh; and now when you *have* rented, to be quarrelling about the very thing you did of your own accord?"

"Dere you didst dell 'em a goot t'ing; and vhat might der 'Squire say to dat?"

"Oh! he was quite dumb-founded, at first; then he said that in old times, when people first rented these lands, they didn't *know* as much as they do now, or they never would have done it."

"Und you could answer dat; or vast it your durn to be dum-founded?"

"I pitched it into him, as they says; I did. Says I, how's this, says I—you are for ever boasting how much you Americans know—and how the people knows every-thing that ought to be done, about politics and religion—and you proclaim far and near that your yeomen are the salt of the earth—and yet you don't know how to bargain for your leases! A pretty sort of wisdom is this, says I!—I had him

15 *

there; for the people round about here is only too sharp at
a trade."

"Did he own dat you vast right, and dat he vast wrong,
dis Herr 'Squire Newcome?"

"Not he; he will never own anything that makes against
his own doctrine, unless he does it ignorantly. But I haven't
told you half of it. I told him, says I, how is it you talk
of one of the Littlepage family cheating you, when, as you
knows yourselves, you had rather have the word of one of
that family than have each other's bonds, says I. You
know, sir, it must be a poor landlord that a tenant can't and
won't take his word: and this they all know to be true;
for a gentleman as has a fine estate is raised above temptation, like, and has a pride in him to do what is honourable
and fair; and, in my opinion, it is good to have a few such
people in a country, if it be only to keep the wicked one
from getting it altogether in his own keeping."

"Und did you say dat moch to der 'Squire?"

"No; that I just says to you two, seeing that we are
here, talking together in a friendly way; but a man needn't
be ashamed to say it anywhere, for it's a religious truth.
But I says to him, Newcome, says I, you, who has been
living so long on the property of the Littlepages, ought to
be ashamed to wish to strip them of it; but you 're not satisfied with keeping gentlemen down quite as much out of
sight as you can, by holding all the offices yourselves, and
taking all the money of the public you can lay your hands
on for your own use, but you wants to trample them under
your feet, I says, and so take your revenge for being what
you be, says I."

, "Vell, my friend," said my uncle, "you vast a bolt man
to dell all dis to der beoples of dis coontry, vhere, I have
heard, a man may say just vhat he hast a mind to say, so
dat he dost not sbeak too moch trut!"

-"That's it—that's it; you have been a quick scholar, I
find. I told this Mr. Newcome, says I, you 're bold enough
in railing at kings and nobles, for you very well know, says
I, that they are three thousand miles away from you, and
can do you no harm; but you would no more dare get up
before your masters, the people, here, and say what you
really think about 'em, and what I have heard you say of

.hem in private, than you would dare put your head before
a cannon, as the gunner touched it off. Oh! I gave him a
lesson, you may be sure !"——

Although there was a good deal of the English footman in
John's logic and feeling, there was also a good deal of truth
in what he said. The part where he accused Newcome of
holding one set of opinions in private, concerning *his* masters, and another in public, is true to the life. There is not,
at this moment, within the wide reach of the American bor-
ders, one demagogue to be found who might not, with justice, be accused of precisely the same deception. There is
not one demagogue in the whole country, who, if he lived
in a monarchy, would not be the humblest advocate of men
in power, ready to kneel at the feet of those who stood in
the sovereign's presence. There is not, at this instant, a
man in power among us a senator or a legislator, who is
now the seeming advocate of what he wishes to call the
rights of the tenants, and who is for overlooking principles
and destroying law and right, in order to pacify the anti-
renters by extraordinary concessions, that would not be
among the foremost, under a monarchial system, to recommend and support the freest application of the sword and the
bayonet to suppress what would then be viewed, ay, and be
termed, " the rapacious longings of the disaffected to enjoy
the property of others without paying for it." All this is
certain ; for it depends on a law of morals that is infallible.
Any one who wishes to obtain a clear index to the true characters of the public men he is required to support, or oppose, has now the opportunity ; for each stands before a
mirror that reflects him in his just proportions, and in which
the dullest eye has only to cast a glance, in order to view
him from head to foot.

The entrance of my grandmother put a stop to John's
discourse. He was sent out of the room on a message, and
then I learned the object of this visit. My sister had been
let into the secret of our true characters, and was dying to
embrace me. My dear grandmother, rightly enough, had
decided it would be to the last degree unkind to keep her in
ignorance of our presence ; and, the fact known, nature had
.ongings which must be appeased. I had myself been

tempted twenty times, that morning, to snatch Patt to my
heart and kiss her, as I used to do just after my beard began to grow; and she was so much of a child as to complain.
The principal thing to be arranged, then, was to obtain an
interview for me without awakening suspicion in the observers.　My grandmother's plan was arranged, however,
and she now communicated it to us. .

There was a neat little dressing-room annexed to Martha's bed-room ; in that the meeting was to take place.

" She and Mary Warren are now there, waiting for your
appearance, Hugh——"

" Mary Warren !—Does she, then, know who I am?"

" Not in the least ; she has no other idea than that you
are a young German, of good connections and well educated,
who has been driven from his own country by political troubles, and who is reduced to turn his musical taste and ac-
quisitions to account, in the way you seem to do, until he
can find some better employment.　All this she had told us
before we met you, and you are not to be vain, Hugh, if I
add, that your supposed misfortunes, and great skill with
the flute, and good behaviour, have made a friend of one of
the best and most true-hearted girls I ever had the good fortune to know.　I say good *behaviour*, for little, just now,
can be ascribed to good *looks*."

" I hope I am not in the least revolting in appearance, in
this disguise. For my sister's sake——"

The hearty laugh of my dear old grandmother brought
me up, and I said no more ; colouring, I believe, a little, at
my own folly.　Even uncle Ro joined in the mirth, though
I could see he wished Mary Warren even safely translated
along with her father, and that the latter was Archbishop of
Canterbury.　I must acknowledge that I felt a good deal
ashamed of the weakness I had betrayed.

" You are very well, Hugh, darling," continued my grandmother ; " though I must think you would be more interesting in your own hair, which is curling, than in that lank
wig.　Still, one can see enough of your face to recognise
it, if one has the clue ; and I told Martha, at the first, that
I was struck with a certain expression of the eyes and smile
that reminded me of her brother. But, there they are, Mary

and Martha, in the drawing-room, waiting for your appearance. The first is so fond of music, and, indeed, is so practised in it, as to have been delighted with your flute ; and she has talked so much of your skill as to justify us in seeming to wish for a further exhibition of your skill. Henrietta and Ann, having less taste that way, have gone together to select bouquets, in the green-house, and there is now an excellent opportunity to gratify your sister. I am to draw Mary out of the room, after a little while, when you and Martha may say a word to each other in your proper characters. As for you, Roger, you are to open your box again, and I will answer for it *that* will serve to amuse your other wards, should they return too soon from their visit to the gardener.''

Everything being thus explained, and our dinner ended, all parties proceeded to the execution of the plan, each in his or her designated mode. When my grandmother and I reached the dressing-room, however, Martha was not there, though Mary Warren was, her bright but serene eyes full of happiness and expectation. Martha had retired to the inner room for a moment, whither my grandmother, suspecting the truth, followed her. As I afterwards ascertained, my sister, fearful of not being able to suppress her tears on my entrance, had withdrawn, in order to struggle for self-command without betraying our secret. I was told to commence an air, without waiting for the absent young lady, as the strain could easily be heard through the open door.

I might have played ten minutes before my sister and grandmother came out again. Both had been in tears, though the intense manner in which Mary Warren was occupied with the harmony of my flute, probably prevented her from observing it. To me, however, it was plain enough ; and glad was I to find that my sister had succeeded in commanding her feelings. In a minute or two my grandmother profited by a pause to rise and carry away with her Mary Warren, though the last left the room with a reluctance that was very manifest. The pretence was a promise to meet the divine in the library, on some business connected with the Sunday-schools.

" You can keep the young man for another air, Martha,"
observed my grandmother; " and I will send Jane to you,
as I pass her room."

Jane was my sister's own maid, and her room was close
at hand, and I dare say dear grandmother gave her the order,
in Mary Warren's presence, as soon as she quitted the room,
else might Mary Warren well be surprised at the singularity
of the whole procedure; but Jane did not make her appearance, nevertheless. As for myself, I continued to play as
long as I thought any ear was near enough to hear me;
then I laid aside my flute. In the next instant Patt was in
my arms, where she lay some time weeping, but looking
inexpressibly happy.

" Oh! Hugh, what a disguise was this to visit your own
house in!" she said, as soon as composed enough to speak.

" Would it have done to come here otherwise? You
know the state of the country, and the precious fruits our
boasted tree of liberty is bringing forth. The owner of the
land can only visit his property at the risk of his life!"

Martha pressed me in her arms in a way to show how
conscious she was of the danger I incurred in even thus visiting her; after which we seated ourselves, side by side,
on a little divan, and began to speak of those things that
were most natural to a brother and sister who so much loved
each other, and who had not met for five years. My grandmother had managed so well as to prevent all interruption
for an hour, if we saw fit to remain together, while to others
it should seem as if Pat had dismissed me in a few minutes.

" Not one of the other girls suspect, in the least, who you
are," said Martha, smiling, when we had got through with
the questions and answers so natural to our situation. " I
am surprised that Henrietta has not, for *she* prides herself
on her penetration. She is as much in the dark as the
others, however."

" And Miss Mary Warren—the young lady who has just
left the room—has she not some *small* notion that I am not
a common Dutch music-grinder ?"

Patt laughed, and that so merrily as to cause the tones
of her sweet voice to fill me with delight, as I remembered
what she had been in childhood and girlhood five years be-

fore, and she shook her bright tresses off her cheeks ere she would answer.

"No, Hugh," she replied, "she fancies you an *uncommon* Dutch music-grinder; an *artiste* that not only grinds, but who dresses up his harmonies in such a way as to be palatable to the most refined taste. How came Mary to think you and my uncle two reduced German gentlemen?"

"And does the dear girl believe—that is, does Miss Mary Warren do us so much honour, as to imagine that?"

"Indeed she does, for she told us as much as soon as she got home; and Henrietta and Ann have made themselves very merry with their speculations on the subject of Miss Warren's great incognito. They call you Herzog von Geige."

"Thank them for that." I am afraid I answered a little too pointedly, for I saw that Patt seemed surprised. "But your American towns are just such half-way things as to spoil young women; making them neither refined and polished as they might be in real capitals, while they are not left the simplicity and nature of the country."

"Well, Master Hugh, this is being very cross about a very little, and not particularly complimentary to your own sister. And why not *your* American towns, as well as *ours?*—are you no longer one of us?"

"Certainly; one of *yours*, always, my dearest Patt, though not one of every chattering girl who may set up for a *belle*, with her Dukes of Fiddle! But, enough of this; —you like the Warrens?"

"Very much so; father and daughter. The first is just what a clergyman should be; of a cultivation and intelligence to fit him to be any man's companion, and a simplicity like that of a child. You remember his predecessor— so dissatisfied, so selfish, so lazy, so censorious, so unjust to every person and thing around him, and yet so exacting; and, at the same time, so——"

"What? Thus far you have drawn his character well; I should like to hear the remainder."

"I have said more than I ought already; for one has an idea that, by bringing a clergyman into disrepute, it brings religion and the church into discredit, too. A priest must

be a *very* bad man to have injurious things said of him, in
this country, Hugh."

" That is, perhaps, true. But you like Mr. Warren better
than him who has left you ?"

" A thousand times, and in all things. In addition to
having a most pious and sincere pastor, *we* have an agreeable and well-bred neighbour, from whose mouth, in the five
years that he has dwelt here, I have not heard a syllable at
the expense of a single fellow-creature. You know how it
is apt to be with the other clergy and ours, in the country—
for ever at swords' points ; and if not actually quarrelling,
keeping up a hollow peace."

" That is only too true—or used to be true, before I went
abroad."

" And it is so now, elsewhere, I 'll answer for it, though
it be so no longer here. Mr. Warren and Mr. Peck seem
to live on perfectly amicable terms, though as little alike a'
bottom as fire and water."

" By the way, how do the clergy of the different sects, up
and down the country, behave on the subject of anti-rent ?"

" I can answer only from what I hear, with the exception
of Mr. Warren's course. *He* has preached two or three
plain and severe sermons on the duty of honesty in our
worldly transactions, one of which was from the tenth commandment. Of course he said nothing of the particular
trouble, but everybody must have made the necessary application of the home-truths he uttered. I question if another voice has been raised, far and near, on the subject,
although I have heard Mr. Warren say the movement
threatens more to demoralize New York than anything that
has happened in his time."

" And the man down at the village ?"

" Oh, he goes, of course, with the majority. When was
one of that set ever known to oppose his parish, in anything ?"

" And Mary is as sound and as high-principled as her
father ?"

" Quite so ; though there has been a good deal said about
the necessity of Mr. Warren's removing, and giving up St.
Andrew's, since he preached against covetousness. All the

anti-renters say, I hear, that they know he meant *them*, and that they won't put up with it."

" I dare say ; each one fancying he was almost called out by name : that is the way, when conscience works."

" I should be very, very sorry to part with Mary ; and almost as much so to part with her father. There is one thing, however, that Mr. Warren himself thinks we had better have done, Hugh ; and that is to take down the canopy from over our pew. You can have no notion of the noise that foolish canopy is making up and down the country."

" I shall *not* take it down. It is my property, and there it shall remain. As for the canopy, it was a wrong distinction to place in a church, I am willing to allow ; but it never gave offence until it has been thought that a cry against it would help to rob me of my lands at half price, or at no price at all, as it may happen."

" All that may be true ; but if improper for a church, why keep it ?"

" Because I do not choose to be bullied out of what is my own, even though I care nothing about it. There might have been a time when the canopy was unsuited to the house of God, and that was when those who saw it might fancy it canopied the head of a fellow-creature who had higher claims than themselves to divine favour ; but, in times like these, when men estimate merit by beginning at the other end of the social scale, there is little danger of any one's falling into the mistake. The canopy shall stand, little as I care about it : now, I would actually prefer it should come down, as I can fully see the impropriety of making any distinctions in the temple ; but it shall stand until concessions cease to be dangerous. It is a right of property, and as such I will maintain it. If others dislike it, let them put canopies over their pews, too. The best test, in such a matter, is to see who could bear it. A pretty figure Seneca Newcome would cut, for instance, seated in a canopied pew ! Even his own set would laugh at him, which, I fancy, is more than they yet do at me."

Martha was disappointed ; but she changed the subject. We next talked of our own little private affairs, as they were connected with smaller matters.

" For whom is that beautiful chain intended, Hugh ?"

16

asked Patt, laughingly. "I can now believe the pedlar when he says it is reserved for your future wife. But who is that wife to be? Will her name be Henrietta or Ann?"

"Why not ask, also, if it will be Mary? — why exclude one of your companions, while you include the other two?"

Patt started—seemed surprised; her cheeks flushed, and then I saw that pleasure was the feeling predominant.

"Am I too late to secure that jewel, as a pendant to my chain?" I asked, half in jest, half seriously.

"Too soon, at least, to attract it by the richness and beauty of the bauble. A more natural and disinterested girl than Mary Warren does not exist in the country."

"Be frank with me, Martha, and say at once; has she a favoured suitor?"

"Why, this seems really serious!" exclaimed my sister, laughing. "But, to put you out of your pain, I will answer; I know of but one. One she has certainly, or female sagacity is at fault."

"But is he one that is favoured? You can never know how much depends on your answer."

"Of that you can judge for yourself. It is 'Squire Seneky Newcome, as he is called hereabouts — the brother of the charming Opportunity, who still reserves herself for you."

"And they are as rank anti-renters as any male and female in the country."

"They are rank Newcomites; and that means that each is for himself. Would you believe it, but Opportunity really gives herself airs with Mary Warren!"

"And how does Mary Warren take such an assumption?"

"As a young person should—quietly and without manifesting any feeling. But there is something quite intolerable in one like Opportunity Newcome's assuming a superiority over any true lady! Mary is as well educated and as well connected as any of us, and is quite as much accustomed to good company; while Opportunity—" here Patt laughed, and then added, hurriedly, "but you know Opportunity as well as I do."

"Oh! yes; she is *la* vertue, or *the* virtue, and *je suis venue, pour*."

The latter allusion Patt understood well enough, having
laughed over the story a dozen times; and she laughed again
when I explained the affair of " *the* solitude."

Then came a fit of sisterly feeling. Patt insisted on taking
off my wig, and seeing my face in its natural dress. I
consented to gratify her, when the girl really behaved like a
simpleton. First she pushed about my curls until they were
arranged to suit the silly creature, when she ran back several steps, clapped her hands in delight, then rushed into my
arms and kissed my forehead and eyes, and called me " her
brother"— her " only brother" — her " dear, *dear* Hugh,"
and by a number of other such epithets, until she worked
herself, and me too, into such an excess of feeling that we
sat down, side by side, and each had a hearty fit of crying.
Perhaps some such burst as this was necessary to relieve
our minds, and we submitted to it wisely.

My sister wept the longest, as a matter of course; but,
as soon as she had dried her eyes, she replaced the wig, and
completely restored my disguise, trembling the whole time
lest some one might enter and detect me.

" You have been very imprudent, Hugh, in coming here
at all," she said, while thus busy. " You can form no notion of the miserable state of the country, or how far the
anti-rent poison has extended, or the malignant nature of
its feeling. The annoyances they have attempted with dear
grandmother are odious; *you* they would scarcely leave
alive."

" The country and the people must have strangely altered,
then, in five years. Our New York population has hitherto
had very little of the assassin-like character. Tar and feathers are the blackguards', and have been the petty tyrants'
weapons, from time immemorial, in this country; but not
the knife."

" And can anything sooner or more effectually alter a
people than longings for the property of others? Is not the
' love of money the root of all evil?'— and what right have
we to suppose our Ravensnest population is better than another, when that sordid feeling is thoroughly aroused? You
know you have written me yourself, that all the American
can or does live for is money."

" I have written you, dear, that the country, in its pro-

sent condition, leaves no other incentive to exertion, and
therein it is cursed. Military fame, military rank, even,
are unattainable, under our system : the arts, letters and
science, bring little or no reward ; and there being no poli-
litical rank that a man of refinement would care for, men
must live for money, or live altogether for another state of
being. But I have told you, at the same time, Martha, that,
notwithstanding all this, I believe the American a less mercenary being, in the ordinary sense of the word, than the
European ; that two men might be bought, for instance, in
any European country, for one here. This last I suppose
to be the result of the facility of making a living, and the
habits it produces." ·

"Never mind causes ; Mr. Warren says there is a desperate intention to rob existing among these people, and that
they are dangerous. As yet they do a little respect women,
but how long they will do that one cannot know."   ·.

"It may all be so. It *must* be so, respecting what I have
heard and read ; yet this vale looks as smiling and as sweet,
at this very moment, as if an evil passion never sullied it!
But, depend on my prudence, which tells me that we ought
now to part. I shall see you again and again before I quit
the estate, and you will, of course, join us somewhere — at
the Springs, perhaps — as soon as we find it necessary or
expedient to decamp."

Martha promised this, of course, and I kissed her, previously to separating. No one crossed my way as I descended to the piazza, which was easily done, since I was
literally at home. I lounged about on the lawn a few minutes, and then, showing myself in front of the library windows, I was summoned to the room, as I had expected. ·

Uncle Ro had disposed of every article of the fine jewelry
that he had brought home as presents for his wards. The
pay was a matter to be arranged with Mrs. Littlepage,
which meant no pay at all ; and, as the donor afterwards
told me, he liked this mode of distributing the various ornaments better than presenting them himself, as he was now
certain each girl had consulted her own fancy.

As the hour of the regular dinner was approaching, we
took our leave soon after, not without receiving kind and
pressing invitations to visit the Nest again ere we left the

township. Of course we promised all that was required, intending most faithfully to comply. On quitting the house we returned towards the farm, though not without pausing on the lawn to gaze around us on a scene so dear to both, from recollection, association, and interest. But I forget, this is aristocratical; the landlord has no right to sentiments of this nature, which are feelings that the sublimated liberty of the law is beginning to hold in reserve solely for the benefit of the tenant!

CHAPTER XII.

"There shall be, in England, seven half-penny loaves sold for a penny: the three-hooped pot shall have ten hoops; and I will make it felony to drink small beer: all the realm shall be in common, and in Cheapside shall my palfrey go to grass."

Jack Cade.

"I do not see, sir," I remarked, as we moved on from the last of these pauses, "why the governors and legislators, and writers on this subject of anti-rentism, talk so much of feudality, and chickens, and days' works, and durable leases, when we have none of these, while we have all the disaffection they are said to produce."

"You will understand that better as you come to know more of men. No party alludes to its weak points. It is just as you say; but the proceedings of your tenants, for instance, give the lie to the theories of the philanthropists, and must be kept in the back-ground. It is true that the disaffection has not yet extended to one-half, or to one-fourth of the leased estates in the country, perhaps not to one-tenth, if you take the number of the landlords as the standard, instead of the extent of their possessions, but it certainly *will*, should the authorities tamper with the rebels much longer."

"If they tax the incomes of the landlords under the durable rent system, why would not the parties aggrieved have

16 *

the same right to take up arms to resist such an act of oppression as our fathers had, in 1776?"

"Their cause would be better; for that was only a constructive right, and one dependent on general principles, whereas this is an attempt at a most mean evasion of a written law, the meanness of the attempt being quite as culpable as its fraud. Every human being knows that such a tax, so far as it has any object beyond that of an election-sop, is to choke off the landlords from the maintenance of their covenants, which is a thing that no State *can* do directly, without running the risk of having its law pronounced unconstitutional by the courts of the United States, if, indeed, not by its own courts."

"The Court of Errors, think you?"

"The Court of Errors is doomed, by its own abuses. Catiline never abused the patience of Rome more than that mongrel assembly has abused the patience of every sound lawyer in the State. "Fiat justitia, ruat cœlum," is interpreted, now, into "Let justice be done, and the court fall." No one wishes to see it continued, and the approaching convention will send it to the Capulets, if it do nothing else to be commended. It was a pitiful imitation of the House of Lords system, with this striking difference: the English lords are men of education, and men with a vast deal at stake, and their knowledge and interests teach them to leave the settlement of appeals to the legal men of their body, of whom there are always a respectable number, in addition to those in possession of the woolsack and the bench; whereas our Senate is a court composed of small lawyers, country doctors, merchants, farmers, with occasionally a man of really liberal attainments. Under the direction of an acute and honest judge, as most of our true judges actually are, the Court of Errors would hardly form such a jury as would allow a creditable person to be tried by his peers, in a case affecting character, for instance, and here we have it set up as a court of the last resort, to settle points of law!"

"I see it has just made a decision in a libel suit, at which the profession sneers."

"It has, indeed. Now look at that very decision, for instance, as the measure of its knowledge. An editor of a newspaper holds up a literary man to the world as one anxious to obtain a small sum of money, in order to put it into Wall street, for 'shaving purposes.' Now, the only material question raised was the true signification of the word shaving.' If to say a man is a 'shaver,' in the sense in which it is applied to the use of money, be bringing him into discredit, then was the plaintiff's declaration sufficient; if not, it was insufficient, being wanting in what is called an 'innuendo.' The dictionaries, and men in general, understand by 'shaving,' 'extortion,' and nothing else. To call a man a 'shaver' is to say he is an 'extortioner,' without going into details. But, in Wall street, and among money-dealers, certain transactions that, in their eyes, and by the courts, are not deemed discreditable, have of late been brought within the category of 'shaving.' Thus it is technically, or by convention among brokers, termed "shaving" if a man buy a note at less than its face, which is a legal transaction. On the strength of this last circumstance, *as is set forth in the published opinions*, the highest Court of Appeals in New York has decided it does not bring a man into discredit to say he is a 'shaver!'—thus making a conventional signification of the brokers of Wall street higher authority for the use of the English tongue than the standard lexicographers, and all the rest of those who use the language! On the same principle, if a set of pick-pockets, at the Five Points, should choose to mystify their trade a little by including in the term ' to filch' the literal *borrowing* of a pocket-handkerchief, it would not be a libel to accuse a citizen of ' filching his neighbour's handkerchief!' "

" But the libel was uttered to the *world*, and not to the brokers of Wall street only, who might possibly understand their own terms."

" Very true; and was uttered in a newspaper that carried the falsehood to Europe; for the writer of the charge, when brought up for it, publicly admitted that he had no ground for suspecting the literary man of any such practices. *He* called it a '*joke*.' Every line of the context, however, showed it was a malicious charge. The decision is very much as if a man who is sued for accusing another of ' stealing' should set up a defence that he meant ' stealing' hearts, for the word is sometimes used in *that* sense. When

men use epithets that convey discredit in their general mean
ing, it is their business to give them a special signification
in their own contexts, if such be their real intention.   But
I much question if there be a respectable money-dealer, even
in Wall street, who would not swear, if called on in a court
of justice so to do, that *he* thought the general charge of
' shaving' discreditable to any man."   · ·

" And you think the landlords whose rents were taxed,
sir, would have a moral right to resist ?"

" Beyond all question ; as it would be an income tax on
them only, of all in the country.   What is more, I am fully
persuaded that two thousand men embodied to resist such
tyranny would look down the whole available authority of
the State ; inasmuch as I do not believe citizens could be
found to take up arms to enforce a law so flagrantly unjust.
Men will look on passively and see wrongs inflicted, that
would never come out to support them by their own acts.
But we are approaching the farm, and there is Tom Miller
and his hired men waiting our arrival."   ·

It is unnecessary to repeat, in detail, all that passed in
this our second visit to the farm-house.   Miller received us
in a friendly manner, and offered us *a* bed, if we would pass
the night with him.   This business of *a* bed had given us
more difficulty than anything else, in the course of our pe-
regrinations.   New York has long got over the " two-man"
and " three-man bed" system, as regards its best inns.   At
no respectable New York inn is a gentleman now asked to
share even his room, without an apology and a special necessity, with another, much less his bed ; but the rule does
not hold good as respects pedlars and music-grinders.   We
had ascertained that we were not only expected to share
the same bed, but to occupy that bed in a room filled with
other beds.   There are certain things that get to be second
nature, and that no masquerading will cause to go down ;
and, among others, one gets to dislike sharing his room and
his tooth-brush.   This little difficulty gave us more trouble
that night, at Tom Miller's, than anything we had yet encountered.   At the taverns, bribes had answered our purpose ; but this would not do so well at a farm residence.
At length the matter was got along with by putting me in
the garret, where I was favoured with a straw bed under

my own roof, the decent Mrs. Miller making many apologies for not having a feather-smotherer, in which to "squash"
me. I did not tell the good woman that I never used feathers, summer or winter ; for, had I done so, she would have
set me down as a poor creature from " oppressed" Germany,
where the " folks" did not know how to live. Nor would
she have been so much out of the way *quoad* the beds, for
in all my journeyings I never met with such uncomfortable
sleeping as one finds in Germany, off the Rhine and out of
the large towns.*

While the negotiation was in progress I observed that
Josh Brigham, as the anti-rent disposed hireling of Miller's
was called, kept a watchful eye and an open ear on what
was done and said. Of all men on earth, the American of
that class is the most " distrustful," as he calls it himself,
and has his suspicions the soonest awakened. The Indian
on the war-path — the sentinel who is posted in a fog, near
his enemy, an hour before the dawn of day — the husband
that is jealous, or the priest that has become a partisan, is
not a whit more apt to fancy, conjecture, or assert, than the
American of that class who has become " distrustful." This
fellow, Brigham, was the very beau ideal of the suspicious
school, being envious and malignant, as well as shrewd,
observant, and covetous. The very fact that he was connected with the " Injins," as turned out to be the case, added
to his natural propensities the consciousness of guilt, and
rendered him doubly dangerous. The whole time my uncle
and myself were crossing over and figuring in, in order to
procure for each a room, though it were only a closet, his
watchful, distrustful looks denoted how much he saw in our
movements to awaken curiosity, if not downright suspicion.
When all was over, he followed me to the little lawn in
front of the house, whither I had gone to look at the familiar scene by the light of the setting sun, and began to betray the nature of his own suspicions by his language.

" The old man" (meaning my uncle Ro) " must have
plenty of gold watches about him," he said, " to be so plaguy

---

* As the "honourable gentleman from Albany" does not seem to
understand the precise signification of " provincial," I can tell him that
one sign of such a character is to admire a bed at an American country inn.—EDITOR.

partic'lar consarnin' his bed. Pedlin' sich matters is a tick
lish trade, I guess, in some parts?" ·

"Ja; it ist dangerous somevhere, but it might not be so
in dis goot coontry."

"Why did the old fellow, then, try so hard to get that
little room all to himself, and shove you off into the garret?
We hired men don't like the garret, which is a hot place in
summer."

"In Charmany one man hast ever one bed," I answered,
anxious to get rid of the subject.

I bounced a little, as "one has one-half of a bed" would
be nearer to the truth, though the other half might be in
another room.

"Oh! that's it, is't? Wa-a-l, every country has its
ways, I s'pose. Jarmany is a desp'ate aristocratic land, I
take it."

"Ja; dere ist moch of de old feudal law, and feudal coos-
tum still remaining in Charmany."

"Landlords a plenty, I guess, if the truth was known.
Leases as long as my arm, I calkerlate?"

"Vell, dey do dink, in Charmany, dat de longer might
oe de lease, de better it might be for de denant."

As that was purely a German sentiment, or at least not
an American sentiment, according to the notions broached
by statesmen among ourselves, I made it as Dutch as possible by garnishing it well with d's.

"That's a droll idee! Now, we think, here, that a lease
is a bad thing; and the less you have of a bad thing, the
better."

"Vell, dat ist queer; so queer ast I don't know! Vhat
vill dey do as might help it?"

"Oh! the Legislature will set it all right. They mean
to pass a law to prevent any more leases at all."

"Und vill de beople stand dat? Dis ist a free coontry,
effery body dells me, and vilt der beoples agree not to hire
lands if dey vants to?"

"Oh! you see we wish to choke the landlords off from
their present leases; and, by and bye, when *that* is done,
the law can let up again."

"But ist dat right? Der law should be joost, und not
hold down und let oop, as you calls it."

" You don't understand us yet, I see. Why that's the prettiest and the neatest legislation on airth! That's just what the bankrupt law did."

" Vhat did der bankroopt law do, bray? Vhat might you mean now? — I don't know."

" Do! why it did wonders for some on us, I can tell you! It paid our debts, and let us up when we was down; and that's no trifle, I can tell you. I took 'the benefit,' as it is called, myself."

" You! — you might take der benefit of a bankroopt law! You, lifing here ast a hiret man, on dis farm!"

" Sartain; why not? All a man wanted, under *that* law, was about $60 to carry him through the mill; and if he could rake and scrape that much together, he might wipe off as long a score as he pleased. I had been dealin' in speckylation, and that's a make or break business, I can tell you. Well, I got to be about $423.22 wuss than nothin'; but, having about $90 in hand, I went through the mill without getting cogged the smallest morsel! A man doos a good business, to my notion, when he can make 20 cents pay a whull dollar of debt."

" Und you did dat goot business?"

" You may say that; and now I means to make antirentism get me a farm cheap—what *I* call cheap; and that an't none of your $30 or $40 an acre, I can tell you!"

It was quite clear that Mr. Joshua Brigham regarded these transactions as so many Pragmatic Sanctions, that were to clear the moral and legal atmospheres of any atoms of difficulty that might exist in the forms of old opinions, to his getting easily out of debt, in the one case, and suddenly rich in the other. I dare say I looked bewildered, but I certainly felt so, at thus finding myself face to face with a low knave, who had a deliberate intention, as I now found, to rob me of a farm. It is certain that Joshua so imagined, for, inviting me to walk down the road with him a short distance, he endeavoured to clear up any moral difficulties that might beset me, by pursuing the subject.

" You see," resumed Joshua, " I will tell you how it is. These Littlepages have had this land long enough, and it's time to give poor folks a chance. The young spark that pretends to own all the farms you see, far and near, never *did* any thing for 'em in his life; only to be his father's son.   Now, to my notion, a man should do suthin' for his land, and not be obligated for it to mere natur'.   This is a free country, and what right has one man to land more than another ?"

"Or. do his shirt or do his. dobacco, or do his coat, or do anyding else.".

"Well, I don't go as far as that.   A man has a right to his clothes, and maybe to a horse or a cow, but he has no right to all the land in creation.   The law gives a right to a cow as ag'in' execution."

"Und doesn't der law gif a right to der landt, too? You most not depend on der law, if you might succeed."

"We like to get as much law as we can on our side. Americans like law : now, you'll read in all the books—*our* books, I mean, them that's printed here—that the Americans be the most lawful people on airth, and that they'll do more for the law than any other folks known !"

"Vell, dat isn't vhat dey says of der Americans in Europe; nein, nein, dey might not say dat."

"Why, don't you think it is so?   Don't you think this the greatest country on airth, and the most lawful?"

"Vell, I don'ts know.   Das coontry ist das coontry, und it ist vhat it ist, you might see."

"Yes; I thought you would be of my way of thinking, when we got to understand each other."   Nothing is easier than to mislead an American on the estimate foreigners place on them : in this respect they are the most deluded people living, though, in other matters, certainly among the shrewdest.   "That's the way with acquaintances, at first ; they don't always understand one another : and then you talk a little thick, like.   But now, friend, I'll come to the p'int — but first swear you'll not betray me."

"Ja, jä — I oonderstandst; I most schwear I won't bedray you : das ist goot."

"But, hold up your hand.   Stop ; of what religion be you ?"

"Gristian, to be sure.   I might not be a Chew.   Nein, nein ; I am a ferry bat Gristian."

"We are all bad enough, for that matter ; but I lay no stress on *that*.   A little of the devil in a man helps him

along, in this business of ourn. But you must be suthin'
more than a Christian, I s'pose, as we don't call *that* bein'
of any religion at all, in this country. Of what *supportin'*
religion be you?"

"Soobortin'; vell, I might not oonderstands dat. Vhat
ist soobortin' religion? Coomes dat vrom Melanchton und
Luther?—or coomes it vrom der Pope? Vhat ist dat soobortin' religion?"-

"Why, what religion do you *patronize?* Do you patronize the standin' order, or the kneelin' order?—or do
you patronize neither? Some folks thinks its best to lie
down at prayer, as the least likely to divart the thoughts."

"I might not oonderstand. But nefer mindt der religion,
und coome to der p'int dat you mentioned."

"Well, that p'int is this. You're a Jarman, and can't
like aristocrats, and so I'll trust you; though, if you dc
betray me, you'll never play on another bit of music in this
country, or any other! If you want to be an Injin, as good
an opportunity will offer to-morrow as ever fell in a man's
way!"

"An Injin! Vhat goot vill it do to be an Injin? I
dought it might be better to be a vhite man, in America?"

"Oh! I mean only an anti-rent Injin. We've got matters so nicely fixed now, that a chap can be an Injin without any paint at all, or any washin' or scrubbin', but can
convart himself into himself ag'in, at any time, in two minutes. The wages is good and the work light; then we
have rare chances in the stores, and round about among the
farms. The law is that an Injin must have what he wants,
and no grumblin', and we take care to want enough. If
you'll be at the meetin', I'll tell you how you'll know me."

"Ja, ja—dat ist goot; I vill be at der meetin', sartainly.
Vhere might it be?"

"Down at the village. The word came up this a'ter-
noon, and we shall all be on the ground by ten o'clock."

"Vilt der be a fight, dat you meet so bunctually, and wid
so moch spirit?"

"Fight! Lord, no; who is there to fight, I should like to
know? We are pretty much all ag'in the Littlepages, and
there's none of them on the ground but two or three women. I'll tell vou how it's all settled. The meetin' is

17

called on the deliberative and liberty-supportin' plan. I s'pose you know we 've all sorts of meetin's in this coun- try ?"

" Nein ; I dought dere might be meetin's for bolitics, vhen der beople might coome, but I don't know vhat else."

" Is 't possible ! What, have you no ' indignation meetin's' in Jarmany ? We count a great deal on our indignation meetin's, and both sides have 'em in abundance, when things get to be warm. Our meetin' to-morrow is for deliberation and liberty-principles generally. We may pass some indig- nation resolutions about aristocrats, for nobody can bear them critturs in this part of the country, I can tell you."

Lest this manuscript should get into the hands of some of those who do not understand the real condition of New York society, it may be well to explain that " aristocrat" means, in the parlance of the country, no other than a man of gentleman-like tastes, habits, opinions and associations. There are gradations among the aristocracy of the State, as well as among other men. Thus he who is an aristocrat in a hamlet, would be very democratic in a village; and he of the village might be no aristocrat in the town, at all ; though, in the towns generally, indeed always, when their population has the least of a town character, the distinction ceases altogether, men quietly dropping into the traces of civilized society, and talking or thinking very little about it. To see the crying evils of American aristocracy, then, one must go into the country. There, indeed, a plenty of cases exist. Thus, if there happen to be a man whose pro- perty is assessed at twenty-five per cent. above that of all his neighbours — who must have right on his side bright as a cloudless sun to get a verdict, if obliged to appeal to the laws — who pays fifty per cent. more for everything he buys, and receives fifty per cent. less for everything he sells, than any other person near him — who is surrounded by rancorous enemies, in the midst of a seeming state of peace — who has everything he says and does perverted, and added to, and lied about — who is traduced because his dinner-hour is later than that of " other folks" — who don't stoop, but is straight in the back — who presumes to doubt that this country in general, and his own township in par- ticular, is the focus of civilization — who hesitates about

signing his name to any flagrant instance of ignorance, bad
taste, or worse morals, that his neighbours may get up in
the shape of a petition, remonstrance, or resolution—depend
on it that man is a prodigious aristocrat, and one who, for
his many offences and manner of lording it over mankind,
deserves to be banished. I ask the reader's pardon for so
abruptly breaking in upon Joshua's speech, but such very
different notions exist about aristocrats, in different parts of
the world, that some such explanation was necessary in
order to prevent mistakes. I have forgotten one mark of
the tribe that is, perhaps, more-material than all the rest,
which must not be omitted, and is this : — If he happen to
be a man who prefers his own pursuits to public life, and is
regardless of "popularity," he is just guilty of the unpar-
donable sin. The "people" will forgive anything sooner
than this; though there are "folks" who fancy it as infallible a sign of an aristocrat not to chew tobacco. But, unless I return to Joshua, the reader will complain that I cause
him to stand still.

"No, no," continued Mr. Brigham; "anything but an
aristocrat for me. I hate the very name of the sarpents,
and wish there warn't one in the land. To-morrow we are
to have a great anti-rent lecturer out——"

"A vhat?"

"A lecturer; one that lectur's, you understand, on anti-
rentism, temperance, aristocracy, government, or any other
grievance that may happen to be uppermost. Have you
no lecturers in Jarmany?"

"Ja, Ja; dere ist lecturers in das universities — blenty
of dem."

"Well, we have 'em universal and partic'lar, as we happen to want 'em. To-morrow we're to have one, they tell
me, the smartest man that has appeared in the cause. He
goes it strong, and the Injins mean to back him up, with all
sorts of shrieks and whoopin's. Your hurdy-gurdy, there,
makes no sort of music to what our tribe can make when
we fairly open our throats."

"Vell, dis ist queer! I vast told dat der Americans vast
all philosophers, und dat all dey didt vast didt in a t'ought-
ful and sober manner; und now you dells mo dey screams
deir arguments like Injins!"

"That we do! I wish you'd been here in the hard-cider and log-cabin times, and you'd a seen reason and philoso- phy, as you call it! I was a whig that summer, though I went democrat last season. There's about five hundred on us in this county that make the most of things, I can tell you. What's the use of a vote, if a body gets nothin' by it? But to-morrow you'll see the business done up, and matters detarmined for this part of the world, in fine style. We know what we're about, and we mean to carry things through quite to the eend."

"Und vhat do you means to do?"

"Well, seein' that you seem to be of the right sort, and be so likely to put on the Injin shirt, I'll tell you all about it. We mean to get good and old farms at favourable rates. That's what we mean to do. The people's up and in 'ar- nest, and what the people want they'll have! This time they want farms, and farms they must have. What's the use of havin' a government of the people, if the people's obliged to want farms? We've begun ag'in' the Renssa- laers, and the durables, and the quarter-sales, and the chick- ens; but we don't, by no manner of means, think of eending there. What should we get by that? A man wants to get suthin' when he puts his foot into a matter of this 'natur'. We know who's our fri'nds and who's our inimies! Could we have some men I could name for governors, all would go clear enough the first winter. We would tax the land- lords out, and law 'em about in one way and another, so as to make 'em right down glad to sell the last rod of their lands, and that cheap, too!"

"Und who might own dese farms, all oop und down der coontry, dat I sees?"

"As the law now stands, Littlepage owns 'em; but if we alter the law enough, he wun't. If we can only work the Legislature up to the stickin' p'int, we shall get all we want. Would you believe it, the man wun't sell a single farm, they say; but wishes to keep every one on 'em for himself! Is that to be borne in a free country? They'd hardly stand that in Jarmany, I'm thinkin'. A man that is such an aris- tocrat as to refuse to sell anything, I despise."

"Vell, dey stand to der laws in Charmany, und broperty

\s respected in most coontries. You vouldn't do away wiα
der rights of broperty, if you mights, I hopes ?"

  " Not I. If a man owns a watch, or a horse, or a cow,
I'm for having the law such that a poor man can keep 'em,
even ag'in execution. We're getting the laws pretty straight
on them p'ints, in old York, I can tell you ; a poor man, let
him be ever so much in debt, can hold on to a mighty smart lot
of things, now-a-days, and laugh at the law right in its. face !
I've known chaps that owed as much as $200, hold on to
as good as $300 ; though most of their debts was for the
very. things they held on to !"·

  .What a picture is this, yet is it not true ? A state of society in which a man can contract a debt for a cow, or his
household goods, and laugh at his creditor when he . seeks
his pay, on the one hand ; and on the other, legislators and
executives lending themselves to the chicanery of another
set, that are striving to deprive a particular class of its rights
of property, directly in the face of written contracts ! This
is straining at the gnat and swallowing the camel, with a
vengeance ; and all for votes ! Does any one really expect
a community can long exist, favoured by a wise and justice-
dispensing Providence, in which such things are coolly attempted — ay, and coolly done ? It is time that the American began to see things as they are, and not as they are
said to be, in the speeches of governors, fourth of July ora-
tions, and electioneering addresses. I write warmly, I know,
but I feel warmly ; and I write like a man who sees that a
most flagitious attempt to rob him is tampered with by some
in power, instead of being met; as the boasted morals and
intelligence of the country would require, by the stern opposition of all in authority. Curses — deep, deep curses —
ere long, will fall on all who shrink from their duty in such
a crisis. Even the very men who succeed, if succeed they
should, will, in the end, curse the instruments of their own
success.*

---

* That Mr. Hugh Littlepage does not feel or express himself too
strongly on the state of things that has now existed among us for long,
long years, the following case, but one that illustrates the melancholy
truth among many, will show.   At a time when the tenants of an extensive landlord, to whom tens of thousands were owing for rent, were
openly resisting the law, and defeating every attempt to distrain, though
  .17 *

" A first-rate lecturer on feudal tenors," (Joshua was not in the least particular in his language, but, in the substance, he knew what he was talking about as well as some who are in high places,) " chickens and days' works. We ex- pect a great deal from this man, who is paid well for coming.";

" Und who might bay him ? — der State ?

" No — we haven't got to that *yet;* though some think the State will *have* to do it, in the long run. At present the tenants are taxed so much on the dollar, accordin' to rent, or so much an acre, and that way the needful money is raised. But one of our lecturers told us, a time back, that it was money put out at use, and every man ought to keep an account of what he give, for the time was not far off when he would get it back, with double interest. ' It is paid now for a reform,' he said, ' and when the reform is obtained, no doubt the State would feel itself so much indebted to us all, that it would tax the late landlords until we got all our money back again, and more too.";

" Dat vould pe a bretty speculation ; ja, dat might be most bootiful !"

" Why, yes ; it wouldn't be a bad operation, living on the inimy, as a body might say. But you'll not catch our folks livin' on themselves, I can tell you. That they might do without societies. No, we 've an object ; and when folks has an object, they commonly look sharp a'ter it. We don't let on all we want and mean openly : and you'll find folks among us that 'll deny stoutly that anti-renters has anything to do with the Injin system ; but folks an't obliged to believe the moon is *all* cheese, unless they've a mind to. Some among us maintain that no man ought to hold more than a thousand acres of land, while others think natur' has laid down the law on that p'int, and that a man shouldn't hold more than he has need on."

---

two ordinary companies of even armed constables would have put them down, the sheriff entered the house of that very landlord, and levied on his furniture for debt. Had that gentleman, on the just and pervading principle that he owed no allegiance to an authority that did not pro- tect him, resisted the sheriff's officer, *he* would have gone to the State's prison; and there he might have staid until his last hour of service was expended.— EDITOR.

" Und vich side dost you favour ? — vich of dese obinions. might not be yours ?"

" I 'm not partic'lar, so I get a good farm. I should like one with comfortable buildin's on 't, and one that hasn't been worked to death. For them two principles I think I 'd stand out ; but, whether there be four hundred acres, or four hundred and fifty, or even five hundred, I 'm no way onaccomadatin'. I expect there 'll be trouble in the eend, when we come to the division, but I 'm not the man to make it. I s'pose I shall get my turn at the town offices, and other chances, and, givin' me my rights in them, I 'll take up with almost any farm young Littlepage has, though I should rather have one in the main valley here, than one more out of the way; still, I don't set myself down as at all partic'lar."

" Und vhat do you expect to bay Mr. Littlepage for der farm, ast you might choose ?"

" That depends on sarcumstances. The Injins mainly expect to come in cheap. Some folks think it 's best to pay suthin', as it might stand ag'in' law better, should it come to that ; while other some see no great use in paying anything. Them that 's willing to pay, mainly hold out for paying the principal of the first rents."

" I doesn't oonderstandt vhat you means py der brincipal of der first rents."

" It 's plain enough, when you get the lay on 't. You see, these lands were let pretty low, when they were first taken up from the forest, in order to get folks to live here. That 's the way we 're obliged to do in America, or people won't come. Many tenants paid no rent at all for six, eight, or ten years ; and a'ter that, until their three lives run out, as it is called, they paid only sixpence an acre, or six dollars and a quarter on the hundred acres. That was done, you see, to buy men to come here at all ; and you can see by the price that was paid, how hard a time they must have had on 't. Now, some of our folks hold that the whull time ought to be counted — that which was rent free, and that which was not — in a way that I 'll explain to you ; for I 'd have you to know I haven't entered into this business without looking to the right and the wrong on 't."

" Exblain, exblain ; I might hear you exblain, and you
most exblain."

" Why, you 're in a hurry, friend Griezenbach, or whatever your name be. But I 'll explain, if you wish it. S'pose,
now, a lease run 'thirty years — ten on nothin', and twenty
on sixpences. Well, a hundred sixpences make fifty shillings, and twenty times fifty make a thousand, as all the
rent paid in thirty years. If you divide a thousand by thirty,
it leaves thirty-three shillings and a fraction"—Joshua calculated like an American of his class, accurately and with
rapidity—" for the average rent of the thirty years. Calling thirty-three shillings four dollars, and it 's plaguy little
more, we have that for the interest, which, at 7 per cent.,
will make a principal of rather more than fifty dollars,
though not as much as sixty. As sich matters ought to be
done on liberal principles, they say that Littlepage ought to
take fifty dollars, and give a deed for the hundred acres."

" Und vhat might be der rent of a hoondred acres now ?—
he might get more dan sixpence to-day ?"

" That he does. Most all of the farms are running out
on second, and some on third leases. Four shillings an
acre is about the average of the rents, accordin' to circumstances."

" Den you dinks der landtlort ought to accept one year's
rent for der farms ?"

" I don't look on it in that light. He ought to take fifty
dollars for a hundred acres. You forget the tenants have
paid for their farms, over and over again, in rent. They
feel as if they have paid enough, and that it was time to
stop."

Extraordinary as this reasoning may seem in most men's
minds, I have since found it is a very favourite sentiment
among anti-renters. " Are we to go on, and pay rent for
ever ?" they ask, with logical and virtuous indignation !

" Und vhat may be der aferage value of a hoondred acre
farm, in dis part of de coontry ?" I inquired.

" From two thousand five hundred to three thousand dollars. It would be more, but tenants won't put good buildings on farms, you know, seein' that they don't own them.
I heard one of our leaders lamentin' that he didn't foresee

what times was comin' to, when he repaired his old house,
or he would have built a new one. But a man can't fore-
tell everything. I dare say many has the same feelin's,
now."

"Den you dinks Herr Littlebage ought to accept $50 for
vhat is worth $2500 ? Das seem ferry little."

"You forget the back rent that has been paid, and the
work the tenant has done. What would the farm be good
for without the work that has been done on it ?"

"Ja, ja — I oonderstandst ; und vhat vould der work be
goot for vidout der landt on vhich it vast done ?"

This was rather an incautious question to put to a man
as distrustful and rogueish as Joshua Brigham. The fellow
cast a lowering and distrustful look at me ; but ere there was
time to answer, Miller, of whom he stood in healthful awe,
called him away to look after the cows.

Here, then, I had enjoyed an opportunity of hearing the
opinions of one of my own hirelings on the interesting subject of my right to my own estate. I have since ascertained
that, while these sentiments are sedulously kept out of view
in the proceedings of the government, which deals with the
whole matter as if the tenants were nothing but martyrs to
hard bargains, and the landlords their task-masters, of
greater or less lenity, they are extensively circulated in the
" infected districts," and are held to be very sound doctrines
by a large number of the " bone and sinew of the land."
Of course the reasoning is varied a little, to suit circumstances, and to make it meet the facts. But of this school
is a great deal, and a very great deal, of the reasoning that
circulates on the leased property ; and, from what I have
seen and heard already, I make no doubt that there are
quasi legislators among us who, instead of holding the
manly and only safe doctrine which ought to be held on
such a subject, and saying that these deluded men should be
taught better, are ready to cite the very fact that such notions do exist as a reason for the necessity of making concessions, in order to keep the peace at the cheapest rate.
That profound principle of legislation, which concedes the
right in order to maintain quiet, is admirably adapted to
forming sinners ; and, if carried out in favour of all who

may happen to covet their neighbour's goods, would, in a short time, render this community the very paradise of knaves.

As for Joshua Brigham, I saw no more of him that night; for he quitted the farm on leave, just as it got to be dark. Where he went I do not know; but the errand on which he left us could no longer be a secret to me. As the family retired early, and we ourselves were a good deal fatigued, everybody was in bed by nine o'clock, and, judging from myself, soon asleep. Previously to saying "good night," however, Miller told us of the meeting of the next day, and of his intention to attend it.

CHAPTER XIII.

"He knows the game; how true he keeps the wind!"
"Silence."

King Henry VI.

AFTER an early breakfast, next morning, the signs of preparation for a start became very apparent in the family. Not only Miller, but his wife and daughter, intended to go down to " Little Neest," as the hamlet was almost invariably called in that fragment of the universe, in contradistinction to the " Neest" proper. I found afterwards that this very circumstance was cited against me in the controversy, it being thought *lèse majesté* for a private residence to monopolize the major of the proposition, while a hamlet had to put up with the minor; the latter, moreover, including two taverns, which are exclusively the property of the public, there being exclusiveness with the public as well as with aristocrats — more especially in all things that pertain to power or profit. As to the two last, even Joshua Brigham was much more of an aristocrat than I was myself. It must be admitted that the Americans are a humane population, for they are the only people who deem that bankruptcy gives a claim to public favour.*

As respects the two " Nests," had not so much more serious matter been in agitation, the precedence of the names might actually have been taken up as a question of moment. I have heard of a lawsuit in France, touching a name that has been illustrious in that country for a period so long as to extend beyond the reach of man — as, indeed, was apparent by the matter in controversy — and which name has obtained for itself a high place in the annals of even our own republic. I allude to the House of Grasse, which was seated, prior to the revolution, and may be still, at a place called Grasse, in the southern part of the kingdom, the town being almost as famous for the manufacture of pleasant things as the family for its exploits in arms. About a century since, the Marquis de Grasse is said to have had a *procés* with his neighbours of the place, to establish the fact whether the family gave its name to the town, or the town gave its name to the family. The Marquis prevailed in the struggle, but greatly impaired his fortune in achieving that new victory. As my house, or its predecessor, was certainly erected and named while the site of Little Nest was still in the virgin forest, one would think its claims to the priority of possession beyond dispute; but such might not prove to be the case on a trial. There are two histories among us, as relates to both public and private things; the one being as nearly true as is usual, while the other is invariably the fruits of the human imagination. Everything depending so much on majorities, that soon gets to be the most authentic tradition which has the most believers; for, under the system of numbers, little regard is paid to superior advantages, knowledge, or investigation, all depending on 3 as against 2, which makes 1 majority. I find a great deal of this spurious history is getting to be mixed up with the anti-rent controversy, facts coming out daily that long have lain dormant in the graves of the past. These facts affect the whole structure of the historical picture of the

---

* Absurd as this may seem, it is nevertheless true, and for a reason that is creditable, rather than the reverse — a wish to help along the unfortunate. It is a great mistake, however, as a rule, to admit of any other motive for selecting for public trusts, than qualification.—EDITOR.

State and colony, leaving touches of black where the pencil had originally put in white, and placing the high lights where the shadows have before always been understood to be. In a word, men are telling the stories as best agrees with their present views, and not at all as they agree with fact.

It was the intention of Tom Miller to give my uncle Ro and me a dearborn to ourselves, while he drove his wife, Kitty and a *help*, as far as the " Little Neest," in a two-horse vehicle that was better adapted to such a freight. Thus disposed of, then, we all left the place in company, just as the clock in the farm-house entry struck nine. I drove our horse myself; and *mine* he was, in fact, every hoof, vehicle and farming utensil on the Nest farm, being as much my property, under the *old* laws, as the hat on my head. It is true, the Millers had now been fifty years or more, nay, nearly sixty, in possession, and by the *new* mode of construction it is possible some may fancy that we had paid them wages so long for working the land, and for using the cattle and utensils, that the title, in a moral sense, had passed out of me, in order to pass into Tom Miller. If use begets a right, why not to a wagon and horse, as well as to a farm.

As we left the place I gazed wistfully towards the Nest House, in the hope of seeing the form of some one that I loved, at a window, on the lawn, or in the piazza. Not a soul appeared, however, and we trotted down the road a short distance in the rear of the other wagon, conversing on such things as came uppermost in our minds. The distance we had to go was about four miles, and the hour named for the commencement of the lecture, which was to be the great affair of the day, had been named at eleven. This caused us to be in no hurry, and I rather preferred to coincide with the animal I drove, and move very slowly, than hurry on, and arrive an hour or two sooner than was required. In consequence of this feeling on our part, Miller and his family were soon out of sight, it being their wish to obtain as much of the marvels of the day as was possible.

The road, of course, was perfectly well known to my uncle and myself; but, had it not been, there was no danger of missing our way, as we had only to follow the general direction of the broad valley through which it ran. Then Miller had considerately told us that we must pass two churches, or a church and a " meetin'-'us'," the spires of both of which were visible most of the way, answering for beacons. Referring to this term of " meeting-house," does it not furnish conclusive evidence, of itself, of the inconsistent folly of that wisest of all earthly beings, man? It was adopted in contradistinction from, and in direct opposition to, the supposed idolatrous association connected with the use of the word " church," at a time when certain sects would feel offended at hearing their places of worship thus styled; whereas, at the present day, those very sectarians are a little disposed to resent this exclusive appropriation of the proscribed word by the sects who have always adhered to it as offensively presuming, and, in a slight degree, " arisdogradic!" I am a little afraid that your out-and-outers in politics, religion, love of liberty, and other human excellences, are somewhat apt to make these circuits in their eccentric orbits, and to come out somewhere quite near the places from which they started.

· The road between the Nest House and Little Nest, the hamlet, is rural, and quite as agreeable as is usually found in a part of the country that is without water-views or mountain scenery. Our New York landscapes are rarely, nay, never grand, as compared with the noble views one finds in Italy, Switzerland, Spain, and the finer parts of Europe; but we have a vast many that want nothing but a finish to their artificial accessories to render them singularly agreeable. Such is the case with the principal vale of Ravensnest, which, at the very moment we were driving through it, struck my uncle and myself as presenting a picture of rural abundance, mingled with rural comfort, that one seldom sees in the old world, where the absence of enclosures, and the concentration of the dwellings in villages, leave the fields naked and with a desolate appearance, in spite of their high tillage and crops.

" This is an estate worth contending for, now," said my uncle, as we trotted slowly on, " although it has not hitherto been very productive to its owner. The first half century of an American property of this sort rarely brings much to its proprietor beyond trouble and vexation."

18

"·And after that time the tenant is to have it, pretty much at his own price, as a reward for his own labour!"

" What evidences are to be found, wherever the eye rests of the selfishness of man, and his unfitness to be left to the unlimited control of his own affairs! In England they are quarrelling with the landlords, who *do* compose a real aristocracy, and make the laws, about the manner in which they protect themselves and the products of their estates; while here the true owner of the soil is struggling against the power of numbers, with the people, who are the only aristocrats we possess, in order to maintain his right of property in the simplest and most naked form! A common vice is at the bottom of both wrongs, and that is the vice of selfishness."

" But how are abuses like those of which we complain here — abuses of the most formidable character of any that can exist, since the oppressors are so many, and so totally irresponsible by their numbers — to be avoided, if you give the people the right of self-government?"

" God help the nation where self-government, in its literal sense, exists, Hugh! The term is conventional, and, properly viewed, means a government' in which the source of authority is the body of the nation, and does not come from any other sovereign. When a people that has been properly educated by experience, calmly selects its agents, and coolly sets to work to adopt a set of principles to form its fundamental law or constitution, the machine is on the right track, and will work well enough so long as it is kept there; but this running off, and altering the fundamental principles every time a political faction has need of recruits, is introducing tyranny in its worst form — a tyranny that is just as dangerous to real liberty as hypocrisy is to religion!"

We were now approaching St. Andrew's church and the rectory, with its glebe, the latter lying contiguous to the church-yard, or, as it is an Americanism to say, the " graveyard." There had been an evident improvement around the rectory since I had last seen it. Shrubbery had been planted, care was taken of the fences, the garden was neatly and well worked, the fields looked smooth, and everything denoted that it was " new lords and new laws." The last incumbent had been a whining, complaining, narrow-minded, selfish and lazy priest, the least estimable of all human characters, short of the commission of the actual and higher crimes; but his successor had the reputation of being a devout and real Christian—one who took delight in the duties of his holy office, and who served God because he loved him. I am fully aware how laborious is the life of a country priest, and how contracted and mean is the pittance he in common receives, and how much more he merits than he gets, if his reward were to be graduated by things here. But this picture, like every other, has its different sides, and occasionally men do certainly enter the church from motives as little as possible connected with those that ought to influence them.

"There is the wagon of Mr. Warren, at his door," observed my uncle, as we passed the rectory. "Can it be that he intends visiting the village also, on an occasion like this?"

"Nothing more probable, sir, if the character Patt has given of him be true," I answered. "She tells me he has been active in endeavouring to put down the covetous spirit that is getting uppermost in the town, and has even preached boldly, though generally, against the principles involved in the question. The other man, they say, goes for popularity, and preaches and prays with the anti-renters."

No more was said, but on we went, soon entering a large bit of wood, a part of the virgin forest. This wood, exceeding a thousand acres in extent, stretched down from the hills along some broken and otherwise little valuable land, and had been reserved from the axe to meet the wants of some future day. It was mine, therefore, in the fullest sense of the word; and, singular as it may seem, one of the grounds of accusation brought against me and my predecessors was that we had *declined leasing it!* Thus, on the one hand, we were abused for having leased our land, and, on the other, for not having leased it. The fact is, we, in common with other extensive landlords, are expected to use our property as much as possible for the particular benefit of other people, while those other people are expected to use *their* property as much as possible for their own particular benefit.

There was near a mile of forest to pass before we came
out again in the open country, at about a mile and a half's
distance from the hamlet.   On our left this little forest did
not extend more than a hundred rods, terminating at the
edge of the rivulet — or *creek*, as the stream is erroneously
called, and for no visible reason but the fact that it was only
a hundred feet wide — which swept close under the broken
ground mentioned at this point.   On our right, however, the
forest stretched away for more than a mile, until, indeed, it
became lost and confounded with other portions of wood that
had been reserved for the farms on which they grew.   As
is very usual in America, in cases where roads pass through
a forest, a second growth had shot up on each side of this
highway, which was fringed for the whole distance with
large bushes of pine, hemlock, chestnut and maple.   In some
places these bushes almost touched the track, while in others
a large space was given.   We were winding our way through
this wood, and had nearly reached its centre, at a point
where no house was visible — and no house, indeed, stood
within half a mile of us — with the view in front and in
rear limited to some six or eight rods in each direction by
the young trees, when our ears were startled by a low,
shrill, banditti-like whistle.   I must confess that my feelings
were anything but comfortable at that interruption, for I remembered the conversation of the previous night.   I thought
by the sudden jump of my uncle, and the manner he instinctively felt where he ought to have had a pistol, to meet
such a crisis, that he believed himself already in the hands
of the Philistines.

. A half minute sufficed to tell us the truth.   I had hardly
stopped the horse, in order to look around me, when a line
of men, all armed and disguised, issued in single file from
the bushes, and drew up in the road, at right angles to its
course.   There were six of these "Injins," as they are
called, and, indeed, call themselves, each carrying a rifle,
horn and pouch, and otherwise equipped for the field.   The
disguises were very simple, consisting of a sort of loose
calico hunting-shirt and trowsers that completely concealed
the person.   The head was covered by a species of hood,
or mask, equally of calico, that was fitted with holes for the
eyes, nose and mouth, and which completed the disguise

There were no means of recognizing a man thus equipped, unless it might be by the stature, in cases in which the party was either unusually tall or unusually short. A middle-sized man was perfectly safe from recognition, so long as he did not speak and could keep his equipments. Those who did speak altered their voices, as we soon found, using a jargon that was intended to imitate the imperfect English of the native owners of the soil. Although neither of us had ever seen one of the gang before, we knew these disturbers of the public peace to be what in truth they were, the instant our eyes fell on them. One could not well be mistaken, indeed, under the circumstances in which we were placed; but the tomahawks that one or two carried, the manner of their march, and other pieces of mummery that they exhibited, would have told us the fact, had we met them even in another place.

My first impulse was to turn the wagon, and to endeavour to lash the lazy beast I drove into a run. Fortunately, before the attempt was made, I turned my head to see if there was room for such an exploit, and saw six others of these "Injins" drawn across the road behind us. It was now so obviously the wisest course to put the best face on the matter, that we walked the horse boldly up to the party in front, until he was stopped by one of the gang taking him by the bridle.

"Sago, sago," cried one who seemed to act as a chief, and whom I shall thus designate, speaking in his natural voice, though affecting an Indian pronunciation. "How do, how do?—where come from, eh?—where go, eh?—What you say, too—up rent or down rent, eh?"

"Ve ist two Charmans," returned uncle Ro, in his most desperate dialect, the absurdity of men who spoke the same language resorting to such similar means of deception tempting me sorely to laugh in the fellows' faces; "Ve ist two Charmans dat ist goin' to hear a man's sbeak about bayin' rent, und to sell vatches. Might you buy a vatch, goot shentlemans."

Although the fellows doubtless knew who we were, so far as our assumed characters went, and had probably been advised of our approach, this bait took, and there was a general jumping up and down, and a common pow-wowing

18 *

among them, indicative of the pleasure such a proposal gave. In a minute the whole party were around us, with some eight or ten more who appeared from the nearest bushes. We were helped out of the wagon with a gentle violence that denoted their impatience. As a matter of course, I expected that all the trinkets and watches, which were of little value, fortunately, would immediately disappear; for who could doubt that men engaged in attempting to rob on so large a scale as these fellows were engaged in, would hesitate about doing a job on one a little more diminutive. I was mistaken, however; some sort of imperceptible discipline keeping those who were thus disposed, of whom there must have been some in such a party, in temporary order. The horse was left standing in the middle of the highway, right glad to take his rest, while we were shown the trunk of a fallen tree, near by, on which to place our box of wares. A dozen watches were presently in the hands of as many of these seeming savages, who manifested a good deal of admiration at their shining appearance. While this scene, which was half mummery and half nature, was in the course of enactment, the chief beckoned me to a seat on the further end of the tree, and, attended by one or two of his companions, he began to question me as follows: —

"Mind tell truth," he said, making no very expert actor in the way of imitation. "Dis ' Streak o' Lightning,'" laying his hand on his own breast, that I might not misconceive the person of the warrior who bore so eminent a title; "no good lie to him —know ebbery t'ing afore he ask, only ask for fun —what do here, eh?"

"Ve coomes to see der Injins und der beoples at der village, dat ve might sell our vatches."

"Dat all; sartain? — can call ' down rent,' eh?"

"Dat ist ferry easy; ' down rent, eh?'"

"Sartain Jarman, eh?—you no spy?—you no sent here by gubbernor, eh?—landlord no pay you, eh?"

"Vhat might I spy? Dere ist nothin' do spy, but mans vid calico faces. Vhy been you afraid of der governor?— I dinks der governors be ferry goot frients of der anti-rents."

"Not when we act this way. Send horse, send foot a'ter us, den. T'ink good friend, too, when he dare "

." He be d——d !" bawled out one of the tribe, in as good
homely, rustic English as ever came out of the mouth of a
clown. "If he's our friend, why did he send the artillery
and horse down to Hudson? — and why has he had Big
Thunder up afore his infarnal courts?   He be d——d !"

There was no mistaking this outpouring of the feelings ;.
and so "Streak o' Lightning" seemed to think too, for he
whispered one of the tribe, who took the plain-speaking Injin
by the arm and led him away, grumbling and growling, as
the thunder mutters in the horizon after the storm has
passed on. For myself, I made several profitable reflections concerning the inevitable fate of those who attempt
to "serve God and Mammon." This anti-rentism is a question in which, so far as a governor is concerned, there is
but one course to pursue, and that is to enforce the laws by
suppressing violence, and leaving the parties to the covenants of leases to settle their differences in the courts, like
the parties to any other contracts. It is a poor rule that
will not work both ways. Many a landlord has made a
hard bargain for himself; and I happen to know of one
case in particular, in which a family has long been, and is
still, kept out of the enjoyment of a very valuable estate, as
to any benefit of importance, purely by the circumstance
that a weak-minded possessor of the property fancied he
was securing souls for paradise by letting his farms on leases
for ninety-nine years, at nominal rents, with a covenant that
the tenant should go twice to a particular church!. Now,
nothing is plainer than that it is a greater hardship to the citizen who is the owner of many farms so situated, than to the
citizen who is the lessee of only one with a hard covenant;
and, on general principles, the landlord in question would
be most entitled to relief, since one man who suffers a good
deal is more an object of true commiseration than many who
suffer each a little. What would a governor be apt to say
if my landlord should go with his complaints to the foot of
the executive chair, and tell him that the very covenant
which had led his predecessor into the mistake of thus wasting his means was openly disregarded; that farms worth
many thousands of dollars had now been enjoyed by the
tenants for near a century for mere nominal rents, and that
the owner of the land in fee had occasion for his property,

&c. &c. - Would the governor recommend legislative action in that case? Would the *length* of *such* leases induce
him to recommend that no lease should exceed five years in
duration? Would the landlords who should get up a corps
of Injins to worry their tenants into an abandonment of their
farms be the objects of commiseration?—and wou'd the law
slumber for years over *their* rebellions and depredations,
until two or three murders aroused public indignation? Let
them answer that know. As a landlord, I should be sorry
to incur the ridicule that would attend even a public complaint of the hardships of such a case. A common sneer
would send me to the courts for my remedy, if I had one,
and the whole difference between the " if and ifs" of the two
cases would be that a landlord gives but one vote, while his
tenants may be legion.*

" He be d——d," muttered the plain-speaking Injin, as
long as I could hear him. As soon as released from his
presence, Streak of Lightning continued his examination,
though a little vexed at the undramatical character of the
interruption.

" Sartain no spy, eh?—sartain gubbernor no send him,
eh?—sartain come to sell watch, eh?"

" I coomes, as I tell ye, to see if vatches might be solt,
und not for der gobbernor; I neffer might see der mans."

As all this was true, my conscience felt pretty easy on
the score of whatever there might be equivocal about it.

" What folks think of Injin down below, eh?—what folks
say of anti-rent, eh?—hear him talk about much?"

" Vell, soome does dink anti-rent ist goot, und soome
does dink anti-rent ist bad. Dey dinks as dey wishes."

Here a low whistle came down the road, or rather down
the bushes, when every Injin started up; each man very
fairly gave back the watch he was examining, and in less
than half a minute we were alone on the log. This movement was so sudden that it left us in a little doubt as to the
proper mode of proceeding. My uncle, however, coolly set
about replacing his treasures in their box, while I went to

* This is no invented statement, but strictly one that is true, the
writer having himself a small interest in a property so situated; though
he has not yet bethought him of applying to the Legislature for relief.
—EDITOR.

the horse, which had shaken off his head-stall, and was quietly grazing along the road-side. A minute or two might
have been thus occupied, when the trotting of a horse and
the sound of wheels announced the near approach of one
of those vehicles which have got to be almost national; a
dearborn, or a one-horse wagon. As it came out from behind a screen of bushes formed by a curvature in the road,
I saw that it contained the Rev. Mr. Warren and his sweet
daughter.

The road being narrow, and our vehicle in its centre, it
was not possible for the new-comers to proceed until we got
out of the way, and the divine pulled up as soon as he
reached the spot where we stood.

"Good morning, *gentlemen*," said Mr. Warren, cordially,
and using a word that, in *his* mouth, I felt meant all it expressed. "Good morning, *gentlemen*. Are you playing
Handel to the wood-nymphs, or reciting eclogues?"

"Neider, neider, Herr Pastor; we meet wid coostomers
here, und dey has joost left us," answered uncle Ro, who
certainly enacted his part with perfect *aplomb*, and the most
admirable mimicry as to manner. "*Guten tag, guten tag*
Might der Herr Pastor been going to der village?"

"We are. I understand there is to be a meeting there
of the misguided men called anti-renters, and that several
of my parishioners are likely to be present. On such an
occasion I conceive it to be my duty to go among my own
particular people, and whisper a word of advice. Nothing
can be farther from my notions of propriety than for a clergyman to be mingling and mixing himself up with political
concerns in general, but this is a matter that touches morality, and the minister of God is neglectful of his duty who
keeps aloof when a word of admonition might aid in preventing some wavering brother from the commission of a
grievous sin. This last consideration has brought me out
to a scene I could otherwise most heartily avoid."

This might be well enough, I said to myself, but what
has your daughter to do in such a scene? Is the mind of
Mary Warren, then, after all, no better than vulgar minds
in general?—and can she find a pleasure in the excitement
of lectures of this cast, and in that of public meetings? No
surer test can be found of cultivation, than the manner in

which it almost intuitively shrinks from communion unnecessarily with tastes and principles below its own level;
yet here was the girl with whom I was already half in love—
and that was saying as little as could be said, too—actually
going down to the "Little Neest" to hear an itinerant lecturer on political economy utter his crudities, and to see
and be seen! I was grievously disappointed, and would at
the moment have cheerfully yielded the best farm on my
estate to have had the thing otherwise. My uncle must
have had some similar notion, by the remark he made.

"Und doost das *jung frau* go to see der Injins, too; to
bersuade 'em dey ist fery vicked?"

Mary's face had been a little pale for her, I thought, as
the wagon drew up; but it immediately became scarlet. She
even suffered her head to droop a little, and then I perceived
that she cast an anxious and tender glance at her father. I
cannot say whether this look were or were not intended for
a silent appeal, unconsciously made; but the father, without
even seeing it, acted as if he fancied it might be.

"No, no," he said, hurriedly; "this dear girl is doing
violence to all her feelings but one, in venturing to such a
place. Her filial piety has proved stronger than her fears
and her tastes, and when she found that go I would, no argument of mine could persuade her to remain at home. I
hope she will not repent it."

The colour did not quit Mary's face, but she looked grateful at finding her true motives appreciated; and she even
smiled, though she said nothing. My own feelings under-
went another sudden revulsion. There was no want of
those tastes and inclinations that can alone render a young
woman attractive to any man of sentiment, but there was
high moral feeling and natural affection enough to overcome
them in a case in which she thought duty demanded the
sacrifice! It was very little probable that anything would
or could occur that day to render the presence of Mary
Warren in the least necessary or useful; but it was very
pleasant to me and very lovely in her to think otherwise,
under the strong impulses of her filial attachment.

Another idea, however, and one far less pleasant, suggested itself to the minds of my uncle and myself, and almost at the same instant; it was this: the conversation was

carried on in a high key, or loud enough to be heard at
some little distance, the horse and part of the wagon inter-
posing between the speakers; and there was the physical
certainty that some of those whom we knew to be close at
hand, in the bushes, must hear all that was said, and might
take serious offence at it. Under this apprehension, therefore, my uncle directed me to remove our own vehicle as
fast as possible, in order that the clergyman might 'pass.
Mr. Warren, however, was in no hurry to do this, for he
was utterly ignorant of the audience he had, and entertained
that feeling towards us that men of liberal acquirements are
apt to feel when they see others of similar educations reduced by fortune below their proper level. He was consequently desirous of manifesting his sympathy with us, and
would not proceed, even after I had opened the way for
him.

"It is a painful thing," continued Mr. Warren, "to find
men mistaking their own cupidity for the workings of a
love of liberty. To me nothing is more palpable than that
this anti-rent movement is covetousness incited by the father
of evil; yet you will find men among us who fancy they
are aiding the cause of free institutions by joining in it,
when, in truth, they are doing all they can to bring them
into discredit, and to insure their certain downfall, in the
end."

This was sufficiently awkward; for, by going near enough
to give a warning in a low voice, and have that warning
followed by a change in the discourse, we should be betraying ourselves, and might fall into serious danger. At the
very moment the clergyman was thus speaking I saw the
masked head of Streak o' Lightning appearing through an
opening in some small pines that grew a little in the rear of
the wagon, a position that enabled him to hear every syllable that was uttered. I was afraid to act myself, and trusted
to the greater experience of my uncle. Whether the last
also saw the pretended chief was more than I knew, but he
decided to let the conversation go on, rather leaning to the
anti-rent side of the question, as the course that could do no
serious evil, while it might secure our own safety. It is
scarcely necessary to say all these considerations glanced

through our minds so swiftly as to cause no very awkward or suspicious pause in the discourse.

"B'rhaps dey doosn't like to bay rent?" put in my uncle, with a roughness of manner that was in accordance with the roughness of the sentiment. "Beoples might radder haf deir landts for nuttin', dan bay rents for dem."

"In that case, then, let them go and buy lands for them-selves; if they do not wish to pay rent; why did they agree to pay rent?"

"May be dey changes deir minds. Vhat is goot to-day doosn't always seem goot to-morrow."

"That may be true; but we have no right to make others suffer for our own fickleness. I dare say, now, that it might be better for the whole community that so large a tract of land as that included in the Manor of Rensselaerwyck, for instance, and lying as it does in the very heart of the State, should be altogether in the hands of the occupants, than have it subject to the divided interest that actually exists; but it does not follow that a change is to be made by violence, or by fraudulent means. In either of the latter cases the injury done the community would be greater than if the present tenures were to exist a thousand years. I dare say much the larger portion of those farms can be bought off at a moderate advance on their actual money-value; and that is the way to get rid of the difficulty; not by bullying owners out of their property. If the State finds a political conside-ration of so much importance for getting rid of the tenures, let the State tax itself to do so, and make a liberal offer, in addition to what the tenants will offer, and I'll answer for it the landlords will not stand so much in their own way as to decline good prices."

"But, maybes dey won't sell all der landts; dey may wants to keep some of dem."

"They have a right to say yes or no, while we have no right to juggle or legislate them out of their property. The Legislature of this State has quite lately been exhibiting one of the most pitiable sights the world has seen in my day. It has been struggling for months to find a way to get round the positive provisions of laws and constitutions, in order to

make a sacrifice of the rights of a few, to secure the votes
of the many."

" Votes ist a goot ding, at election dime — haw, haw,
haw !" exclaimed my uncle.

, Mr. Warren looked both surprised and offended. The
coarseness of manner that my uncle had assumed effected
its object with the Injins, but it almost destroyed the divine's
previous good opinion of our characters, and quite upset his
notions of our refinement and principles. There was no
time for explanations, however; for, just as my uncle's
broad and well-acted " haw, haw, haw" was ended, a shrill
whistle was heard in the bushes, and some forty or fifty of
the Injins came whooping and leaping out from their cover,
filling the road in all directions, immediately around the
wagons.

Mary Warren uttered a little scream at this startling
scene, and I saw her arm clinging to that of her father, by
a sort of involuntary movement, as if she would protect him
at all hazards. Then she seemed to rally, and from that
instant her character assumed an energy, an earnestness,
a spirit and an intrepidity that I had least expected in one
so mild in aspect, and so really sweet in disposition.

All this was unnoticed by the Injins. They had their
impulses, too, and the first thing they did was to assist Mr.
Warren and his daughter to alight from their wagon. This
was done, not without decorum of manner, and certainly not
without some regard to the holy office of one of the parties,
and to the sex of the other. Nevertheless, it was done neatly
and expeditiously, leaving us all, Mr. Warren and Mary,
my uncle and myself, with a cluster of some fifty Injins
around us, standing in the centre of the highway.

CHAPTER XIV.

"No toil in despair,
No tyrant, no slave,
No bread-tax is there,
With a maw like the grave."

ALL this was so suddenly done as scarce to leave us time to think. There was one instant, notwithstanding, while two Injins were assisting Mary Warren to jump from the wagon, when my incognito was in great danger. Perceiving that the young lady was treated with no particular disrespect, I so far overcame the feeling as to remain quiet, though I silently changed my position sufficiently to get near her elbow, where I could and did whisper a word or two of encouragement. But Mary thought only of her father, and had no fears for herself. She saw none but him, trembled only for him, dreaded and hoped for him alone.

As for Mr. Warren himself, he betrayed no discomposure. Had he been about to enter the desk, his manner could not have been more calm. He gazed around him, to ascertain if it were possible to recognise any of his captors, but suddenly turned his head away, as if struck with the expediency of not learning their names, even though it had been possible. He might be put on the stand as a witness against some misguided neighbour, did he know his person. All this was so apparent in his benevolent countenance, that I think it struck some among the Injins, and still believe it may have had a little influence on their treatment of him. A pot of tar and a bag of feathers had been brought into the road when the gang poured out of the bushes, but whether this were merely accidental, or it had originally been intended to use them on Mr. Warren, I cannot say. The offensive materials soon and silently disappeared, and with them every sign of any intention to offer personal injury.

"What have I done that I am thus arrested in the public highway, by men armed and disguised, contrary to law?" demanded the divine, as soon as the general pause which

succeeded the first movement invited him to speak. "This
is a rash and illegal step, that may yet bring repentance."

"No preachee now," answered Streak o' Lightning;
"preachee for meetin', no good for road."

Mr. Warren afterwards admitted to me that he was much
relieved by this reply, the substitution of the word "meeting" for "church" giving him the grateful assurance that
this individual, at least, was not one of his own people.

"Admonition and remonstrance may always be useful
when crime is meditated. You are now committing a felony,
for which the State s prison is the punishment prescribed by
the laws of the land, and the duties of my holy office direct
me to warn you of the consequences. The earth itself is
but one of God's temples, and his ministers need never hesitate to proclaim his laws on any part of it."

It was evident that the calm severity of the divine, aided,
no doubt, by his known character, produced an impression
on the gang, for the two who had still hold of his arms released them, and a little circle was now formed, in the centre of which he stood.

"If you will enlarge this circle, my friends," continued
Mr. Warren; "and give room, I will address you here, where
we stand, and let you know my reasons why I think your
conduct ought to be——""

"No, no—no preachee here," suddenly interrupted Streak
o' Lightning; "go to village, go to meetin'-'us'—preachee
there.—Two preacher, den.—Bring wagon and put him in.
March, march; path open." '

Although this was but an "Injin" imitation of "Indian"
sententiousness, and somewhat of a caricature, everybody
understood well enough what was meant. Mr. Warren offered no resistance, but suffered himself to be placed in Miller's wagon, with my uncle at his side, without opposition.
Then it was, however, that he bethought himself of his
daughter, though his daughter had never ceased to think of
him. I had some little difficulty in keeping her from rushing into the crowd, and clinging to his side. Mr. Warren
rose, and, giving her an encouraging smile, bade her be
calm, told her he had nothing to fear, and requested that
she would enter his own wagon again and return home,

promising to rejoin her as soon as his duties at the village were discharged.

" Here is no one to drive the horse, my child, but our young German acquaintance. The distance is very short, and if he will thus oblige me, he can come down to the village with the wagon, as soon as he has seen you safe at our own door."

Mary Warren was accustomed to defer to her father's opinions, and she so far submitted, now, as to permit me to assist her into the wagon, and to place myself at her side, whip in hand, proud of and pleased with the precious charge thus committed to my care. These arrangements made, the Injins commenced their march, about half of them preceding, and the remainder following the wagon that contained their prisoner. Four, however, walked on each side of the vehicle, thus preventing the possibility of escape. No noise was made, and little was said ; the orders being given by signs and signals, rather than by words.

Our wagon continued stationary until the party had got at least a hundred yards from us, no one giving any heed to our movements. I had waited thus long for the double purpose of noting the manner of the proceedings among the Injins, and to obtain room to turn at a spot in the road a short distance in advance of us, and which was wider than common. To this spot I now walked the horse, and was in the act of turning the animal's head in the required direction, when I saw Mary Warren's little gloved hand laid hurriedly on the reins. She endeavoured to keep the head of the horse in the road.

" No, no," said the charming girl, speaking earnestly, as if she would not be denied, " we will follow my father to the village. I may not, must not, *cannot* quit him !"

The time and place were every way propitious, and I determined to let Mary Warren know who I was. By doing it I might give her confidence in me at a moment when she was in distress, and encourage her with the hope that I might also befriend her father. At any rate, I was determined to pass for an itinerant Dutch music-grinder with *her* no longer.

" Miss Mary, Miss Warren," I commenced, cautiously,

and with quite as much hesitation and diffidence of feeling as of manner, " I am not what I seem — that is, I am no music-grinder."

The start, the look, and the alarm of my companion, were all eloquent and natural. Her hand was still on the reins, and she now drew on them so hard as actually to stop the horse. I thought she intended to jump out of the vehicle, as a place no longer fit for her.

" Be not alarmed, Miss Warren," I said, eagerly, and, I trust, so earnestly as to inspire a little confidence. " You will not think the worse of me at finding I am your countryman instead of a foreigner, and a gentleman instead of a music-grinder. I shall do all you ask, and will protect you with my life."

" This is so extraordinary ! — so unusual ! — The whole country appears unsettled ! Pray, sir, if you are not the person whom you have represented yourself to be, who are you ?"

" One who admires your filial love and courage — who honours you for them both. I am the brother of your friend, Martha — I am Hugh Littlepage !"

The little hand now abandoned the reins, and the dear girl turned half round on the cushion of the seat, gazing at me in mute astonishment ! I had been cursing in my heart the lank locks of the miserable wig I was compelled to wear, ever since I had met with Mary Warren, as unnecessarily deforming and ugly, for one might have as well a becoming as a horridly unbecoming disguise. Off went my cap, therefore, and off went the wig after it, leaving my own shaggy curls for the sole setting of my face.

Mary made a slight exclamation as she gazed at me, and the deadly paleness of her countenance was succeeded by a slight blush. A smile, too, parted her lips, and I fancied she was less alarmed.

" Am I forgiven, Miss Warren ?" I asked ; " and will you recognise me for the brother of your friend ?"

" Does Martha — does Mrs. Littlepage know of this ?" the charming girl at length asked.

" Both ; I have had the happiness of being embraced by both my grandmother and my sister. You were taken out

19 *

of the room, yesterday, by the first, that I might be left alone with the last, for that very purpose!"

"I see it all, now; yes, I thought it singular then, though I felt there could be no impropriety in any of Mrs. Littlepages' acts. Dearest Martha! how well she played her part, and how admirably she has kept your secret!"

"It is very necessary. You see the condition of the country, and will understand that it would be imprudent in me to appear openly, even on my own estate. I have a written covenant authorizing me to visit every farm near us, to look after my own interests; yet, it may be questioned if it would be safe to visit one among them all, now that the spirits of misrule and covetousness are up and doing."

"Replace your disguise at once, Mr. Littlepage," said Mary, eagerly; "do—do not delay an instant."

I did as desired, Mary watching the process with interested, and, at the same time, amused eyes. I thought she looked as sorry as I felt myself when that lank, villanous wig was again performing its office.

"Am I as well arranged as when we first met, Miss Warren? Do I appear again the music-grinder?"

"I see no difference," returned the dear girl, laughing. How musical and cheering to me were the sounds of her voice in that little burst of sweet, feminine merriment. "Indeed, indeed, I do not think even Martha could know you now, for the person you the moment before seemed."

"My disguise is, then, perfect. I was in hopes it left a little that my friends might recognise, while it effectually concealed me from my enemies."

"It does—oh! it does. Now I know who you are, I find no difficulty in tracing in your features the resemblance to your portrait in the family gallery, at the Nest. The eyes, too, cannot be altered without artificial brows, and those you have not."

This was consoling; but all that time Mr. Warren and the party in front had been forgotten.— Perhaps it was excusable in two young persons thus situated, and who had now known each other a week, to think more of what was just then passing in the wagon, than to recollect the tribe that was marching down the road, and the errand they were on. I felt the necessity, however, of next consulting my companion as to our future movements. Mary heard me in evident anxiety, and her purpose seemed unsettled, for she changed colour under each new impulse of her feelings.

"If it were not for one thing," she answered, after a thoughtful pause, "I should insist on following my father."

"And what may be the reason of this change of purpose?"

"Would it be altogether safe for *you*, Mr. Littlepage, to venture again among those misguided men?"

"Never think of me, Miss Warren. You see I have been among them already undetected, and it is my intention to join them again, even should I first have to take you home. Decide for yourself."

"I will, then, follow my father. My presence may be the means of saving him from some indignity."

I was rejoiced at this decision, on two accounts; of which one might have been creditable enough to me, while the other, I am sorry to say, was rather selfish. I delighted in the dear girl's devotion to her parent, and I was glad to have her company as long as possible that morning. Without entering into a very close analysis of motives, however, I drove down the road, keeping the horse on a very slow gait, being in no particular hurry to quit my present fair companion.

Mary and I had now a free, and, in some sense, a confidential dialogue. Her manner towards me had entirely changed; for, while it maintained the modesty and *retenue* of her sex and station, it displayed much of that frankness which was the natural consequence of her great intimacy at the Nest, and, as I have since ascertained, of her own ingenuous nature. The circumstance, too, that she now felt she was with one of her own class, who had opinions, habits, tastes and thoughts like her own, removed a mountain of restraint, and made her communications natural and easy. I was near an hour, I do believe, in driving the two miles that lay between the point where the Injins had been met and the village, and in that hour Mary Warren and I became better acquainted than would have been the case, under ordinary circumstances, in a year.

In the first place, I explained the reasons and manner of my early and unexpected return home, and the motives by which I had been governed in thus coming in disguise on my own property. Then I said a little of my future intentions, and of my disposition to hold out to the last against every attempt on my rights, whether they might come from the open violence and unprincipled designs of those below, or the equally unprincipled schemes of those above. A spurious liberty and political cant were things that I despised, as every intelligent and independent man must; and I did not intend to be persuaded I was an aristocrat, merely because I had the habits of a gentleman, at the very moment when I had less political influence than the hired labourers in my own service.

Mary Warren manifested a spirit and an intelligence that surprised me. She expressed her own belief that the proscribed classes of the country had only to be true to themselves to be restored to their just rights, and that on the very principle by which they were so fast losing them. The opinions she thus expressed are worthy of being recorded.

"Everything that is done in that way," said this gentle, but admirable creature, "has hitherto been done on a principle that is quite as false and vicious as that by which they are now oppressed. We have had a great deal written and said, lately, about uniting people of property, but it has been so evidently with an intention to make money rule, and that in its most vulgar and vicious manner, that persons of right feelings would not unite in such an effort; but it does seem to me, Mr. Littlepage, that if the gentlemen of New York would form themselves into an association in defence of their rights, and for nothing else, and let it be known that they would not be robbed with impunity, they are numerous enough and powerful enough to put down this anti-rent project by the mere force of numbers. Thousands would join them for the sake of principles, and the country might be left to the enjoyment of the fruits of liberty, without getting any of the fruits of its cant."

This is a capital idea, and might easily be carried out. It requires nothing but a little self-denial, with the conviction of the necessity of doing something, if the downward tendency is to be ever checked short of civil war, and a revolution that is to let in despotism in its more direct form; despotism, in the indirect, is fast appearing among us, as it is.

" I have heard of a proposition for the Legislature to appoint special commissioners, who are to settle all the difficulties between the landlords and tenants," I remarked, " a scheme in the result of which some people profess to have a faith. I regard it as only one of the many projects that have been devised to evade the laws and institutions of the country, as they now exist."

Mary Warren seemed thoughtful for a moment; then her eye and face brightened, as if she were struck with some thought suddenly; after which the colour deepened, on her cheek, and she turned to me as if half doubting, and yet half desirous of giving utterance to the idea that was uppermost.

" You wish to say something, Miss Warren ?"

" I dare say it will be very silly—and I hope you won't think it pedantic in a girl, but really it does look so to me—what difference would there be between such a commission and the Star-Chamber judges of the Stuarts, Mr. Littlepage ?"

" Not much in general principles, certainly, as both would be the instruments of tyrants; but a very important one in a great essential. The Star-Chamber courts were legal, whereas this commission would be flagrantly illegal; the adoption of a special tribunal to effect certain purposes that could exist only in the very teeth of the constitution, both in its spirit and its letter. Yet this project comes from men who prate about the ' spirit of the institutions,' which they clearly understand to be their own spirit, let that be what it may."

" Providence, I trust, will not smile on such desperate efforts to do wrong !" said Mary Warren, solemnly.

" One hardly dare look into the inscrutable ways of a Power that has its motives so high beyond our reach. Providence permits much evil to be done, and is very apt to be, as Frederic of Prussia expressed it, on the side of strong battalions, so far as human vision can penetrate. Of one thing, however, I feel certain, and that is that they who are now the most eager to overturn everything to effect present purposes, will be made to repent of it bitterly, either in their own persons, or in those of their descendants."

"That is what is meant, my father says, by visiting 'the sins of the fathers upon the children, unto the third and fourth generations.' But there is the party, with their prisoners, just entering the village. Who is your companion, Mr. Littlepage?—One hired to act as an assistant?"

"It is my uncle, himself. You have often heard, I should think, of Mr. Roger Littlepage?"

Mary gave a little exclamation at hearing this, and she almost laughed. After a short pause she blushed brightly, and turned to me as she said—

"And my father and I have supposed you, the one a pedlar, and the other a street-musician!"

"But bedlars and moosic-grinders of goot etications, as might be panishet for deir bolitics."

Now, indeed, she laughed out, for the long and frank dialogue we had held together made this change to broken English seem as if a third person had joined us. I profited by the occasion to exhort the dear girl to be calm, and not to feel any apprehension on the subject of her father. I pointed out how little probable it was that violence would be offered to a minister of the gospel, and showed her, by the number of persons that had collected in the village, that it was impossible he should not have many warm and devoted friends present. I also gave her permission to, nay, requested she would, tell Mr. Warren the fact of my uncle's and my own presence, and the reasons of our disguises, trusting altogether to the very obvious interest the dear girl took in our safety, that she would add, of her own accord, the necessary warning on the subject of secresy. Just as this conversation ended we drove into the hamlet, and I helped my fair companion to alight.

Mary Warren now hastened to seek her father, while I was left to take care of the horse. This I did by fastening him to the rails of a fence, that was lined for a long distance by horses and wagons drawn up by the way-side. Surprisingly few persons in the country, at this day, are seen on horseback. Notwithstanding the vast difference in the amount of the population, ten horsemen were to be met with forty years ago, by all accounts, on the highways of

the State, for one to-day. The well-known vehicle, called
a dearborn, with its four light wheels and mere shell of a
box, is in such general use as to have superseded almost
every other species of conveyance. Coaches and chariots
are no longer met with, except in the towns; and even the
coachee, the English sociable, which was once so common,
has very generally given way to a sort of carriage-wagon,
that seems a very general favourite. My grandmother, who
did use the stately-looking and elegant chariot in town, had
nothing but this carriage-wagon in the country; and I question if one-half of the population of the State would know
what to call the former vehicle, if they should see it.

As a matter of course, the collection of people assembled
at Little Nest on this occasion had been brought together in
dearborns, of which there must have been between two and
three hundred lining the fences and crowding the horse-
sheds of the two inns. The American countryman, in the
true sense of the word, is still quite rustic in many of his
notions; though, on the whole, less marked in this particular than his European counterpart. As the rule, he has
yet to learn that the little liberties which are tolerated in a
thinly-peopled district, and which are of no great moment
when put in practice under such circumstances, become oppressive and offensive when reverted to in places of much
resort. The habits of popular control, too, come to aid in
making them fancy that what everybody does in their part
of the country can have no great harm in it. It was in
conformity with this *tendency* of the institutions, perhaps,
that very many of the vehicles I have named were thrust
into improper places, stopping up the footways, impeding
the entrances to doors, here and there letting down bars
without permission, and garnishing orchards and pastures
with one-horse wagons. Nothing was meant by all these
liberties beyond a desire to dispose of the horses and vehicles in the manner easiest to their owners. Nevertheless,
there was some connection between the institutions and
these little liberties which some statesmen might fancy existed in the *spirit* of the former. This, however, was a
capital mistake, inasmuch as the *spirit* of the institutions
is to be found in the laws, which prohibit and punish all
sorts of trespasses, and which are enacted expressly to curb

the *tendencies* of human nature! No, no, as my uncle Ro
says, nothing can be less alike, sometimes, than the *spirit*
of institutions and their *tendencies.*

I was surprised to find nearly as many females as men
had collected at the Little Nest on this occasion. As for
the Injins, after escorting Mr. Warren as far as the village,
as if significantly to admonish him of their presence, they
had quietly released him, permitting him to go where he
pleased. Mary had no difficulty in finding him, and I saw
her at his side, apparently in conversation with Opportunity
and her brother, Seneca, as soon as I moved down the road,
after securing the horse. The Injins themselves kept a little
aloof, having my uncle in their very centre; not as a prisoner, for it was clear no one suspected his character, but
as a pedlar. The watches were out again, and near half
of the whole gang seemed busy in trading, though I thought
that some among them were anxious and distrustful.

It was a singular spectacle to see men who were raising
the cry of "aristocracy" against those who happened to be
richer than themselves, while they did not possess a single
privilege or power that, substantially, was not equally shared
by every other man in the country, thus openly arrayed in
defiance of law, and thus violently trampling the law under
their feet. What made the spectacle more painful was the
certainty that was obtained by their very actions on the
ground, that no small portion of these Injins were mere
boys, led on by artful and knavish men, and who considered the whole thing as a joke When the laws fall so
much into disrepute as to be the subjects of jokes of this
sort, it is time to inquire into their mode of administration.
Does any one believe that fifty landlords could have thus
flown into the face of a recent enactment, and committed
felony openly, and under circumstances that had rendered
their intentions no secret, for a time long enough to enable
the authorities to collect a force sufficient to repress them?
My own opinion is, that had Mr. Stephen Rensselaer, and
Mr. William Rensselaer, and Mr. Harry Livingston, and
Mr. John Hunter, and Mr. Daniel Livingston, and Mr. Hugh
Littlepage, and fifty more that I could name, been caught
armed and disguised, in order to *defend* the rights of property that are solemnly guarantied in these institutions, of

which it would seem to be the notion of some that it is the
" spirit" to dispossess them, we should all of us have been
the inmates of States' prisons, without legislators troubling
themselves to pass laws for our liberation ! This is another
of the extraordinary features of American aristocracy, which
almost deprives the noble of the every-day use and benefit
of the law. It would be worth our while to lose a moment
in inquiring into the process by which such strange results
are brought about, but it is fortunately rendered unnecessary by the circumstance that the principle will be amply
developed in the course of the narrative.

A stranger could hardly have felt the real character of
this meeting by noting the air and manner of those who had
come to attend it. The " armed and disguised" kept themselves in a body, it is true, and maintained, in a slight degree, the appearance of distinctness from " the people," but
many of the latter stopped to speak to these men, and were
apparently on good terms with them. Not a few of the
gentler sex, even, appeared to have acquaintances in the
gang ; and it would have struck a political philosopher from
the other hemisphere with some surprise, to have seen the
" people" thus tolerating fellows who were openly trampling
on a law that the " people" themselves had just enacted !
A political philosopher from among ourselves, however,
might have explained the seeming contradiction by referring
it to the " spirit of the institutions." If one were to ask
Hugh Littlepage to solve the difficulty, he would have been
very apt to answer that the " people" of Ravensnest wanted
to compel him to sell lands which he did not wish to sell,
and that not a few of them were anxious to add to the compulsory bargains conditions as to price that would rob him
of about one-half of his estate ; and that what the Albany
philosophers called the " spirit of the institutions," was, in
fact, a " spirit of the devil," which the institutions were ex
pressly designed to hold in subjection !

There was a good deal of out-door management going on,
as might be seen by the private discussions that were held
between pairs, under what is called the " horse-shedding"
process. This " horse-shedding" process, I understand, is
well known among us, and extends not only to politics, but
to the administration of justice. Your regular " horse-
20

shedder" is employed to frequent taverns where jurors stay, and drops hints before them touching the merits of causes known to be on the calendars; possibly contrives to get into a room with six or eight beds, in which there may accidentally be a juror, or even two, in a bed, when he drops into a natural conversation on the merits of some matter at issue, praises one of the parties, while he drops dark hints to the prejudice of the other, and makes his own representations of the facts in a way to scatter the seed where he is morally certain it will take root and grow. All this time he is not conversing with a juror, not he; he is only assuming the office of the judge by anticipation, and dissecting evidence before it has been given, in the ear of a particular friend. It is true there is a law against doing anything of the sort; it is true there is law to punish the editor of a newspaper who shall publish anything to prejudice the interests of litigants; it is true the "horse-shedding process" is flagrantly wicked, and intended to destroy most of the benefits of the jury-system; but, notwithstanding all this, the "spirit of the institutions" carries everything before it, and men regard all these laws and provisions, as well as the eternal principles of right, precisely as if they had no existence at all, or as if a freeman were above the law. He makes the law, and why should he not break it? Here is another effect of the "spirit of the institutions."

At length the bell rang, and the crowd began to move towards the "meetin'-us." This building was not that which had been originally constructed, and at the raising of which I have heard it said, my dear old grandmother, then a lovely and spirited girl of nineteen, had been conspicuous for her coolness and judgment, but a far more pretending successor. The old building had been constructed on the true model of the highest dissenting spirit—a spirit that induced its advocates to quarrel with good taste as well as religious dogmas, in order to make the chasm as wide as possible—while in this, some concessions had been made to the temper of the times. I very well remember the old "meetin'-us" at the "Little Nest," for it was pulled down to give place to its more pretending successor after I had attained my sixteenth year. A description of both may let the reader into the secret of our rural church architecture.

The " old Neest meetin'-us," like its successor, was of a hemlock frame, covered with pine clap-boards, and painted white. Of late years, the paint had been of a most fleeting quality, the oil seeming to evaporate, instead of striking in and setting, leaving the colouring matter in a somewhat decomposed condition, to rub off by friction and wash away in the rains. The house was a stiff, formal parallelogram, resembling a man with high shoulders, appearing to be " stuck up." It had two rows of formal, short and ungraceful windows, *that* being a point in orthodoxy at the period of its erection. It had a tower, uncouth, and in some respects too large and others too small, if one can reconcile the contradiction; but there are anomalies of this sort in art, as well as in nature. On top of this tower stood a long-legged belfry, which had got a very dangerous, though a very common, propensity in ecclesiastical matters ; in other words, it had begun to " cant." It was this diversion from the perpendicular which had suggested the necessity of erecting a new edifice, and the building in which the " lecture" on feudal tenures and aristocracy was now to be delivered.

The new meeting-house at Little Nest was a much more pretending edifice than its predecessor. It was also of wood, but a bold diverging from " first principles" had been ventured on, not only in physical, but in the moral church. The last was " new-school;" as, indeed, was the first. What " new-school" means, in a spiritual sense, I do not exactly know, but I suppose it to be some improvement on some other improvement of the more ancient and venerable dogmas of the sect to which it belongs. These improvements on improvements are rather common among us, and are favourably viewed by a great number under the name of progress ; though he who stands at a little distance can, half the time, discover that the parties in progress very often come out at the precise spot from which they started.

For my part, I find so much wisdom in the bible—so profound a knowledge of human nature, and of its tendencies—counsel so comprehensive and so safe, and this solely in reference to the things of this life, that I do not believe everything is progress in the right direction because it sets us in motion on paths that are not two thousand years old ! I

believe that we have quite as much that ought to be kept,
as of that which ought to be thrown away; and while I
admit the vast number of abuses that have grown up in the
old world, under the "spirit of *their* institutions," as our
philosophers would say, I can see a goodly number that
are also growing up here, certainly not under the same
"spirit," unless we refer them both, as a truly wise man
would, to our common and miserable nature.

The main departure from first principles, in the sense of
material things, was in the fact that the new meeting-house
had only *one* row of windows, and that the windows of that
row had the pointed arch. The time has been when this
circumstance would have created a schism in the theological world; and I hope that my youth and inexperience
will be pardoned, if I respectfully suggest that a pointed
arch, or any other arch in *wood*, ought to create another in
the world of taste.

But in we went, men, women and children; uncle Ro.
Mr. Warren, Mary, Seneca, Opportunity, and all, the Injins
excepted. For some reason connected with their policy,
those savages remained outside, until the whole audience
had assembled in grave silence. The orator was in, or on
a sort of stage, which was made, under the new-light system in architecture, to supersede the old, inconvenient, and
ugly pulpit, supported on each side by two divines, of what
denomination I shall not take on myself to say. It will be
sufficient if I add Mr. Warren was not one of them. He
and Mary had taken their seats quite near the door, and
under the gallery. I saw that the rector was uneasy the
moment the lecturer and his two supporters entered the pulpit, and appeared on the stage; and at length he arose, and
followed by Mary, he suddenly left the building. In an
instant I was at their side, for it struck me indisposition
was the cause of so strange a movement. Fortunately, at
this moment, the whole audience rose in a body, and one
of the ministers commenced an extempore prayer.

At that instant, the Injins had drawn themselves up
around the building, close to its sides, and under the open
windows, in a position that enabled them to hear all that
passed. As I afterwards learned, this arrangement was
made with an understanding with those within, one of the

ministers having positively refused to address the throne of Grace so long as any of the tribe were present. Well has it been said, that man often strains at a gnat. and swallows a camel!

CHAPTER· XV

"I tell thee, Jack Cade, the clothier means to to dress the common wealth, and turn it, and put a new nap upon it."
King Henry VI.

As I knew Mary must have communicated to her father my real name, I did not hesitate, as I ought to have done in my actual dress and in my assumed character, about following them, in order to inquire if I could be of any service. I never saw distress more strongly painted in any man's countenance than it was in that of Mr. Warren, when I approached. So very obvious, indeed, was his emotion, that I did not venture to obtrude myself on him, but followed in silence; and he and Mary slowly walked, side by side, across the street to the stoop of a house, of which all the usual inmates had probably gone in the other direction. Here, Mr. Warren took a seat, Mary still at his side, while I drew near, standing before him.

"I thank you, Mr. Littlepage," the divine at length said, with a smile so painful it was almost haggard, "for, so Mary tells me you should be called—I thank you for this attention, sir—but, it will be over in another minute—I feel better now, and shall be able to command myself." -

No more was then said, concerning the reason of this distress; but Mary has since explained to me its cause. When her father went into the meeting-house, he had not the smallest idea that anything like a religious service would be dragged into the ceremonies of such a day. The two mi nisters on the stage first gave him the alarm; when a most painful struggle occurred in his mind, whether or not he should remain, and be a party to the mockery of addressing
20 *

God in prayer, in an assembly collected to set at naught
one of the plainest of his laws — nay, with banded felons
drawn up around the building, as principal actors, in the
whole mummery. The alternative was for him, a minister
of the altar, to seem to quit those who were about to join in
prayer, and to do this moreover under circumstances which
might appear to others as if he rejected all worship but that
which was in accordance with his own views of right, a
notion that would be certain to spread far and near, greatly
to the prejudice of his own people. But the first, as he
viewed the matter, involved a species of blasphemy; and
yielding to his feelings, he took the decided step he had, intending to remain out of the building, until the more regular
business of the day commenced.

It is certain Mr. Warren, who acted under the best impulse of christian feeling, a reverence for God, and a profound wish not to be a party in offending him with the
mockery of worship under such circumstances, has lost
much influence, and made many enemies, by the step he
then took. The very same feeling which has raised the
cry of aristocracy against every gentleman who dwells in
sufficiently near contact with the masses to distinguish his
habits from those around him; which induces the eastern
emigrant, who comes from a state of society where there
are no landlords, to fancy those he finds here ought to be
pulled down, because he is not a landlord himself; which
enables the legislator to stand up in his place, and unblush-
ingly talk about feudal usages, at the very instant he is
demonstrating that equal rights are denied to those he would
fain stigmatize as feudal lords, has extended to religion, and
the church of which Mr. Warren was a minister, is very
generally accused of being aristocratic, too! This charge
is brought because it has claims which other churches affect
to renounce and reject as forming no part of the faith; but
the last cannot remain easy under their own decisions;
and while they shout, and sing that they have found " a
church without a bishop," they hate the church that has a
bishop, because it has something they do not possess themselves, instead of pitying its deluded members, if they believe them wrong. This will not be admitted generally, but
it is nevertheless true; and betrays itself in a hundred ways.

It is seen in the attempt to *call* their own priests bishops, in the feeling so manifest whenever a cry can be raised against their existence, and in the *general* character of these theological rallies, whenever they do occur.

For one, I see a close analogy between my own church, as it exists in this country, and comparing it with that from which it sprung, and to those which surround it, and the true political circumstances of the two hemispheres. In discarding a vast amount of surplusage, in reducing the orders of the ministry in practice, as well as in theory, to their primitive number, three, and in rejecting all connection with the State, the American branch of the Episcopal Church has assumed the position it was desirous to fill; restoring, as near as may be, the simplicity of the apostolical ages, while it does not disregard the precepts and practices of the apostles themselves. It has not set itself above antiquity and authority, but merely endeavoured to sustain them, without the encumbrances of more modern abuses. Thus, too, has it been in political things. No attempt has been made to create new organic social distinctions in this country, but solely to disencumber those that are inseparable from the existence of all civilized society, of the clumsy machinery with which the expedients of military oppressors had invested them. The real sages of this country, in founding its institutions, no more thought of getting rid of the landlords of the country, than the church thought of getting rid of its bishops. The first knew that the gradations of property were an inevitable incident of civilization; that it would not be wise, if it were possible, to prevent the affluent from making large investments in the soil; and that this could not be done in practice, without leaving the relation of landlord and tenant. Because landlords, in other parts of the world, possessed privileges that were not necessary to the natural or simple existence of the character, was no reason for destroying the character itself; any more than the fact that the bishops of England possess an authority the apostles knew nothing of, rendered it proper for the American branch of the church to do away with an office that came from the apostles. But, envy and jealousy do not pause to reflect on such things; it is enough for *them*, in the one case, that you and yours have estates, and occupy social

positions, that I and mine do not, and cannot easily, occupy
and possess ; *therefore* I will oppose you, and join my voice
to the cry of those who wish to get their farms for nothing;
and in the other, that you have bishops when we can have
none, without abandoning our present organization and doctrines.

I dwell on these points at some little length, because the
movements of Mr. Warren and myself, at that moment, had
a direct influence on the circumstances that will soon be
related.   It is probable that fully one-half of those collected
in the Little Nest meeting-house, that morning, as they stood
up, and lent a sort of one-sided and listless attention to the
prayer, were thinking of the scandalous and aristocratical
conduct of Mr. Warren, in " goin' out o' meetin' just as
meetin' went to prayers !"   Few, indeed, were they who
would be likely to ascribe any charitable motive for the
act ; and probably not one of those present thought of the
true and conscientious feeling that had induced it.   So the
world wags !   It is certain that a malignant and bitter feeling was got up against the worthy rector on that occasion,
and for that act, which has not yet abated, and which will
not abate in many hundreds, until the near approach of
death shall lay bare to them the true character of. so many
of their own feelings.

It was some minutes before Mr. Warren entirely regained
his composure.   At length he spoke to me, in his usual benevolent and mild way, saying a few words that were complimentary, on the subject of my return, while he expressed
his fears that my uncle Ro and myself had been imprudent in thus placing ourselves, as it might be, in the lion's
jaws.

" You have certainly made your disguises so complete,"
he added, smiling, " as to have escaped wonderfully well so
far.   That you should deceive Mary and myself is no great
matter, since neither of us ever saw you before ; but, the
manner in which your nearest relatives have been misled,
is surprising.   Nevertheless, you have every inducement to
be cautious, for hatred and jealousy have a penetration that
does not belong even to love."

" We think we are safe, sir," I answered, " for we are
certainly within the statute.   We are too well aware of our

miserable aristocratical condition to place ourselves within
the grasp of the law, for such are our eminent privileges as
a landed nobility, that we are morally certain either of us
would not only be sent to the state's prison were he to be
guilty of the felony those Injins are committing, and will
commit, with perfect impunity, but that he would be kept
there, as long as a single tear of anguish could be wrung
from one of those who are classed with the aristocracy. Democracy alone finds any sympathy in the ordinary administration of American justice."

"I am afraid that your irony has only too much truth in
it. But the movement around the building would seem to
say that the real business of the day is about to commence,
and we had better return to the church."

"Those men in disguise are watching us, in a most unpleasant and alarming manner," said Mary Warren, delight-
ing me far more by the vigilance she thus manifested in my
behalf, than alarming me by the fact.

That we were watched, however, became obviously apparent, as we walked towards the building, by the actions of
some of the Injins. They had left the side of the church
where they had posted themselves during the prayer, and
head was going to head, among those nearest to us; or, it
would be nearer to appearances, were I to say bunch of
calico was going to bunch of calico, for nothing in the form
of a head was visible among them. Nothing was said to
Mr. Warren and Mary, however, who were permitted to go
into the meeting-house, unmolested; but two of these disguised gentry placed themselves before me, laying their
rifles across my path, and completely intercepting my advance.

"Who you?" abruptly demanded one of the two; —
"where go—where come from?"

The answer was ready, and I trust it was sufficiently
steady.

"I coomes from Charmany, und I goes into der kerch,
as dey say in mine coontry; what might be callet meetin'-
'us, here."

What might have followed, it is not easy to say, had not
the loud, declamatory voice of the lecturer just then been
heard, as he commenced his address. This appeared to be

a signal for the tribe to make some movement, for the two
fellows who had stopped me, walked silently away, though
bag of calico went to bag of calico, as they trotted off together, seemingly communicating to each other their suspicions. I took advantage of the opening, and passed into
the church, where I worked my way through the throng,
and got a seat at my uncle's side.

I have neither time, room, nor inclination to give anything like an analysis of the lecture. The speaker was
fluent, inflated, and anything but logical. Not only did he
contradict himself, but he contradicted the laws of nature.
The intelligent reader will not require to be reminded of the
general character of a speech that was addressed to the
passions and interests of such an audience, rather than to
their reason. He commented, at first, on the particular
covenants of the leases on the old estates of the colony,
alluding to the quarter-sales, chickens, days' work, and du
rable tenures, in the customary way. The reservation of
the mines, too, was mentioned as a tyrannical covenant,
precisely as if a landlord were obliged to convey any more
of the rights that were vested in him, than he saw fit; or the
tenant could justly claim more than he had hired! This
man treated all these branches of the subject, as if the
tenants had acquired certain mysterious interests by time
and occupation, overlooking the fact that the one party got
just as good a title as the other by this process; the lease
being the instrument between them, that was getting to be
venerable. If one party grew old as a tenant, so did the
other as a landlord. I thought that this lecturer would have
been glad to confine himself to the Manor leases, that being
the particular branch of the subject he had been accustomed
to treat; but, such was not the precise nature of the job he
was now employed to execute. At Ravensnest, he could
not flourish the feudal grievance of the quarter-sales, the
"four fat fowls," the "days' works," and the *length* of the
leases. Here it was clearly his cue to say nothing of the
three first, and to complain of the *shortness* of the leases, as
mine were about to fall in, in considerable numbers. Finding it was necessary to take new ground, he determined it
should be bold ground, and such as would give him the least
trouble to get along with.

As soon as the lecturer had got through with his general heads, and felt the necessity of coming down to particulars, he opened upon the family of Littlepage, in a very declamatory way. What had they ever done for the country, he demanded, that *they* should be lords in the land? By some process known to himself, he had converted landlords into ords in the land, and was now aiming to make the tenants occupy the latter station—nay, both stations. Of course, some services of a public character, of which the Littlepages might boast, were not touched upon at all, everything of that nature being compressed into what the lecturer and his audience deemed serving the people, by helping to indulge them in all their desires, however rapacious or wicked. As everybody who knows anything of the actual state of matters among us, must be aware how rarely the " people" hear the truth, when their own power and interests are in question, it is not surprising that a very shallow reasoner was enabled to draw wool over the eyes of the audience of Ravensnest on that particular subject.

But my interest was most awakened when this man came to speak of myself. It is not often that a man enjoys the same opportunity as that I then possessed to hear his own character delineated, and his most private motives analyzed. In the first place, the audience were told that this " young Hugh Littlepage had never done anything for the land that he proudly, and like a great European noble, he calls his ' estate.' Most of you, fellow-citizens, can show your hard hands, and recall the burning suns under which you have opened the swarth, through those then lovely meadows yonder, as *your* titles to these farms. But, Hugh Littlepage never did a day's work in his life"—ten minutes before he had been complaining of the " days' work" in the Manor leases, as indignities that a freeman ought not to submit to— " no, fellow-citizens, he never had that honour, and never will have it, until by a just division of his property, or what he now *calls* his property, you reduce him to the necessity of labouring to raise the crops he wants to consume."

" Where is this Hugh Littlepage at this very moment? In Paris, squandering *your* hard earnings in riotous living, according to the best standards of aristocracy. He lives in the midst of abundance, dresses richly and fares richly,

while *you* and *yours* are eating the sweat of your brows.
He is no man for a pewter spoon and two-pronged fork!
No, my countrymen! He must have a *gold* spoon for some
of his dishes, and you will find it hard to believe—plain,
unpretending, republican farmers as you are, but it is not
the less true—he must have forks of *silver!* Fellow-citizens, Hugh Littlepage would not put his knife into his
mouth, as you and I do, in eating—as all plain, unpretending republicans do—for the world. It would choke him;
no, he keeps *silver* forks to touch his anointed lips!" Here
there was an attempt to get up something like applause, but
it totally failed. The men of Ravensnest had been accustomed all their lives to see the Littlepages in the social station they occupied; and, after all, it did not seem so very
extraordinary that we should have silver forks, any more
than that others should have silver spoons. The lecturer
had the tact to see that he had failed on this point, and he
turned to another.

The next onset was made against our title. Whence
did it come? demanded the lecturer. From the king of
England; and the people had conquered the country from
that sovereign, and put themselves in his place. Now, is it
not a good principle in politics, that to the victors belong
the spoils? He believed it was; and that in conquering
America, he was of opinion that the people of America had
conquered the land, and that they had a right to take the
land, and to keep it. Titles from kings he did not respect
much; and he believed the American people, generally, did
not think much of them. If Hugh Littlepage wished an
"estate," as he called it, let him come to the people and
"sarve *them*," and see what sort of an estate *they* would
give him.

But there was one portion of his speech which was so
remarkable, that I must attempt to give it, as it was uttered.
It was while the lecturer was expatiating on this subject of
titles, that he broke out in the following language:—" Don't
talk to me," he bellowed — for by this time his voice had
risen to the pitch of a methodist's, in a camp-meeting —
" Don't talk to me of antiquity, and time, and length of possession, as things to be respected. They're nawthin'—jest
nawthin' at all. Possession 's good in law, I 'll admit; and

I contind that's jest what the tenants has. They've got the lawful possession of this very property, that layeth (not eggs, but) up and down, far and near, and all around; a rich and goodly heritage, when divided up among hard-working and honest folks; but too much, by tens of thousands of acres, for a young chap, who is wasting his substance in foreign lands, to hold. I contind that the tenants has this very, precise, lawful possession, at this blessed moment, only the law won't let 'em enj'y it. It's all owing to that accursed law, that the tenant can't set up a title ag'in his landlord. You see by this one fact, fellow-citizens, that they are a privileged class, and ought to be brought down to the level of gin'ral humanity. You can set up title ag'in anybody else, but you shan't set up title ag'in a landlord. I know what is said in the primisis," shaking his head, in derision of any arguments on the other side of this particular point; "I know that circumstances alter cases. I can see the hardship of one neighbour's coming to another, and asking to borrow or hire his horse for a day, and then pretendin' to hold him on some other ketch. But horses isn't land; you must all allow *that*. No, if horses *was* land, the case would be altered. Land is an element, and so is fire, and so is water, and so is air. Now, who will say that a freeman hasn't a right to air, hasn't a right to water, and, on the same process, hasn't a right to land? He *has*, fellow-citizens—he *has*. These are what are called in philosophy elementary rights; which is the same thing as a right to the elements, of which land is one, and a principal one. I say a principal one.; for, if there was no land to stand on, we should drop away from air, and couldn't enj'y *that*; we should lose all our water in vapour, and couldn't put it to millin' and manafacterin' purposes; and where could we build our fires? No; land is the *first* elementary right, and connected with it comes the first and most sacred right to the elements.

"I do not altogether disregard antiquity, neither. No; I respect and revere pre-emption rights; for they fortify and sustain the right to the elements. Now, I do not condemn squattin', as some doos. It's actin' accordin' to natur', and natur' is right. I respect and venerate a squatter's posses-sion; for it's held under the sacred principle of usefulness.

It says, 'go and make the wilderness blossom as the rose, and means 'progress.' That's an antiquity I respect. I respect the antiquity of your possessions here, *as tenants;* for it is a hard-working and useful antiquity — an antiquity that increases and multiplies. If it be said that Hugh Littlepage's ancestors — your noble has his 'ancestors,' while us 'common folks' are satisfied with forefathers"—[this hit took with a great many present, raising a very general laugh]—" but if this Hugh's ancestors did pay anything for the land, if I was you, fellow-citizens, I'd be gin'rous, and let him have it back ag'in. Perhaps his forefathers gave a cent an acre to the king — may be, two; or say sixpence, if you will. I'd let him have his sixpence an acre back again, by way of shutting his mouth. No; I'm for nawthin' that's ungin'rous."

"Fellow-citizens, I profess to be what is called a Democrat. I know that many of you be what is called Whigs—but I apprehend there is'nt much difference between us on the subject of this system of leasing land. We are all republicans, and leasing farms is anti-republican. Then, I wish to be liberal even to them I commonly oppose at elections, and I will freely admit, then, on the whull, the Whigs have rather out-done us Democrats, on the subject of this anti-rentism. I am sorry to be obliged to own in it, but it must be confessed that, while in the way of governors, there hasn't been much difference—yes, put 'em in a bag, and shake 'em up, and you'd hardly know which would come out first—which has done himself the most immortal honour, which has shown himself the most comprehensive, profound and safe statesman; I know that some of our people complain of the governors for ordering out troops ag'in the Injins, but they could not *help* that—they wouldn't have done it, in my judgment, had there been any way of getting round it; but the law was too strong for them, so they druv' in the Injins, and now they join us in putting down aristocracy, and in raising up gin'ral humanity. No; I don't go ag'in the governors, though many doos."

" But I profess to be a Democrat, and I'll give an outline of my principles, that all may see why they can't, and don't, and never will agree with aristocracy or nobility, in any form or shape. I believe one man is as good as an other in all things. Neither birth, nor law, nor edication, nor riches, nor poverty, nor anything else can ever make any difference in this principle, which is sacred, and fundamental, and is the chief stone of the corner in true Democracy. One man is as good as another, I say, and has just the same right to the enj'yment of 'arth and its privileges, as any other man. I think the majority ought to rule in all things, and that it is the duty of the minority to submit. Now, I've had this here sentiment thrown back upon me, in some places where I have spoken, and been asked ' how is this— the majority must rule, and the minority must submit—in that case, the minority is'nt as good as the majority in practice, and, hasn't the same right. They are made to own what they think ought not to be done?' The answer to this is so plain, I wonder a sensible man can ask the question, for all the minority has to do, is to join the majority, to have things as they want 'em. The road is free, and it is this open road that makes true liberty. Any man can fall in with the majority, and sensible folks commonly do, when they can find it, and that makes a person not only a man, as the saying is, but a FREEMAN, a still more honourable title."

" Fellow-citizens, a great movement is in progress, " Go ahead!" is the cry, and the march is onward; our thoughts already fly about on the wings of the lightning, and our bodies move but little slower, on the vapour of steam—soon our principles will rush ahead of all, and let in the radiance of a glorious day of universal reform, and loveliness, and virtue and charity, when the odious sound of *rent* will never be heard, when every man will set down under his own apple, or cherry tree, if not under his own fig tree.

" I am a Democrat,—yes, a Democrat. Glorious appellation! I delight in it! It is my pride, my boast, my very virtue. Let but the people truly rule, and all must come well. The people has no temptation to do wrong. If they hurt the state, they hurt themselves, for they are the state. Is a man likely to hurt himself? Equality is my axiom. Nor, by equality, do I mean your narrow pitiful equality before the law, as it is sometimes tarmed, for that may be no equality at all; but, I mean an equality that is substantial, and which must be restored. when the working of the law has deranged it. Fellow-citizens, do vou know what leap-year means? I dare say some of you don't, the ladies in partic'lar not giving much attention to astronomy. Well, I have inquired, and it is this:—The 'arth revolves around the sun in a year, as we all know. And we count three hundred and sixty-five days in a year, we all know. But, the 'arth is a few hours longer than three hundred and sixty-five days, in making its circuit—nearly six hours longer. Now, everybody knows that 4 times 6 makes 24, and so a twenty-ninth day is put into February, every fourth year, to restore the lost time; another change being to be made a long distance ahead to settle the fractions. Thus will it be with Democracy. Human natur' can't devise laws yet, that will keep all things on an exactly equal footing, and political leap-years must be introduced into the political calendar, to restore the equilibrium. In astronomy, we must divide up anew the hours and minutes; in humanity, we must, from time to time, divide up the land."

But, I cannot follow this inflated fool any longer; for he was quite as much of fool as of knave, though partaking largely of the latter character. It was plain that he carried many of his notions much farther than a good portion of his audience carried theirs; though, whenever he touched upon anti-rentism, he hit a chord that vibrated through the whole assembly. That the tenants ought to own their farms, and pay no more rents, AND POCKET ALL THE BENE-FITS OF THEIR OWN PREVIOUS LABOURS, THOUGH THESE LABOURS HAD BEEN CONSIDERED IN THE EARLIER RENTS, AND WERE, INDEED, STILL CONSIDERED, IN THE LOW RATES AT WHICH THE LANDS WERE LET, was a doctrine all could understand; and few were they, I am sorry to say, who did not betray how much self-love and self-interest had ob-scured the sense of right.

The lecture, such as it was, lasted more than two hours; and when it was done, an individual rose, in the character of a chairman—when did three Americans ever get together to discuss anything, that they had not a chairman and se-cretary, and all the parliamentary forms?—and invited any one present, who might entertain views different from the speaker, to give his opinion. Never before did I feel so tempted to speak in public. My first impulse was to throw away the wig, and come out in my own person, and expose the shallow trash that had just been uttered. I believe even I, unaccustomed as I was to public speaking, could easily have done this, and I whispered as much to my uncle, who was actually on his feet, to perform the office for me, when the sound of " Mr. Chairman," from a different part of the church, anticipated him. Looking round, I recognised at once the face of the intelligent mechanic, named Hall whom we had met at Mooseridge, on our way to the Nest. I took my seat, at once, perfectly satisfied that the subject was in good hands.

This speaker commenced with great moderation, both of manner and tone, and, indeed, he preserved them throughout. His utterance, accent and language, of course, were all tinctured by his habits and associations; but his good sense and his good principles were equally gifts from above. More of the " true image of his maker" was to be found in that one individual than existed in fifty common men. He saw clearly, spoke clearly, and demonstrated effectively. As he was well known in that vicinity and generally respected, he was listened to with profound attention, and spoke like a man who stood in no dread of tar and feathers. Had the same sentiments been delivered by one in a fine coat, and a stranger, or even by myself, who had so much at stake, very many of them would have been incontinently set down as aristocratic, and not to be tolerated, the most sublimated lover of equality occasionally falling into these little contradictions.

Hall commenced by reminding the audience that they all knew him, and knew he was no landlord. He was a mechanic, and a labouring man, like most of themselves, and had no interest that could be separate from the general good of society. This opening was a little homage to prejudice, since reason is reason, and right right, let them come whence they will. " I, too, am a democrat," he went on to say, " but I do not understand democracy to mean anything like that which has been described by the last speaker. I tell that gentleman plainly, that if he is a democrat, I am none, and if I am a democrat, he is none. By democracy I understand a government in which the sovereign power resides in the body of the nation ; and not in a few, or in one. But

21 *

this principle no more gives the body of the people authority
to act wrong, than in a monarchy, in which the sovereign
power resides in one man, that one man has a right to act
wrong. By equality, I do not understand anything more
than equality before the law—now, if the law had said that
when the late.Malbone Littlepage died, his farms should go
not to his next of kin, or to his devisee, but to his neighbours, then that would have been the law to be obeyed,
although it would be a law destructive of civilization, since
men would never accumulate property to go to the public.
Something nearer home is necessary to make men work,
and deny themselves what they like.

"The gentleman has told us of a sort of political leap-
year that is to regulate the social calender. I understand
him to mean that when property has got to be unequal, it
must be divided up, in order that men may make a new
start. I fear he will have to dispense with leap years, and
come to leap months, or leap weeks, ay, or even to leap
days; for, was the property of this township divided up this
very morning, and in this meetin'-us, it would get to be unequal before night. Some folks can't keep money when
they have it; and others can't keep their hands off it.

"Then, again, if Hugh Littlepage's property is to be
divided, the property of all of Hugh Littlepage's neighbours
ought to be divided too, to make even an *appearance* of
equality; though it would be but an *appearance* of equality,
admitting that were done, since Hugh Littlepage has more
than all the rest of the town put together. Yes, fellow-
citizens, Hugh Littlepage pays, at this moment, one-twen-
tieth of the taxes of this whole county. That is about the
proportion of Ravensnest; and that tax, in reality, comes
out of his pockets, as much the greater part of the taxes of
Rensselaer and Albany counties, if you will except the cities
they contain, are paid by the Rensselaers. It wun't do to
tell me the tenants pay the taxes, for I know better. We
all know that the probable amount of the taxes is estimated
in the original bargain, and is so much deducted from the
rent, and comes out of the landlord if it come out of anybody. There is a good reason why the tenant should pay
it, and a reason that is altogether in his interest; because
the law would make his oxen, and horses, and carts liable

for the taxes, should the landlord neglect to pay the taxes.
The collector always sells personals for a tax if he can find
them on the property; and by deducting it from the rent,
and paying it himself, the tenant makes himself secure
against that loss. To say that a tenant don't take any
account of the taxes he will be likely to pay, in making his
bargain, is as if one should say he is *non com.* and not fit
to be trusted with his own affairs. There are men, in this
community, I am sorry to say, who wish a law passed to
tax the rents on durable leases, or on all leases, in order to
choke the landlords off from their claims, but such men are
true friends to neither justice nor their country. Such a
law would be a tax on the incomes of a particular class of
society, and on no other. It is a law that would justify the
aggrieved parties in taking up arms to resist it, unless the
law would give 'em relief, as I rather think it would. By
removing into another State, however, they would escape
the tax completely, laugh at those who framed it, who would
incur the odium of doing an impotent wrong, and get laughed
at as well as despised, besides injuring the State by drawing
away its money to be spent out of its limits. Think, for
one moment, of the impression that would be made of New
York justice, if a hundred citizens of note and standing were
to be found living in Philadelphia or Paris, and circulating
to the world the report that they were exiles to escape a
special taxation! The more the matter was inquired into,
the worse it must appear; for men may say what they
please, to be ready ag'in election time, as there is but one
piece, or parcel of property to tax, it is an income tax, and
nothing else. What makes the matter still worse is, that
every man of sense will know that it is taxing the same
person twice, substantially for the same thing, since the
landlord has the direct land tax deducted from the rent in
the original bargain.

"As for all this cry about aristocracy, I don't understand
it. Hugh Littlepage has just as good a right to his ways as
I have to mine. The gentleman says he needs gold spoons
and silver forks to eat with. Well, what of that? I dare
say the gentleman himself finds a steel knife and fork useful, and has no objection to a silver, or, at least, to a pewter

spoon. Now, there are folks that use wooden forks, or no forks, and who are glad to get horn spoons; and *they* might call that gentleman himself an aristocrat. This setting of ourselves up as the standard in all things is anything but liberty. If I don't like to eat my dinner with a man who uses a silver fork, no man in this country can compel me. On the other hand, if young Mr. Littlepage don't like a companion who chews tobacco, as I do, he ought to be left to follow his own inclination.

" Then, this doctrine that one man's as good as another has got two sides to it. One man ought to have the same general rights as another, I am ready to allow; but if one man is as *good* as another, why do we have the trouble and cost of elections? We might draw lots, as we do for jurors, and save a good deal of time and money. We all know there is ch'ice in men, and I think that so long as the people have their ch'ice in sayin' who shall and who shall not be their agents, they've got all they have any right to. So long as this is done, the rest of the world may be left to follow their own ways, provided they obey the laws.

" Then, I am no great admirer of them that are always telling the people they 're parfect. I know this county pretty well, as well as most in it; and if there be a parfect man in Washington county, I have not yet fallen in with him. Ten millions of imparfect men won't make one parfect man, and so I don't look for perfection in the people any more than I do in princes. All I look for in democracy is to keep the reins in so many hands as to prevent a few from turning everything to their own account; still, we mustn't forget that, when a great many do go wrong, it is much worse than when a few go wrong.

" If my son didn't inherit the property of Malbone Littlepage, neither will Malbone Littlepage's son inherit mine. We are on a footing in that respect. As to paying rent, which some persons think so hard, what would they do if they had no house to live in, or farm to work? If folks wish to purchase houses and farms, no one can prevent them if they have money to do it with; and if they have not, is it expected other people are to provide them with such things out of their own——"

Here the speaker was interrupted by a sudden whooping, and the Injins came pressing into the house in a way to drive in all the'aisles before them. Men, women and children leaped from the windows, the distance being trifling, while others made their escape by the two side-doors, the Injins coming in only by the main entrance. In less time than it takes to record the fact, the audience had nearly all d . persed.

CHAPTER XVI.

" And yet it is said, — Labour in thy vocation : which is as much as to say, — let the magistrates be labouring men ; and therefore should we be magistrates."

King Henry VI.

In a minute or two the tumult ceased, and a singular scene presented itself. The church had four separate groups or parties left in it, besides the Injins, who crowded the main isle. The chairman, secretary, two ministers and lecturer, remained perfectly tranquil in their seats, probably understanding quite well *they* had nothing to fear from the intruders. Mr. Warren and Mary were in another corner, under the gallery, he having disdained flight, and prudently kept his daughter at his side. My uncle and myself were the *pendants* of the two last named, occupying the opposite corner, also under the gallery. Mr. Hall, and two or three friends who stuck by him, were in a pew near the wall, but about half way down the church, the former erect on a seat, where he had placed himself to speak.

" Proceed with your remarks, sir," coolly observed the chairman, who was one of those paradoxical anti-renters who has nothing to do with the Injins, though he knew all about them, and, as I have been told, was actually foremost in collecting and disbursing their pay. At this instant Seneca Newcome sneaked in at a side door, keeping as far as possible from the " disguised and armed," but curious to ascertain what would come next.

As for Hall, he behaved with admirable self-possession. He probably knew that his former auditors were collecting under the windows, and by raising his voice he would be easily heard. At all events, he did elevate his voice, and went on as if nothing had happened.

"I was about to say a word, Mr. Chairman, on the natur' of the two qualities that have, to me, at least, seemed uppermost in the lecturer's argooment"—yes, this sensible, well-principled man actually used that detestable sound, just as I have written it, calling 'argument' 'argooment'—what a pity it is that so little attention is paid to the very first principles of speaking the language well in this country, the common schools probably doing more harm than they do good in this respect—"that have, to me, at least, seemed uppermost in the lecturer's argooment, and they are both those that God himself has viewed as of so great importance to our nature as to give his express commandments about them. He has commanded us not to steal, and he has commanded us not to covet our neighbour's goods; proof sufficient that the possession of property is sanctioned by divine authority, and that it is endowed with a certain sanctity of privilege. Now for the application.

"You can do nothing as to leases in existence, because the State can't impair a contract. A great deal is said about this government's being one of the people, and that the people ought to do as they please. Now, I'm a plain man, and am talking to plain men, and mean to talk plainly. That this is a government of the people, being a democracy, or because the sovereign power, in the last resort, resides in the body of the people, is true; but that this is a government of the people, in the common signification, or as too many of the people themselves understand it, is not true. This very interest, about which there is so much commotion, or the right to interfere with contracts, is put beyond the people of the State by a clause in the constitution of the United States. Now, the constitution of the United States might be altered, making another provision saying that 'no State shall ever pass any law to do away with the existence of durable leases,' and every man, woman and child in New York be opposed to such a change, but they would have to swallow it. Come, let us see what figures will do. There are twenty-seven States in actual existence, and soon will be thirty. I don't care 'on which number you calculate;

say thirty, if you please, as that is likely to be the number before the constitution could be altered. Well, twenty-three of these States can put a clause into the constitution, saying you shan't meddle with leases. This might leave the seven most popular States, with every voter, opposed to the change. I 've made a calculation, and find what the seven most populous States had in 1840, and I find that more than half of all the population of the country is contained in them seven States, which can be made to submit to a minority. Nor is this all; the alteration may be carried by only one vote in each of the twenty-three States, and, deducting these from the electors in the seven dissenting States, you might have a constitutional change made in the country against a majority of say two millions! It follows that the people, in the common meaning, are not as omnipotent as some suppose. There's something stronger than the people, after all, and that's principles, and if we go to work to tear to pieces our own——"

It was impossible to hear another word that the speaker said. The idea that the people are not omnipotent, was one little likely to find favour among any portion of the population that fancies themselves to be peculiarly the people. So much accustomed to consider themselves invested with the exercise of a power which, in any case, can be rightfully exercised by only the whole people, have local assemblages got to be, that they often run into illegal excesses, fancying even their little fragment of the body politic infallible, as well as omnipotent, in such matters at least. To have it openly denied, therefore, that the popular fabric of American institutions is so put together, as to leave it in the power of a decided minority to change the organic law, as is unquestionably the fact in theory, however little likely to occur in practice, sounded in the ears of Mr. Hall's auditors like political blasphemy. Those under the windows groaned, while the gang in the aisle whooped and yelled, and that in a fashion that had all the exaggeration of a caricature. It was very apparent that there was an end of all the deliberative part of the proceedings of the day.

Hall seemed neither surprised nor uneasy. He wiped his face very coolly, and then took his seat, leaving the Injins to dance about the church, flourishing their rifles and knives,

in a way that might have frightened one less steady.   As
for Mr. Warren, he led Mary out, though there was a move-'
ment that threatened to stop him.   My uncle and myself
followed, the whooping and screaming being really unpleasant to the ear.   As to the chairman, the secretary, and the
two ministers of the gospel, they kept their stations on the
stage, entirely self-possessed and unmolested.   No one went
near them, a forbearance that must have been owing to the
often alleged fact that the real anti-renters, the oppressed
tenantry of New York, and these vile masqueraders, had
nothing to do with each other !

  One of the astounding circumstances of the times, is the
general prevalence of falsehood among us, and the almost
total suppression of truth.   No matter what amount of evidence there may be to contradict a statement, or how often
it has been disproved, it is reaffirmed, with just as much
assurance, as if the matter had never been investigated ; ay,
and believed, as if its substance were uncontradicted.   I am
persuaded there is no part of the world, in which it is more
difficult to get a truth into the public mind, when there is a
motive to suppress it, than among ourselves.   This may
seem singular, when it is remembered how many journals
there are, which are uttered with the avowed purpose to
circulate information.   Alas ! the machinery which can be
used to give currency to truth, is equally efficient in giving
currency to falsehood.   There are so many modes, too, of
diluting truth, in addition to the downright lies which are
told, that I greatly question if one alleged fact, out of twenty
that goes the rounds of the public prints, those of the com-
moner sort excepted, is true in all its essentials.   It requires
so much integrity of purpose, so much discrimination, such
a sensitiveness of conscience, and often so large a degree of
self-sacrifice in men to speak nothing but truth, that one is
not to expect that their more vulgar and irresponsible agents
are to possess a quality that is so very rare among the very
best of the principals.

  If I was glad to get out of the church myself, the reader
may depend on it, I was rejoiced when I saw Mr. Warren
leading Mary towards the place where I had left his wagon,
as if about to quit a scene that now promised nothing but
clamour and wrangling, if not something more serious.

Uncle Ro desired me to bring out the wagon in which we had left the farm; and, in the midst of a species of general panic, in which the women, in particular, went flying about in all directions, I proceeded to comply. It was at this moment that a general pause to all movements was produced by the gang of Injins pouring out of the church, bringing in their centre the late speaker, Mr. Hall. - As the chairman, secretary, lecturer, and the two " ministers of the gospel," followed, it was conclusive as to the termination of anything like further discussion.

My uncle called me back, and I thought was disposed to assist Hall, who, manfully supported by the two or three friends that had stood by him the whole day, was now moving towards us, surrounded by a cluster of wrangling and menacing Injins; the whole party bearing no little resemblance to a pack of village curs that sets upon the strange dog that has ventured in among them.

Oaths and threats filled the air; and poor Hall's ears were offended by an imputation that, I dare say, they then heard for the first time. He was called a " d——d aristocrat," and a hireling in the pay of " d——d aristocrats." To all this, however, the sturdy and right-thinking blacksmith was very indifferent; well knowing there was not a fact connected with his existence, or a sentiment of his moral being, that would justify any such charge. It was in answer to this deadly imputation, that I first heard him speak again, after he had been interrupted in the church.

" Call me what you please," he cried, in his clear, full voice; " I don't mind hard names. There isn't a man among you who thinks I 'm an aristocrat, or the hireling of any one; but I hope I am not yet so great a knave as to wish to rob a neighbour because he happens to be richer than I am myself."

" Who gave Hugh Littlepage his land?" demanded one, in the midst of the gang, speaking without the affectation of mimicry, though the covering to his head sufficiently changed his voice. " You know, yourself, it came from the king."

" He never worked for an acre of it!" bawled another.

' If he was a hard-working, honest man, like yourself, Tim

22

Hall, we might bear it; but you know he is not. He's a
spendthrift and an aristocrat."   ,   ,

"I know that hard hands don't make a man honest, any
more than soft hands make him a rogue," answered Tim
Hall, with spirit. "As for the Littlepages, they are gentlemen in every sense of the word, and always have been.
Their word will pass even now, when the bond of many a
man who sets himself up ag'in them wouldn't be looked at."

I was grateful and touched with this proof that a character, which I fully believed to be merited, was not lost on
one of the most intelligent men of his class, in that part of
the country. Envy, and covetousness, and malignancy,
may lie as they will, but the upright recognize the upright;
the truly poor know who most assuage their sorrows and
relieve their wants; and the real lover of liberty understands that its privileges are not to be interpreted altogether
in his own favour. I did not like the idea of such a man's
being ill-treated by a gang of disguised blackguards — fellows, who added to the crime of violating a positive law,
the high moral offence of prostituting the sacred principles
of liberty, by professing to drag them into the service of a
cause, which wanted very little, in its range, to include all
the pickpockets and thieves in the land.   ..

"They will do that noble fellow some injury, I fear," I
whispered to my uncle.

"If it were not for the mortification of admitting our disguise, I would go forward at once, and attempt to bring him
out of the crowd," was the answer. "But that will not do,
under the circumstances. Let us be patient, and observe
what is to follow."

"Tar and feathers!" shouted some one among the Injins;
"Tar and feather him!" "Crop him, and send him home!"
answered others. "Tim Hall has gone over to the enemy,"
added the Injin who asked whence I had my lands.

I fancied I knew that voice, and when its tones had been
repeated two or three times, it struck me it was that of
Seneca Newcome. That Seneca was an anti-renter, was
no secret; but that he, a lawyer, would be guilty of the great
indiscretion of committing felony, was a matter about which
one might well entertain a doubt. To urge others to be
guilty, was a different matter, but to commit himself seemed

unlikely. With a view to keep an eye on the figure I distrusted, I looked out for some mode by which he might be known. A patch, or rather goar in the calico, answered admirably, for on looking at others, I saw that this goar was accidental, and peculiar to that particular dress, most probably owing to a deficiency in the material originally supplied.

All this time, which indeed was but a minute or two, the tumult continued. The Injins seemed undetermined what to do; equally afraid to carry out their menaces against Hall, and unwilling to let him go. At the very instant when we were looking for something serious, the storm abated, and an unexpected calm settled on the scene. How this was effected, I never knew; though it is reasonable to suppose an order had been communicated to the Injins, by some signal that was known only to themselves. Of the result there was no doubt; the crowd around Hall opened, and that sturdy and uncompromising freeman came out of it, wiping his face, looking heated and a little angry. He did not yield, however, remaining near the spot, still supported by the two or three friends who had accompanied him from Mooseridge.

My uncle Ro, on reflection, conceived it wisest not to seem in a hurry to quit the village, and as soon as I had ascertained that Mr. Warren had come to a similar decision, and had actually taken refuge in the house of a parishioner, I 'was agreeable,' as the English say. While the pedlar, therefore, made a new display of his watches, I strolled round among the crowd, Injins and others intermixed, to see what could be seen, and to glean intelligence. In the course of my wanderings, chance brought me close to the side of the masquer in the dress with the goar. Tickling him gently on the elbow, I induced him to step a little aside with me, where our conversation would not be overheard.

"Why might you be Injin—gentleman as you be?" I asked, with as much of an air of simplicity, as I could assume.

The start with which this question was met, convinced me I was right; and I scarce needed farther confirmation of the justice of my suspicion. If I had, however, it was afforded.

"Why ask Injin dat?" returned the man with the goar.

"Vell, dat might do, and it might not do, 'Squire New-come; but it might not do wid one as knows you as vell as I know you.   So dell me; vy might you be Injin?"

"Harkee," said Seneca, in his natural speech, and evi-dently much disturbed by my discovery; "you must, on no account, let it be known who I am.   You see, this Injin busi-ness is ticklish work, and the law might—that is—*you* could get nothing by mentioning what you know, but as you have said, as I'm a gentleman, and an attorney at·law, it wouldn't sound well to have it said that I was caught dressed up in this manner, playing Injin."

"Ja — ja — I oonderstänts — gentlemans might not do sich dings, und not be laughed at—dat's all."

"Ye-e-e-s—that's all, as you say, so be careful what you say, or hint about it.   Well, since you've found me out, it's my treat.   What shall 't be?"

This was not very elegant for a 'gentleman,' and 'an at-torney at law,' certainly, but, as it belonged to the school of Mr. Newcome, it struck me it might not be prudent for me to betray that I belonged to one of a different sort.   Affect-ing contentment, therefore, I told him what he pleased, and he led me to a store of all business, that was kept by his brother, and in which, as I afterwards found, he himself was a partner.   Here he generously treated me to a glass of fiery whiskey, which I managed to spill in a way that prevented my being choked.   This was adroitly enough effected, as a refusal to drink would have been taken as a most suspicious circumstance in a German.   As respects Americans of my assumed class, I am happy to say it is now more possible for one to refuse a glass than to accept it.   It says a good deal in favour of the population of a country, when even the coachman declines his whet.   Nevertheless, a nation may become perfectly sober, and fall away with fearful rapidity on other great essentials.   On the subject of sobriety, I agree altogether with my uncle, in thinking that the Americans drink much less than most, if not less than any European nation; the common notion that long prevailed to the contrary in the country, being no more than the fruits of the general disposition, in other people, to decry demo-

cracy, aided somewhat, perhaps, by the exaggerations that
are so common in all the published statistics of morals.

I remarked that very few even of the Injins drank, though
they now began to circulate freely among the crowd and in
the stores. Seneca left me as soon as he fancied he had
clenched my discretion with a treat, and I stood looking
round at the manner in which the "armed and disguised"
conducted themselves. One fellow, in particular, attracted
my attention; and his deportment may be taken as a specimen of that of many of his comrades.

I was soon struck by the fact that Orson Newcome, Seneca's brother and partner, was obviously desirous of having as little to do with any of the Injins as possible. As
soon as one entered his store, he appeared uneasy; and
whenever one left it, he seemed glad. At first, I was inclined to think that Orson,—what names will not the great
eastern family adopt, before they have got through with their
catalogue!—really, they seem to select their appellations
as they do so many other things, or to prove that they'll
do as they please;—but, Orson, I fancied at first, was influenced by principle, and did not care to conceal the disgust
he felt at such audacious and illegal proceedings. But I
soon discovered my mistake, by ascertaining the true cause
of his distaste for the presence of an Injin.

"Injin want calico, for shirt"—said one of these worthies
significantly, to Orson, who, at first, affected not to hear
him.

The demand was repeated, however, with additional significance, when the cloth was reluctantly thrown on the
counter.

"Good," said the Injin, after examining the quality,
"cut Injin twenty yard—good measure, hear!"

The calico was cut, with a sort of desperate submission;
the twenty yards were folded, enveloped, and handed to the
customer, who coolly put the bundle under his arm, saying,
as he turned to leave the store—"Charge it to Down Rent."

The mystery of Orson's sullenness was now explained.
As invariably follows the abandonment of principle, the
fomenters of wrong were suffering smartly through the en-
croachments of their own agents. I ascertained, afterwards,
that these very Injins, who had been embodied in hundreds,

22*

with a view to look down law, and right, and the sacred
character of contracts, had begun to carry out their main
principle; and were making all sorts of demands, on the
pockets and property of their very employers, under one
pretence or another, but with very obvious tendencies towards their own benefit. The "Spirit of anti-Rentism" was
beginning to develope itself in this form, under the system
of violence; as, under that of legislative usurpation, and
legislative truckling to numbers, which is most to be feared
from the character of our representatives, it will as certainly be developed, unless suppressed in the bud, by such
further demands on its complaisant ministers, as will either
compel them to repent of their first false step, will drive the
State to civil war, or will drive all the honest men out of it.

I did not remain long in the store. After quitting it, I
went in quest of Mr. Warren and Mary, anxious to know
if I could be of any service to them. The father thanked
me for this attention, and let me know that he was now
about to quit the village, as he saw others beginning to go
away, among whom were Hall, who was an old and much
valued acquaintance of his, and whom he had invited to stop
at the rectory to dine. He advised us to imitate the example, as there were strangers among the Injins, who might
be addicted to drinking.

On this information I hunted up my uncle, who had actually sold most of his trinkets, and all his watches but one,
the secret of his great success being the smallness of his
prices. He sold for what he had bought, and in some instances for even less, quitting the place with the reputation
of being the *most reasonable* jewel-pedlar who had ever
appeared in it.

The road was beginning to be lined with vehicles carrying home the people who had collected to hear the lecture.
As this was the first occasion which offered for witnessing
such an exhibition, since my return, I examined the different parties we passed, with a view to comparison. There
is a certain air of rusticity, even in the large towns of America, which one does not meet with in the capitals of the old
world. But the American country is less rustic than any
part of the world with which I am acquainted, England
alone excepted. Of course, in making such a remark, no

allusion is intended to the immediate environs of very large towns; though I am far from certain that the population of St. Ouen, the Runnymede of France, and which stands within a league of the walls of Paris, would not have offered a more decidedly rustic spectacle, than that which we then saw. As respects females, this was very strikingly true; scarce one being visible who had that air of coarseness, and ignorance, and vulgarity, which denotes a degraded condition and a life of hardships. There was little apparent that marked a peasantry in the moral sense of the word; but the whole population seemed to be at their ease, using neat and well-kept vehicles; solid, active horses; and being themselves reasonably well, though not very tastefully clad. Yet, all this was on a leased estate, under the dire oppression of a landlord, and beneath the shadow of aristocracy! A short dialogue which took place between my uncle and two sturdy weather-beaten husbandmen, who drove their horses to a short distance, on a walk at the side of ours, made the impression produced by such facts deeper than it might otherwise have been. I will relate it.

"You are Jarmans, I b'lieve," commenced the oldest of the two men, a grey-headed tenant of my own, of the name of Holmes, who was well known to us both — "Jarmans, from the old countries, I hear?"

"Ja — we bees from der olt coontries; und dat is a great vay off."

"Ye-e-s, I s'pose it is—I've heern tell of them countries, often. Doos the landlord system exist there?"

"Ja — dere ist landtlorts all ofer dis worlt, I do dinks; und denants, doo."

"Well, and how is the plan liked there; or be folks thinking of getting red (rid) on't?"

"Nein — how might dey gets red of it? It ist der law, you might see, und vhat ist der law moost be done."

This answer puzzled old Holmes a good deal. He passed a hand over his face, and turned to his companion, one Tubbs, also a tenant on my estate, as if to ask assistance. Tubbs was one of the new school; a school that makes more laws than it respects, and belongs to the movement. He is a man that fancies the world never knew anything

of principles, facts, or tendencies, until the commencement
of this century.

"What sort of a government had you, in your own country?" demanded Tubbs.

"Bretty goot. Mein coontry was Preussen; und dat might
be t'ought a bretty goot gofernment."

"Yes, but it's a kingly government, I take it;—it seems
to me, I have heern tell of kings in that land."

"Ja, ja—dere ist ein koenig—one king. De last might
be der goet koenig Vilhelm, und now dere ist his son, who
ist a goot koenig, too, as I might dink. Ja, ja—dere ist a
king."

"That explains it all," cried Tubbs, with a sort of triumph. "You see, they have a king, and so they have
tenants; but, here we have no king, and we have no need
of landlords. Every man, in a free country, should be his
own landlord; that's my doctrine, and to that I'll stick.

"There is some reason in that, fri'nd; isn't that your
idee?" asked Holmes.

"Vell, I might not oonderstandt. Dost der shentlemans
object to landlordts, in his coontry, because dere might be
landlordts in dem coontries ast might haf kings?"

"That's it! That's just the reason on't, and the true
principle!" answered Tubbs. "Kings and liberty can't go
together, and landlords and liberty can't go together."

"But, might not der law in dis coontry be to haf landlordts, too? I hear dat it ist so."

"Yes, that is the law, as it stands; but we mean to alter
it, all. We have got so many votes, now, as to be sure
to have both parties with us, at a gin'ral election; and give
us the governor on our side, with the sartainty of votes
enough to turn an election, and we're pretty confident of success. Votes is all that is wanting, in a truly free country,
for men to have things pretty much in their own way."

"Und dost you mean to haf not'in dat might be in do
coontries ast haf kings?"

"To be sure not. What do we want of any of your
lordly contrivances, to make the rich richer, and the poor
poorer."

"Vell, you moost alter de law of nature, if do rich vilt

not get riches, und de poor vill not feel dey be poor. Do piple dells us dat de misery of de poor ist deir poverty."

" Ay, ay, bible talk don't go for much in politics. Sabba' days are set aside for the bible, and week days for public and private matters. Now, here is Hugh Littlepage, of the same flesh and blood as my neighbour Holmes and myself be—no better and no worse; yes, I'm willing to allow he's no worse, in the main, though in some things L do think we might claim the preference; but I'll allow he's no worse, for the sake of argooment. Each on us rents a farm of this Littlepage, of a hundred acres good. Wa-al, this land we till, and crop, and labour, with our hands, and the hands of our sons, and hired help, perhaps; and yet we have to pay fifty dollars a-piece, annually, to that youngster Hugh Littlepage, for rent; which money he takes and squanders where he pleases, in riotous livin', for 't we know. Now, is that right, I ask; and isn't it an onsuitable state of things for a republican country?"

" Und you dinks yoong Littlebage might spend his money in riotous lifin' in foreign landts?"

" Sartain—that's the tale, hereabouts; and I have seen a man who knows another, that has an acquaintance who has been in Paris, and who tells the people of his neighbourhood that he stood at the door of the king's palace one day, and actually saw both the Littlepages going in to pay ' tribute unto Cæsar,' as it is called—I suppose you know; and they tell me that all that goes to see a king, has to kneel and kiss his hand—some say his toe. Do you happen to know how it is in the old countries?"

" It ist not so; I haf seen more kings as half a dozen, und dey dost not kneel down and kiss deir hants, except on sartain business. Dey might not allvays hear what ist true, n dis coontry."

" Wa-a-l, I don't know — I never was there to see," answered Tubbs, in that peculiar manner, which, whenever it is used by an American, may safely be interpreted to mean, " I'll not contradict you, but I'll believe what I please." That is what I've heern say. But, why should we pay rent to young Littlepage to spend in riotous living?"

" I might not know, oonless you haf hiret his landt, und

agree't to pay him rent; in which case you might do as you agree't."

"But when the bargain's of a kingly natur', I say no. Every country has its natur', and every government has its natur', and all things should be, in conformity with natur'. Now its ag'in natur' to pay rent in a republican country. We want nothing here, that's in common with lords and kings."

"Vell, den, you most alter your whole country. You might not haf wifes und children; you might not lif in houses, and plough de landt; you might not eat und drink, und you might not wear any shirt."

Tubbs looked a little astonished. Like the *Bourgeois Gentilhomme*, he was amazed to find he had been talking prose all his life without knowing it. There is no question that laws unsuitable to the institutions of a republic might exist in a kingdom, but it is equally certain that the law which compels the tenant to pay for the use of his house, or farm, is not one of the number. Tubbs, however, had been so thoroughly persuaded, by dint of talking, there was something exceedingly anti-republican in one man's paying rent to another, that he was not disposed to give the matter up so easily.

"Ay, ay," he answered, "we have many things in common with kingdoms, as *men*, I must allow; but why should we have anything in common of this aristocratic natur'? A free country should contain freemen, and how *can* a man be free if he doesn't own the land out of which he makes his living?"

"Und if he makes his lifin' out of anoder man's land, he might be honest enough to pay for its use, I dinks."

"But, we hold it *ought* not to be another man's land, but the land of him who works it."

"Dell me dis—dost you efer let out a field to a poor neighbour on shares?"

"Sartain; we all do that, both to accommodate folks, and to get crops when we are crowded with work ourselves."

"Und why might not all dat crop pelong to him dat works de field?"

"Oh! that's doin' business on a small scale, and can't do anybody harm. But the American institutions never in-ended that there should be a great privileged class among us, like the lords in Europe."

"Did you efer haf any difficulty in getting your hire for a field dat might be so let out?"

"Sartain. There's miserable neighbours as well as them that isn't. I had to sue the very last chap I had such dealin's with."

"Und dit das law let you haf your money?"

"To be sure it did! What would law be good for, if it didn't help a body to his rights?"

"Und dost den tenants of dis broperty let Hugh Littlebage haf his rents, ast might be due?"

"That's a different thing, I tell you. Hugh Littlepage has more than he wants, and spends his money in riotous livin' in foreign parts."

"Vell, und sooppose your neighpours might vants to ask you what you do wit' your tollars after you shall sell your pork and beef, to see you mate goot use of it—might dat be liperty?"

"That! Why, who do you think would trouble himself about my 'arnin's. It's the big fish, only, that folks talk about, and care about, in such matters."

"Den folks make Hugh Littlebage a big fish, by dair own mettlin', und enfy, und cofetousness—is it not so?"

"Harkee, fri'nd, I some think you're leanin' yourself to kingly ways, and to the ideas in which you was brought up. Take my advice, and abandon all these notions as soon as you can, for they'll never be popular in this part of the world."

Popular! How broad has the signification of this word got to be! In the eyes of two-thirds of the population it already means, 'what is right.' *Vox populi, vox dei.* To what an extent is this little word made to entwine itself around all the interests of life! When it is deemed expedient to inculcate certain notions in the minds of the people, the first argument used is to endeavour to persuade the inhabitants of New York that the inhabitants of Pennsylvania are already of that mind. A simulated public opinion is the strongest argument used, indeed, on every occasion of the public discussion of any disputed point. He that can count the most voices is a better man than he who can give the

most reasons; numbers carrying more weight with them,
than facts, or law. It is evident, that, while in some things,
such a system may work well, there are others, and those
of overshadowing importance, in which its tendency is direct
and fearful towards corruption.

As soon as Tubbs had given his admonition, he applied
the whip to his horse, and trotted on, leaving us to follow at
the best gait we could extort from Tom Miller's hack.

CHAPTER XVII.

"If he were with me, King of Tuscarora,
　Gazing as I upon thy portrait now,
In all its medalled, fringed, and bearded glory,
　Its eyes' dark beauty, and its thoughtful brow —

Its brow, half-martial and half-diplomatic;
　Its eye, upsoaring, like an eagle's wings;
Well might he boast that we, the democratic,
　Outrival Europe—even in our kings."

                                    Red Jacket.

My uncle Ro. said nothing, when the two tenants left us;
though I saw, by his countenance, that he felt all the absurdity of the stuff we had just been listening to. We had
got within half a mile of the woods, when eight Injins came
galloping up to a wagon that was directly behind us, and
which contained another of my tenants, with his eldest son,
a lad of sixteen, whom he had brought with him as a scholar, in having his sense of right unsettled by the selfish
mystification that was going on in the land; a species of
fatherly care that was of very questionable merit. I said
there were eight of these Injins, but there were only four
horses, each beast carrying double. No sooner did the
leaders of the party reach the wagon I have mentioned
than it was stopped, and its owner was commanded to alight.
The man was a decided down-renter, but he obeyed the
order with a very ill grace; and did not obey at all, indeed,
until he was helped out of the wagon, by a little gentle

violence of this fragment of his own *corps d'armée*. The boy was soon put into the highway, when two of the "disguised and armed" leaped into the vacant places, and drove on, passing us at a furious pace, making a parting nod to the owner of the vehicle, and consoling him for its temporary loss, by calling out, "Injin want him—Injin good fellow—you know."

Whether the discomfited farmer *knew* or not, we could not tell; but he *looked* as if he wished the Injins anywhere but in their "happy hunting grounds." We drove on laughing, for it was in human nature to be amused at such an exhibition of the compulsory system, or of "liberty and equality carried out;" and more particularly so, when I was certain that the "honest, hard-working, horny-hand tiller of the soil," wanted to cheat me out of a farm; or, to put his case in the most favourable point of view, wanted to compel me to sell him one at his own price. Nor did our amusement stop here. Before we reached the woods, we found Holmes and Tubbs in the highway, too; the other two worthies who had been mounted *en croupe* having dispossessed them of their wagon also, and told them to "charge it to Injin." We afterwards learned that this practice was very general; the owner recovering his horse and team, in the course of a few days, by hearing it had been left, secretly, at some tavern within a few miles of his residence. As for old Holmes, he was in an honest indignation when we came up with him, while even Tubbs looked soured and discontented, or as if he thought friends were entitled to better treatment.

"Vhat ist der matter?" cried out uncle Ro, who could hardly keep from laughing the whole time; "vhat ist der matter now? Vhere might be your hantsome vaggin and your gay horse?"

"It's too bad!—yes, it's eeny most too bad!" grunted Holmes. "Here am I, past three-score-and-ten, which is the full time of man; the bible says—and what the bible says *must* be true, you know!—here have they trundled me into the highway, as they would a sack of potatoes, and left me to walk every step of four miles to reach my own door! It's too bad—it's eeny most too bad!"

23

"Oh! dat might be a trifle, compared to vhat it vould be to haf peen drundelled out of your farm."

"I know 't!—I know 't!—I understand!—i 's all meant for the good cause — to put down aristocracy, and make men raa'ly equal, as the law intends them to be — but this, I say, is œny most too bad!"

"Und you so olt!"

"Seventy-six, if I 'm a day. My time can't be long, and my legs is weak, they be. Yes, the bible says a man's time is limited pretty much to three-score-and-ten—and I 'll never stand out ag'in the bible."

"Und vhat might der piple say apout vanting to haf your neighpours' goots?"

"It cries that down dreadfully! Yes, there 's plenty of that in the good book, I know from havin' heard it read — ay, and havin' read it myself, these three-score years; it doos cry it down, the most awfully. I shall tell the Injins this, the next time they want my wagon. There's bible ag'in all sich practices."

"Der piple ist a goot pook."

"That it is—that it is—and great is the consolation and hope that I have known drawn from its pages. I'm glad to find that they set store by the bible in Jarmany. I was pretty much of the notion, we had most of the religion that's goin', in Ameriky, and it's pleasant to find there is some in Jarmany."

All this time old Holmes was puffing along on foot, my uncle Ro walking his horse, in order to enjoy his discourse.

"Oh! ja—ja, ja—dere might be some religion left in der olt worlt—de puritans, as you might call dem, did not pring it all away."

"Desp'rate good people them! We got all our best sarcumstances from our puritan forefathers. Some folks say that all Ameriky has got, is owing to them very saints!"

"Ja—und if it bees not so, nefer mind; for dey will be sartain to get all Ameriky."

Holmes was mystified, but he kept tugging on, casting wistful glances at our wagon, as he endeavoured to keep up with it. Fearful we might trot on and leave him, the old man continued the discourse. "Yes," he said, "our authority for everything must come from the bible, a'ter all.

It tells us we hadn't ought to bear malice, and that's a rule I endivour to act up to; for an old man, you see, can't indulge his sinful natur' if he would. Now, I've been down to Little Nest to attend a Down Rent Meetin',—but I bear no more malice ag'in Hugh Littlepage, not I, no more than if he wern't a bit of my landlord! All I want of him is my farm, on such a lay as I can live by, and the b'ys a'ter me. I look on it as dreadful hard and oppressive that the Littlepages should refuse to let us have the place, seein' that I have worked it now for the tarm of three whull lives."

"Und dey agreet dat dey might sell you de farm, when dem dree lifes wast up?"

"No, not in downright language they didn't, as I must allow. In the way of bargain, I must own the advantage is altogether on the side of Littlepage. That was his grand'ther's act; and if you wun't drive quite so fast, as I'm getting a little out of wind, I'll tell you all about it. That is just what we complain on; the bargain being so much in his favour. Now, my lives *have* hung on desp'rately, haven't they, Shabbakuk?" appealing to Tubbs. "It's every hour of forty-five years sin' I tuck that lease, and one life, that of my old woman, is still in bein', as they call it, though it's a sort of bein' that a body might as well not have as have. She can't stand it a great while longer, and then that farm that I set so much store by, out of which I've made my livelihood most of my life, and on which I've brought up fourteen children, will go out of my hands to enrich Hugh Littlepage, who's got so much now he can't spend it at hum like honest folks, but must go abroad, to waste it in riotous living, as they tell us. Yes, onless the governor and the legislature helps me out of my difficulty, I don't see but Hugh Littlepage must get it all, making the 'rich richer, and the poor poorer.'"

"Und vhy must dis cruel ding come to pass? Vhy might not mans keep his own in Ameriky?"

"That's jest it, you see. It isn't my own, in law, only by natur', like, and the 'speret of the Institutions,' as they call it. I'm sure I don't kear much how I get it, so it only comes. If the governor can only make the landlords sell, or even give away, he may sartainly count on my support,

providin' they don't put the prices too high.   I hate high
prices, which is onsuitable to a free country."

"Fery drue.   I soopoose your lease might gif you
dat farm quite reasonaple, as it might be mate so long
ago?"

"Only two shillings the acre," answered the old fellow,
with a knowing look, which as much as boasted of the
capital bargain he had in the affair, "or twenty-five dollars
a year for a hundred acres.   That's no great matter, I'm
ready to allow; but my lives havin' held on so desp'rately,
until land's got up to forty dollars an acre about here, I
can't no more expect sich another lay than I can expect to
go to Congress.   I can rent that place, to-morrow mornin',
for $150 of as good money as any man can pay."

"Und how much might you expect 'squire Littlebage
woult ask on a new lease?"

"Some think as much as $62.50; though other some
think he would let it go to *me* for $50, for three lives longer.
The old gin'ral told me when he signed the lease that I was
gettin' a bargain, ' but, niver mind,' said he, ' if I give you
good tarms, ' you'll make the better tenant, and I look to
posterity and their benefit as much as I do to my own.   If
I don't get the advantage I might,' says he, ' my children,
or my children's children, will.   A man mustn't altogether
live for himself in this world, especially if he has children.'
Them was good idees, wasn't they?"

"You might not dink differently.   Und, how moch woult
you love to bay for a deet of de farm?"

"Wa-a-l, there's differences of opinion on that subject.
The most approved notion is, that Hugh Littlepage ought to
be made to give warrantees, with full covenants, as it's called; and covenants is all in all, in a deed, you know ——"

"But might not be in a lease?" put in uncle Ro, somewhat drily.

"That depinds—But, some say them deeds ought to be
given, if the tenants allow the landlords the worth of the
land, when the patentee got it, and interest down to the present day.   It does seem a desp'rate price to pay for land, to
give principal and interest, and to throw in all that has been
paid beside?"

"Haf you made a calculation, to see vhat it might come to?"

"Shabbakuk has—tell the gentleman, Shabbakuk, how much you made it come to, the acre."

Shabbakuk was a far deeper rogue than his neighbour Holmes. The last was merely a man of selfish and narrow views, who, from passing a long life with no other object before him than that of scraping together property, had got his mind completely ensnared in the meshes of this world's net; whereas, his companion took the *initiative*, as the French have it, in knavery, and not only carried out, but invented the schemes of the wicked. He clearly did not like this appeal to his arithmetic, but having no suspicion to whom he was talking, and fancying every man in the lower conditions of life must be an ally in a plan to make the "rich, poorer; and the poor, richer;" he was a little more communicative than might otherwise have been the case. After reflecting a moment, he gave us his answer, reading from a paper in his hand, on which the whole sum had been elaborately worked for the occasion of the late meeting.

"The land was worth ten cents an acre, maybe, when the first Littlepage got it, and that is a liberal price. Now, that was eighty years since, for we don't count old Herman Mordaunt's time, as anything; seeing that the land was worth next to nothin', in his time. The interest on ten cents at 7 per cent. is 7 mills a year, or 560 mills for 80 years. This is without compound; compound being unlawful, and nothin' ag'in law should be taken into the account. Add the 10 cents to the 560 mills, and you get 660 mills, or 66 cents. Now this sum, or a sum calculated on the same principles, all the tenants are willing to pay for their farms,* and if justice prevails they will get them."

"Dat seems but little to bay for landt dat might now rent for a dollar an acre, each year."

"You forgit that the Littlepages have had the rent these eighty years, the whull time."

---

* In order that the reader may understand Mr. Hugh Littlepage is not inventing, I will add that propositions still more extravagant than these have been openly circulated among the anti-renters, up and down the country.—EDITOR.

23*

" Und de denants haf hat de farms dese eighty years, do whole time, too."

" Oh ! we put the land ag'in the work. If my neighbour Holmes, here, has had his farm forty-five years, so the farm has had his work forty-five years, as an off-set. You may depind on 't the governor and the legislature understand all that."

"If dey does," answered Uncle Ro, whipping his horse into a trot, " dey must be fit for deir high stations. It is goot for a country to haf great governors, and great legisladürs. *Guten Tag.*"

Away he went, leaving neighbour Holmes, Shabbakuk Tubbs, the governor and legislature, with their joint morals, wisdom, logic and philosophy, in the highway, together. My uncle Ro shook his head, and then he laughed, as the absurdity of what had just passed forced itself on his imagination.

I dare say many may be found, who have openly professed principles and opinions identical, in substance, with what has just been related here, who will be disposed to deny them, when they are thrown into their faces. There is nothing unusual in men's refusing to recognise their own children, when they are ashamed of the circumstances tha brought them into being. But, in the course of this controversy, I have often heard arguments in discourse, and have often read them in the journals, as they have been put into the mouths of men in authority, and that too in their public communications, which, stripped of their very thin coverings, are pretty much on the level with those of Holmes and Tubbs. I am aware that no governor has, *as yet*, alluded to the *hardships* of the tenants, under the limited leases, but it would be idle to deny that the door has been opened to principles, or, a want of principles, that must sweep away all such property in the current of reckless popular clamour, unless the evil be soon arrested. I say *evil*, for it must prove a curse to any community to break down the securities of property, as it is held in what has hitherto been thought its most secure form, and, what is still of more importance in a moral point of view, all to appease the cravings of cupidity, as they are exhibited in the masses.

We were soon out of sight of Holmes and Tubbs, and in

the woods. I confess that I expected, each instant, to overtake Hall in the hands of the Injins; for the movement
among that class of persons had appeared to me as one directed particularly against him. We saw nothing of the
sort, however, and had nearly reached the northern limits
of the bit of forest, when we came in sight of the two
wagons which had been so cavalierly taken possession of,
and of the two horses ridden by the mounted men. The
whole were drawn up on one side of the highway, under the
charge of a single Injin, in a manner to announce that we
were approaching a point of some interest.

My uncle and myself fully expected to be again stopped,
as we drove up to the place just mentioned; not only was
he track of the road left clear, however, but we were suf
fered to pass without a question. All the horses had been
in a lather, as if driven very hard; though, otherwise, there
was nothing to indicate trouble, if we except the presence
of the solitary sentinel. From this fellow, neither sign, nor
order molested us; but on we went, at Tom Miller's horse's
favourite amble, until we were so near the verge of the
wood, as to get a view into the open fields beyond. Here,
indeed, we obtained a sight of certain movements that, I
confess, gave me some little concern..

Among the bushes that lined the highway, and which
have been already mentioned, I got a glimpse of several of
the "disguised and armed," who were evidently lying in
ambush. Their number might have been twenty in all,
and, it was now sufficiently apparent, that those who had
pressed the wagons had been hurrying forward to re-enforce
their party. At this point, I felt quite certain we should
be stopped; but we were not. We were suffered to pass
without question, as we had just passed the wagons and
horses, though it must have been known to the party that
we were fully aware of their presence at that particular
spot. But, on we went, and were soon, unmolested, in the
open country.

It was not long, however, before the mystery was explained. A road descended from the higher ground, which
lay to the westward of us, a little on our left, and a party
of men was coming down it, at a quick walk, which, at
the first glance, I mistook for a detachment of the Injins:

but which, at a second look, I ascertained to be composed
of Indians, or real red men. The difference between the
two is very great, as every American will at once admit,
though many who read this manuscript will be obliged to
me-for an explanation. There is "Indian" and "Injin."
The Injin 'is a white man, who, bent on an unworthy and
illegal purpose, is obliged to hide his face, and to perform
his task in disguise. The Indian is a red man, who is neither afraid, nor ashamed, to show his countenance, equally
to friend or enemy. The first is the agent of designing
demagogues, the hireling of a discontented and grasping
spirit, who mocks at truth and right by calling himself one
who labours to carry out " the spirit of those Institutions"
which he dishonours and is afraid to trust ; while the other
erves himself only, and is afraid of nothing. One is skulking from, and shirking the duties of civilization, while the
other, though a savage, is, at least, true to his own professions.

   There they were, sure enough, a party of some sixteen
or eighteen of the real aborigines. It is not an uncommon
thing to meet with an Indian, or two, strolling about the
country selling baskets — formerly it was brooms of birch,
but the march of improvement has nearly banished so rude
a manufacture from the country—with a squaw, or two, in
company; but it is now very unusual to meet a true Indian
warrior in the heart of the State, carrying his rifle and
tomahawk, as was the case with all those who were so
swiftly descending the road. My uncle Ro was quite as
much astonished as I was myself; and he pulled up at the
junction of the two highways, in order to await the arrival
of the strangers.

   " These are real Redskins, Hugh—and of a noble tribe,"
cried my uncle, as a still nearer approach gave him a better
and better view. " Warriors of the West, out of all question,
with one white man in attendance—what can such a party
possibly want at Ravensnest !"

   " Perhaps the anti-renters intend to enlarge their plans,
and have a scheme to come out upon us, with an alliance
formed with the true sons of the forest—may they not intend
intimidation ?"

   " Whom could they thus intimidate, but their own wives

and children? But, here they come, in a noble body, and we can speak to them."

There they did come, indeed; seventeen of the finer specimens of the Redskins, as they are now sometimes seen passing among us in bodies, moving to or from their distant prairies; for the white man has already forced the Indian, with the bears, and the elk, and the moose, out of the forests of America, upon those vast plains.

What is to be the end of the increase of this nation, is one of the mysteries of Divine Providence. If faithful to the right, if *just*, not in the sense of yielding to the clamours of the many, but in the sense of good laws, if true to themselves, the people of this republic may laugh at European interference and European power, when brought to bear on their home interests, as so much of the lumbering policy of ages no longer suited to the facts and feelings of our own times, and push on to the fulfilment of a destiny, which, if carried out on the apparent designs of the ruler of the earth, will leave that of all other States which have preceded us, as much in the shade, as the mountain leaves the valley. But, it must not be forgotten that the brightest dawns often usher in the darkest days; that the most brilliant youths frequently precede manhoods of disappointment and baffled wishes; that even the professed man of God can fall away from his vows and his faith, and finish a career that was commenced in virtue and hope, in profligacy and sin. Nations are no more safe from the influence of temptation than individuals, and this has a weakness peculiarly its own. Instead of falling back on its popular principle, in extremities, as its infallible safeguard, it is precisely in the irresponsible and grasping character of that principle that its danger is to be apprehended. That principle, which, kept within the limits of right, is so admirably adapted to restraining the ordinary workings of cupidity and selfishness, as they are familiarly seen in narrow governments, when permitted to overrun the boundaries placed for its control, becomes a torrent that has broken out of its icy bed, in the Spring, and completely defaces all that is beneficial or lovely, in either nature or art, that may happen to lie in its course. As yet, the experience of two centuries has offered nothing so menacing to the future prosperity of this country, as the social fermenta-

tion which is at this moment at work, in the State of New
York.   On the result of this depends the solution of the all-
important question, whether principles are to rule this republic, or men ; and these last, too, viewed in their most vulgar
and repulsive qualities, or as the mere creatures of self, in-
tead of being the guardians and agents of that which ought
to be.   It is owing to this state of things, that we have already seen a legislature occupied with discussing the modes
of evading the provisions of its own laws, and men who
ought to stand before the world, stern and uncompromising
in their public morals, manifesting a most pernicious ingenuity in endeavouring to master and overreach each other
in wielding the arts of the demagogue.

As the Indians entered the north and south road, or that
in which we had stopped, the whole party came to a halt,
with characteristic courtesy, as if to meet our wish to speak
to them.   The foremost of the band, who was also the oldest,
being a man of sixty, if not older, nodded his head, and uttered the usual conventional salutation of " Sago, sago."

" Sago," said my uncle, and " Sago" put in I.

" How do ?" continued the Indian, who we now discovered
spoke English.   " What call this country ?"

" This is Ravensnest.   The village of Little Nest is about
a mile and a half on the other side of that wood."

The Indian now turned, and in his deep guttural tones
communicated this intelligence to his fellows.   The information obviously was well received, which was as much as
saying that they had reached the end of their journey. Some
conversation next succeeded, delivered in brief, sententious
remarks, when the old chief again turned to us.   I call him
chief, though it was evident that the whole party was composed of chiefs.   This was apparent by their medals, their
fine appearance generally, and by their quiet, dignified, not
to say lofty, bearing.   Each of them was in a light summer
attire, wearing the moccasin and leggings, &c. ; the calico
shirt, or a thin blanket, that was cast around the upper part
of the person, much as the Roman may be supposed to have
worn his toga ; all carrying the rifle, the bright, well-scoured
tomahawk, and the sheathed knife.   Each, too, had his horn
and his bullet-pouch, and some of the more youthful were a
little elaborate in their ornaments, in the way of feathers,

and such presents as they had received on their long journey. Not one of them all, however, was painted.

"This Raven-nest, eh?" continued the old chief, speaking directly, but with sufficient courtesy.

"As I have said. The village lies on the other side of that wood; the house from which the name is taken is a mile and a half in the other direction."

This, too, was translated, and a low, but general expression of pleasure was given.

"Any Injins 'bout here, eh?" demanded the chief, looking so earnestly at the same time as to surprise us both.

"Yes," answered my uncle. "There *are* Injins—a party is in the edge of the wood, there, within thirty rods of you at this moment."

With great rapidity this fact was communicated to the eager listeners, and there was a sensation in the party, though it was a sensation betrayed as such feelings are only betrayed among the aborigines of this part of the world; quietly, reservedly, and with a coldness amounting nearly to indifference. We were amused, however, at noting how much more interest this news awakened than would probably have been excited had these red-men been told a town like London was on the other side of the wood. As children are known to feel most interest in children, so did these children of the forest seem to be most alive to an interest in these unexpected neighbours, brethren of the same habits and race, as they unquestionably imagined. After some earnest discourse among themselves, the old chief, whose name turned out to be Prairiefire, once more addressed himself to us.

"What tribe, eh? Know tribe?"

"They are called Anti-rent Injins—a new tribe in this part of the country, and are not much esteemed."

"Bad Injin, eh?"

"I am afraid so. They are not honest enough to go in paint, but wear shirts over their faces."

Another long and wondering conference succeeded. It is to be supposed that such a *tribe* as that of the Anti-renters was hitherto unknown among the American savages. The first intelligence of the existence of such a people would naturally awaken great interest, and we were soon requested to show them the way to the spot where this unheard of tribe might be found. This was going somewhat further than my uncle had anticipated, but he was not a man to beat a retreat when he had once undertaken an enterprise. After a short deliberation with himself, he signified his assent; and alighting from our wagon, we fastened Tom Miller's horse to a stake of one of the fences, and set off, on foot, as guides to our new brethren, in seeking the great tribe of the Anti-renters! .We had not gone half the distance to the woods before we met Holmes and Tubbs, who, getting a cast in another wagon, until they reached the place where their own vehicle was stationed, had recovered that, and were now on their way home, apprehensive that some new freak of their great allies might throw them out into the highway again. This wagon, our own excepted, was the only one that had yet emerged from the wood, the owners of some twenty others preferring to remain in the back-ground until the development of the meeting between the tribes should occur.

"What, in natur', does all this mean?" exclaimed old Holmes, as we approached him, reining in his horse, for the purposes of a conference. "Is the governor sending out ra-al Injins ag'in' us, in order to favour the landlords?"

This was taking a harsh and most uncharitable view of the course of the governor, for an anti-renter; but that func-tionary having made the capital blunder of serving, altoge-ther, neither "God nor Mammon" in this great question, must expect to take it right and left, as neither God nor Mammon will be very likely to approve of his course.

"Vell, I don't know," was my uncle's answer. "Dese ist ra-al red-men, und dem younder ist ra-al Injins, dat's all. Vhat might bring dese warriors here, joost now, you must ask of demselves, if you wants to l'arn."

"There can be no harm in asking; I'm no way skeary about redskins, having seen 'em often, and my father fit 'em in his day, as I've heern him tell. Sago, Sago."

"Sago," answered Prairiefire, with his customary cour-tesy.

"Where, in natur', do you red-men all come *from*, and where *can* ye be goin'?"

It was apparent that Holmes belonged to a school that

never hesitated about putting any question; and that would have an answer, if an answer was to be got. The old chief had probably met with such pale-faces before, the untrained American being certainly among the most diligent of all the human beings of that class. But, on the other hand, the red-man regards the indulgence of a too eager curiosity as womanish, and unworthy of the self-command and dignity of a warrior. The betraying of surprise, and the indulgence of a curiosity fit only for squaws, were two things that Prairiefire had doubtless been early told were unworthy of his sex; for to some such in-and-in breeding alone could be referred the explanation of the circumstance that neither Holmes' manner, address, nor language, caused in him the least expression of emotion. He answered the questions, however, and that with a coldness that seemed of proof.

"Come from setting sun — been to see Great Father, at Washington — go home," was the sententious reply.

"But, how come ye to pass by Ravensnest?—I'm afeared the governor, and them chaps at Albany, must have a hand in this, Shabbakuck?"

What Shabbakuck thought of the "governor, and them chaps at Albany" is not known, as he did not see fit to make any reply. His ordinary propensity to meddle was probably awed by the appearance of these real Redskins.

"I say, *why* do ye come this-a-way?" Holmes continued, repeating his question. "If you've been to Washington, and found him to hum (Anglice, 'at home'), why didn't ye go back by the way ye come?"

"Come here to find Injin; got no Injin here, eh?"

"Injin? why, of one sort we've got more of the critturs tnan a body can very well git along with. Of what colour be the Injins you want to find? — Be they of the pale-face natur', or be they red like yourselves?"

"Want to find red-man. He ole, now; like top of dead hemlock, wind blow t'rough his branches till leaf all fall off."

"By George, Hugh," whispered my uncle, "these redskins are in search of old Susquesus!" Then entirely forgetting the necessity of maintaining his broken English in the presence of his two Ravensnest listeners, Shabbakuck Tubbs, in particular, he turned, somewhat inconsiderately

24,

for one of his years, to the Prairiefire, and hastily re•
marked—

"I can help you in your search. You are looking for a
warrior of the Onondagoes; one who left his tribe a hundred summers ago, a red-man of great renown for finding
his path in the forest, and who would never taste fire-water
His name is Susquesus.".

Until this moment, the only white man who was in company with this strange party — strange at least in our portion of the State of New York, though common enough,
perhaps, on the great thoroughfares of the country—broke
silence. This man was an ordinary interpreter, who had
been sent with the party in case of necessity; but being little more acquainted with the ways of civilization than those
whom he was to guide, he had prudently held his tongue
until he saw that he might be of some use. We afterwards
learned that the sub-agent who had accompanied the chiefs
to Washington, had profited by the wish of the Indians to
pay their passing homage to the "Withered Hemlock, that
still stands," as they poetically called Susquesus in their
own dialects—for Indians of several tribes were present—to
pay a visit to his own relatives in Massachusetts, his presence not being deemed necessary in such a purely pious
pilgrimage.

"You're right," observed the interpreter. "These chiefs
have not come to look up any *tribe*, but there are two of
the ancient Onondagoes among them, and their traditions
tell of a chief, called Susquesus, that has outlived everything but tradition; who left his own people long, long ago,
and who left a great name behind him for vartue, and that
is a thing a red-skin never forgets."

"And all these warriors have come fifty miles out of their
way, to pay this homage to Susquesus?"

"Such has been their wish, and I asked permission of the
Bureau at Washington, to permit them to come. It costs
Uncle Sam $50 or a $100 more than it otherwise might,
but such a visit will do all the warriors of the West a million of dollars of good; no men honour right and justice
more than redskins, though it's in their own fashion."

"I am sure Uncle Sam has acted no more than right-
eously, as I hope he always may act as respects these peo•

ple. Susquesus is an old friend of mine, and I will lead you to him."

"And who in natur' be *you*?" demanded Holmes, his curiosity starting off on a new track.

"Who am I?—You shall know who I am," answered uncle Ro, removing his wig, an action that I imitated on the spot,—"I am Roger Littlepage, the late trustee of this estate, and this is Hugh Littlepage, its owner." Old Holmes was good pluck in most matters; of far better stuff at the bottom, than the sneaking, snivelling, prating demagogue at his side; but by this discovery he was dumbfounded! He looked at my uncle, then he looked at me; after which, he fastened a distressed and inquiring gaze on Shabbakuck. As for the Indians, notwithstanding their habitual self-command, a common "hugh!" was uttered among them, when they saw two men, as it might be, thus scalping themselves. Uncle Ro was excited, and his manner was, in the least degree, theatrical, as with one hand he removed his cap, and with the other his wig; holding the last, with an extended arm, in the direction of the Indians. As a redman is rarely guilty of any act of rudeness, unless he mean to play the brute in good earnest, it is possible that the Chippewa towards whom the hand which held the wig was extended, mistook the attitude for an invitation to examine that curious article, for himself. It is certain he gently forced it from my uncle's grasp, and, in the twinkling of an eye, all the savages were gathered round it, uttering many but low and guarded expressions of surprise. Those men were all chiefs, and they restrained their astonishment at this point. Had there been any of the ignoble vulgar among them, there is little doubt that the wig would have passed from hand to hand, and been fitted to a dozen heads, already shaved to receive it.

CHAPTER XVIII.

The Gordon is gude in a hurry,
  An' Campbell is steel to the bane,
An' Grant, an' Mackenzie, an' Murray,
  An' Cameron will truckle to nane."

                                        Hogg.

THE interruption of this scene came from old Holmes, who
cried to his companion, on the high key in which it was
usual for him to speak :—

"This is downright bad, Shabbakuk — we'll never get
our leases a'ter this !"

"Nobody can say"—answered Tubbs, giving a loud hem,
as if determined to brazen the matter out. "Maybe the
gentleman will be glad to compromise the matter. It's
ag'in law, I believe, for any one to appear on the highway
disguised—and both the 'Squire Littlepages, you'll notice,
neighbour Holmes, be in the very *middle* of the road, and
both was disguised, only a minute ago."

"That's true.—D'ye think anything can be got out o'
that ? I want profitable proceedin's."

Shabbakuk gave another hem, looked behind him, as if
to ascertain what had become of the Injins, for he clearly
did not fancy the real ' article' before him, and then he answered:

"We may get our farms, neighbour Holmes, if you'll
agree, as I'm willin' to do, to be reasonable about this matter, so long as 'Squire Littlepage wishes to hearken to his
own interests."

My uncle did not deign to make any answer, but, knowing we had done nothing to bring us within the view of the
late statute, he turned towards the Indians, renewing his
offer to them to be their guide.

"The chiefs want very much to know who you are, an
how you two came by double scalps," said the interpreter,
smiling like one who understood for his own part, the nature
of a wig very well.

" Tell them that this young gentleman is Hugh Littlepage, and that I am his uncle. Hugh Littlepage is the
owner of the land that you see on every side of you."

The answer was communicated, and we waited for its
effect on the Indians. To our surprise, several of them soon
gathered around, evidently regarding us both, with interest
and respect.

" The claims of a landlord seem to be better understood
among these untutored savages, than among your own
tenants, Hugh," said my uncle. " But there goes old
Holmes, the inbred rogue, and his friend Shabbakuk, back
to the woods; we may have an affair on hand with *his*
Injins."

" I think not, sir. It does not appear to me that there is
valour enough in that tribe, to face this. In general, the
white man is fully a match for the redskin; but it may be
doubted whether chiefs like these, would not prove too much
for twice their number of varlets, of the breed of yonder
skulking scoundrels."

" Why do the chiefs manifest so much interest in us?"
asked my uncle, of the interpreter. " Is it possible that they
pay so much respect to us, on account of our connection
with this estate?"

" Not at all—not at all. They know the difference between a chief and a common man well enough, it is true,"
was the answer; " and twenty times, as we have come
down through the country, have they expressed their surprise to me, that so many common men should be chiefs,
among the pale-faces; but, they care nothing for riches.
He is the greatest man among them, who is best on a war
path, and at a council-fire; though they *do* honour them
that has had great and useful ancestors.".

" But, they seem to betray some unusual and extraordinary interest in us, too; perhaps they are surprised at seeing gentlemen in such dresses?"

" Lord, sir, what do men care for dresses, that are used
to see the heads of factories and forts, half the time dressed
in skins. They know that there be holidays and workin'-
days; times for every-day wear, and times for feathers and
paint. No—no—they look at you both, with so much in-
erest, on account of their traditions."

24*

"Their traditions!   What can these have to do with us?
We have never had anything to do with Indians."

'That's true of you, and may be true of your fathers;
but it's not true of some of your ancestors. Yesterday, after
we had got to our night's stopping-place, two of the chiefs,
this smallish man with the double plate on his breast, and
that elderly warrior, who has been once scalped, as you can
see by his crown, began to tell of some of the treacheries of
their own tribe, which was once a Canada people.   The
elderly chief related the adventures of a war-path, that led
out of Canada, across the large waters, down to a settlement where they expected to get a great many scalps, but
where in the end they lost more scalps than they found;
and where they met Susquesus, the upright Onondago, as
they call him in that tongue, as well as the Yengeese owner
of the land, at this very spot, whom they called by a name
something like your own, who was a warrior of great courage and skill by their traditions.   They suppose you to be
the descendants of the last, and honour you accordingly;
that's all."

"And, is it possible that these untutored beings have traditions as reliable as this?"

"Lord, if you could hear what they say among themselves, about the lies that are read to them out of the pale-
face prints, you would l'arn how much store they set by
truth!   In my day, I have travelled through a hundred
miles of wilderness, by a path that was no better, nor any
worse, than an Indian tradition of its manner of running;
and a tradition that must have been, at least, a hundred
summers old.   They know all about your forefathers, and
they know something about you, too, if you be the gentleman
that finds the upright Onondago, or the Withered Hemlock,
in his old age, with a wigwam, and keeps it filled with food
and fuel."-

"Is this possible!   And all this is spoken of, and known
among the savages of the Far West?"

"If you call these chiefs, savages," returned the interpreter, a little offended at hearing such a term applied to his
best friends and constant associates.   "To be sure they
have their ways, and so have the pale-faces; but Injin ways
be not so very savage, when a body gets a little used to

them. Now, I remember it was a long time before I could get reconciled to seeing a warrior scalp his enemy; but as I reasoned on it, and entered into the spirit of the practice, I began to feel it was all right."

I was walking just in front of my uncle, for we were in motion again on our way to the wood, but could not help turning and saying to him with a smile—

"So it would seem that this matter of the 'spirit' is to be found in other places besides the legislature. There is the 'spirit of scalping,' as well as the 'spirit of the institutions!'"

"Ay, Hugh, and the 'spirit of fleecing,' as a consequence of what is profanely termed the last. But, it may be well to go no nearer to the wood, than this spot. The Injins I have told you of are in these bushes in front, and they are armed—I leave you to communicate with them in any manner you please. They are about twenty in number."

The interpreter informed his chiefs of what had been said, who spoke together in earnest consultation for a moment. Then Prairiefire, himself, plucked a branch off the nearest bush, and holding it up he advanced close to the cover, and called out aloud, in some one, or in many of the different dialects with which he was acquainted. I saw by the moving of their branches, that men were in the bushes; but no answer of any sort was made. There was one savage in our band, who betrayed manifest impatience at these proceedings. He was a large, athletic Iowa chief, called in English Flintyheart, and, as we subsequently learned, of great renown for martial exploits. It was always difficult to hold him in, when there was a prospect of scalps, and he was now less restrained than common, from the circumstance of his having no superior of his own particular tribe present. After Prairiefire had called two or three times in vain to the party in the cover, Flintyhead stepped out, spoke a few words, with energy and spirit, terminating his appeal by a most effective, not to say appalling, whoop. That sound was echoed back by most of the band, when they all broke off, right and left, stealing more like snakes than bipeds to the fences, under cover of which they glanced forward to the wood, in which every man of them buried himself, in the twinkling of an eye In vain had the interpreter called to

them, to remind them where they were, and to tell them
that they might displease their Great Father, at Washington;
and Prairiefire stood his ground, exposed to any shot the
supposed foe might send at him; on they went, like so many
hounds that have struck a scent too strong to be held in restraint by any whipper-in.

. " They expect to find Injins," said the interpreter, in a
sort of despair, " and there's no holdin' 'em back. There
can be no enemies of their'n down here-a-way, and the agent
will be awfully angry if blood is drawn; though I shouldn't
mind it a bit if the party was some of them scoundrels, the
Sauks and Foxes, whom it's often a marcy to kill. It's
different down here, however, and I must say I wish this
nadn't happened."

My uncle and myself just waited long enough to hear
this, when we rushed forward, along the highway, and entered the wood, joined by Prairiefire, who, fancying by our
movement that all was right, now raised such a whoop himself as to demonstrate it was not for want of ' knowing how'
that he had hitherto been silent. The road made a curve
at the very point where it penetrated the forest, and being
fringed with the bushes already mentioned, the two circumstances shut out the view of what was passing behind the
scenes, until we reached the turn, where a common halt of
the wagons had been made, when the whole view burst
upon us at once in all its magnificence.

A rout of a ' grand army' could scarcely have been more
picturesque! The road was lined with vehicles, in full
retreat, to use a military term, or, to speak in the more
common parlance, scampering off. Every whip was in
active use, every horse was on the run, whilst half the
faces were turned behind their owners, the women sending
back screams to the whoops of the savages. As for the
Injins, they had instinctively abandoned the woods, and
poured down into the highway, speed like theirs demanding
open ground for its finest display. Some had leaped into
wagons, piling themselves up among those virtuous wives
and daughters of that portion of the honest yeomanry who
had collected to devise the means of cheating me out of my
property. But, why dwell on this scene, since the exploits
of these Injins, for the last six years, have amply proved

that the only .thing in which they excel, is in running away.
They are heroes when a dozen can get round a single man
to tar and feather him ; valiant as a hundred against five or
six, and occasionally murderers, when each victim can be
destroyed by five or six bullets, to make sure of him. The
very cowardice of the scoundrels should render them loath-
some to the whole community ; the dog that has spirit only
to hunt in packs being cur at the bottom.

, I must add one other object to the view, however. Holmes
and Shabbakuk brought up the rear, and both were flogging
their devoted beast as if his employers—I dare not call them
masters,' as I might be accused of aristocracy for using so
offensive a term in this age of common-sense liberty, while
' employers' is a very significant expression for the particular occasion—as if his ' employers,' then, had left something behind them, at ' Little Neest,' and were hurrying
back to obtain it before it fell into other hands. Old Holmes
kept looking behind, as if chased by the covenants of forty
leases, while the " Spirit of the Institutions," headed by two
governors, and " the honourable gentleman from Albany,"
was in full pursuit. If the " Spirit of the Institutions" was
really there, it was quite alone ; for I looked in vain for the
exhibition of any other spirit. In much less time than it has
taken me to write this account, the road was cleared, leaving
my uncle, myself, and Prairiefire, in quiet possession ; the
latter uttering a very significant " hugh !" as the last wagon
went out of sight in a cloud of dust..   .

It was but a moment, however, before our own tribe, or
tribes would be more accurate, came down upon us, collecting in the road at the very spot where we stood. The victory had been bloodless, but it was complete. Not only had
the savage Indians completely routed the virtuous and much-
oppressed-by-aristocracy Injins, but they had captured two
specimens of virtue and depression in the persons of as
many of the band. So very significant and expressive was
the manner of the captives, that Flintyheart, into whose
hands they had fallen, not only seemed to hold their scalps
in contempt, but actually had disdained to disarm them
There they stood, bundles of calico, resembling children in
swaddling-clothes, with nothing partaking of that natural
freedom of which their party love to boast, but their legs,

which were left at perfect liberty, by way of a *dernier re-sort*. My uncle now assumed a little authority, and com-manded these fellows to take off their disguises. He might as well have ordered one of the oaks, or maples, to lay down its leaves before the season came round ; for neither would obey.

The interpreter, however, whose name was Manytongues, rendered into English from the Indian dialects, was a man of surprisingly few words, considering his calling, on an occasion like this. Walking up to one of the prisoners, he first disarmed him, and then removed his calico hood, ex-posing the discomfited countenance of Brigham, Tom Mil-ler's envious labourer. The " hughs !" that escaped the Indians were very expressive, on finding that not only did a pale-face countenance appear from beneath the covering, but one that might be said to be somewhat paler than com-mon. Manytongues had a good deal of frontier waggery about him, and, by this time he began to comprehend how the land lay. Passing his hand over Josh's head, he coolly remarked—

" That scalp would be thought more of, in Iowa, than it 's ra-ally worth, I 'm thinking, if truth was said. But let us see who we have here."

Suiting the action to the words, as it is termed, the inter-preter laid hold of the hood of the other captive, but did not succeed in removing it without a sharp struggle. He effected his purpose, assisted by two of the younger chiefs, who stepped forward to aid him. I anticipated the result, for I had early recognised the goar ; but great was the surprise of my uncle when he saw Seneca Newcome's well-known face developed by the change !

Seneca—or, it might be better now to use his own favour-ite orthoepy, and call him Sene*ky*, at once, for he had a particularly sneaking look as he emerged from under the calico, and this would be suiting the sound to appearances—Seneky, then, was in a " mingled tumult," as it is called, of rage and shame. The first predominated, however, and, as is only too common in cases of military disasters, instead of attributing his capture to circumstances, the prowess of his enemies, or any fault of his own, he sought to mitigate his own disgrace by heaping disgrace on his comrade. Indeed,

he manner in which these men went at each other, as
soon as unsacked, reminded me of two game cocks that are
let out of their bags within three feet of each other, with this
exception — neither crowed.

"This is all your fault, you cowardly dog," said Seneky,
almost fiercely, for shame had filled his face with blood.
"Had you kept on your feet, and not run me down, in your
haste to get off, I might have retreated, and got clear with
the rest of them."

This assault was too much for Joshua, who gained spirit
to answer by its rudeness and violence, not to say injus
tice; for, as we afterwards ascertained, Newcome had actu
ally fallen in his eagerness to retreat; and Brigham, so far
from being the cause of his coming down, had only prevented his getting up, by falling on top of him. In this
prostrate condition they had further fallen into the hands of
their enemies.

"I want nothin' from you, 'Squire Newcome," answered
Joshua, quite decidedly as to tone and manner; "*your* character is well known, all up and down the country."

"What of my character? — What have *you* got to say
ag'in' me or my character?" demanded the attorney at law,
in a tone of high defiance. "I want to see the man who
can say anything ag'in' my character."

This was pretty well, considering that the fellow had actually been detected in the commission of a felony; though
I suppose that difficulty would have been gotten over, in a
moral sense, by the claim of being taken while struggling
in defence of human rights, and the "spirit of the institutions." The defiance was too much for Brigham's patience,
and being fully assured, by this time, that he was not in
much danger of being scalped, he turned upon Seneca, and
cried, with something more than spirit, with downright ran-
cour—

"You're a pretty fri'nd of the poor man, and of the
people, if truth must be said, an't you? Everybody in the
county that's in want of money knows what *you* be, you
d——d shaver."

As the last words came out, Seneky's fist went in upon
Brigham's nose, causing the blood to flow freely. My uncle

Ro now thought it time to interfere, and he rebuked the irritated lawyer with dignity.

" Why did he call me a d——d shaver, then ?" retorted Seneky, still angry and red. " I'll stand *that* from no man."

- " Why, what harm can there be in such a charge, Mr. Newcome ? You are a member of the bar, and ought to understand the laws of your country, and cannot stand in need of being told that it has been decided by the highest tribunal of your State that it is no reproach to be called a shaver! Some of the honourable members of that learned body, indeed, seem to think, on the contrary, that it is matter of commendation and congratulation. I am ashamed of you, Mr. Newcome—I'm quite ashamed of you."

Seneky muttered something, in which I fancied I understood the words " the Court of Errors be d——d," or " the Court of Errors" might go to some very bad place, which I will not name; but I will not take on myself that any man of decency could really use such irreverent language about a body so truly eminent, though a person in a passion is sometimes disposed to forget propriety. My uncle now thought it time to put an end to this scene; and, without deigning to enter into any explanations, he signified to Many-tongues his readiness to lead his chiefs to the point where they desired to go.

" As to these two Injins," he added, " their capture will do us no honour ; and now we know who they are, they can be taken at any time by the deputy sheriffs or constables. It is hardly worth while to encumber your march with such fellows."

The chiefs assented to this proposal, too, and we quitted the woods in a body, leaving Seneky and Joshua on the ground. As we subsequently learned, our backs were no sooner turned, than the last pitched into the first, and pounded him not only until he owned he was " a shaver," but that he was " a d——d shaver" in the bargain. Such was the man, and such the class, that the deluded anti-renters of New York wish to substitute, in a social sense, for the ancient landlords of the country! A pretty top-sheaf they would make to the stack of the community, and admirably would the grain be kept that was protected by their covering! One would like to see fellows of this moral calibre interpreting *their* covenants; and it would be a useful, though a painful lesson, to see the change effected for a twelvemonth, in order to ascertain, after things had got back into the old natural channel, how many would *then* wish to " return, like the dog to his vomit, or the sow to her wallowing in the mire."

.. After giving some directions to Manytongues, my uncle and I got into our wagon and drove up the road, leaving the Indians to follow. The rendezvous was at the Nest, whither we had now determined to proceed at once, and assume our proper characters. In passing the rectory we found time to stop and run in, to inquire after the welfare of Mr. and Miss Warren. Great was my joy at learning they had gone on to the Nest, where they were all to dine. This intelligence did not tend to lessen the speed of Miller's horse, or my horse it would be better to say, for I am the real owner of everything on the Nest Farm, and shall probably so remain, unless the " spirit of the Institutions" gets at my property there, as well as in other places. In the course of half an hour we drove on the lawn, and stopped at the door. It will be recollected that the Indians had our wigs, which had been left by my uncle and myself in their hands, as things of no further use to us. Notwithstanding our dresses, the instant we presented ourselves without these instruments of disguise we were recognized, and the cry went through the house and grounds that " Mr. Hugh had come home!" I confess I was touched with some signs of interest and feeling that escaped the domestics, as well as those who belonged out of doors, when they saw me again standing before them in health, if not in good looks. My uncle, too, was welcome; and there were a few minutes during which I forgot all my grounds for vexation, and was truly happy.

Although my grandmother, and sister, and Mary Warren, all knew what the cry of " Mr. Hugh has got home" meant, it brought everybody out upon the piazza. Mr. Warren had related the events of the day, as far as he was acquainted with them; but even those who were in the secret, were surprised at our thus returning unwigged, and in

25

our proper characters. As for myself, I could not but note
the manner in which the four girls came out to meet me.
Martha flew into my embrace, cast her arms around my
neck, kissing me six or eight times without stopping. Then
Miss Colebrooke came next, with Ann Marston leaning on
her arm, both smiling, though greatly surprised, and both
bright, and pretty, and lady-like. They were glad to see
me, and met my salutations frankly and like old friends;
though I could see they did not fancy my dress in the least.
Mary Warren was behind them all, smiling, blushing, and
shy ; but it did not require two looks from me to make certain that *her* welcome was as sincere as that of my older
friends. Mr. Warren was glad to have it in his power to
greet us openly, and to form an acquaintance with those, to
whose return he had now been looking with anxiety and
hope, for three or four years.

A few minutes sufficed for the necessary explanations, a
part of which, indeed, had already been made by those who
were previously in the secret ; when my dear grandmother
and Patt insisted on our going up to our old room, and of
dressing ourselves in attire more suitable to our stations.
A plenty of summer clothes had been left behind us, and
our wardrobes had been examined that morning in anticipation of our soon having need of them ; so that no great time
was necessary to make the change. I was a little fuller
than when I left home, but the clothes being loose, there
was no difficulty in equipping myself. I found a handsome
blue dress coat, that did very well, and vests and pantaloons,
ad libitum. Clothing is so much cheaper in Europe than
at home, that Americans who are well supplied, do not often
carry much with them when they go abroad ; and this had
been a rule with my uncle all his life. Each of us, moreover, habitually kept a supply of country attire at the Nest,
which we did not think of removing. In consequence of
these little domestic circumstances, as has been said, there
was no want of the means of putting my uncle and myself
on a level with others of our class, as respects outward appearance, in that retired part of the country, at least.

The apartments of my uncle and myself were quite near
each other, in the north wing of the house ; as that which
looked in the direction of a part of the meadows under the

cliff, the wooded ravine, and the wigwam, or cabin, of the
" Upright Onondago." The last was very plainly in view,
from the window of my dressing-room ; and I was standing
at the latter, contemplating the figures of the two old fellows,
as they sat basking in the sun, as was their practice of an
afternoon, when a tap at the door proved to be the announcement of the entrance of John.

" Well, John, my good fellow," I said, laughingly ; " I
find a wig makes a great difference with your means of recognizing an old friend. I must thank you, nevertheless,
for the good treatment you gave me in my character of a
music-grinder."

" I am sure, Mr. Hugh, you are heartily welcome to my
services, come as you may to ask them. It was a most
surprisingest deception, sir, as I shall ever hadmit ; but I
thought the whole time you wasn't exactly what you seemed
to be, as I told Kitty as soon as I went down stairs : ' Kitty,'
says I, ' them two pedlars is just the two genteelest pedlars
as hever I see in this country, and I shouldn't wonder if
they had known better days.' But, now you have been to
see the hanti-renters with your own eyes, Mr. Hugh, what
do you think of them, if I may be so bold as to ask tho
question ?" -

" Very much as I thought, before I had been to see them.
They are a set of fellows who are canting about liberty, at
the very moment when they are doing all they can to discredit its laws, and who mistake selfishness for patriotism ;
just as their backers in the State government are doing, by
using the same cant, when their object is nothing but votes.
If no tenant had a vote, this question would never have
been raised, or dreamt of—but I see those two old fellows,
Jaaf and Sus, seem to enjoy themselves still."

" Indeed they do, sir, in the most surprisingest manner !
They was both antiquities, as we says in Hengland, when
I came to this country, sir — and that was before you was
born, Mr. Hugh — an age agone. But there they sits, sir,
day in and day out, looking like monumentals of past
times. The nigger"— John had been long enough in tho
country to catch the vernacular—" The nigger grows uglier
and uglier every year, and that is most of a change I can
see in him ; while I do think, sir, that the Indian grows

'andsomer 'and 'andsomer. ⸗ He 's the 'andsomest old gentleman, sir, as I knows of, far and near !"

"Old *gentleman !*"   What an expressive term that was,
in this case !   No human being would ever think of calling
Jaaf an " old gentleman," even in these " aristocratic"·days,
when " gentlemen" are plentier than blackberries ; while
any one might feel disposed thus to describe Susquesus.
The Onondago *was* a gentleman, in the best meaning of the
word ; though he may, and certainly did, want a great
deal in the way of mere conventional usages.   As for John,
he never would have used the word to me, except in a case
in which he felt the party had a claim to the appellation.

" Susquesus · is a magnificent sight, with his grey or
white head, fiery eyes, composed features, and impressive
air," I answered ; " and Jaaf is no beauty.   How do the
old men get on together ?"

· " Why, sir, they quarrel a good deal—that is, the nigger
quarrels ; though the Indian is too much above him to mind
what he says.   Nor will I say that Yop actually quarrels,
sir, for he has the greatest possible regard for his friend ;
but he aggravates in the most surprisingest manner — just
like a nigger, howsever, I do suppose."

" They have wanted for nothing, I trust, during my absence.   Their table and other comforts have been seen to
carefully, I hope ?"

" No fear of that, sir, so long as Mrs. Littlepage lives !
She has the affection of a child for the old men, and has
everything provided for them that they can possibly want.
Betty Smith, sir—you remember Betty, the widow of the old
coachman, that died when you was at college, sir — well,
Betty has done nothing, these four years, but look after
them two old men.   She keeps everything tidy in their
hut, and washes it out twice a week, and washes their
clothes for them, and darns, and sews, and cooks, and
looks after all their comforts.   She lives hard by, in the
other cottage, sir, and has everything handy."

" I am glad of that.   Does either of the old men ever
stray over as far as the Nest House now, John ?"   Before
I went abroad, we had a visit from each, daily."

" That custom has fallen away a little, sir ; though the
nigger comes much the oftenest.   He is sure to be here

once or twice a week, in good weather. Then he walks
into the kitchen, where he will sit sometimes for a whole
morning, telling the hardest stories, sir — ha, ha, ha! — yes,
sir, just the hardest stories one ever heard!"

"Why what can he have to say of that nature, that it
seems to amuse you so?"

"According to his notion, sir, everything in the country
is falling away, and is inferior like to what it may have
been in his young days. The turkeys arn't so large, sir;
and the fowls is poorer, sir; and the mutton isn't so fat,
sir; and sich sort of enormities."

Here John laughed very heartily, though it was plain
enough he did not much fancy the comparisons.

"And Susquesus," I said, "he does not share in his
friend's criticisms?"

"Sus never enters the kitchen, sir, at all. He knows that
all the quality and upper class come to the great door of the
house, and is too much of a gentleman to come in at any
other entrance. No, sir, I never saw Sus in the kitchen or
hoffices, at all; nor does Mrs. Littlepage 'ave his table set
anywhere but in the hupper rooms, or on the piazza, when
she wishes to treat him to anything nice. The old gentleman has what he calls his traditions, sir, and can tell a great
many stories of old times; but they ar'n't about turkeys, and
'orses, and garden-stuff, and such things as Yop dwells on
so much, and so uncomfortably."

I now dismissed John, after again thanking him for his
civilities to one of my late appearance, and joined my uncle.
When we entered the little drawing-room, where the whole
party was waiting to meet us, previously to going to the
table, a common exclamation of pleasure escaped them all.
Martha again kissed me, declaring I was now Hugh; that
I looked as she had expected to see Hugh; that she would
now know me for Hugh, and many other similar things;
while my dear grandmother stood and parted my hair, and
gazed into my face with tears in her eyes, for I reminded
her of her first-born, who had died so young! As for the
other ladies, the two heiress-wards of Uncle Ro seemed
smiling and friendly, and willing to renew our ancient amicable relations; but Mary Warren still kept herself in the
25*

back-ground, though I thought by her modest and half
averted eye, and flushed cheeks, that she sympathized as
deeply in her friend Patt's present happiness as any of the
others ; possibly more deeply. .

Before we went to the table I sent a servant to the top of
the house, with orders to look down the road, in order to
ascertain when my red friends might be expected. -This
man reported that they were advancing along the highway,
and would probably reach the door in the course of half an
hour. They had stopped ; and he thought that he could
perceive, by means of his glass, that they were painting their
faces, and otherwise arranging their toilets, in preparation
for the anticipated interview. On receiving this information
we took our seats at table, expecting to be ready to receive
the chiefs, as soon as they should arrive.

Ours was a happy dinner. For the moment, the condi
tion of the country and the schemes of my tenants were for
gotten, and we chatted of those nearer interests and feelings
that naturally presented themselves to our minds at such a
time. At length dear grandmother pleasantly remarked—

· " You must have an instinct for the discovery of discretion, Hugh, for no one could have made a better choice of
a confidant than you did, while going to the village, this
morning."   ,

Mary blushed like an Italian sky at eventide, and looked
down, to conceal her confusion.

" I do not know whether it was discretion or vanity,
grandmother," was my answer, " for I am conscious of
feeling an unconquerable reluctance to passing for a com
mon music-grinder in Miss Warren's eyes."

" Nay, Hugh," put in the saucy Patt, " I had told you
before that you passed for a very uncommon music-grinder
in her eyes. As for the grinding, she said but little ; for it
was of the flute, and of the manner in which it was played,
that Miss Warren spoke the most eloquently."

The ". Martha !" of Mary Warren, lowly, but half-re-
proachfully uttered, showed that the charming girl was beginning to be really distressed, and my observant parent
changed the discourse by a gentle and adroit expedient
such as a woman alone knows, thoroughly how to put in

practice. It was simply handing Mr. Warren a plate of greengages; but the act was so performed as to change the discourse.

During the whole of that meal I felt certain there was a secret, mysterious communication between me and Mary Warren, which, while it probably did escape the notice of others, was perfectly evident to ourselves. This fact I *felt* to be true; while there was a consciousness betrayed in Mary's blushes, and even in her averted eyes, that I found extremely eloquent on the same subject.

CHAPTER XIX.

" With look, like patient Job's, eschewing evil;
. With motions graceful as a bird's in air;
Thou art, in sober truth, the veriest devil
That e'er clinched fingers in a captive's hair."

Red Jacket.

ALTHOUGH an immense progress has been made in liberating this country from the domination of England, in the way of opinion and usages, a good deal remains to be done yet. Still, he who can look back forty years, must see the great changes that have occurred in very many things; and it is to be hoped that he who lives forty years hence, will find very few remaining that have no better reasons for their existence among ourselves than the example of a people so remote, with a different climate, different social organization, and different wants. I am for no more condemning a usage, however, simply because it is English, than I am for approving it, simply because it is English. I wish everything to stand on its own merits, and feel certain that no nation ever can become great, in the higher signification of the term, until it ceases to imitate, because it is imitation of a certain fixed model. One of the very greatest evils of this imitative spirit is even now developing itself in what is called the " progress" of the country, which is assailing principles that are as old as the existence of man, and which may almost be said to be eternal as social truths, at the very moment that notions derived from our ancestors are submitted to in the highest places, the Senate of the United States for example, that are founded in facts which not only have no existence among ourselves, but which are positively antagonist to such as have. So much easier is it to join in the hurrah! of a " progress," than to ascertain whether it is making in the right direction, or whether it be progress at all. But, to return from things of moment to those of less concern.

Among other customs to be condemned that we have derived from England, is the practice of the men sitting at table after the women have left it. Much as I may wish to see this every-way offensive custom done away with, and the more polished and humanizing usage of all the rest of christendom adopted in its stead, I should feel ashamed at finding, as I make no doubt I should find it, that our custom would be abandoned within a twelvemonth after it might be understood it was abandoned in England. My uncle had long endeavoured to introduce into our own immediate circle the practice of retaining the ladies at table for a reasonable time, and of then quitting it with them at the expiration of that time ; but it is hard to ' kick against the pricks.' Men who fancy it ' society' to meet at each other's houses to drink wine, and taste wine, and talk about wine, and to outdo each other in giving their guests the most costly wines, are not to be diverted easily from their objects. The hard-drinking days are past, but the hard ' talking days' are in their vigour. If it could be understood, generally, that even in England it is deemed vulgar to descant on the liquor that is put upon the table, perhaps we might get rid of the practice too. Vulgar in England! It is even deemed vulgar here, by the right sort, as I am ready to maintain, and indeed know of my own observation. That one or two friends who are participating in the benefits of some particularly benevolent bottle, should say a word in commendation of its merits, is natural enough, and well enough ; no one can reasonably find any fault with such a sign of grateful feeling ; but I know of nothing more revolt-

ing than to see twenty grave faces arrayed round a table,
employed as so many tasters at a Rhenish wine sale, while
the cheeks of their host look like those of Boreas, owing to
the process of sucking syphons.

When my dear grandmother rose, imitated by the four
bright-faced girls, who did as she set the example, and
said, as was customary with the old school, "Well; gen
tlemen, I leave you to your wine; but you will recollect
that you will be most welcome guests in the drawing-
room," my uncle caught her hand, and insisted she
should not quit us. There was something exceedingly
touching, to my eyes, in the sort of intercourse, and in the
affection which existed between my uncle Ro and his mother.
A bachelor himself, while she was a widow, they were particularly fond of each other; and many is the time that I
have seen him go up to her, when we were alone, and pat
her cheeks, and then kiss them, as one might do so to a
much-beloved sister. My grandmother always received
these little liberties with perfect good-humour, and with evident affection. In her turn, I have frequently known her to
approach 'Roger,' as she always called him, and kiss his
bald head, in a way that denoted she vividly remembered
the time when he was an infant in her arms. On this occasion she yielded to his request, and resumed her seat, the
girls imitating her, nothing loth, as they had done in rising.
The conversation then, naturally enough, reverted to the
state of the country.

"It has much surprised me, that the men in authority
among us have confined all their remarks and statements to
the facts of the Rensselaer and Livingston estates," observed
my grandmother, "when there are difficulties existing in
so many others."

"The explanation is very simple, my good mother,"
answered uncle Ro. "The Rensselaer estates have the
quarter-sales, and chickens, and days' works; and there is
much of the *ad captandum* argument about such things, that
does very well to work up for political effect; whereas, on
the other estates, these great auxiliaries must be laid aside.
It is just as certain, as it is that the sun has risen this day,
that an extensive and concerted plan exists to transfer the
freehold rights of the landlords, on nearly every property

in the State, to the tenants; and that, too, on conditions unjustly favourable to the last; but you will find nothing of the sort in the messages of governors, or speeches of legislators, who seem to think all is said, when they have dwelt on the expediency of appeasing the complaints of the tenants, as a high political duty, without stopping to inquire whether those complaints are founded in right or not. The injury that will be done to the republic, by showing men how much can be effected by clamour, is of itself incalculable. It would take a generation to do away the evil consequences of the example, were the anti-rent combination to be utterly defeated to-morrow."

" I find that the general argument against the landlords is a want of title, in those cases in which nothing better can be found," observed Mr. Warren. " The lecturer, to-day, seemed to condemn any title that was derived from the king, as defeated by the conquest over that monarch, by the war of the revolution."

" A most charming consummation that would have been for the heroic deeds of the Littlepages! There were my father, grandfather, and great-grandfather, all in arms, in that war; the two first as general officers, and the last as a major; and the result of all their hardships and dangers is to be to rob themselves of their own property! I am aware that this silly pretence has been urged, even in a court of justice; but folly, and wrong, and madness, are not yet quite ripe enough among us, to carry such a doctrine down. As ' coming events cast their shadows before,' it is possible we are to take this very movement, however, as the dawn of the approaching day of American reason, and not as a twilight left by the departed rays of a sun of a period of mental darkness."

" You surely do not apprehend, uncle Ro, that these people can really get Hugh's lands away from him !" exclaimed Patt, reddening with anxiety and anger.

" No one can say, my dear; for, certainly, no one is safe when opinions and acts, like those which have been circulated and attempted among us of late years, can be acted on without awakening very general indignation. Look to the moneyed classes at this very moment, agonized and excited on the subject of a war about Oregon—a thing very ittle likely to occur, though certainly possible; while they manifest the utmost indifference to this anti-rentism, though the positive existence of everything connected with just social organization is directly involved in its fate. One is a bare possibility, but it convulses the class I have named; while the other is connected with the existence of civilized society itself; yet it has ceased to attract attention, and is nearly forgotten! Every man in the community, whose means raise him at all above the common level, has a direct interest in facing this danger, and in endeavouring to put it down; but scarcely any one appears to be conscious of the importance of the crisis. We have only one or two more steps to make, in order to become like Turkey; a country in which the wealthy are obliged to conceal their means, in order to protect it from the grasp of the government; but no one seems to care at all about it!"

"Some recent travellers among us have said that we have nearly reached that pass already, as our rich affect great simplicity and plainness in public, while they fill their houses in private with all the usual evidences of wealth and luxury. I think de Tocqueville, among others, makes that remark."

"Ay, that is merely one of the ordinarily sagacious remarks of the European, who, by not understanding the American history, confounds causes and makes mistakes. The plainness of things in public is no more than an ancient habit of the country, while the elegance and luxury in private are a very simple and natural consequence of the tastes of women who live in a state of society in which they are limited to the very minimum of refined habits and intellectual pleasures. The writer who made this mistake is a very clever man, and has exceeding merit, considering his means of ascertaining truth; but he has made very many similar blunders."

"Nevertheless, Mr. Littlepage," resumed the rector, who was a gentleman, in all the senses of the word, and knew the world, and the best part of it, too, even while he had preserved an admirable simplicity of character, "changes *have* certainly taken place among us, of the nature alluded to by M. de Tocqueville."

"That is quite true, sir; but they have also taken place elsewhere. When I was a boy, I can well remember to have seen coaches-and-six in this country, and almost every

man of fortune drove his coach-and-four; whereas, now
such a thing is of the rarest occurrence possible. But the
same is true all over christendom; for when I first went to
Europe, coaches-and-six, with outriders, and all that sort of
state, was an every-day thing; whereas it is now never, or
at least very seldom, seen. Improved roads, steam-boats,
and railroads, can produce such changes, without having
recourse to the oppression of the masses."

"I am sure," put in Patt, laughing, "if publicity be what
Mons. de Tocqueville requires, there is publicity enough in
New York! All the new-fashioned houses are so constructed, with their low balconies and lower windows, that anybody can see in at their windows. If what I have read and
heard of a Paris house be true, standing between *cour et
jardin*, there is infinitely more of privacy there than here;
and one might just as well say that the Parisians bury themselves behind *porte cochères*, and among trees, to escape the
attacks of the Faubourg St. Antoine, as to say we retreat
into our houses to be fine, lest the mobocracy would not
tolerate us."

"The girl has profited by your letters, I see, Hugh," said
my uncle, nodding his head in approbation; "and what is
more, she makes a suitable application of her tuition, or
rather, of yours. No, no, all that is a mistake; and, as
Martha says, no houses are so much in the street as those
of the new style in our own towns. It would be far more
just to say that, instead of retiring within doors to be fine,
as Patt calls it, unseen by envious neighbours, the Manhattanese, in particular, turn their dwellings wrong side out,
lest their neighbours should take offence at not being permitted to see all that is going on within. But, neither is
true. The house is the more showy because it is most under
woman's control; and it would be just as near the truth to
say that the reason why the American men appear abroad
in plain blue, and black, and brown clothes, while their
wives and daughters are at home in silks and satins — ay,
even in modern brocades—is an apprehension of the masses,
as to ascribe the plainness of street life, compared to that
within doors, to the same cause. There is a good deal of
difference between a *salon* in the Faubourg, or the Chaussée
d'Autin, and even on the Boulevard des Italiens. But, John

is craning with his neck, out there on the piazza, as if our red brethren were at hand."

So it was, in point of fact, and everybody now rose from table, without ceremony, and went forth to meet our guests. We had barely time to reach the lawn, the ladies having run for their hats in the meantime, before Prairiefire, Flintyheart, Manytongues, and all the rest of them, came up, on the sort of half trot that distinguishes an Indian's march.

Notwithstanding the change in our dresses, my uncle and myself were instantly recognised, and courteously saluted by the principal chiefs. Then our wigs were gravely offered to us, by two of the younger men; but we declined receiving them, begging the gentlemen who had them in keeping, to do us the honour to accept them, as tokens of our particular regard. This was done with great good will, and with a pleasure that was much too obvious to be concealed. Half an hour later, I observed that each of the young forest dandies had a wig on his otherwise naked head, with a peacock's feather stuck quite knowingly in the lank hair. The effect was somewhat ludicrous; particularly on the young ladies; but I saw that each of the warriors himself looked round, as if to ask for the admiration that he felt his appearance ought to awaken!

No sooner were the salutations exchanged, than the redmen began to examine the house—the cliff on which it stood —the meadows beneath, and the surrounding ground. At first, we supposed, that they were struck with the extent and solidity of the buildings, together with a certain air of finish and neatness, that is not everywhere seen in America, even in the vicinity of its better-class houses; but Manytongues soon undeceived us. My uncle asked him, why all the redmen had broken off, and scattered themselves around the buildings, some looking here, others pointing there, and all manifestly earnest and much engaged with something; though it was not easy to understand what that something was; intimating his supposition that they might be struck with the buildings.

"Lord bless ye, no sir," answered the interpreter; "they don't care a straw about the house, or any house. There's Flintyheart, in particular; he's a chief that you can no more move with riches, and large housen, and sich like matters,

26

.han·you can make the Mississippi run up stream. When
we went to Uncle Sam's house, at Washington, he scarce
condescended to look at it; and the Capitol had no more effect on any on 'em, than if it had been a better sort of wigwam; not so much, for that matter, as Injins be curious in
wigwams. What's put 'em up, on a trail like, just now, is
he knowledge that this is the spot where a battle was fit,
something like ninety seasons ago, in which the Upright
Onondago was consarned, as well as some of their own people on t'other side—that's what's put 'em in commotion."

"And·why does Flintyheart talk to those around him
with so much energy; and point to the flats, and the cliff,
and the ravine yonder, that lies beyond the wigwam of
Susquesus?"

"Ah! Is that, then, the wigwam of the Upright Onondago!" exclaimed the interpreter, betraying some such interest as one might, manifest on unexpectedly being told that
he saw Mount Vernon or Monticello, for the first time in his
life. "Well, it's something to have seen. *that;* though it
will be more to see the man himself; for all the tribes on the
upper prairies, are full of his story and his behaviour. No
Injin, since the time of Tamenund himself, has made as
much talk, of late years, as Susquesus, the Upright Onondago, unless it might be Tecumthe, perhaps. But, what oc-
cupies Flintyheart, just at this moment, is an account of the
battle, in which his father's grandfather lost his life, though
he did not lose his scalp. That disgrace he is now telling
on 'em, he escaped, and glad enough is his descendant, that
it was so. It's no great matter to an Injin to be killed; but
he'd rather escape losing his scalp, or being struck at all by
the inimy, if it can possibly be made to turn out so. Now
he's talking of some young pale-face that was killed, whom
he calls Lover of Fun—and, now he's got on some nigger,
who he says fit like a devil." ·

"All these persons are known to us, by *our* traditions,
also!" exclaimed my uncle, with more interest than I had
known him manifest for many a day. "But I'm amazed to
find that the Indians retain so accurate an account of such
small matters, for so long a time."

"It isn't a small matter to them. Their battles is seldom
on a very great scale, and they make great account of any

skrimmage in which noted warriors have fallen." Here Manytongues paused for a minute, and listened attentively to the discourse of the chiefs; after which he resumed his explanations. "They have met with a great difficulty in the house," he continued, "while everything else is right. They understand the cliff of rocks, the position of the buildings themselves, that ravine thereaway, and all the rest of the things hereabouts, except the house."

"What may be the difficulty with the house? Does it not stand in the place it ought to occupy?".

"That's just their difficulty. It *does* stand where it ought to stand, but it isn't the right sort of house, though they say the shape agrees well enough — one side out to the fields, like; two sides running back to the cliff, and the cliff itself for the other. But their traditions say that their warriors indivour'd to burn out your forefathers, and that they built a fire again' the side of the buildin', which they never would have done had it been built of stone, as this house is built. *That's* what partic'larly puzzles them."

"Then their traditions are surprisingly minute and accurate! The house which then stood on, or near this spot, and which did resemble the present building in the ground plan, *was* of squared logs, and might have been set on fire, and an attempt was actually made to do so, but was successfully resisted. Your chiefs have had a true account; but changes have been made here. The house of logs stood near fifty years, when it was replaced by this dwelling, which was originally erected about sixty years ago, and has been added to since, on the old design. No, no — the traditions are surprisingly accurate.".

This gave the Indians great satisfaction, as soon as the fact was communicated to them; and from that instant all their doubts and uncertainty were ended. Their own knowledge of the progress of things in a settlement, gave them the means of comprehending any other changes; though the shape of this building having so nearly corresponded with that of which their traditions spoke, they had become embarrassed by the difference in the material. While they were still continuing their examinations, and ascertaining localities to their own satisfaction, my uncle and myself continued the discourse with Manytongues.

"I am curious to know," said my uncle, "what may be he history of Susquesus, that a party of chiefs like those should travel so far out of their way, to pay him the homage of a visit. Is his great age the cause?"

"That is one reason, sartainly; though there is another, that is of more account, but which is known only to themselves. I have often tried to get the history out of them, but never could succeed. As long as I can remember, the Onondagoes, and Tuscaroras, and the Injins of the old New York tribes, that have found their way up to the prairies, have talked of the Upright Onondago, who must have been an old man when I was born. Of late years, they have talked more and more of him; and so good an opportunity offering to come and see him, there would have been great disappointment out West, had it been neglected. His age is, no doubt, one principal cause; but there is another, though I have never been able to discover what it is."

"This Indian has been in communication, and connected with my immediate family, now near, if not quite ninety years. He was with my grandfather, Cornelius Littlepage, in the attack on Ty, that was made by Abercrombie, in 1758; and here we are within twelve or thirteen years of a century from that event. I believe my great-grandfather, Herman Mordaunt, had even some previous knowledge of him. As long as I can remember, he has been a grey-headed old man; and we suppose both he and the negro who lives with him, to have seen fully a hundred and twenty years, if not more."

"Something of importance happened to Susquesus, or the Trackless, as he was then called, about ninety-three winters ago; that much I've gathered from what has fallen from the chiefs at different times; but, what that something was, it has exceeded my means to discover. At any rate, it has quite as much to do with this visit as the Withered Hemlock's great age. Injins respect years; and they respect wisdom highly; but they respect courage and justice most of-all. The tarm 'Upright' has its meaning, depend on't."

We were greatly interested by all this, as indeed were my grandmother and her sweet companions. Mary Warren, in particular, manifested a lively interest in Susquesus' history, as was betrayed in a brief dialogue I now had with her, walking to and fro in front of the piazza, while the rest of the party were curiously watching the movements of the still excited savages.

"My father and I have often visited the two old men, and have been deeply interested in them," observed this intelligent, yet simple-minded girl, — "with the Indian, in particular, we have felt a strong sympathy, for nothing is plainer than the keenness with which he still feels on the subject of his own people. We have been told that he is often visited by red-men—or, at least, as often as any come near him; and they are said ever to exhibit a great reverence for his years, and respect for his character."

"This I know to be true, for I have frequently seen those who have come to pay him visits. But they have usually been merely your basket-making, half-and-half sort of savages, who have possessed the characteristics of neither race, entirely. This is the first instance in which I have heard of so marked a demonstration of respect—how is that, dear grandmother? can you recall any other instance of Susquesus's receiving such a decided mark of homage from his own people as this?"

"This is the third within my recollection, Hugh. Shortly after my marriage, which was not long after the revolution, as you may know, there was a party here on a visit to Susquesus. It remained ten days. The chiefs it contained were said to be Onondagoes altogether, or warriors of his own particular people; and something like a misunderstanding was reported to have been made up; though what it was, I confess I was too thoughtless then to inquire. Both my father-in-law, and my uncle Chainbearer, it was always believed, knew the whole of the Trackless' story, though neither ever related it to me. I do not believe your grandfather knew it," added the venerable speaker, with a sort of tender regret; "or I think I should have heard it. But that first visit was soon after Susquesus and Jaaf took possession of their house, and it was reported, at the time, that the strangers remained so long, in the hope of inducing Sus to rejoin his tribe. If such was their wish, however, it failed; for there he is now, and there he has ever been since he first went to the hut."

26*

"And the second visit, grandmother — you mentioned
that there were three."

"Oh! tell us of them all, Mrs. Littlepage," added Mary
earnestly, blushing up to the eyes the moment after at her
own eagerness. My dear grandmother smiled benevo-
lently on both, and I thought she looked a little archly at
us, as old ladies sometimes will, when the images of their
own youth recur to their minds.

"You appear to have a common sympathy in these red-
men, my children," she answered, Mary fairly blushing
scarlet at hearing herself thus coupled with me in the term
' children,'—" and I have great pleasure in gratifying your
curiosity. The second great visit that Susquesus received
from Indians occurred the very year you were born, Hugh,
and then we really felt afraid we might lose the old man ;
so earnest were his own people in their entreaties that he
would go away with them. But he would not. Here he
has remained ever since, and a few weeks ago he told me
that here he should die. If these Indians hope to prevail
any better, I am sure they will be disappointed."

"So he told my father, also," added Mary Warren, "who
has often spoken to him of death, and has hoped to open
his eyes to the truths of the gospel."

"With what success, Miss Warren? That is a consummation which would terminate the old man's career most
worthily."

"With little, I fear," answered the charming girl, in a
low, melancholy tone. "At least, I know that my father
has been disappointed. Sus listens to him attentively, but
he manifests no feeling beyond respect for the speaker. Attempts have been made to induce him to enter the church
before, but——"

"You were about to add something, Miss Warren, which
still remains to be said."

"I can add it for her," resumed my grandmother, "for
certain I am that Mary Warren will never add it herself.
The fact is, as you must know, Hugh, from your own obser
vation, that Mr. Warren's predecessor was an unfaithful and
selfish servant of the church—one who did little good to
any, not even himself. In this country it takes a good deal

in a clergyman, to wear out the patience of a people; but it can be done; and when they once get to look at him through the same medium as that with which other men are viewed, a reaction follows, under which he is certain to suffer. We could all wish to throw a veil over the conduct of the late incumbent of St. Andrew's, but it requires one so much thicker and larger than common, that the task is not easy. Mary has merely meant that better instruction, and a closer attention to duty, might have done more for Trackless twenty years ago, than they can do to-day."

"How much injury, after all, faithless ministers can do to the church of God! One such bad example unsettles more minds than twenty good examples keep steady."

"I do not know that, Hugh; but of one thing I am cer tain—that more evil is done by pretending to struggle for the honour of the church, by attempting to sustain its unworthy ministers, than could be done by at once admitting their offences, in cases that are clear. We all know that the ministers of the altar are but men, and as such are to be expected to fall—certain to do so without Divine aid—but if we cannot make its ministers pure, we ought to do all we can to keep the altar itself from contamination."

"Yes, yes, grandmother—but the day has gone by for *ex officio* religion in the American branch of the church"—here Mary Warren joined the other girls—" at least. And it is so best. Suspicions may be base and unworthy, but a blind credulity is contemptible. If I see a chestnut forming on yonder branch, it would be an act of exceeding folly in me to suppose that the tree was a walnut, though all the nursery-men in the country were ready to swear to it."

My grandmother smiled, but she also walked away, when I joined my uncle again.

"The interpreter tells me, Hugh," said the last, "that the chiefs wish to pay their first visit to the hut this evening. Luckily, the old farm-house is empty just now, since Miller has taken possession of the new one; and I have directed Mr. Manytongues to establish himself there, while he and his party remain here. There is a kitchen, all ready for their use, and it is only to send over a few cooking utensils, that is to say, a pot or two, and fifty bundles of straw, to set them up in housekeeping. For all this I have just given orders, not wishing to disturb you, or possibly unwilling to lay down a guardian's authority; and there is the straw already loading up in yonder barn-yard. In half an hour they may rank themselves among the pot-wollopers of Ravensnest."

"Shall we go with them to the house before, or after they have paid their visit to Susquesus?"

"Before, certainly. John has volunteered to go over and let the Onondago know the honour that is intended him, and to assist him in making his toilet; for the red-man would not like to be taken in undress any more than another. While this is doing, we can instal our guests in their new abode, and see the preparations commenced for their supper. As for the '*Injins*,' there is little to apprehend from them, I fancy, so long as we have a strong party of the real Simon Pures within call."

After this, we invited the interpreter to lead his chiefs towards the dwelling they were to occupy, preceding the party ourselves, and leaving the ladies on the lawn. At that season, the days were at the longest, and it would be pleasanter to pay the visit to the hut in the cool of the evening than to go at an earlier hour. My grandmother ordered her covered wagon before we left her, intending to be present at an interview which everybody felt must be most interesting.

The empty building which was thus appropriated to the use of the Indians was quite a century old, having been erected by my ancestor, Herman Mordaunt, as the original farm-house on his own particular farm. For a long time it had been used in its original character; and when it was found convenient to erect another, in a more eligible spot, and of more convenient form, this old structure had been preserved as a relic, and from year to year its removal had been talked of, but not effected. It remained, therefore, for me to decide on its fate, unless, indeed, the ' spirit of the Institutions' should happen to get hold of it, and take its control out of my hands, along with that of the rest of my property, by way of demonstrating to mankind how thoroughly the great State of New York is imbued with a love of rational liberty!

As we walked towards the " old farm-house," Miller came

from the other building to meet us. He had learned that
his friends, the pedlars, were his—what shall I call myself?
'Master' would be the *legal* term, and it would be good
English; but it would give the "honourable gentleman"
and his friends mortal offence, and I am not now to learn
that there are those among us who deny facts that are as
plain as the noses on their faces, and who fly right into the
face of the law whenever it is convenient: I shall not,
however, call myself a "boss" to please even these eminent
statesmen, and therefore must be content with using a term
that, if the moving spirits of the day can prevail, will soon
be sufficiently close in its signification, and call myself Tom
Miller's———nothing.

It was enough to see that Miller was a good deal embarrassed with the dilemma in which he was placed. For a
great many years he and his family had been in the employment of me and mine, receiving ample pay, as all such men
ever do—when they are so unfortunate as to serve a malignant aristocrat—much higher pay than they would get in
the service of your Newcomes, and Holmeses, and Tubbses,
besides far better treatment in all essentials; and now he had
only to carry out the principles of the anti-renters to claim
the farm he and they had so long worked, as of right. Yes,
the same principles would just as soon give this hireling my
home and farm as it would give any tenant on my estate
that which he worked. It is true, one party received wages,
while the other paid rent; but these facts do not affect the
principle at all; since he who received the wages got no
other benefit from his toil, while he who paid the rent was
master of all the crops—I, beg pardon, the *boss* of all the
crops. The common title of both—if any title at all exist—
is the circumstance that each had expended his labour on a
particular farm, and consequently had a right to own it for
all future time.

Miller made some awkward apologies for not recognising
me, and endeavoured to explain away one or two little things
that he must have felt put him in rather an awkward position, but to which neither my uncle nor myself attached any
moment. We knew that poor Tom was human, and that
the easiest of all transgressions for a man to fall into were
those connected with his self-love; and that the temptation

to a man who has the consciousness of not being anywhere near the summit of the social ladder, is a strong inducement to err when he thinks there is a chance of getting up a round or two; failing of success in which, it requires higher feelings, and perhaps a higher station, than that of Tom Miller's, not to leave him open to a certain demoniacal gratification which so many experience at the prospect of beholding others dragged down to their own level. - We heard Tom's excuses kindly, but did not commit ourselves by promises or declarations of any sort.

CHAPTER XX.

"Two hundred years! two hundred years!
How much of human power and pride,
What glorious hopes, what gloomy fears,
Have sunk beneath their noiseless tide!" -
PIERPONT.

IT wanted about an hour to sunset,—or sun-*down*, to use our common Americanism—when we all left the new quarters of our red brethren, in order to visit the huts. As the moment approached, it was easy to trace in the Indians the evidence of strong interest; mingled, as we fancied, with a little awe. Several of the chiefs had improved the intervening time, to retouch the wild conceits that they had previously painted on their visages, rendering their countenances still more appalling. Flintyheart, in particular, was conspicuous in his grim embellishments; though Prairiefire had not laid any veil between the eye and his natural hue.

As the course of my narrative will now render it necessary to relate conversations that occurred in languages and dialects of which I know literally nothing, it may be well to say here, once for all, that I got as close a translation of everything that passed, as it was possible to obtain, from Manytongues; and wrote it all down, either on the spot, or immediately after returning to the Nest. This explanation may be ne-

cessary in order to prevent some of those who may read
this manuscript, from fancying that I am inventing.

The carriage of my grandmother had left the door, filled
with its smiling freight, several minutes before we took up
our line of march. This last, however, was not done without a little ceremony, and some attention to order. As Indians rarely march except in what is called "Indian file,"
or singly, each man following in the footsteps of his leader,
such was the mode of advancing adopted on the present occasion. The Prairiefire led the line, as the oldest chief, and
the one most distinguished in council. Flintyheart was
second, while the others were arranged by some rule of
precedency that was known to themselves. As soon as the
line had formed, it commenced its march; my uncle, the
interpreter, and myself walking at the side of Prairiefire,
while Miller, followed by half-a-dozen of the curious from
the Nest House and the farm, followed in the rear.

It will be remembered that John had been sent to the hut
to announce the intended visit. His stay had been much
longer than was anticipated; but when the procession had
gone about half the distance it was to march, it was met by
this faithful domestic, on his return. The worthy fellow
wheeled into line, on my flank, and communicated what he
had to say while keeping up with the column.

"To own the truth, Mr. Hugh," he said, "the old man
was more moved by hearing that about fifty Indians had
come a long distance to see him—"

"Seventeen—you should have said seventeen, John; that
being the exact number."

"Is it, sir? Well, I declare that I thought there might
be fifty—I once thought of calling 'em forty, sir, but it then
occurred to me that it might not be enough." All this time
John was looking over his shoulder to count the grave-look-
ing warriors who followed in a line; and satisfied of his
mistake, one of the commonest in the world for men of his
class, that of exaggeration, he resumed his report. "Well,
sir, I *do* believe you are right, and I have been a little hout.
But old Sus was quite moved, sir, when I told him of the
intended visit, and so I stayed to help the old gentleman to
dress and paint; for that nigger, Yop, is of no more use
now, you know, sir, than if he had never lived in a gentle-

man's family at all. It must have been hawful times, sir
when the gentry of York had nothing but niggers to serve
'em, sir."

"We did pretty well, John, notwithstanding," unswered
my uncle, who had a strong attachment to the old black
race, that once so generally filled all the menial stations of
the country, as is apt to be the case with all gentlemen
of fifty ; "we did pretty well, notwithstanding. Jaaf, however, never acted strictly as a body-servant, though he was
my grandfather's own man."

"Well, sir, if there had been nobody but Yop at the hut,
Sus would never have been decently dressed and painted for
this occasion. As it is, I hope that you will be satisfied,
sir, for the old gentleman looks remarkably well ;—Indian
fashion, you know, sir."

"Did the Onondago ask any questions ?"

"Why, you know how it is with him in that particular,
Mr. Hugh. He's a very silent person, is Susquesus ; most
remarkable so when he 'as any one has can entertain him
with conversation. I talked most of the time myself, sir,
has I commonly does when I pays him a wisit. Indians is
remarkably silent, in general, I believe, sir."

"And whose idea was it to paint and dress—yours, or
the Onondago's ?"

"Why, sir, I supposes the hidear to be Indian, by origin,
though in this case it was my surgestion. Yes, sir, I
surgested the thought ; though I will not take it on myself
to say Sus had not some hinclination that way, even before
I 'inted my hopinion."

"Did you think of the paint ?" put in uncle Ro. "I do
not remember to have seen the Trackless in his paint these
thirty years. I once asked him to paint and dress on a
Fourth of July ; it was about the time you were born,
Hugh—and I remember the old fellow's answer as well as
if it were given yesterday. 'When the tree ceases to bear
fruit,' was the substance of his reply, ' blossoms only remind
the observer of its uselessness.' "

"I have heard that Susquesus was once considered very
eloquent, even for an Indian."

"I remember him to have had some such reputation,
though I will not answer for its justice. Occasionally, I

have heard strong expressions in his brief, clipping manner
of speaking English,—but, in common, he has been content to be simple and taciturn. I remember to have heard
my father say that when he first made the acquaintance of
Susquesus, and that must have been quite sixty years since,
the old man had great apprehension of being reduced to
the mortifying necessity of making baskets and brooms;
but, his dread on that subject once removed, he had ever
after seemed satisfied and without care."

"Without care is the condition of those who have least,
I believe, sir. It would not be an easy matter for the
government of New York to devise ways and means to
deprive Sus of *his* farms, either by instituting suits for title,
destroying quarter-sales, laying taxes, or resorting to any
other of the ingenious expedients known to the Albany
politics."

My uncle did not answer for quite a minute; when he
did, it was thoughtfully and with great deliberation of
manner.

"Your term of 'Albany Politics' has recalled to my
mind," he said, "a consideration that has often forced itself
upon my reflections. There is doubtless an advantage—
nay, there may be a necessity for cutting up the local affairs
of this country, by entrusting their management to so many
local governments; but there is, out of all question, one
great evil consequent on it. When legislators have the
great affairs of state on their hands, the making of war and
peace, the maintaining of armies, and the control of all those
interests which connect one country with another, the mind
gets to be enlarged, and with it the character and disposition of the man. But, bring men together, who *must* act,
or appear incapable of acting, and set them at work upon
the smaller concerns of legislation; and it's ten to one but
they betray the narrowness of their education by the narrowness of their views. This is the reason of the vast difference that every intelligent man knows to exist between
Albany and Washington."

"Do you then think our legislators so much inferior to
those of Europe?"

"Only, as they are provincial; which nine in ten neces
sarily are, since nine Americans in ten, even among the
27

educated classes, are decidedly provincial. This term ' provincial' covers quite one-half of the distinctive sins of the
country, though many laugh at a deficiency, of which, in
the nature of things, they can have no notion, as purely
a matter of the imagination... The active communications
of the Americans certainly render them surprisingly little
obnoxious to such a charge, for their age and geographical
position. These last disadvantages produce effects, nevertheless, that are perhaps unavoidable. When you have had
an opportunity of seeing something of the society of the
towns, for instance, after your intercourse with the world of
Europe, you will understand what I mean, for it is a difference much more readily *felt* than *described*. Provincialism, however, may be defined as a general tendency to
the narrow views which mark a contracted association, and
an ignorance of the great world—not in the sense of station solely, but in the sense of liberality, intelligence, and a
knowledge of all the varied interests of life. But, here we
are, at the hut."

There we were, sure enough. The evening was delightful. Susquesus had seated himself on a stool, on the green
sward that extended for some distance around the door of
his habitation, and where he was a little in shade, protected
from the strong rays of a setting, but June, sun. A tree
cast its shadow over his person. Jaaf was posted on one
side, as no doubt, he himself thought best became his colour
and character. It is another trait of human nature, that
while the negro affects a great contempt and aversion for the
red-man, the Indian feels his own mental superiority to the
domestic slave. I had never seen Susquesus in so grand
costume, as that in which he appeared this evening. Habitually he wore his Indian vestments; the leggings, moca-
sin, breech-piece, blanket or calico shirt, according to the
season; but I had never before seen him in his ornaments
and paint. The first consisted of two medals which bore
the images, the one of George III, the other of his grandfather—of two more, bestowed by the agents of the republic;
of large rings in his ears, that dropped nearly to his shoulders, and of bracelets formed of the teeth of some animal,
that, at first, I was afraid was a man. A tomahawk that
was kept as bright as friction could make it, and a sheathed

knife, were in his girdle, while his well-tried rifle stood leaning against a tree; weapons that were now exhibited as
emblems of the past, since their owner could scarcely render either very effective. The old man had used the paint
with unusual judgment for an Indian, merely tinging his
cheeks with a colour that served to give brightness to eyes
that had once been keen as intense expression could render
them, but which were now somewhat dimmed by age. In
other respects, nothing was changed in the customary neat
simplicity that reigned in and around the cabin, though Jaaf
had brought out, as if to sun, an old livery coat of his own,
that he had formerly worn, and a cocked hat, in which I
have been told he was wont actually to exhibit himself of
Sundays, and holidays; reminders of the superiority of a
" nigger" over an " Injin."

Three or four rude benches, which belonged to the establishment of the hut, were placed at a short distance in front
of Susquesus, in a sort of semicircle, for the reception of
his guests. Towards these benches, then, Prairiefire led the
way, followed by all the chiefs. Although they soon ranged
themselves in the circle, not one took his seat for fully a
minute. That time they all stood gazing intently, but reve-
rently, towards the aged man before them, who returned
their look, as steadily and intently as it was given. Then,
at a signal from their leader, who on this occasion was Prairiefire, every man seated himself. This change of position,
however, did not cause the silence to be broken; but there
they all sat, for quite ten minutes, gazing at the Upright
Onondago, who, in his turn, kept his look steadily fastened
on his visiters. It was during this interval of silence that
the carriage of my grandmother drove up, and stopped just
without the circle of grave, attentive Indians, not one of
whom even turned his head to ascertain who or what caused
the interruption. No one spoke; my dear grandmother
being a profoundly attentive observer of the scene, while all
the bright faces around her, were so many eloquent pictures
of curiosity, blended with some gentler and better feelings,
exhibited in the most pleasing form of which humanity is
susceptible.

At length Susquesus himself arose, which he did with
great dignity of manner, and without any visible bodily

effort, and spoke. His voice was a little tremulous, i
thought; though more through feeling than age; but, on the
whole, he was calm, and surprisingly connected and clear
considering his great age. Of course, I was indebted to
Manytongues for the interpretation of all that passed.

"Brethren," commenced Susquesus, "you are welcome.
You have travelled on a long, and crooked, and thorny path,
to find an old chief, whose tribe ought ninety summers ago
to have looked upon him as among the departed. I am
sorry no better sight will meet your eyes at the end of so
long a journey. I would make the path back toward the
setting sun broader and straighter if I knew how. But I
do not know how. I am old. The pine in the woods is
scarce older; the villages of the pale-faces, through so
many of which you have journeyed, are not half so old;
I was born when the white race were like the moose on the
hills; here and there one; now they are like the pigeons
after they have hatched their young. When I was a boy
my young legs could never run out of the woods into a
clearing; now, my old legs cannot carry me into the woods,
they are so far off. Everything is changed in the land,
but the red-man's heart. *That* is like the rock which never
alters. My children, you are welcome."

That speech, pronounced in the deep husky tones of extreme old age, yet relieved by the fire of a spirit that was
smothered rather than extinct, produced a profound impression. A low murmur of admiration passed among the
guests, though neither rose to answer, until a sufficient time
had seemed to pass, in which the wisdom that they had just
been listeners to might make its proper impression. When
this pause was thought to be sufficiently long to have produced its effect, Prairiefire, a chief more celebrated in council even than in the field, arose to answer. His speech,
freely translated, was in the following words.

"Father;—your words are always wise—they are always true. The path between your wigwam and our villages *is* a long one—it is a crooked path, and many thorns
and stones have been found on it. But all difficulties may
be overcome. Two moons ago, we were at one end of it;
now we are at the other end. We have come with two
notches on our sticks. One notch told us to go to the Great

Council House of the Pale-face, to see our great pale-face Father—the other notch told us to come here, to see our great Red Father. We have been to the great Council House of the Pale-faces; we have seen Uncle Sam. His arm is very long; it reaches from the salt lake, the water of which we tried to drink, but it is too salt, to our own lakes, near the setting sun, of which the water is sweet. We never tasted water that was salt before, and we do not find it pleasant. We shall never taste it again; it is not worth while to come so far to drink water that is salt.

"Uncle Sam is a wise chief. He has many counsellors. The council at his council-fire must be a great council—it has much to say. Its words ought to have some good in them, they are so many. We thought of our Red Father, while listening to them, and wanted to come here. We *have* come here. We are glad to find our Red Father still alive and well. The Great Spirit loves a just Indian, and takes care of him. A hundred winters, in his eyes, are like a single winter. We are thankful to him for having led us by the crooked and long path, at the end of which we have found the Trackless—the Upright of the Onondagoes. I have spoken."

A gleam of happiness shot into the swarthy lineaments of Susquesus, as he heard, in his own language, a well-merited appellation that had not greeted his ears for a period as long as the ordinary life of man. It was a title, a cognomen that told the story of his connection with his tribe; and neither years, nor distance, nor new scenes, nor new ties, nor wars, nor strifes had caused him to forget the smallest incident connected with that tale. I gazed at the old man with awe, as his countenance became illuminated by the flood of recollections that was rushing into it, through the channel of his memory, and the expressive glance my uncle threw at me, said how much he was impressed, also. One of the faculties of Manytongues was to be able to interpret, *pari passu* with the speaker; and, standing between us and the carriage, he kept up, sentence by sentence, a low accompaniment of each speech, so that none of us lost a syllable of what was said.

As soon as Prairiefire resumed his seat, another silence succeeded. It lasted several minutes, during which the only

27*

audible sounds were various discontented grunts, accompanied by suppressed mutterings on the part of old Jaaf, who
never could tolerate any Indian but his companion. That
the negro was dissatisfied with this extraordinary visit was
sufficiently apparent to us, but not one of all the red men
took heed of his deportment. Sus, who was nearest to him,
must have heard his low grumbling, but it did not induce
him to change his look from the countenances of those in
his front for a single moment. On the other hand, the visiters themselves seemed totally unconscious of the negro's
presence, though in fact they were not, as subsequently appeared. In a word, the Upright Onondago was the centre
of attraction for them, all other things being apparently forgotten for the time.

At length there was a slight movement among the redskins, and another arose. This man was positively the
least well-looking of the whole party. His stature was lower
than that of the rest of the Indians; his form was meagre
and ungraceful—the last, at least, while his mind was in a
state of rest; and his appearance, generally, was wanting
in that nobleness of exterior which so singularly marked
that of every one of his companions. As I afterwards
learned, the name of this Indian was Eaglesflight, being so
called from the soaring character of the eloquence in which
he had been known to indulge. On the present occasion,
though his manner was serious and his countenance interested, the spirit within was not heaving with any of its extraordinary throes. Still, such a man could not rise to
speak, and avoid creating some slight sensation among his
expectant auditors. Guarded as are the red-men in general on the subject of betraying their emotions, we could
detect something like a suppressed movement among his
friends when Eaglesflight stood erect. The orator commenced in a low but solemn manner, his tones changing
from the deep, impressive guttural, to the gentle and pa-
thetic, in a way to constitute eloquence of itself. As I
listened, I fancied that never before did the human voice
seem to possess so much winning power. The utterance
was slow and impressive, as is usually the case with true
orators.

"The Great Spirit makes men differently," commenced

Eaglesflight. "Some are like willows, that bend with the breeze and are broken in the storm. Some are pines, with slender trunks, few branches, and a soft wood. Now and then there is an oak among them, which grows on the prairie, stretching its branches a great way, and making a pleasant shade. This wood is hard; it lasts a long time. Why has the Great Spirit made this difference in trees?—why does the Great Spirit make this difference in men? There is a reason for it. *He* knows it, though we may not. What he does is always right?

"I have heard orators at our Council Fires complain that things should be as they are. They say that the land, and the lakes, and the rivers, and the hunting-grounds, belong to the red-man only, and that no other colour ought ever to be seen there. The Great Spirit has thought otherwise, and what he thinks happens. Men are of many colours. Some are red, which is the colour of my father. Some are pale, which is the colour of my friends. Some are black, which is the colour of my father's friend. He is black, though old age is changing his skin. All this is right; it comes from the Great Spirit, and we must not complain.

"My father says he is very old—that the pine in the woods is scarce older. We know it. That is one reason why we have come so far to see him, though there is another reason. My father knows what that other reason is, so do we. For a hundred winters and summers, that reason has not gone out of our minds. The old men have told it to the young men; and the young men, when they have grown older, have told it to their sons. In this way it has reached our ears. How many bad Indians have lived in that time, have died, and are forgotten! It is the good Indian that lives longest in our memories. We wish to forget that the wicked ever were in our tribes. We never forget the good.

"I have seen many changes. I am but a child, compared with my father; but I feel the cold of sixty winters in my bones. During all that time, the red-men have been travelling towards the setting sun. I sometimes think I shall live to reach it! It must be a great way off, but the man who never stops goes far. Let us go there, pale-faces will follow. Why all this is, I do not know. My father is

wiser than his son, and he may be able to tell us. I sit
down to hear his answer."

Although Eaglesflight had spoken so quietly, and concluded in a manner so different from what I had expected,
there was a deep interest in what was now going on. The
particular reason why these red-men had come so far out
of their way to visit Susquesus had not yet been revealed,
as we all hoped would be the case ; but the profound reverence that these strangers, from the wilds of the far west,
manifested for our aged friend, gave every assurance that
when we did learn it, there would be no reason for disappointment. As usual, a pause succeeded the brief address
of the last speaker; after which, Susquesus once more
arose, and spoke.

"My children," he said, "I am very old. Fifty autumns
ago, when the leaves fell, I thought it was time for me to
pass on to the Happy Hunting-Grounds of my people, and
be a redskin again.- But my name was not called. I have
been left alone here, in the midst of the pale-face fields,
and houses, and villages, without a single being of my own
colour and race to speak to. My head was almost grown
white. Still, as years came on my head, the spirit turned
more towards my youth. I began to forget the battles, and
hunts, and journeys of middle life, and to think of the
things seen when a young chief among the Onondagoes.
My day is now a dream, in which I dream of the past.
Why is the eye of Susquesus so far-seeing, after a hundred
winters and more? Can any one tell? I think not. We
do not understand the Great Spirit, and we do not understand his doings. Here I am, where I have been for half
my days. That big wigwam is the wigwam of my best
friends. Though their faces are pale, and mine is red, our
hearts have the same colour. I never forget *them* — no,
not one of them. I see them all, from the oldest to the
youngest. They seem to be of my blood. This comes
from friendship, and many kindnesses. These are all the
pale-faces I now see. Red-men stand before my eyes in
all other places. My mind is with them.

"My children, you are young. Seventy winters are a
great many for one of you. It is not so with me. Why
I have been left standing alone here, near the hunting-

grounds of our fathers, is more than I can say. So it is, and it is right. A withered hemlock is sometimes seen, standing by itself, in the fields of the pale-faces. I am such a tree. It is not cut down, because the wood is of no use, and even the squaws do not like it to cook by. When the winds blow, they seem to blow around it. It is tired of standing there alone, but it cannot fall. That tree wishes for the axe, but no man puts the axe to its root. Its time has not come. So it is with me — my time has not come.

"Children, my days now are dreams of my tribe. I see the wigwam of my father. It was the best in the village. He was a chief, and venison was never scarce in his lodge. I see him come off the war-path with many scalps on his pole. He had plenty of wampum, and wore many medals. The scalps on his pole were sometimes from red-men, sometimes from pale-faces. He took them all himself. I see my mother, too. She loved me as the she-bear loves her cubs. I had brothers and sisters, and I see them, too. They laugh and play, and seem happy. There is the spring where we dipped up water in our gourds, and here is the hill where we lay waiting for the warriors to come in from the war-paths and the hunt. Everything looks pleasant to me. That was a village of the Onondagoes, my own people, and I loved them a hundred and twenty winters ago. I love them now, as if the time were but one winter and one summer. The mind does not feel time. For fifty seasons I thought but little of my own people. My thoughts were on the hunt and the war-path, and on the quarrels of the pale-faces, with whom I lived. Now, I say again, I think most of the past, and of my young days. It is a great mystery why we can see things that are so far off so plainly, and cannot see things that are so near by. Still, it is so.

"Children, you ask why the red-men keep moving towards the setting sun, and why the pale-faces follow? You ask if the place where the sun sets will be ever reached, and if pale-men will go there to plough and to build, and to cut down the trees. He that has seen what *has* happened, ought to know what *will* happen again. I am very old, but I see nothing new. One day is like another. The same fruits come each summer, and the winters are alike. The bird builds in the same tree many times.

"My children, I have lived long among the pale-faces.
Still, my heart is of the same colour as my face. I have
never forgotten that I am a red-man; never forgotten the
Onondagoes. When I was young, beautiful woods covered
these fields. Far and near the buck and the moose leaped
mong the trees. Nothing but the hunter stopped them. It
is all changed! The plough has frightened away the deer.
The moose will not stay near the sound of the church-bell.
He does not know what it means. The deer goes first.
The red-man keeps on his trail, and the pale-face is never
far behind. So it has been since the big canoes of the
stranger first came into our waters; so it will be until
another salt lake is reached beneath the setting sun. When
that other lake is seen, the red-man must stop, and die in
the open fields, where rum, and tobacco, and bread are
plenty, or march on into the great salt lake of the west and
be drowned. Why this is so I cannot tell. That it has been
so; I know; that it will be so, I believe. There is a reason for it; none can tell what that reason is but the Great
Spirit."

Susquesus had spoken calmly and clearly, and Manytongues translated as he proceeded, sentence by sentence.
So profound was the attention of the savage listeners that I
heard their suppressed breathings. We white men are so
occupied with ourselves, and our own passing concerns, look
on all other races of human beings as so much our inferiors,
that it is seldom we have time or inclination to reflect on the
consequences of our own acts. Like the wheel that rolls
along the highway, however, many is the inferior creature
that we heedlessly crush in our path. Thus has it been with
the red-man, and, as the Trackless had said, thus will it
continue to be. He will be driven to the salt lake of the far
west, where he must plunge in and be drowned, or turn and
die in the midst of abundance.

My uncle Ro knew more of the Indians, and of their habits, than any one else of our party, unless it might be my
grandmother. She, indeed, had seen a good deal of them
in early life; and when quite a young girl, dwelling with
that uncle of her own who went by the *sobriquet* of the
"Chainbearer," she had even dwelt in the woods, near the
tribe of Susquesus, and had often heard him named there

as an Indian in high repute, although he was even at that distant day an exile from his people. When our old friend resumed his seat, she beckoned her son and myself to the side of the carriage, and spoke to us on the subject of what had just-been uttered, the translation of Manytongues having been loud enough to let the whole party hear what he said.

"This is not a visit of business, but one of ceremony only," she said. "To-morrow, probably, the real object of the strangers will be made known. All that has passed, as yet, has been complimentary, mixed with a little desire to hear the wisdom of the sage. The red-man is never in a hurry, impatience being a failing that he is apt to impute to us women. Well, though we are females, we can wait. In the mean time, some of us can weep, as you see is particularly the case with Miss Mary Warren."

This was true enough; the fine eyes of all four of the girls glistening with tears, while the cheeks of the person named were quite wet with those that had streamed down them. At this allusion to such an excess of sympathy, the young lady dried her eyes, and the colour heightened so much in her face, that I thought it best to avert my looks. While this by-play was going on, Prairiefire arose again, and concluded the proceedings of that preliminary visit, by making another short speech :

"Father," he said, "we thank you. What we have heard will not be forgotten. All red-men are afraid of that Great Salt Lake, under the setting sun, and in which some say it dips every night. What you have told us, will make us think more of it. We have come a great distance, and are tired. We will now go to our wigwam, and eat, and sleep. To-morrow, when the sun is up here," pointing to a part of the heavens that would indicate something like nine o'clock, "we will come again, and open our ears. The Great Spirit who has spared you so long, will spare you until then, and we shall not forget to come. It is too pleasant to us to be near you, for us to forget. Farewell."

The Indians now rose in a body, and stood regarding Susquesus fully a minute, in profound silence, when they filed off at a quick pace, and followed their leader towards their quarters for the night. As the train noiselessly wound its way from before him, a shade passed athwart the dark countenance of the Trackless, and he smiled no more that day.

All this time the negro, the contemporary of the Indian, kept muttering his discontent at seeing so many redskins in his presence, unheeded and indeed unheard by his friend.

"What you do wid dem Injin," he growled, as the party disappeared. "No good ebber come of sich as dem. How many time dey work debbletry in a wood, and you and I not werry far off, Sus. How ole you got, redskin; and forgetful! Nobody can hold out wid colour' man. Gosh! I do b'lieve I lib for ebber, sometime! It won'erful to think of, how long I stay on dis werry 'arth!"

Such exclamations were not uncommon with the aged Jaaf, and no one noted them. He did not seem to expect any answer himself, nor did any one appear to deem it at all necessary to make one. As for the Trackless, he arose with a saddened countenance, and moved into his hut like one who wished to be left alone with his thoughts. My grandmother ordered the carriage to move on, and the rest of us returned to the house on foot.

CHAPTER XXI.

"With all thy rural echoes come,
Sweet comrade of the rosy day,
Wafting the wild bee's gentle hum,
Or cuckoo's plaintive roundelay."
                                        CAMPBELL.

THAT night was passed under my own roof, in the family circle. Although my presence on the estate was now gene- rally known, to all who were interested in it, I cannot say that I thought much of the anti-renters, or of any risks in- curred by the discovery. The craven spirit manifested by the 'Injins' in presence of the Indians, the assumed before the real, had not a tendency to awaken much respect for the disaffected, and quite likely disposed me to be more indiffercnt to their proceedings, than I might otherwise have been. At all events, I was happy with Patt, and Mary, and my uncle's wards, and did not give the disorganizers a thought, until quite at the close of the evening. The manner in which John went about to barricade the doors and windows, after the ladies had retired, struck me unpleasantly, however, and it did not fail to produce the same effect on my uncle. This seemingly important duty was done, when my faithful *maitre-d'hotel*, for such, in a measure, was the Englishman's station, came to me, and my uncle, who were waiting for his appearance in the library, armed like Robinson Crusoe. He brought us each a revolving pistol, and a rifle, with a proper allowance of ammunition.

"Missus," so John persevered in calling my grandmother, though it was very unlike an English servant to do so, after he had been in the country three months—"Missus as hordered harms to be laid in, in quantities, Mr. Hugh, and hall of us has our rifles and pistols, just like these. She keeps some for herself and Miss Martha, in her own room still, but as she supposes you can make better use of these than the maids, I had her orders to bring them down out of the maids' room, and hoffer them to yourselves, gentlemen. They are hall loaded, and smart weapons be they."

"Surely there has been no occasion as yet, for using such things as these!" exclaimed my uncle.

"One doesn't know, Mr. Roger, when the hinimy may come. We have had only three alarms since the ladies arrived, and most luckily no blood was shed; though we fired at the hinimy, and the hinimy fired at us. When I says no blood was spilt, I should add, on our side; for there was no way to know how much the anti's suffered, and they hadn't good stone walls to cover them, as we 'ad on our side."

"Gracious Providence! I had no notion of this! Hugh, the country is in a worse state than I had supposed, and we ought not to leave the ladies here an hour after to-morrow!"

As the ladies who came within my uncle's category, did not include Mary Warren, I did not take exactly the same view of the subject as he did himself. Nothing further was said on the subject, however; and shortly after each shouldered his rifle, and retired to his own room.

28

It was past midnight when I reached my apartment, but I felt no inclination for sleep. That had been an important day to me, one full of excitement, and I was still too much under the influence of its circumstances to think of my bed. There was soon a profound silence in the house, the closing of doors and the sound of footsteps having ceased, and I went to a window, to gaze on the scene without. There was a three-quarters' moon, which gave light enough to render all the nearer objects of the landscape distinctly visible. Tho view had nothing remarkable in it, but it was always rural and pretty. The little river, and the broad meadows, were not to be seen from my side of the house, which commanded the carriage road that wound through the lawn—the farm-house—the distant church—the neat and pretty rectory—the dwelling of Mary, and a long reach of farms, that lay along the valley, and on the broad breast of the rising ground to the westward.

Everything, far and near, seemed buried in the quiet of deep night. Even the cattle in the fields had lain down to sleep; for, like man, they love to follow the law of nature, and divide the hours by light and darkness. John had placed the candles in my dressing-room, and closed the inner shutters; but I had taken a seat by a window of the bed-room, and sat in no other light but that which came from the moon, which was now near setting. I might have been ruminating on the events of the day half an hour or more, when I fancied some object was in motion on a path that led towards the village, but which was quite distinct from the ordinary highway. This path was private, indeed, running fully a mile through my own farm and grounds, bounded for a considerable distance by high fences on each side of it, and running among the copses and thickets of the lawn, as soon as it emerged from the fields. It had been made in order to enable my grandfather to ride to his fields, uninterrupted by gates or bars; and issuing into the bit of forest already described, it passed through that by a short cut, and enabled us to reach the hamlet by a road that saved nearly a mile in the whole distance. This path was often used by those who left the Nest, or who came to it, in the saddle, but rarely by any but those who belonged to the family. Though old as the place itself, it was little known by others not suit-

ing the general taste for publicity, there not being a solitary
dwelling on it between the Nest House itself and the point
where it emerged into the highway, beyond the wood, which
was quite near to the village.

I could see the whole line of this private path, with the
exception, here and there, of intervals that were hid by trees
and thickets, from the point where it terminated until it entered the wood. There could be no mistake. Late as was
the hour, some one mounted was galloping along that path,
winding his or *her* way among the rails of the fences; now
plainly visible, then lost to view. I had caught a glimpse
of this phantom, (for at that unusual hour, and by that delusive light, it required no great effort of the imagination thus
to fancy the equestrian,) just as it emerged from the wood,
and could not well be mistaken as to the accuracy of my
discovery. The path led through a pretty wooded ravine
in the lawn, and no sooner did I lose sight of this strange
object than I turned my eyes eagerly to the spot where it
ought to reappear, on emerging from its cover.

The path lay in shadow for twenty rods on quitting the
ravine, after which it wound across the lawn to the door,
for about twice that distance, in full moonlight. At the termination of the shadow there was a noble oak, which stood
alone, and beneath its wide branches was a seat much frequented by the ladies in the heats of summer. My eye kept
moving from this point, where the light became strong, to
that where the path issued from the ravine. At the latter
it was just possible to distinguish a moving object, and, sure
enough, there I got my next view of the person I was watching. The horse came up the ascent on a gallop — a pace
that was continued until its rider drew the rein beneath the
oak. Here, to my surprise, a female sprang from the saddle with great alacrity, and secured her steed within the
shadow of the tree. This was no sooner done than she
moved on towards the house, in much apparent haste. Fearful of disturbing the family, I now left my room on tiptoe,
and without a candle, the light of the moon penetrating the
passages in sufficient quantity to serve my purpose, descending as fast as possible to the lower floor. Swift and prompt
as had been my own movement, it had been anticipated by
another. To my great surprise, on reaching the little side-

door to which the path led, and where the ladies had long
been accustomed to get into the saddle, when they used it,
I found a female figure, with her hand on the massive lock,
as if ready to turn its key at some expected summons. To
my great astonishment, on drawing nearer, I recognised, by
the faint light that penetrated through a little window over
the door, the person of Mary Warren!

I certainly started at this unexpected discovery, but, if she
who caused that start in me submitted to any similar emotion, I did not discover it. She may have heard my step,
however, descending the stairs, and have been prepared for
the meeting.

"You have seen her, too, have you, Mr. Littlepage!"
exclaimed Mary, though she used the precaution to speak in
a suppressed tone. "What *can* have brought her here at
this late hour?"

"You know who it is, then, Miss Warren?" I answered,
feeling an indescribable pleasure succeed my surprise, as I
remembered the dear girl, who was fully dressed, just as
she had left the drawing-room an hour before, must have
been gazing out upon the moonlight view as well as myself;
a species of romance that proved something like a similarity
of tastes, if not a secret sympathy between us.

"Certainly," returned Mary, steadily. "I cannot well
be mistaken in the person, I think. It is Opportunity Newcome."

"My hand was on the key, and I turned it in the lock.
A bar remained, and this I also removed, when we opened
the door. Sure enough, there came the person just named,
within ten feet of the steps, which she doubtless intended to
ascend. She manifested surprise on ascertaining who were
her porters, but hastened into the house, looking anxiously
behind her, as if distrustful of pursuit or observation. I led
the way to the library, lighted its lamp, and then turned to
my two silent companions, looking a request for explanation.

Opportunity was a young woman, in her twenty-sixth
year, and was not without considerable personal charms.
The exercise and excitement through which she had just
gone had heightened the colour in her cheeks, and rendered
her appearance unusually pleasing. Nevertheless, Oppor-

tunity was not a woman to awaken anything like the passion of love in me, though I had long been aware such was
her purpose. I suspected that her present business was
connected with this scheme, I will own, and was prepared
to listen to her communication with distrust. As for Oppor
tunity herself, she hesitated about making her disclosures,
and the very first words she uttered were anything but delicate or feminine.

" Well, I declare!" exclaimed Opportunity, " I did not
expect to find you two alone at this time of night !".

I could have given her tongue a twitch to cure it of its
propensity to speak evil, but concern for Mary Warren, induced me to turn anxiously towards her. Never did the
steady self-possession of perfect innocence better assert itself
than in the dear girl at this rude assault ; the innocence
which can leave no latent intention, or wish, to alarm the
feelings.

. " We had all retired," answered the pure-minded girl,
" and everybody on my side of the house is in bed and
asleep, I believe ; but I did not feel any drowsiness, and was
sitting at a window, looking out upon the view by this lovely
moonlight, when I saw you ride out of the woods, and follow
.he lane. As you came up to the oak I knew who it was,
Opportunity, and ran down to admit you ; for I was certain
something extraordinary must bring you here at this late
hour."

" Oh! nothing extraordinary, at all !" cried Miss Oppor
tunity, in a careless way. " I love moonlight as well as
yourself, Mary, and am a desperate horsewoman, as you
know. I thought it would be romantic to gallop over to the
Nest, and go back between one and two in the morning.
Nothing more, I can assure you."

The coolness with which this was said amazed me not a
little, though I was not so silly as to believe a syllable of it.
Opportunity had a great deal of vulgar sentimentalism
about her, it is true — such as some girls are apt to mistake
for refinement ; but she was not quite so bad as to travel
that lane, at midnight, and alone, without some special
object. It occurred to me that this object might be connected with her brother, and that she would naturally wish
to make her communications privately. We had all taken

28*

seats at a table which occupied the centre of the room, Mary
and myself quite near each other, and Opportunity at a distant angle.   I wrote on a slip of paper a short request for
Mary to leave me alone with our visiter, and laid it under
her eyes, without exciting Opportunity's suspicion; talking
to her, the whole time, about the night, and the weather,
and her ride.   While we were thus engaged, Miss-Warren
rose, and quietly glided out of the room.   So silently was
this done, that I do not believe my remaining companion
was conscious of it at the moment.

" You have driven Mary Warren away, Miss Opportunity," I remarked, " by the hint about our being alone together."

" Lord! there's no great harm in that! I am used to
being alone with gentlemen, and think nothing of it.   But,
are we really alone, Mr. Hugh, and quite by ourselves?"

" Quite, as you see.   Our two selves and Mary Warren
I believe to be the only persons in the house, out of our
beds.   She has left us, a little hurt, perhaps, and we are
quite alone."

" Oh! As for Mary Warren's feelings, I don't mind
them much, Mr. Hugh.   She's a good critter" — yes, this
elegant young lady actually used that extraordinary word
— "and as forgiving as religion.   Besides, she's only the
episcopal clergyman's daughter; and, take your family
away, that's a denomination that would not stand long at
Ravensnest, I can tell you."

" I am very glad, then, my family is not away, for it is
a denomination I both honour and love.   So long as the
grasping and innovating spirit of the times leaves the Littlepages anything, a fair portion of their means shall be
given to support that congregation.   As for Miss Warren,
I am pleased to hear that her temperament is so forgiving."

" I know that well, and did not speak in the hope of
making any change in your views, Mr. Hugh.   Mary Warren, however, will not think much of my remark to-morrow,
I do not believe she thought half as much about it to-night
as I should have done, had it been made to *me*."

I fancy this was quite true; Mary Warren having listened to the insinuation as the guileless and innocent hear
innuendos that bring no consciousness with them, while Op-

portunity's spirit would have been very apt to buckle on the armour which practice had rendered well-fitting.

"You have not taken this long ride merely to admire the moon, Miss Opportunity," I now carelessly remarked, willing to bring things to a head. "If you would favour me with its real object, I should be pleased to learn it."

"What if Mary should be standing at the keyhole, listening?" said this elegant 'critter,' with the suspicion of a vulgar mind. "I wouldn't have her hear what I 've got to tell you, for a mint of money."

"I do not think there is much danger of that," I answered, rising notwithstanding, and throwing open the door. "You perceive there is no one here, and we can converse in safety."

Opportunity was not so easily satisfied. Of a gossiping, craving disposition herself, in all things that pertain to curiosity, it was not easy for her to imagine another could be less guided by that feeling than herself. Rising, therefore, she went on tiptoe to the passage, and examined it for herself. Satisfied, at length, that we were not watched, she returned to the room, closed the door softly, motioned for me to be seated, placed herself quite near me, and then appeared disposed to proceed to business.

"This has been a dreadful day, Mr. Hugh," the young woman now commenced, actually looking sorrowful, as I make little doubt she really felt. "Who could have thought that the street-musician was you, and that old German pedlar of watches, Mr. Roger! I declare, the world seems to be getting upside-down, and folks don't know when they 're in their right places?"

"It was a foolish adventure, perhaps; but it has let us into some most important secrets."

"That 's just the difficulty. I defend you all I can, and tell my brothers that you 've not done anything they would n't do in a minute, if only half a farm depended on it, while, in your case, it may be more than a hundred."

"Your brothers then complain of my having appeared among the anti-renters, in disguise?"

"They do, desperately, Mr. Hugh, and seem quite put out about it. They say it was ungenerous to come in that way into your own country, and steal their secrets from them! I say all I can in your favour, but words wont pass for much with men in such a taking. You know, Mr. Hugh, I've always been your friend, even from our childish days, having got myself into more than one scrape to get you out of them."

As Opportunity made this declaration, one a little loose as to facts, by the way, she sighed gently, dropped her eyes, and looked as conscious and confused as I believe it was at all in her nature to appear. It was not my cue to betray undue bashfulness at such a moment, and as for any scruples on the subject of misleading a confiding heart, I should as soon have thought of feeding an anaconda or a boá constrictor with angle-worms. I took the young lady's hand, therefore, squeezed it with as sentimental a pressure as I knew how to use, and looked green enough about the eyes, I dare say.

"You are only too good, Opportunity," I answered "Yes, I have ever relied on you as a friend, and have never doubted you would defend me, when I was not present to defend myself."

Here I released the hand, a little apprehensive I might have the young lady sobbing on my shoulder, unless some little moderation were observed. Opportunity manifested a reluctance to let go her hold, but what could a young woman do, when the gentleman himself exhibited so much discretion?

"Yes, Seneky, in particular, is in a dreadful taking," she resumed, "and to pacify him, I consented to ride over my self, at this time of night, to let you know what is threatened."

"That is most kind of you, Opportunity; and, as it is so late, had you not better tell your story at once, and then go to a room and rest yourself, after so sharp a ride?"

"Tell my tale I will, for it's high time you heard it; but, as for rest, I must jump on my horse and gallop back the moment the moon sets; sleep I must in my own bed this night. Of course you and Mary Warren will both be silent as to my visit, since it has been made for your good."

I promised for myself and Mary, and then pressed my companion to delay no longer in imparting the information she had ridden so far to bring. The story was soon told and proved to be sufficiently alarming. One portion of the facts I got directly from Opportunity herself, while another has been subsequently gleaned from various sources, all being certain. The particular circumstances were these :—

When Seneca followed the band of " Injins" and his co-anti-renters, in their precipitate retreat on the hamlet, his revelations produced a general consternation. It then became known that the young Paris spendthrift was on his own estate, that he had actually been among the disaffected that day, had learned many of their secrets, and had probably made black marks against certain of the tenants, whose leases were nearly expired. Bad as this was, of itself, it was not the worst of the matter. Nothing was more certain than the fact that this young landlord knew a few of those who had committed felony, and might have sundry highly probable suspicions as to others. The guilty lay at his mercy, as a matter of course ; and there was a sufficiency of common sense left among these conspirators, to understand that a man, who must feel that attempts were making to rob him of his estate, would be very likely to turn the tables on his assailants, did an occasion offer. When men embark in an undertaking as innately nefarious as that of anti-rentism certainly is, when it is stripped of its pretensions and stands in its naked deformity, they are not apt to stop at trifles. To this desperate character of its mischief, the country owes the general depression of truth that has accompanied its career, its false and dangerous principles, its confusion between right and wrong, and finally its murders. It has been the miserable prerogative of demagogues alone, to defend its career and its demoralization. Thus has it happened, that the country has seen the same quasi legislators—legislators, by the vote of a party and the courtesy of the country, if by no other tenure—supporting, with an air of high pretension, the very doubtful policy of attempting to make men moral by statute law, on the one side, while they go the full length of these property-depredators, on the other ! In such a state of society, it is not surprising that any expedient should be adopted to intimidate and bully me nto silence. It was consequently determined, in a conclave of the chiefs, that a complaint should be made against my uncle and myself, before an anti-rent justice of the peace,

for felony under the recent statute, in appearing " diguised
and armed," as a means of preventing our complaints
against the real offenders.   It is true, we were not in masks ·
but our disguises, nevertheless, were so effectual as possibly
to meet the contingency contemplated by the law, had we
been armed. As to weapons, however, we had been totally
and intentionally without anything of the sort ; but oaths
cost villains, like those engaged in this plot, very little.
Those oaths had been taken, and warrants were actually
signed by the magistrate, of which the service was suspended
at Seneca's solicitation, merely to enable the last to effect
a compromise.   It was not thought sufficient, however, to
menace my uncle and myself with a prosecution of this
nature ; intimidation of another sort was to be put in requi-
sition, to enforce the dread of the legal proceedings ; a measure which should let us see that our assailants were in
downright earnest. Opportunity had ascertained that something serious was to be attempted, and she believed that very
night, though what it was precisely was more than she knew;
or, knowing, was willing to communicate.

The object of this late visit, then, was to make terms for
her brother, or brothers ; to apprize me of some unknown
but pressing danger, and to obtain all that influence in my
breast that might fairly be anticipated from services so material. Beyond a question, I was fortunate in having such
a friend in the enemy's camp, though past experience had
taught me to be wary how I trusted my miserable and sensitive heart within the meshes of a net that had been so often
cast.   .   .

" I am very sensible of the importance of your services,
Miss Opportunity," I said, when the voluble young lady had
told her tale, " and shall not fail to bear it in mind.· · As for
making any direct arrangement with your brother Seneca,
that is out of the question, since it would be compromising
felony, and subject me to punishment ;. but I can be passive,
if I see fit, and your wishes will have great weight with me.
The attempt to arrest my uncle and myself, should it ever
be made, will only subject its instigators to action for malicious prosecutions, and gives me no concern. It is v?ry
doubtful how far we were disguised, in the sense of the
statute, and it is certain we were not armed, in any

sense. Without perjury, therefore, such a prosecution must fail——"

"Folks take desperate oaths in anti-rent times!" interrupted Opportunity, with a significant look.

"I am quite aware of that. Human testimony,'at the best, is very frail, and often to be distrusted; but in seasons of excitement, and passion, and cupidity, it is common to find it corrupt. The most material thing, at present, is to know precisely the nature of the evil they meditate against us."—

Opportunity's eye did not turn away, as mine was fastened on her while she answered this question, but retained all the steadiness of sincerity.

"I wish I could tell you, Mr. Hugh," she said; "but I can say no more than I have. Some injury will be attempted this night, I feel certain; but what that injury will be, is more than I know myself. I must now go home; for the moon will be nearly down, and it would never do for me to be seen by any of the antis. The little I *have* said in favour of the Littlepages has made me enemies, as it is; but I never should be forgiven, was this ride to be known."

Opportunity now rose, and smiling on me, as any other rover might be supposed to fire a parting broadside, in order to render the recollection of her presence as memorable as possible, she hurried away. I accompanied her to the oak, as a matter of course, and assisted her into her saddle. Sundry little passages of country coquetry occurred during these movements, and the young lady manifested a reluctance to depart, even when all was ready, though she was in so great a hurry. Her game was certainly as desperate as that of the anti-renters themselves, but it was a game she was determined to play out. The moon was not yet quite down, and that circumstance served as a pretence for delay, while I fancied that she might still have something in reserve to communicate.

"This has been so kind in you, dear Opportunity," I said, laying my hand gently on the one of hers which held the bridle—"so like old times—so like yourself, indeed—that I scarce know how to thank you. But we shall live to have old-fashioned times again, when the former communications can be opened among us. Those were happy days,

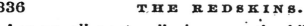

when we all went galloping over the hills. together; mere
boys and girls, it is true, but delighted boys and girls I hope
you will allow."

"That they was"—Opportunity's education and graces
did not extend to good grammar, in her ordinary discourse,
which many persons among us seem to fancy is anti-republican—"That they was! And I should like to live 'em over
again. Never mind, Hugh; you'll live to put down these
people, and then you'll settle and marry.- You mean to
marry, of course?"

This was a pretty plain demonstration; but I was used to
it, as what young man of fortune is not?—and a danger
known is a danger avoided. I pressed the hand I held gently, relinquished it, and then observed, in a somewhat disappointed tone—

"Well, I ought not to ask again, what is the particular
injury I am to expect to-night. A brother is nearer than a
friend, I know; and I can appreciate your difficulties."

Opportunity had actually given the spirited beast she
rode the rein, and was on the point of galloping off, when
these last words touched her heart. Leaning forward, and
bending her head down, so as to bring our faces within a
foot of each other, she said, in a low voice—

"*Fire* is a good servant, but a hard master. A tea-kettle
of water-thrown on it, at first, would have put out the last
great conflagration in York."

These words were no sooner uttered than the bold young
woman struck her horse a smart blow, and away she went
galloping over the turf with an almost noiseless hoof. I
watched her for a moment, and saw her descend into the
ravine; when, left quite alone, there was abundant opportu-
nity-for reflection, though no longer any Opportunity to
look at.

"Fire!"—That *was* an ominous word. It is the instrument of the low villain, and is an injury against which it is
difficult, indeed, to guard. It had been used in these anti-rent
troubles, though less, perhaps, than would have been the
case in almost any other country; the institutions of this,
even if they have introduced so many false and exaggerated
notions of liberty, having had a most beneficial effect in
essening some of the other evils of humanity. Still, fire

had been resorted to, and the term of ' barn-burner' had got
to be common among us; far more common, I rejoice to
say, than the practice which gave it birth. Nevertheless,
it was clearly of the last importance to certain persons at
Ravensnest to frighten me from complaining, since their
crimes could only lead them to the State's prison, were justice done. I determined, therefore, not to lay my head on
a pillow that night, until assured that the danger was past.

The moon had now set, but the stars shed their twinkling
rays on the dusky landscape. I was not sorry for the
change, as it enabled me to move about with less risk of
being seen. The first thing was to seek some auxiliaries to
aid me in watching, and I at once decided to look for them
among my guests, the Indians. If " fire will fight fire,"
' Indian' ought to be a match for ' Injin' any day. There
is just the difference between these two classes of men, that
their names would imply. The one is natural, dignified,
polished in his way—nay, gentleman-like; while the other
is a sneaking scoundrel, and as vulgar as his own appellation. No one would think of calling these last masquerading rogues " Indians ;" by common consent, even the most
particular purist in language terms them " Injins." " *Il y a
chapeau et chapeau*," and there are " Indian and Injin."

Without returning to the house, I took my way at once
towards the quarters of my red guests. Familiar with every
object around me, I kept so much within the shadows, and
moved across the lawn and fields by a route so hidden, that
there was not much risk of my being seen, even had there
been enemies on the look-out. The distance was not great,
and I soon stood at the foot of the little knoll on which the
old farm-house stood, sheltered in a manner by a dark row
of aged currants, which lined the bottom of an old and half-
deserted garden. Here I paused to look about me, and to
reflect a moment, before I proceeded any further.

There stood the good, old, substantial residence of my
fathers, in shadowy outline, looming large and massive in its
form and aspect. It might be fired, certainly, but not with
much facility, on its exterior. With the exception of its
roof, its piazza, and its outside-doors, little wood was exposed
to an incendiary without; and a slight degree of watchfulness might suffice against such a danger. Then the law
29

punished arson of an inhabited dwelling with death, as it should do, and your sneaking scoundrels seldom brave such a penalty in this country. Much is said about the impotency of the punishment of the gallows, but no man can tell how many thousand times it has stayed the hand and caused the heart to quail. Until some one can appear among us, who is able to reveal this important secret, it is idle to talk about the few cases in which it is known that the risk of death has been insufficient to prevent crime. One thing we all know; other punishments exist, and crime is perpetrated directly in *their* face, daily and hourly; and I cannot see why such a circumstance should not be just as much of an argument against the punishment of the penitentiary, as against punishment by the gallows. For one, I am clearly for keeping in existence the knowledge that there is a power in the country, potent to sweep away the offender, when cases of sufficient gravity occur to render the warning wholesome.

CHAPTER XXII.

" O, time and death! with certain pace,
Though still unequal, hurrying on,
O'erturning, in your awful race,
The cot, the palace, and the throne!

" Not always in the storm of war,
Nor by the pestilence that sweeps
From the plague-smitten realms afar,
Beyond the old and solemn deeps."
SANDS.

BESIDES the house with its walls of stone, however, there were numerous out-buildings. The carriage-house, stables, and home-barn, were all of stone also; but a brand thrown into a hay-mow would easily produce a conflagration. The barns, hay-ricks, &c., on the flats, and near the dwelling of Miller, were all of wood, according to the custom of the country, and it was not death to set fire to a barn. The disguised and armed'·who should commit this last offence. would incur no other risk than that which had already been ncurred in carrying out his desperate plans. I thought of hese things for a moment, when I opened a passage through the currant-bushes, intending to pass by a breach in the decayed fence into the garden, and thus by a private way to the house. To my astonishment, and in a slight degree to my alarm, a man stood before me the instant I emerged from the thicket.

" Who be—where go—what want?" demanded one of the real red-skins, significantly ; this being a sentinel of the party whose vigilance even my guarded approach had not eluded.

I told him who I was, and that I came to seek the interpreter, Manytongues. No sooner was I recognised, than my red friend offered me his hand to shake, American fashion, and seemed satisfied. He asked no question, manifested no curiosity at this visit at an hour so unusual, and took it all as one in ordinary life would receive a call in a morning between the permitted hours of twelve and three. *Something* had brought me there, he must have known ; but, what that something was appeared to give him no concern. This man accompanied me to the house, and pointed to the spot where I should find the person I sought, snoring on his well-shaken bundles of straw.

At the first touch of my finger, Manytongues awoke, and stood erect. He recognised me in an instant, dark as was the room, and touching my arm as a signal to follow, led the way into the open air. After moving out of ear-shot, he stopped and proceeded to business himself, like one accustomed to such interruptions.

" Anything stirring to-night?" demanded this frontierman, with the coolness of one who was ever ready. " Am I to call my red-skins ; or is it only a notice that is to be given?" ·

" Of that you shall judge for yourself. You doubtless know the condition of this part of the country, and the troubles that exist on the subject of the rents paid for the use of the farms. What you saw to-day is a specimen of the scenes that are now constantly acted among us."

" Colonel, I can't say I do rightly understand the state of

things down here-a-way," drawled out the interpreter, after
yawning like a hound, and giving me the most favourite title
of the frontiers. "It seems to be neither one thing nor
t'other; nuther tomahawk nor law. I can understand both
of *them*, but this half-and-half sort of thing bothers me, and
puts me out. You ought to have law, or you hadn't ought;
but what you have should be stuck to."

"You mean that you do not find this part of the country
either civilized or savage. Not submitting to the laws, nor
yet permitting the natural appeal to force?"

"Something of that sort. The agent told me, when I
came on with this party of red-skins, that I was comin' down
into a quarter of the country where there was justices of the
peace, and that no man, red or pale, could or should right
himself. So we've all on us indivour'd to go by that rule;
and I can qualify that not a critter has been shot or scalped
since we crossed the Mississippi. Some sich law was necessary among us, as we came from different and hostile tribes,
and nothing would be easier than to breed a quarrel among
ourselves, if a body was so disposed. But, I must say, that
I'm not only disapp'inted myself, but most of my chiefs be
dreadfully disapp'inted likewise."

"In what particular have you been most disappointed?"

"In many matters. The first thing that set me a-think-
in' was to hear folks read them newspapers. The way men
talk of each other, in them things, is wonderful, and to me
it's a surprise any's left, at the end of the year, to begin the
same game the next. Why, Colonel Littlepage—"

"I am no colonel—not even an ensign—you must be
confounding me with some other of my family."

"You *ought* to be, sir, and I shall not do you the injustice to call you by any lower title. I've known gentlemen
of not one-quarter your pretensions tarmed gin'rals, out
West. I've hunted on the prer-ies these twenty-five years,
and have now crossed the Upper Lakes six times, and know
what is due to a gentleman as well as any man. And so,
as I was sayin', Colonel Littlepage, was men to *talk* of each
other out on the prer-ies as they *print* of each other down
here among the meetin-'uses, scalps would be so plenty as
to fall considerable in valie. I'm not at all spiteful, but my
'eelin's has been r'iled at only just *hearin*' 'em things *read*,

for, as for reading myself, that's a thing I never condescended to. This somewhat prepared me for findin' things
different as I got deeper into the settlements, and I've not
been disapp'inted so far as them expectations went—it's the
old idee that's been crossed."

"I am not astonished to hear this, and agree with you
entirely in thinking that the nations which can withstand a
press of which the general character is as degraded as that
of this country, must be composed of beings of a higher
order than man. But, to come to business; you must have
some notions of these mock savages, and of the people called
anti-renters ?"

"Sort o', and sort o' not. I can't understand when a
man has agreed to pay rent, why he should not pay it. A
bargain is a bargain, and the word of a gentleman is as
good as his bond."

"These opinions would surprise some among us, a few
legislators included. *They* appear to think that the moral
test of every engagement is whether the parties like it or
not."

"One word, if you please, Colonel. Do they give in as
much to complaints of the owners of the sile as to the complaints of them that hire the land in order to work it ?"

"Not at all. The complaints of the landlords would not
find a single sympathetic chord in the breast of the softest
nearted politician in America, let them be ever so well-
founded. Surely, *you*, who are a rover on the prairies, can
have no great respect for land titles ?"

"The prer-ie is the prer-ie, Colonel, and men live and
act by prer-ie law on prer-ie ground. But right is right, too,
Colonel, as well as prer-ie is prer-ie; and I like to see it
per\ail. I do not think you will find a red-skin among all
the chiefs who are asleep under that roof who will not give
his voice ag in flying from the tarms of a solemn bargain.
A man must be well steeped in the ways of the law, I
should judge, to bring his mind to such an act."

"Do these red-men, then, know anything of the nature
of the difficulties that exist here ?"

"They have heard on 'em, and have talked a good deal
together on the subject. It's opposyte to the very natur' of
an Indian, like, to agree to one thing, and to do another.

29*

But, here is a Chippewa, who is on the look-out. I will ask him a question, and you shall hear his answer."

Manytongues now spoke to the sentinel, who was sauntering near. After a brief exchange of questions and answers in the tongue of the latter, the interpreter communicated what had passed.

"This Chippewa has heard somewhere," he said, "that there are folks in this part of the world who get into wigwams, by agreeing to pay rent for them, and, when once in possession, they want to fly from their agreements, and make the man they got it from prove his right to it. Is that true, Colonel?"

"It is true, out of all question, and not only do the tenants wish to enact this treachery, but they have found others, that call themselves legislators, who are willing to sustain them in the fraud. It is much as if you should borrow, or hire a rifle for a day's sporting, and when the man who let you have it, came to claim it at night, you should tell him to prove he was the right owner."

"What's that to me? I got the rifle of him; have no right but such as he had; and am bound to stand by my bargain. No, no. Colonel; not a redskin on the prer-ies but would revolutionize at that! But, what may have brought you here, at this time o' night? Them that sleep in beds, don't like to quit them 'till mornin' comes to tell 'em to rise."

I then gave Manytongues an account of the visit I had received, without mentioning the name of Opportunity, however, and related the nature of the warning I had heard. The interpreter was, in no wise, disturbed at this prospect of a collision with the Injins, against whom he had a grudge, not only on account of the little affair of the preceding day, but mainly in consequence of their having brought real savages into discredit, by the craven and clumsy manner in which they had carried out their imitation.

"Nothin' better is to be expected from such critturs," he observed, after we had discussed the matter together, at some little length, "though fire is held to be lawful warfare, even on the prer-ies. For my part, I'm not at all sorry there is something to do; nor will my chiefs be melancholy on this account, for it is dull work to be doing nothing, for months and months at a time, but smoking at councils making speeches to folks who live by talking, and eating and drinking. Activity is the natur' of a prer-ie man, and he's always glad to pick his flint, after a spell of considerable quiet. I'll tell the Chippewa to step in, and bring out the redskins, a'ter which you can give your orders."

"I could wish watchfulness rather than violence. The men can lie in watch, near the principal buildings, and it might be well to have some water ready, to extinguish any flames that may be lighted, before they get too far ahead."

"Just as you say, Colonel, for you are my Captain-General. But, I can tell you how I did once, out on the prer-ies, when I caught a rascal of a Sioux blowing a fire he had kindled at one of my own lodges. I just laid him on the flames, and let him put them out himself by bleeding on them."

"We must have no violence, unless it become indispensable to save the buildings. The law will not justify us, in using our arms, except in the last extremity. Prisoners I wish you to take; for they may serve as hostages, besides furnishing examples to intimidate other offenders. I rely on you to give due warning to our red friends, on this subject."

The interpreter gave a sort of grunt, but he said nothing. The conversation went no farther, however, just then; for, by this time, the Indians came stealing out of the house, every man of them armed, looking dusky, prepared and full of wariness. Manytongues did not keep them long, but soon told his story. After this, his authority appeared, in a great measure, to cease. Flintyheart was now the most prominent of the party, though Prairiefire, and another warrior, were also connected with the orders given to the rest. I observed that Eaglesflight had no part in these arrangements, which were peculiarly military, though he appeared, armed and ready, and went forth on the sudden call, like the rest. In five minutes the Indians were all off, principally in pairs, leaving the interpreter and myself still standing together, in front of the deserted house.

It was, by this time, past one o'clock, and I thought it probable my enemies would soon appear, if they came that night. Accompanied by the interpreter, I took the way towards the Nest House, it occurring to me that arms might be wanted, in the course of the morning. On quitting my room, the rifle and pistol provided by John had been left there, and I thought of stealing into the house again, obtaining those weapons, extinguish my lights, and rejoin my present companion, without giving alarm to any of the sleepers.

This plan was successfully executed, so far as ascending to my room and descending to the door were concerned, but there it met with an interruption. While in the very act of closing the little postern, as we used to call it, by way of pleasantry, I felt a small soft hand laid on the one of my own which was drawing to the door after me. In an instant I had turned, and was at the side of Mary Warren. I expressed my surprise at finding her still up, and concern lest she might suffer in health, in consequence of so much unusual watchfulness.

"I could not sleep after what has passed to-night," she answered, "without knowing the meaning of all these movements. I have been looking from my window, and saw you assist Opportunity to get on her horse, and afterward walk towards the old farm-house, where the Indians are lodged. Tell me frankly, Mr. Littlepage, is there any danger to be apprehended?"

"I shall be frank with you, Mary"—how easy and pleasant it was to me to use this gentle familiarity, which might now be assumed without appearing to be presumptuous, under all the circumstances of our intercourse; "I shall be frank with you, Mary; for I know that your prudence and self-command will prevent any unnecessary alarm, while your watchfulness may be of use. There is some reason to fear the brand."

"The brand!"

"So Opportunity has given me reason to suppose; and I do not think she would have ridden the distance she did, at such an hour, unless her business were serious. The brand is the proper instrument of the anti-renter, and renders his disguise convenient. I have got all the red-men on the look-out, however; and I do not think that mischief can be done to-night, without its being detected. To-morrow, we can appeal to the authorities for protection."

"I will not sleep this night!" exclaimed Mary, drawing the light shawl she wore, as a protection against the air of that summer-night, more closely, around her person, as a sterner being might be supposed to gird on his armour in a moment of peril. "I care not for rest. They ought not, they *shall* not, Mr. Littlepage, do you this wrong. Have you apprehensions for this house?"

"One never knows. This house is not easily set fire to from without, and I scarcely think there can be any enemy within. The domestics are old and tried, and I do not believe that either of them could be bought. I feel little apprehension, therefore, from any within, while I confess to a good deal from those without. Fire is such a dreadful foe, and one is usually so helpless against its ravages in the country! I will not ask you to retire, for I know you will not —nay, cannot sleep; but, by passing from window to window, for the next hour, or until I rejoin you, your mind will be occupied, and possibly some injury might be prevented. An unseen observer from a window might detect an attempt that would escape those on the watch without."

"I will do so," said Mary, eagerly; "and should I discover anything, I will open a leaf of the shutter of my own room. You can then see the light of the candle within, and by coming at once to this door, you will find me here, ready to let you know my discovery."

With this understanding we parted, but not until I had shaken hands affectionately with this gentle-looking, but really resolute and clear-headed girl. I rejoined Manytongues, who stood in the shadows of the piazza, where there was no possibility of his being seen, except by one quite near his person. After a brief explanation, we parted, one taking the north side of the buildings, and the other the south, in order to make certain no incendiary was at work on either of the wings.

The Nest House was much less exposed to attempts like those we apprehended, than most American dwellings. The structure being of stone, left but little inflammable material accessible; and the doors, on the exterior, were only two— those already mentioned. There was a great gate, it is true; one large enough to admit a cart into the inner court, on the southern face of the wing, beneath the arch of which an incendiary might, indeed, make his attempt, though a practised rogue would at once see the difficulties. Little wood was even there, beyond that of-the massive gate itself which, once burnt, would leave no further fuel for flames. I examined the place, notwithstanding; and finding all safe on my side of the building, I went to rejoin the interpreter, who was to meet me at the foot of a fine beech, which spread its broad arms over the lawn, at the distance of about a hundred yards from the house, and so nearly in its front, as to afford us, in all respects, the most eligible position for sentinels on duty like ours, far or near.

At the foot of that beech I found Manytongues, and the deep obscurity in which his form was embedded, was, of itself, a high recommendation of the position. I did not see him until almost near enough to touch him. He was seated on a bench, and seemed entirely at his ease, like one accustomed to ambushes, vigilance, and midnight assaults. We exchanged reports, ascertained all was well, and then I took my seat at the interpreter's side, willing to beguile the time by such discourse as occurred to my mind.

"That was a most interesting scene, last evening," I remarked; "the interview between Old Trackless and your red companions! I own a lively curiosity to know what particular claim our aged friend has on those distant tribes that chiefs of note have come so far to see him?"

"They have not come all the way from the prer-ies, to this spot, on any such ar'n'd, though I do not question their readiness to do so. In the first place, old age, when accompanied by wisdom, and sobriety, and a good character, goes a great way with savages, in gin'ral. But, there is something partic'lar about the acts of Susquesus that I do not know, which raises him higher than common in redskin eyes. I intend to l'arn what it is before we quit this country."

A pause succeeded; then I spoke of the "prer-ies," as almost all western men pronounce the word. I drew such an outline of the life as I supposed my companion passed there, thinking it might be agreeable to hear his own habits and enjoyments extolled.

"I'll tell you how it is, Colonel," returned the interpreter, with a little show of feeling; much more than he had previously manifested on any occasion during our short acquaintance; "yes, I'll jist tell you how it is. Prer-ie life is delightsome to them that loves freedom and justice."

"Freedom I can understand," said I, interrupting him, in my surprise—"but as for justice, I should think that laws are absolutely necessary."

"Ay, that's a settlement idee, I know; but it's not as true as some supposes. There is no court and jury like *this*, Colonel," slapping the breech of his rifle with energy, "and eastern powder conspired with Galena lead, makes the best of attorneys. I've tried both, and speak on sartainty. Law druv' me out upon the prer-ies, and love for them keeps me there. Down this-a-way, you're neither one thing nor tuther—law nor rifle; for, if you *had* law, as law *ought* to be, you and I wouldn't be sitting here, at this time of night, to prevent your mock Injins from setting fire to your houses and barns."

There was only too much truth in this last position of the straightforward interpreter to be gainsaid. After making some proper allowances for the difficulties of the case, and the unexpected circumstances, no impartial man could deny that the laws had been trifled with, or things never would have reached the pass they had: as Manytongues affirmed, we had neither the protection of the law, nor the use of the rifle. It ought to be written in letters of brass in all the highways and places of resort in the country, that A STATE OF SOCIETY WHICH PRETENDS TO THE PROTECTION THAT BELONGS TO CIVILIZATION, AND FAILS TO GIVE IT, ONLY MAKES THE CONDITION OF THE HONEST PORTION OF THE COMMUNITY SO MUCH THE WORSE, BY DEPRIVING IT OF THE PROTECTION CONFERRED BY NATURE, WITHOUT SUPPLYING THE SUBSTITUTE.

I dare say the interpreter and I sat an hour under that tree, conversing in low voices, on such matters and things as came uppermost in our minds. There was a good deal of true prer-ie philosophy in the opinions of my companion, which is much as if one should say his notions were a mixture of clear natural justice and strong local prejudices. The last sentiment he uttered was so very characteristic as to merit particular notice.

"I'll tell you how it is, Colonel," he said, "right is right, and nonsense is nonsense. If so be, we should happen to catch one of these mocking rascals firing your house or barn, it would be a smart chance at justice to settle things on the spot. · If I had *my* way, I should just tie the fellow, hands and feet, and toss him into the flames to help him along with his own work. A rascal makes the best of kindling-wood!"

Just at that instant I saw an upper leaf of the inside shutter of Mary Warren's room open, for my eye was resting on the window at that very moment. The light had been brought so near the opening as plainly to show the change, leaving no doubt that my fair sentinel within had made some important discovery. At such a summons I could not hesitate; but, telling Manytongues to continue his watchfulness, I went across the lawn with the steps of youth and haste.· In two minutes my hand was on the latch of the little door ; and, in two seconds more, it was open, and I found myself standing in front of Mary Warren. A gesture from her hand induced me to be cautious, and closing the door silently, I asked an explanation.

" Speak not too loud," whispered the anxious girl, pre- serving a wonderful self-command, nevertheless, for the extraordinary circumstances in which she was placed." I have discovered them; they are here!"

" Here !—not in the house, surely ?"

" In the house itself!—in the kitchen, where they are kindling a fire on the floor at this instant. Come quickly; —there is not a moment to lose."

It may be well to explain here the arrangement of the kitchens and offices, in order to render what is to follow the more intelligible. The gateway mentioned cut the southern wing of the house into two equal parts, the chambers, how- ever, extending the whole length, and of course passing over it. ·On the western side of this gateway were certain offices connected with the· eating-rooms, and those eating- rooms themselves. On the eastern side were the kitchen, servants' hall, scullery, &c., and a flight of narrow stairs that led to the chambers occupied by the domestics. The outside door to this latter portion of the building was be- neath the arch of the gateway, one corresponding to it opening on its opposite side, and by means of which the service was ordinarily made. There was a court, environed on three of its sides by the main edifice, and by the two long, low wings that have been so often mentioned, while it was open on the fourth to the cliff. This cliff was low, and, while it was nearly perpendicular, it was possible for an active man to ascend, or even to descend it, by clinging to the rocks, which were sufficiently ragged to admit of such an adventure. When a boy I had done both fifty times, and it was a somewhat common experiment among the male domestics and hirelings of the household. It occurred to me at once that the incendiaries had most probably entered the house by ascending the cliff, the kitchen of itself furnishing all the materials to light a conflagration.

The reader will be assured that, after receiving the startling communication of Mary Warren, I did not stop to discuss all these matters with her. My first impulse was to desire her to run to the beech, and bid Manytongues join me, but she refused to quit my side.

"No—no—no. You must not go to the kitchen alone," she said, hurriedly. " There are *two* of them, and desperate looking wretches are they, with their faces blackened, and they have muskets. No—no—no. Come, *I* will accompany you."

I hesitated no longer, but moved forward, Mary keeping close at my side. Fortunately, I had brought the rifle with me, and the revolving pistol was in my pocket. We went by the eating-rooms and offices, the course taken by Mary herself on her watch; and who, in looking through a small window of one of the last, that opened beneath the gateway, had discovered what was going on, by means of a similar window in the kitchen. As we went, the noble girl told me that she had kept moving through the lower rooms of the whole house during the time I had been on watch out of doors, and, attracted by the light that gleamed through these windows, she had distinctly seen two men, with blackened faces, kindling a fire in a corner of the kitchen, where the flames must soon communicate with the stairs, by means of which they would speedily reach the attics and the wood work of the roof. Fortunately, the floors of all that part of the house were made of bricks; that of the servants' hall excepted, which was a room beyond the narrow passage that contained the stairs. As soon as apprised of the danger, Mary Warren had flown to the window of her own room, to make the signal to me, and then to the door to meet me. But three or four minutes had elapsed between the time

30

when she became apprised of the danger and that when we were walking hurriedly to the window beneath the gateway.

A bright light, which shone through the opposite window, announced the progress made by the incendiaries. Requesting Mary to remain where she was, I passed through the door, and descended to the pavement of the gateway. The little window beneath the arch was too high for my purposes, when on that level, but there was a row of low windows that opened on the court. To one of these I moved swiftly, and got a clear view of all that was passing within.

"There they are!" exclaimed Mary, who, neglectful of my request, still kept close at my side. "Two men with blackened faces, and the wood of which they have made their fire is blazing brightly."

The fire, now I saw it, did not confirm the dread I felt when I had it before me only in imagination. The stairway had an open plaze beneath it, and on the brick floor below had the incendiaries built their pile. It was constructed, at the bottom, of some of the common wood that was found there, in readiness for the wants of the cook in the morning, lighted by coals taken from the fire-place. A considerable pile had been made with the wood, which was now burning pretty freely, and the two rascals were busy piling on the chairs when I first saw them. They had made a good beginning, and in ten or fifteen minutes longer there is no doubt that all that portion of the house would have been in flames.

"You said they had muskets," I whispered to Mary. "Do you see them now?"

"No: when I saw them, each held his musket in one hand, and worked with the other."

I could have shot the villains without difficulty or risk to myself, but felt deeply averse to taking human life. Still, there was the prospect of a serious struggle before me, and I saw the necessity of obtaining assistance.

"Will you go to my uncle's room, Mary, and tell him to rise immediately. Then to the front door of the house, and call out, 'Manytongues, come here as fast as possible.' It will take but two minutes to do both, and I will watch these rascals in the mean time."

"I dread leaving you here alone with the wretches, Mr.
Littlepage," whispered Mary, gently.

An earnest entreaty on my part, however, induced her
to comply ; and, no sooner did the dear girl set about the
accomplishment of the task, than she flew rather than ran.
It did not seem to me a minute ere I heard her call to the interpreter. The night was so still, that, sweet as were those
tones, and busy as were the incendiaries, they heard them
too ; or fancied they heard something which alarmed them.
They spoke to each other, looked intently at their infernal
work for a single instant, sought their arms, which were
standing in the corner of the kitchen, and were evidently
preparing to depart.

The crisis was near. There was not time to receive assistance before the two fellows would be out, and I must
either meet them in conflict, or suffer them to escape. My
first·impression was to shoot down the leading man, and
grapple with the other ere he had time to prepare his arms.
But a timely thought prevented this hazardous step. The
incendiaries were retiring, and I had a doubt of the legality
of killing a retreating felon. I believed that *my* chances
before a jury would be far less than those of an ordinary
pick-pocket or highway robber, and had heard and read
enough to be certain there were thousands around me who
would fancy it a sufficient moral provocation ·for all which
had passed, that I held the fee, of farms that other men desired to possess.

A majority of my countrymen will scout this idea as forced
and improbable. But, majorities are far from being infallible in their judgments. Let any discreet and observant man
take a near view of that which is daily going on around him.
If he do not find in men this disposition to distort principles,
to pervert justice, and to attain their ends regardless of the
means, then will I admit I do not understand human nature,
as human nature exhibits its deformity in this blessed republic of ours.

There was no time to lose, however ; and the course I
actually decided to take will be soonest told by relating
things as they occurred. I heard the door open, and was
ready for action. Whether the incendiaries intended to
retreat by the cliff, or to open the gate, which was barred

within, I could not tell; but I was ready for either alternative.

. No sooner did I hear a step on the pavement of the gateway than I discharged my rifle in the air. This was done
as an alarm-signal. Clubbing the piece, I sprang forward,
and felled the foremost of the two, with a sharp blow on his
hat. The fellow came down on the pavement like an ox
under the axe of the slaughter-house. Dropping the rifle, I
bounded over his body, and grappled with his companion.
All this was done so rapidly as to take the rascals completely by surprise. So sudden, indeed, was my assault on
the fellow who stood erect, that he was under the necessity
of dropping his rifle, and at it we went, clenched like bears
in the death-hug. I was young and active, but my antagonist was the stronger man of the two. He had also the
advantage of being practised in wrestling, and I soon went
down, my enemy falling on top of me. Luckily, I fell on
the body of the other incendiary, who was just beginning to
discover signs of consciousness after the crushing blow he
had received. My chance would now have been small but
for assistance. The incendiary had caught my neck-hand-
kerchief, and was twisting it to choke me, when I felt a
sudden relief. The light of the fire shone through the
kitchen doors, rendering everything distinct beneath the arch.
Mary came flying back just in time to rescue me. With a
resolution that did her honour, she caught up the rifle I had
dropped, and passed its small end between the bent arms of
my antagonist and his own back, raising it at the same time
like a lever. In the brief interval of breathing this ready
expedient gave me, I rallied my force, caught my enemy by
the throat, made a desperate effort, threw him off, and over
on his side, and was on my feet in an instant. Drawing the
pistol, I ordered the rascal to yield, or to take the consequences. The sight of this weapon secured the victory, the
black-faced villain shrinking back into a corner, begging
piteously not to be shot. At the next moment, the interpreter appeared under the arch, followed by a stream of redskins, which had been turned in this direction by the alarm
given by my rifle.

CHAPTER XXIII.

" Ye say they all have passed away,
That noble race and brave ;
That their light canoes have vanish'd
From off the crested wave ; ,
That 'mid the forests where they roam'd
There rings no hunter's shout ;
But their name is on your waters,
Ye may not wash it out."

MRS. SIGOURNEY.

DIRECTING Manytongues to secure the two incendiaries, sprang into the kitchen to extinguish the flames. It was nigh time, though Mary Warren had already anticipated me here, too. She had actually thrown several dippers of water upon the fire, which was beginning to crackle through the pile of chairs, and had already succeeded in lessening the flames. I knew that a hydrant stood in the kitchen itself, which gave a full stream of water. Filling a pail, I threw the contents on the flames ; and repeating the application, in half a minute the room was filled with vapour, and to the bright light succeeded a darkness that was so deep as to suggest the necessity of finding lamps and candles.

The tumult produced by the scene just described soon brought all in the house to the spot. The domestics, male and female, came tumbling down the stairs, under which the fire had been lighted, and presently candles were seen glancing about the house, in all directions.

"I declare, Mr. Hugh," cried John, the moment he had taken a survey of the state of the kitchen, "this is worse than Hireland, sir ! The Hamericans affect to laugh at the poor Hirish, and calls their country savage, and hunfit to be in'abited, but nothing worse passes in it than is beginning to pass 'ere. Them stairs would have been all in flames in a few minutes, and them stairs once on fire, not one of hus, up in the hattics, could 'ave escaped death ! Don't talk of Hireland, after this !"

Poor John ! his prejudices are those of an Englishman of

30*

his class, and that is saying as much in favour of their strength as *can* be well said of any prejudices. But, how much truth was there in his remark! The quiet manner in which we assume superiority, in morals, order, justice, and virtue, over all other nations, really contains an instructive lesson, if one will only regard things as they really are. I have no wish to exaggerate the faults of my own country, but certainly I shall not remorselessly conceal them, when the most dangerous consequences are connected with such a mistake. As a whole, the disorders, disturbances, and convulsions of America have certainly been much fewer than those of most, perhaps of all other Christian nations, comparing numbers, and including the time since the great experiment commenced. But, such *ought* to have been the result of our facts, quite independently of national character. The institutions leave nothing for the masses to struggle for, and famine is unknown among us. But what does the other side of the picture exhibit? Can any man point to a country in Europe in which a great political movement has com menced on a principle as barefacedly knavish as that of transferring property from one class of men to another. That such a project does exist here, is beyond all just con tradiction; and it is equally certain that it has carried its devices into legislation, and is fast corrupting the govern ment in its most efficient agents. John was right in saying we ought not to turn up our noses at the ebullitions of abused and trodden-on "Hireland," while our own skirts are to be cleared of such sins against the plainest dictates of right.

The fire was extinguished, and the house was safe. The kitchen was soon cleared of the steam and smoke, and in their places appeared a cloud of redskins. Prairiefire, Ea glesflight, and Flintyheart, were all there, examining the effects of the fire, with stern and interested countenances. I looked round for Mary Warren; but that gentle and singu- larly feminine girl, after manifesting a presence of mind and decision that would have done honour to a young man of her own age, had shrunk back with sensitive consciousness, and now concealed herself among the others of her sex. Her duty, so eminently useful and protective, had been per- formed, and she was only anxious to have it all forgotten This I discovered only next day, however

Manytongues had secured the incendiaries, and they were now in the kitchen, also, with their hands tied together, and arms bound behind their backs, at the elbows. As heir faces remained black, it was out of my power to recognise either. The rascal who had been felled by the blow of the rifle was yet confused in manner, and I ordered the domestics to wash him, in the double expectation of bringing him more completely to his senses, and of ascertaining who he might be.

The work was soon done, and both objects were attained. The cook used a dishcloth with so much dexterity, that the black-a-moor came out a white man, at the first application, and he was soon as clean as a child that is about to be sent to school, fresh from the hands of its nurse. The removal of the disguise brought out the abashed and frightened physiognomy of Joshua Brigham, Miller's hired man — or *my* hired man, in effect, as I paid him his wages.

Yes! such was one of the effects of the pernicious opinions that had been so widely circulated in the land, during the profound moral mania that was working its ravages among us, with a fatality and danger that greatly exceed those which accompanied the cholera. A fellow, who was almost an inmate of my family, had not only conspired with others to rob me of my property, on a large scale, but he had actually carried his plot so far as to resort to the brand and the rifle, as two of the agents to be employed in carrying out his virtuous objects. Nor was this the result of the vulgar disposition to steal; it was purely a consesequence of a widely-extended system, that is fast becoming incorporated with the politics of the land, and which men, relying on the efficacy of majorities, are bold enough to stand up, in legislative halls, to defend.*

---

* In order that the reader who is not familiar with what is passing in New York may not suppose that exaggerated terms are here used, the writer will state a single expedient of the anti-renters in the legislature to obtain their ends. It is generally known that the Constitution of the United States prevents the separate States from passing laws impairing the obligations of contracts. But for this provision of the Federal Constitution, it is probable, numbers would have succeeded, long ago, in obtaining the property of the few on their own terms, amid shouts in honour of liberty! This provision, however, has proved

I confess that the discovery of the person of Joshua Brigham rendered me a little curious to ascertain that of his companion. Hester, the cook, was directed to take the other child in hand, as soon as she had well wiped the countenance of the one first unmasked. Nothing loth, the good housewife set about her task, and the first dab of water she applied revealed the astounding fact that I had again captured Seneca Newcome! It will be remembered, that the last time I saw these two men together, I left them fighting in the highway.

I admit that this discovery shocked me. There never had been a being of the Newcome tribe, from the grandfather, who was its root at Ravensnest, down to Opportunity, who had ever been esteemed, or respected among us. Trick— trick—trick—low cunning, and overreaching management, had been the family trait, from the day Jason, of that name, had rented the mill lot, down to the present hour. This I had heard from my grandfather, my grandmother, my own father, my uncle, my aunts and all, older than myself, who belonged to me. Still, *there* they had been, and habit had created a sort of feeling for them. There had, also, been a species of pretension about the family, which brought them more before us, than most of the families of the tenantry.

---

a stubborn obstacle, until the world, near the middle of the nineteenth century, has been favoured with the following notable scheme to effect the ends of those who 'want farms and must have them.' The State *can* regulate, by statute, the law of descents. It has, accordingly, been solemnly proposed in the legislature of New York, that the statute of descents should be so far altered, that when a landlord, holding lands subject to certain leasehold tenures, dies, or a descent is cast, that it shall be lawful for the tenants, on application to the chancellor, to convert these leasehold tenures into mortgages, and to obtain the fee-simple of the estates in payment of the debt ! In other words, A leases a farm to B for ever, reserving a ground-rent, with covenants of re-entry, &c. &c. B wishes a deed, but will not pay A's price. The United States says the contract shall not be impaired, and the Legislature of New York is illustrated by the expedient we have named, to get over the provision of the Constitution !

Since writing the foregoing, this law has actually passed the Assembly, though it has not been adopted by the Senate. The provision included all leased property, when the leases were for more than twenty-one years, or were on lives. — EDITOR.

The grandfather had received a sort of an education, and
.his practice had been continued, after a manner, down to
the unfortunate wretch who now stood a prisoner taken
flagrante delictu, and for a capital crime. Seneca could
never have made a gentleman, as the term is understood
among gentlemen ; but he belonged to a profession which
ought to raise a man materially above the level of the vulgar.
Opportunity, too, had received her *quasi* education, a far
more pretending one than that of my own Patt, but nothing
had been well taught to her ; not even reading, inasmuch as
she had a decided provincial pronunciation, which sometimes grated on my nerves. But, Opportunity had feelings,
and could not have anticipated her own brother's intentions,
when she communicated the important information she had.
Opportunity, moreover, had more refinement than Seneca,
in consequence of having a more limited association, and she
might fall into despair, at this unexpected result of her
own acts !

·I was still reflecting on these things, when summoned to
my. grandmother. She was in her own dressing-room, surrounded by the four girls ; just so many pictures of alarm,
interest, and female loveliness. Mary Warren, alone, was in
regular *toilette ;* but the others, with instinctive coquetry, had
contrived to wrap themselves up, in a way to render them
handsomer than ever. As for my dear grandmother herself, she had been told that the house was safe, but felt that
vague desire to see me, that was perhaps natural to the circumstances.

" The state of the country is frightful," she said, when I
had answered a few of her questions, and had told her who
the prisoners really were ; " and we can hardly remain here,
in safety. Think of one of the Newcomes—and of Seneca,
in particular, with ·his profession and education, being engaged in such a crime !"

" Nay, grandmother," put in Patt, a little archly, " I never
yet heard you speak well of the Newcomes : you barely
tolerated Opportunity, in the hope of improving her."

" It is true, that the race is a bad one, and the circumstances show what injury a set of false notions, transmitted
from father to son, for generations, may do in a family.
We cannot think of keeping these dear girls, here, one

hour after to-morrow, Hugh.   To-morrow, or to-day, for it
is now past two o'clock, I see ;—to-day is Sunday, and we
can go to church ; to-night we will be watchful, and Monday morning, your uncle shall start for Satanstoe, with all
three of the girls."

"I shall not leave my dear grandmother," rejoined Patt—
"nor do I think it would be very kind to leave Mary Warren behind us, in a place like this."

"I cannot quit my father," said Mary, herself, quietly,
but very firmly.   "It is his duty to remain with his parishioners, and more so, now, that so many of them are misguided, than at any other time ; and it is always my duty,
and my pleasure, to remain with *him*."

Was that acting?   Was that Pharisaical?   Or was it
genuine nature ; pure filial affection and filial piety?   Beyond all question, it was the last ; and had not the simple
tone, the earnest manner, and the almost alarmed eagerness,
with which the dear girl spoke, proclaimed as much, no one
could have looked in at that serene and guileless eye and
doubted.   My grandmother smiled on the lovely earnest
speaker, in her kindest manner, took her hand, and charmingly observed—

"Mary and I will remain together.   Her father is in no
danger, for even anti-renters will respect a minister of the
gospel, and can be made to understand it is his duty to rebuke even their sins.   As for the other girls, I think it is
our duty to insist that your uncle's wards, at least, should
no longer be exposed to dangers like those we have gone
through to-night."

The two young ladies, however, protested in the prettiest
manner possible, their determination not to quit "grandmamma," as they affectionately termed their guardian's
mother; and while they were thus employed, my uncle Ro
entered the room, having just paid a visit to the kitchen.

"Here's a charming affair !" exclaimed the old bachelor,
as soon as in our midst.   "Arson, anti-rentism, attempts at
murder, and all sorts of enormities, going hand in hand, in
the very heart of the wisest and best community that earth
ever knew ; and the laws as profoundly asleep the whole
time, as if such gentle acts were considered meritorious.
This out-does repudiation twenty-fold, Hugh.

"Ay, my dear sir, but it will not make a tithe of the talk. Look at the newspapers that will be put into your hands to-morrow morning, fresh from Wall and Pine and Anne streets. They will be in convulsions, if some unfortunate wight of a Senator speak of adding an extra corporal to a regiment of foot, as an alarming war-demonstration, or quote the fall of a fancy stock that has not one cent of intrinsic value, as if it betokened the downfall of a nation; while they doze over this volcano, which is raging and gathering strength beneath the whole community, menacing destruction to the nation itself, which is the father of stocks."

"The intense selfishness that is uppermost is a bad symptom, certainly; and no one can say to what it will lead. One thing is sure; it causes men to limit all their calculations to the present moment; and to abate a nuisance that presses on our existing interests, they will jeopard everything that belongs to the future. But what are we to do with Seneca Newcome, and his co-rascal, the other incendiary?"

"I had thought of referring that to your discretion, sir. They have been guilty of arson, I suppose, and must take their chances, like every-day criminals."

"Their chances will be very good ones, Hugh. Had *you* been caught in Seneca Newcome's kitchen, setting fire to his house, condign and merciless punishment would have been *your* lot, beyond all controversy; but *their* cases will be very different. I'll bet you a hundred that they'll not be convicted; and a thousand that they are pardoned, if convicted."

"Acquitted, sir, will be out of the question—Miss Warren and I saw them both, in the very act of building their fire; and there is plenty of testimony, as to their identity."

This indiscreet speech drew every eye on my late companion; all the ladies, old and young, repeating the name of "Mary!" in the pretty manner in which the sex expresses surprise. As for Mary, herself, the poor blushing girl shrunk back abashed, ashamed of she knew not what, unless it migh. be in connection with some secret consciousness, at finding herself so strangely associated with me.

"Miss Warren is, indeed, in her evening dress," said my

grandmother, a little gravely, "and cannot have been in bed this night. How has this happened, my dear?"

Thus called on, Mary Warren was of too guileless and pure a mind, to hesitate in telling her tale. Every incident, with which she had been connected, was simply and clearly related, though she suppressed the name of our midnight visiter, out of tenderness to Opportunity. All present were too discreet to ask the name, and, I may add, all present heard the narrative with a marked and approving interest. When Mary had done, my grandmother kissed her, and Patt, the generous creature, encircled her waist, with the tenderness and affection of a sister, who felt for all the trials the other had endured.

"It seems, then, we owe our safety to Mary, after all!" exclaimed my good grandmother; "without her care and watchfulness, Hugh might, most probably *would*, have remained on the lawn, until it was too late to save the house, or us."

"That is not all," added uncle Ro. "Any one could have cried 'fire,' or given a *senseless* alarm, but it is evident from Miss Warren's account, unpremeditated and artless as it is that, but for the cool and discreet manner in which she played her part, not one-half of that which has been done, would have been effected, and that the house might have been lost. Nay, had these fellows surprised Hugh, instead of Hugh's surprising them, we might have been called on to deplore his loss."

I saw a common shudder in Patt and Mary, as they stood encircling each other with their arms; but the last was evidently so pained, that I interfered for her relief.

"I do not see any possibility of escape for these incendiaries," I said, turning to my uncle, "under the testimony that can be offered, and am surprised to hear you suggest a doubt of the result of the trial."

"You feel and reason like a very young man, Hugh; one, who fancies things are much nearer what they ought to be than facts will sustain. Justice is blind, now-a-days, not as a proof of impartiality, but as a proof that she too often sees only one side of a question. How will they escape? Perhaps the jury may fancy setting fire to a pile of wood, and certain chairs, is not setting fire to a house, let the *animus* be as plain as the noses on their faces. Mark me, Hugh Littlepage; one month will not go by, before the events of this very night will be tortured into an argument in favour of anti-rentism."

A common exclamation, in which even my grandmother joined, expressed the general dissent from this opinion.

"It is all very well, ladies," answered my uncle Ro, coolly—"all well enough, Master Hugh; but let the issue tell its own story.. I have heard already *other* abuses of the anti-renters urged as a reason why the laws should be changed, in order that men may not be tempted beyond their strength; and why not use the same reasoning in favour of this crime, when it has been used already, in cases of murder? 'The leasehold tenures make men commit murder,' it is said, 'and they ought to be destroyed,' themselves. 'The leasehold tenures make men commit arson,' it will now be said, 'and who desires to retain laws that induce men to commit arson?'"

"On the same principle it might be pretended there should be no such thing as personals, as they tempt men, beyond what they can bear, to commit petty larceny."

"No doubt it could, and no doubt it *would*, if political supremacy were to be the reward. There is nothing—no fallacy, no moral sophism, that would not be used to attain such an end. But, it is late, and we ought to bethink us of disposing of the prisoners for the night—what means this light? The house is not on fire, after all!"

Sure enough, notwithstanding the closed shutters, and drawn curtains of my grandmother's dressing-room, an unusual light had penetrated to the place, filling us with sudden and intense alarm. I opened the door, and found the passages illuminated, though all within appeared tranquil and safe. There was a clamour in the court, however, and presently the fearful war-whoop of the savages rose on the night air. The cries came from without, as I fancied, and rushing to the little door, I was on the lawn in a moment, when the mystery was solved. An extensive hay-barn, one well filled with the remainder of the last year's crops, was on fire, sending its forked and waving tongues of flame at least a hundred feet into the air. It was merely a new ar-

31

gument against the leasehold tenures, and in favour of the
" spirit of the institutions,": a little vividly pressed on the
human senses.   Next year, it may figure in the message of
a governor, or the philanthropical efforts of some Albany
orator, if the same " spirit" prevail in the " institutions," as
would seem to prevail this!   Is a contract to be tolerated
which induces freemen to set barns on fire? ·

The barn that had been set on fire stood on the flats, below the cliff, and fully half a mile from the Nest. The conflagration made a most brilliant blaze, and, as a matter of
course, produced an intense light.   The loss to myself did
not exceed a few hundred dollars ; and, while this particular argument in favour of anti-rentism was not entirely
agreeable, it was not so grave as it might have been, had it
been urged on other buildings, and in the same mode.   In
other words, I was not so much distressed with my loss as
not to be able to see the beauty of the scene; particularly
as my uncle Ro whispered that Dunning had caused an in-
surance to be effected in the Saratoga Mutual Assurance,
which would probably place a considerable portion of the
tenants in the unlooked-for category of those who were to
pay for their own frolic.

As it was too late to think of saving the barn and ricks,
and Miller, with his people, had already descended to the
spot to look after the fences, and any other object that might
be endangered by the flying embers, there was nothing for
us to do but to remain passive spectators. Truly, the scene
was one worthy of being viewed, and is not altogether unfit
for description.

The light of that burning barn extended for a great distance, shining like what it was, an " evil deed in a naughty
world;" for, notwithstanding the high authority of Shakspeare, it is your "evil deeds," after all, that produce the
brightest blazes, and which throw their beams the farthest,
in this state of probation in which we live.

The most remarkable objects in that remarkable scene
were the true and the false redskins—the " Indians" and the
" Injins"—both of whom were in motion on the meadows,
and both of whom were distinctly visible to us where we
stood, on the cliffs (the ladies being at their chamber win-

dows), though I dare say they were not quite so obvious to each other.

The Indians had formed themselves into a very open order, and were advancing towards the other party in a stealthy manner, by creeping on all-fours, or crouching like catamounts to the earth, and availing themselves of everything like a cover that offered. The burning barn was between the two parties, and was a principal reason that the "Injins" were not sooner aware of the risk they ran. The last were a whooping, shouting, dancing, leaping band, of some forty or fifty of the "disguised and armed," who were quite near enough to the conflagration to enjoy it, without being so near as to be necessarily connected with it. We understood their presence and antics to be intended as so many intimations of the secret agency they had had in the depredations of the night, and as so many warnings how I withstood the " spirit of the Institutions."

Manytongues, who had certain vague notions of the necessity of his keeping on the windy side of the law, did not accompany his red brethren, but came through the gateway and joined my uncle and myself, as we stood beneath the cover of a noble chestnut, on the verge of the cliff, watching the course of things on the meadow. I expressed my surprise at seeing him there, and inquired if his presence might not be needed by Flintyheart or Prairiefire.

" Not at all, not at all, Colonel," he answered with perfect coolness. " The savages have no great need of an intarpreter in the business they are on ; and if harm comes of the meetin', it's perhaps best that the two parties should not understand each other, in which case it might all be looked on as an accident. I hope they'll not be particular about scalps,—for I told Flintyheart, as he was leaving us, the people of this part of the world did not like to be scalped."

This was the only encouragement we received from the interpreter, who appeared to think that matters were now in the right train, and that every difficulty would soon be disposed of, *secundum artem*. The Injins, however, viewed the affair differently, having no wish for a serious brush with any one ; much less with enemies of the known character of red-skins. How they ascertained the presence of their foe I cannot say; though it is probable some one saw them stealing along the meadows, in spite of all their care, and gave the alarm. Alarm it was, sure enough; the party of the previous day scarce retreating through the woods with greater haste than the "disguised and armed" now vanished.

Such has been the fact, as respects these men, in every instance in which they have been brought in contact with armed bodies, though much inferior to their own in numbers. Fierce enough, and even brutal, on a variety of occasions in which individuals have become subject to their power, in all cases in which armed parties, however small, have been sent against them, they have betrayed timidity and a dread of making that very appeal to force, which, by their own previous acts, they had insolently invited. Is it then true, that these soi-disant "Injins" have not the ordinary courage of their race, and that they are less than Americans, with arms in their hands, and below the level of all around them in spirit? Such is not the case. The consciousness of guilt has made them cowards; they have found "that the king's name is a tower of strength," and have shrunk from conflicts, in which the secret warnings that come from on high have told them that they were embodied in a wicked cause, and contending for the attainment of wrong ends by unjustifiable means... Their conduct proves how easy it would have been to suppress their depredations at the earliest day, by a judicious application of the power of the State, and how much *they* have to answer for who have neglected their duty in this particular.

As soon as Flintyheart and his followers ascertained tha the "disguised and armed" were actually off again, and that they were not to pass the morning in a skirmish, as no doubt each man among them had hoped would to be the case, they set up such whoops and cries as had not been heard on those meadows during the last eighty years. The period went beyond the memory of man since Indian warfare had existed at Ravensnest, a few false alarms in the revolution excepted. The effect of these yells was to hasten the retreat, as was quite apparent to us on the cliffs; but the sagacious warriors of the Prairies knew too much to expose their persons by approaching nearer to the blazing barn than might be prudent. On the contrary; seemingly satisfied that nothing was to be done, and disdaining a parade of service where no service was to be effected, they slowly retired from the meadows, regaining the cliffs by means known to themselves.

This military demonstration, on the part of our red brethren, was not without its useful consequences. It gave the " Injins" an intimation of watchfulness, and of a readiness to meet them that prevented any new alarm that night, and satisfied everybody at the Nest that our immediate danger had come to an end. Not only was this the feeling of my uncle and myself, but it was also the feeling of the females, as we found on returning to the house, who had witnessed all that passed from the upper windows. After a short interview with my grandmother, she consented to retire, and preparations were made for setting a look-out, and dismissing everybody to their beds again. Manytongues took charge of the watch, though he laughed at the probability of there being any further disturbance that night.

"As for the redskins," he said, " they would as soon sleep out under the trees, at this season of the year, as sleep under a roof; and as for waking—cats a'nt their equals. No—no—Colonel; leave it all to me, and I'll carry you through the night as quietly as if we were on the prer-ies and living under good wholesome prer-ie law."

"As quietly, as if we were on the prairies!" We had then reached that pass in New York, that after one burning, a citizen might really hope to pass the remainder of his night as quietly as if he were on the prairies! And there was that frothy, lumbering, useless machine, called a government, at Albany, within fifty miles of us, as placid, as self-satisfied, as much convinced that this was the greatest people on earth, and itself their illustrious representatives, as if the disturbed counties were so many gardens of Eden, before sin and transgression had become known to it! If it was doing anything in the premises, it was probably calculating the minimum the tenant should pay for the landlord's land, when the latter might be sufficiently worried to part with his estate. Perhaps, it was illustrating its notions of liberty, by naming the precise sum that one citi-

31*

zen ought to accept, in order that the covetous longings of
another should be satisfied !

I was about to retire to my bed, for the first time tha
night, when my uncle Ro remarked it might be well to see
one of our prisoners at least. Orders had been given to
unbind the wretched men, and to keep them in an empty
store-room, which had no available outlet but the door.
Thither we then repaired, and of course were admitted by
the sentinels, without a question. Seneca Newcome was
startled at my appearance, and I confess I was myself embarrassed how to address him, from a wish to say nothing
that might appear like exultation on one side, or concession
on the other. My uncle, however, had no such scruples,
probably from better knowing his man ; accordingly, he
came to the point at once.

"The evil spirit must have got great ascendency in the
country, Seneca Newcome, when men of your knowledge,
dip so deeply into his designs," said Mr. Littlepage, sternly.
" What has my nephew ever done to incite *you* to come into
his house, as an incendiary, like a thief in the night ?"

." Ask me no questions, Mr. Littlepage," surlily replied
the attorney, "for I shall answer none."

. " And this miserable misguided creature who has been
your companion. The last we saw of these two men, Hugh,
hey were quarrelling in the highway, like cat and dog, and
there are signs about their faces that the interview became
still more hostile than it had been, after we left them."

" And here we find them together, companions in an enterprise of life and death !" -

. " It is ever thus with rogues. They will push their quarrels to extremities, and make them up in an hour, when the
demon of rapine points to an object for common plunder.
You see the same spirit in politics, ay, and even in religion.
Men that have lived in hostility, for half their lives, contending for selfish objects, will suddenly combine their powers to attain a common end, and work together like the
most true-hearted friends, so long as they see a chance of
effecting their wishes. If honesty were only one-half as
active as roguery, it would fare better than it does. But the
honest man has his scruples ; his self-respect ; his consis
tency, and most of all his principles, to mark out his course.

and he cannot turn aside at each new impulse, like your
pure knave to convert enemies into friends, and friends into
enemies. And you," turning to Josh Brigham, who was
looking surlily on—" who have actually been eating Hugh
Littlepage's bread, what has he done, that you should come
at midnight, to burn him up like a caterpillar in the
spring?"

" He has had his farm long enough"—muttered the fellow—" it's time that poor folks had some chance."

My uncle shrugged his shoulders; then, as if he suddenly
recollected himself, he lifted his hat, bowed like a thorough-
bred gentleman as he was, when he chose to be, wished
Seneca good night, and walked away. As we retired, he
expressed his conviction of the uselessness of remonstrance,
in this case, and of the necessity of suffering the law to take
its own course. It might be unpleasant to see a Newcome
actually hanged, but nothing short of that operation, he felt
persuaded would ever fetch up the breed in its evil courses.
Wearied with all that had passed, I now went to bed, and
slept soundly for the succeeding seven hours. As the house
was kept quiet by orders, everybody repaired the lost time,
the Nest being as quiet as in those days in which the law
ruled in the republic.

CHAPTER XXIV.

" Well may we sing her beauties
This pleasant land of ours,
Her sunny smiles, her golden fruits,
And all her world of flowers.
And well would they persuade us now,
In moments all too dear,
That, sinful though our hearts may be,
We have our Eden here."

SIMMS.

THE following day was Sunday. I did not rise until
nine, and when I withdrew the curtains and opened the shutters of my window, and looked out upon the lawn, and the
fields beyond it, and the blue void that canopied all, I thought
a lovelier day, or one more in harmony with the tranquil
character of the whole scene, never shone from the heavens.
I threw up the sash, and breathed the morning air which
filled my dressing-room, pregnant with the balms and odours
of the hundred sweet-smelling flowers and plants that em-
bellished the shrubberies. The repose of the Sabbath seemed
to rest on man and beast ; the bees and humming-birds that
buzzed about the flowers, even at their usual pursuits seemed
as if conscious of the sanctity of the day. I think no one
can be insensible to the difference there is between a Sabbath
in the country and any other day of the week. Most of
this, doubtless, is the simple consequence of abstaining from
labour ; but, connected with the history of the festival, its
usual observances, and the holy calm that appears to reign
around, it is so very obvious and impressive, that a Sunday
in a mild day in June, is to me ever a delicious resting-place,
as a mere poetical pause in the bustling and turmoil of this
world's time. Such a day was that which succeeded the
night through which we had just passed, and it came most
opportunely to soothe the spirits, tranquillize the apprehensions, and afford a moment for sober reflection.

There lay the smouldering ruins of the barn, it is true ;
a blackened monument of a wicked deed ; but the mood

which had produced this waste and wrong appeared to have passed away; and, in all other respects, far and near, the farms of Ravensnest had never spread themselves before the eye in colours more in consonance with the general benevolence of a bountiful nature. For a moment, as I gazed on the broad view, I felt all my earlier interests in it revive, and am not ashamed to own that a profound feeling of gratitude to God came over me when I recollected it was by his Providence I was born the heir to such a scene, instead of having my lot cast among the serfs and dependants of other regions.

After standing at the window a minute, in contemplation of that pleasing view, I drew back; suddenly and painfully conscious of the character and extent of the combination that existed to rob me of my rights in it. America no longer seemed America to my eyes; but, in place of its ancient submission to the law, its quick distinction between right and wrong, its sober and discriminating liberty, which equally avoided submission to the injustice of power, and the excesses of popular delusion, there had been substituted the rapacity of the plunderer, rendered formidable by the insidious manner in which it was interwoven with political machinery, and the truckling of the wretches entrusted with authority; men who were playing into the hands of demagogues, solely in order to secure majorities to perpetuate their own influence. Was, then, the State really so corrupt as to lend itself to projects as base as those openly maintained by the anti-renters? Far from it: four men out of five, if not a larger proportion, must be, and indeed are, sensible of the ills that their success would entail on the community, and would lift up heart and hand to-morrow to put them down totally and without pity; but they have made themselves slaves of the lamp; have enlisted in the ranks of *party*, and *dare* not oppose their leaders, who wield them as Napoleon wielded his masses, to further private views, apostrophizing and affecting an homage to liberty all the while! Such is the history of man!

When the family met in the breakfast-room, a singular tranquillity prevailed among us. As for my grandmother, I knew her spirit and early experience, and was not so much surprised to find her calm and reasonable; but these quali-

ties seemed imparted to her four young companions also.·
Patt could laugh, and yield to her buoyant spirits, just· tho
same as if nothing had occurred, while my uncle's other
wards maintained a lady-like quiet,.that denoted anything
but apprehension. Mary Warren, however, surprised me·
by her air and deportment. There she sat, in her place at
the· table,· looking, if possible, the most feminine, gentle, and
timid of the four. I could scarcely believe that the blushing,
retiring, modest pretty daughter of the rector could be tho·
prompt, decided, and clear-headed young girl who had been
of so much service to me the past night, and to whose coolness and discretion, indeed, we were all indebted for the roof
that was over our heads, and some of us, most probably, for
our lives.

Notwithstanding this air of tranquillity, the breakfast was
a silent and thoughtful meal. Most of the conversation was
between my uncle and ·grandmother, and a portion of it related to the disposal of the prisoners. There was no magistrate within several miles of the Nest, but those who were
tainted with anti-rentism ; and to carry Seneca and his companion before a justice of the peace of this character, would
be, in effect, to let them go at large. Nominal bail would
be taken, and it is more than probable the constable employed would have suffered a rescue, did they even deem it
necessary to go through this parade of performing their duties. My uncle, consequently, adopted the following plan.
He had caused the two incendiaries to be transferred to the
old farm-house, which happened to contain a perfectly dry
and empty cellar, and which had much of the security of a
dungeon, without the usual defects of obscurity and damp-
ness. The red-men had assumed the office of sentinels, one
having his station at the door, while another watched near
a window which admitted the light, while it was scarcely
large enough to permit the human body to squeeze through
it. The interpreter had received instructions from the agent
to· respect the Christian Sabbath ; and no movement being
contemplated for the day, this little duty just suited their
lounging, idle habits,. when in a state of rest. Food and
water, of course, had not been forgotten ; and there my
uncle Ro had left that portion of the business, intending. to
have the delinquents carried to a distant magistrate,· ono of

the Judges of the County, early on Monday morning. As
for the disturbers of the past night, no signs of them were
any longer visible; and there being little extensive cover
near the Nest, no apprehension was felt of any surprise.

We were still at breakfast, when the tone of St. Andrew's
bell came floating, plaintively, through the air, as a summons to prepare ourselves for the services of the day. It
was little more than a mile to the church, and the younger
ladies expressed a desire to walk. My grandmother, attended by her son, therefore, alone used the carriage, while
we young people went off in a body, on foot, half an hour
before the ringing of the second bell. Considering the state
of the country, and the history of the past night, I was
astonished at my own indifference on this occasion, no less
than at that of my charming companions; nor was it long
before I gave utterance to the feeling.

"This America of ours is a queer place, it must be admitted," I cried, as we crossed the lawn to take a foot-path
that would lead us, by pleasant pastures, quite to the church-
door without entering the high-way, except to cross it once;
' here we have the whole neighbourhood as tranquil as if
crime never disturbed it, though it is not yet a dozen hours
since riot, arson, and perhaps murder, were in the contemplation of hundreds of those who live on every side of us.
The change is wonderful!"

"But, you will remember it is Sunday, Hugh," put in
Patt. "All summer, when Sunday has come, we have had
a respite from disturbances and fears. In this part of the
country, the people are too religious to think of desecrating
the Sabbath by violence and armed bands. The anti-renters
would lose more than they would gain by pursuing a different course."

I had little or no difficulty in believing this, it being no
unusual thing, among us, to find observances of this nature
clinging to the habits of thousands, long after the devout
feeling which had first instilled it into the race has become
extinct. Something very like it prevails in other countries,
and among even higher and more intellectual classes, where it
is no unusual thing to find the most profound outward respect
manifested towards the altar and its rites, by men who live
n the hourly neglect of the first and plainest commands of

the decalogue. 'We are not alone, therefore, in this phari
saical spirit, which exists, in some mode or other, wherevel
man himself is to be found.

But, this equivocal piety was certainly manifested to a
striking degree, that day, at Ravensnest. The very men
who were almost desperate in their covetous longings appeared at church, and went through the service with as
much seeming devotion as if conscious of no evil; and a
general truce appeared to prevail in the country, notwithstanding there must have been much bitterness of feeling
among the discomfited. · Nevertheless, I could detect in the
countenances of many of the old tenants of the family, an
altered expression, and a coldness of the eye, which bespoke
anything but the ancient friendly feeling which had so long
existed between us. The solution was very simple; demagogues had stirred up the spirit—not of the Institutions, but
—of covetousness, in their breasts; and so long as that evil
tendency predominated, there was little room for better
feelings.

"Now, I shall have another look at the canopied pew,"
I cried, as we entered the last field, on our way to the
church. "That offensive, but unoffending, object had
almost gone out of my mind's eye, until my uncle recollected it, by intimating that Jack Dunning, as he calls his
friend and council, had written him it *must* come down."

"I agree with Mr. Dunning altogether," answered Martha, quickly. "I wish with all my heart, Hugh, you would
order that hideous-looking thing to be taken away this very
week." ·

"Why this earnestness, my dear Patt? There has the
hideous thing been ever since the church was built, which
is now these three-score years, and no harm has come of
it, as I know."

· "It is harm to be so ugly. It disfigures the church;
and then I do not think distinctions of that sort are proper
for the house of God. I know this ever has been my
grandmother's opinion; but finding her father-in-law and
husband desirous of such an *ornament*, she consented in
silence, during their lives." ·

"What do *you* say to all this, Miss Warren," I asked
turning to my companion, for by some secret influence I

was walking at her side. "Are you 'up canopy' or 'down canopy'?"

"'Down canopy,'" answered Mary, firmly. "I am of Mrs. Littlepage's opinion, that churches ought to contain as little as possible to mark worldly distinctions. Such distinctions are inseparable from life, I know; but it is to prepare for death that we enter such buildings."

"And your father, Miss Warren — have you ever heard him speak of my unfortunate pew?"

Mary hesitated an instant, changed colour, then looked up into my face with a countenance so ingenuous and lovely, that I would have forgiven her even a severe comment on some act of folly of my own.

"My father is an advocate for doing away with pews altogether," she answered, "and, of course, can have no particular wish to preserve yours. He tells me, that in the churches of the Romanists, the congregation sit, stand, or kneel, promiscuously before the altar, or crowd around the pulpit, without any distinctions of rank or persons. Surely, that is better than bringing into the very temple the most pitiful of all worldly classifications, that of mere money."

"It is better, Miss Warren; and I wish, with all my heart, the custom could be adopted here. But the church that might best dispense with the support obtained from pews, and which, by its size and architecture, is best fitted to set the example of a new mode, has gone on in the old way, I understand, and has its pews as well as another."

"Do we get our custom from England, Hugh?" demanded Martha.

"Assuredly; as we do most others, good, bad and indifferent. The property-notion would be very likely to prevail in a country like England; and then it is not absolutely true that everybody sits in common, even in the churches of the continent of the old world. The Seigneur, under the old régime, in France, had his pew, usually; and high dignitaries of the State in no country are found mingling with the mass of worshippers, unless it be in good company. It is true, a duchesse will kneel in the crowd, in most Romish churches, in the towns, for there are too many such persons to accommodate all with privileged seats, and such honours are reserved for the very great; but in the country, there

32

are commonly pews, in by-places, for the great personages of the neighbourhood. We are not quite so bad as we fancy ourselves, in this particular, though we might be better."

"But, you will allow that a canopied pew is unsuited to this country, brother?"

"Not more to this, than to any other. I agree that it is unsuited to all places of worship, where the petty differences between men, which are created by their own usages, should sink into insignificance, in the direct presence, as it might be, of the power of God. But, in this country, I find a spirit rising, which some persons would call the 'spirit of the Institutions,' that is for ever denying men rewards, and honours, and credit exactly in the degree in which they deserve them. The moment a citizen's head is seen above the crowd of faces around him, it becomes the mark of rotten eggs, as if he were raised in the pillory, and his fellow-creatures would not tolerate any difference in moral stature."

"How do you reconcile that with the great number of Catos, and Brutuses, not to say of the Gracchi, that are to be found among us?" asked Mary Warren, slily.

"Oh! these are the mere creatures of party—great men for the nonce. They are used to serve the purposes of factions, and are be-greated for the occasion. Thus it is, that nine-tenths of the Catos you mention, are forgotten, even by name, every political *lustrum*. But let a man rise, *independently of the people*, by his own merit, and see how the people will tolerate him. Thus it is with my pew—it is a *great* pew, and become great without any agency of the 'folks;' and the 'folks' don't like it."

The girls laughed at this sally, as light-hearted, happy girls will laugh at anything of the sort; and Patt put in her retort, in her own direct, spirited manner.

"It is a *great* ugly thing, if that concession will flatter your vanity," she said, "and I do entreat it may come down *greatly*, this present week. Really, you can have no notion, Hugh, how much talk it has made of late."

"I do not doubt it, my dear. The talk is all aimed at the leases; everything that can be thought of, being dragged into the account against us poor landlords, in order to render our cause unpopular, and thus increase the chances of robbing us with impunity. *The good people of this State little imagine that the very evil that the enemies of the institutions have long predicted, and which their friends have as warmly repudiated, are now actively at work among us, and that the great experiment is in imminent danger of failing, at the very moment the people are loudly exulting in its success.* . Let this attempt on property succeed, ever *so indirectly*, AND IT WILL BE FOLLOWED UP BY OTHERS, WHICH WILL AS INEVITABLY DRIVE US INTO DESPOTISM, AS A REFUGE AGAINST ANARCHY, AS EFFECT SUCCEEDS TO CAUSE. The danger exists, now, in its very worst form—that of political demagogueism—and must be met, face to face, and put down manfully, and on true principles, or, in my poor judgment, we are gone. Cant is a prevailing vice of the nation, more especially political and religious cant, and cant can never be appeased by concessions. My canopy *shall* stand, so long as anti-rentism exists at Ravensnest, or be torn down by violence ; when men return to their senses, and begin to see the just distinctions between *meum* and *tuum*, the cook may have it for oven-wood, any day in the week."

As we were now about to cross the stile that communicated with the highway, directly in front of the church, the conversation ceased, as unsuited to the place and the occasion. The congregation of St. Andrew's was small, as is usually the case with the country congregations of its sect which are commonly regarded with distrust by the descendants of the Puritans in particular, and not unfrequently with strong aversion. The rowdy religion—half-cant, half-blasphemy — that Cromwell and his associates entailed on so many Englishmen, but which was not without a degree of ferocious, narrow-minded sincerity about it, after all, has probably been transmitted to this country, with more of its original peculiarities than exist, at the present day, in any other part of the world. Much of the narrow-mindedness remains ; but, unhappily, when liberality does begin to show itself in these sects, it is apt to take the character of latitudinarianism. In a word, the exaggerations and false principles that were so common among the religious fanatics of the American colonies in the seventeenth century, which burnt witches, hanged Quakers, and denounced all but the elect few, are now running their natural race, with the goal of infidelity in open view before them. Thus will it be, also, with the abuses of political liberty, which must as certainly terminate in despotism, unless checked in season; such being, not the "*spirit* of the Institutions," but the tendency of human nature, as connected with everything in which the right is abandoned to sustain the wrong.

Mr. Warren, I found, was a popular preacher, notwithstanding the disfavour with which his sect was generally regarded. A prejudiced and provincial people was naturally disposed to look at everything that differed from their own opinions and habits with dislike; and the simple circumstance that he belonged to a church that possessed bishops, was of itself tortured into a proof that his sect favoured aristocracy and privileged classes. It is true that nearly every other sect in the country had orders in the church, under the names of ministers, elders, and deacons, and was just as liable to the same criticism; but then they did not possess *bishops*, and having that which we do not happen to have ourselves, usually constitutes the *gist* of an offence, in cases of this sort. Notwithstanding these obstacles to popularity, Mr. Warren commanded the respect of all around him; and, strange as it may seem, none the less because, of all the clergy in that vicinity, he alone had dared to rebuke the spirit of covetousness that was abroad, and which it suits the morals of some among us to style the "spirit of the Institutions;" a duty he had discharged on more than one occasion, with great distinctness and force, though temperately and under the full influence of a profound feeling of Christian charity. This conscientious course had given rise to menaces and anonymous letters, the usual recourse of the mean and cowardly; but it had also increased the weight of his character, and extorted the secret deference of many who would gladly have entertained a different feeling towards him, had it been in their power.

My grandmother and uncle were already seated in the canopied pew when we pedestrians entered the church. Mary Warren turned into another aisle, and proceeded to the pew reserved for the rector, accompanied by my sister, while the other two young ladies passed up to the chancel, and took their customary places. I followed, and for the first time in my life was seated beneath the offensive canopy vested with all the rights of ownership. By the term "canopy," however, the reader is not to imagine anything like festooned drapery — crimson colours and gilded laces; our ambition had never soared so high. The amount of the distinction between this pew and any other in the church was simply this: it was larger and more convenient than those around it, an advantage which any other might have equally enjoyed who saw fit to pay for it, as had been the case with us, and it was canopied with a heavy, clumsy, ill-shaped sort of a roof, that was a perfect caricature of the celebrated *baldachino* of St. Peter's, in Rome. The first of these advantages probably excited no particular envy, for it came within the common rule of the country, of "play and pay;" but as for the canopy, that was aristocratic, and was not to be tolerated. Like the leasehold tenure, it was opposed to the 'spirit of the Institutions.' It is true, it did no real harm, as an existing thing; it is true, it had a certain use, as a memorial of past opinions and customs; it is true, it was property, and could not be touched without interfering with its privileges; it is true, that every person who saw it secretly felt there was nothing, after all, so very inappropriate in such a pew's belonging to a Littlepage; and, most of all, it was true that they who sat in it never fancied for a moment that it made them any better or any worse than the rest of their fellow-creatures. There it was, however; and, next to the feudal character of a lease, it was the most offensive object then existing in Ravensnest. It may be questioned if the cross, which occupied the place that, according to provincial orthodoxy, a weathercock should have adorned, or Mr. Warren's surplice, was one-half as offensive.

When I raised my head, after the private devotions which are customary with us semi-papishes, on entering a place of worship, and looking around me, I found that the building was crowded nearly to overflowing. A second glance told me that nearly every eye was fastened on myself. At first, the canopy having been uppermost so lately in my mind, I fancied that the looks were directed at *that;* but I soon became satisfied that I, in my own unworthy person, was their object. I shall not stop to relate most of the idle and silly reports that had got abroad, in connection with the

32*

manner and reason of my disguised appearance in the hamlet, the preceding day, or in connection with anything else,
though one of those reports was so very characteristic, and
so entirely peculiar to the subject in hand, that I cannot
omit it. That report was simply a rumour that I had caused
one of my own barns to be set on fire, the second night of
my arrival, in order to throw the odium of the act on those
" virtuous and hard-working husbandmen," who only maintained an illegal and armed body on foot, just to bully and
worry me out of my property. Yes, there I sat; altogether
unconscious of the honour done me; regarded by quite half
that congregation as the respected and just-minded youth,
who had devised and carried out precisely such a rascally
scheme. Now, no one who has not had the opportunity to
compare, can form any idea how much more potent and
formidable is the American " folks say," than the vulgar
reports of any other state of society. The French *on dit* is
a poor, pitiful report, placed by the side of this vast lever,
which, like that of Archimedes, only wants a stand for its
fulcrum, to move the world. The American " folks say"
has a certain omnipotence, so long as it lasts, which arises
from, not the spirit, but the *character* of the institutions,
themselves. In a country in which the people rule, ' folks'
are resolved that their ' say' shall not pass for nothing. So
few doubt the justice of the popular decision, that holy writ,
itself, has not, in practical effect, one-half the power that
really belongs to one of these reports, so long as it suits the
common mind to entertain it. Few dare resist it; fewer
still call in question its accuracy ; though, in sober truth,
is hardly ever right. It makes and unmakes reputation, for
the time being *bien entendu;* it even makes and unmakes
patriots, themselves. In short, though never quite truth,
and not often very much like the truth, paradoxical as it
may appear, it *is* truth, and nothing but the truth, *pro hac
vice.* Everybody knows, nevertheless, that there is no per-
manency to what " folks say" about anything; and that
' folks' frequently, nay, almost invariably, " unsay" what
has been said six months before; yet, all submit to the authority of its *dicta,* so long as ' folks' choose to ' say.' The
only exception to this rule, and it merely proves it, is in the
case of political parties, when there are always two " folks

say" which flatly contradict each other; and sometimes
there are half-a-dozen, no two of which are ever precisely
alike!

There I sat, as I afterwards learned, " the observed of
all observers," merely because it suited the purposes of those
who wished to get away my estate to raise various reports to
my prejudice,—not one of which, I am happy to have it in
my power to say, was in any manner true. The first good
look that I took at the congregation satisfied me that very
much the larger part of it consisted of those who did not
belong to St. Andrew's church. Curiosity, or some worse
feeling, had trebled the number of Mr. Warren's hearers
that day,—or, it might be more correct to say, of my observers.

There was no other interruption to the services than that
which was produced by the awkwardness of so many who
were strangers to the ritual. The habitual respect paid to
religious rites kept every one in order; and, in the midst of
a feeling that was as malignant and selfish as well could
exist under circumstances of so little provocation, I was safe
from violence, and even from insult. As for myself, little
was or could be known of my character and propensities at
Ravensnest. School, college, and travelling, with winter
residences in town, had made me a sort of stranger in my
own domain, and I was regarded through the covenants of
my leases, rather than through any known facts. The
same was true, though in a less degree, with my uncle, who
had lived so much abroad as to be considered a sort of half
foreigner, and one who preferred other countries to his own.
This is an offence that is rarely forgiven by the masses in
America, though it is probably the most venial sin that one
who has had the opportunities of comparing can commit. Old
nations offer so many more inducements than young nations
to tempt men of leisure and cultivation to reside in them,
that it is not surprising the travelled American should prefer Europe to his own quarter of the world; but the jealousy
of a provincial people is not apt to forgive this preference.
For myself, I have heard it said, and I believe it to be true,
to a certain extent, that countries on the decline, supposing
them to have been once at the summit of civilization, make
pleasanter abodes for the idler than nations on the advance.

This is one of the reasons why Italy attracts so many more
visiters. than England, though climate must pass for something in such a comparison. But these long absences, and
supposed preferences for foreign life, had made my uncle
Ro, in one sense, unpopular with the mass,-which has been
taught to believe, by means of interested and fulsome eulo-
gies on their own state of. society, that it implies something
more than a.want of taste, almost a want of .principle, to
prefer -any other. This want of popularity, however, was
a good deal relieved by a .wide and deep conviction of my
uncle's probity, as well as of his liberality, his purse having
.no more string to it than General Harrison's door was
thought to have of a latch. But the case was very different
with my grandmother. The early part of her life had been
spent at the .Nest, and it was ·impossible so excellent a wo-
man.could be anything but respected. She had, in truth,
been a sore impediment with the anti-renters ; more especially in carrying out that part of their schemes which is
connected with traduction, and its legitimate offspring, prejudice. It would hardly· do to traduce this noble-minded,
charitable, spirited, and just woman ;- yet, hazardous as the
experiment must and did seem, it was attempted, and not
altogether without success. She was accused of an aristocratic preference of her own family to the families of other
people. Patt and I, it was urged, were only her grandchildren, and had ample provision made for us in other
estates besides this,—and. a woman of. Mrs. Littlepage's
time of life, it was said, who had one foot in the grave,
ought to have too much general philanthropy to give a preference to the interests of mere grandchildren, over the interests of the children of men who had paid her husband and
sons ·rent, now, for quite sixty years. This attack had
come from the pulpit, too, or the. top of a molasses hogs-
head, which was made a substitute for a pulpit, by an itinerant preacher, who had taken a bit of job-work, in which
the promulgation of the tenets of the gospel and those of
anti-rentism was, the great end in view.

As I have said, my good grandmother suffered somewhat
in public estimation, in consequence of this assault. It is
true, had any one openly charged the circulators of this silly
calumny with their offence, they would have stoutly denied

it; but it was none the less certain that this charge, among
a hundred others, varying from it only in degree, and not
at all in character, was industriously circulated in order
to render the Littlepages unpopular; unpopularity being
among us the sin that is apt to entail all the evil consequences
of every other offence.

The reader who is not acquainted with the interior of our
social habits, must not suppose that I am colouring for effect.
So far from this, I am quite conscious of having kept the
tone of the picture down, it being an undeniable truth that
nothing of much interest, now-a-days, is left to the simple
decision of principles and laws, in this part of the country at
least. The supremacy of numbers is so great, that scarce
a private suit of magnitude is committed to a jury without
attempts, more or less direct, to influence the common mind
in favour of one side or the other, in the hope that the jurors
will be induced to think as the majority thinks. In Europe,
it is known that judges were, nay, *are*, visited and solicited
by the parties; but, here, it is the public that must be treated
in the same way. I am far from wishing to blazon the defects of my own country, and I know from observation, that
corresponding evils, differing only in their exterior aspects,
and in their mode of acting, exist elsewhere; but these are
the forms in which some of our defects present themselves,
and he is neither a friend to his country, nor an honest man,
who wishes them to be bundled up and cloaked, instead of
being exposed, understood, and corrected. This notion of
' *nil nisi bene*' has done an infinite degree of harm to the
country; and, through the country, to freedom.

I do not think the worship of the temple amounted to any
great matter that day in St. Andrew's Church, Ravensnest.
Quite half the congregation was blundering through the
liturgy, and every man who lost his place in the prayer-
book, or who could not find it at all, seemed to fancy it was
quite sufficient for the ritual of us semi-papists if he kept his
eye on *me* and my canopied pew. How many pharisees
were present, who actually believed that I had caused my
own barn to be burned, in order to throw opprobrium on the
' virtuous,' ' honest,' and ' hard-working' tenants, and who
gave credit to the stories affecting my title, and all the rest

of the stuff that calculating cupidity had set afloat in the
country, I- have no way of knowing; but subsequent circumstances have given me reason to suppose they were not a
few. ·A great many men left the House of God that morning, I make no doubt, whose whole souls were wrapped up
in effecting an act of the grossest injustice, professing to
themselves' to thank God that they were not as wicked as
the being whom they desired to injure.

I stopped to·say a word to Mr. Warren, in the vestry-
room, after the people were dismissed, for he had not passed
the night with us at the Nest, though his daughter had
After we had said a word about the occurrence of the morning, the good rector, having heard a rumour of the arrest of
certain incendiaries, without knowing who they were, I
made a more general remark or two previously to quitting
the place.

"Your congregation was unusually large this morning,
sir," I said, smiling, " though not altogether as attentive as
it might have been." _ .

"I owe it to your return, Mr. Littlepage, aided by the
events of the past day or two. At one moment I was afraid
that some secret project was on foot, and that the day and
place might be desecrated by some scene of disgraceful violence. · All has ·gone off well in that respect, however, and
I trust that no harm will come of this crowd. We Americans *have* a respect for sacred things which will ordinarily
protect the temple."

"Did you, then, think St. Andrew's ran any risk to-day,
sir?"

Mr. Warren coloured a little, and he hesitated an instant
before he answered.

"You doubtless know, young sir," he said, " the nature
of the feeling that is now abroad in the country. With a
view to obtain its ends, anti-rentism drags every auxiliary
it can find into its ranks, and, among other things, it has
assailed your canopied pew. I own, that, at first, I apprehended some assault might be contemplated on *that*."

· "Let it come, sir; the pew shall be altered on a general
and right principle, but not until it is let alone by envy,
malice, and covetousness. ·It would be worse to make a con-

cession to these than to let the pew stand another half century."

With these words in my mouth, I took my leave, hastening on to overtake the girls in the fields.

CHAPTER XXV.

"There is a pure republic — wild, yet strong —
. A 'fierce democracie,' where all are true
To what themselves have voted, — right or wrong, —
And to their laws denominated blue;
(If red, they might to Draco's code belong.)
HALLECK.

SUCH was my haste in quitting the church, that I did not turn to the right or the left. I saw the light, but well-rounded form of Mary Warren loitering along with the rest of the party, seemingly in waiting for me to join them; and crossing the road, I sprang upon the stile, and thence to the ground, coming up with the girls at the next instant.

"What is the meaning of the crowd, Hugh?" asked my sister, pointing down the road with the stick of her parasol, as she put the question.

"Crowd! I have seen no crowd. Everybody had left the church before I quitted it, and all has gone off peaceably. Ha! sure enough, that does look like a crowd yonder in the highway. It seems an organized meeting, by George! Yes, there is the chairman, seated on the upper rail of the fence, and the fellow with a bit of paper in his hand is doubtless the secretary. Very American, and regular, all that! Some vile project is hatching, I'll answer for it, under the aspect of an expression of public opinion. See, there is a chap speaking, and gesticulating manfully!"

We all stopped, for a moment, and stood looking at the crowd, which really had all the signs of a public meeting about it. There it had been, the girls told me, ever since they had quitted the church, and seemingly engaged much as it was at that moment. The spectacle was curious, and the day being fine, while time did not press, we lingered in

the fields, occasionally stopping to look behind us, and note
what was going on in the highway.

· In this manner, we might have walked half the distance
to the Nest, when, on turning to take another look, we perceived that the crowd had dispersed; some driving off in
the ever-recurring one-horse wagon, some on horseback
and others on foot. Three men, however, were walking
fast in our direction, as if desirous of overtaking us. They
had already crossed the stile, and were on the path in the
field, a route rarely or never taken by any but those who
desired to come to the house. Under the circumstances, I
determined at once to stop and wait for them. First feeling
in my pocket, and making sure of the " revolver," which is
getting to be an important weapon, now that private battles
are fought not only " yard-arm and yard-arm," but by
regular " broadsides," starboard and larboard, I intimated
my intention to the girls.

" As these men are evidently coming in quest of me," I
remarked, " it may be as well, ladies, for you to continue
your walk towards home, while I wait for them on this
stile."

. · " Very true," answered Patt. " They can have little to
say that we shall wish to hear, and you will soon overtake
us. Remember, we dine at two on Sundays, Hugh; the
evening service commencing at four, in this month." ·

. " No, no," said Mary Warren, hurriedly, " we ought not,
cannot, quit Mr. Littlepage. These men may do him some
harm."

I was delighted with this simple, natural manifestation of
interest, as well as with the air of decision with which it
was made. Mary, herself, coloured at her own interest,
but did not the less maintain the ground she had taken.

" Why, of what use can we be to Hugh, dear, even admitting what you say to be true?" answered Patt ; " it were
better for us to hurry on to the house, and send those here
who can assist him in such a case, than stand by idle and
useless."

As if profiting by this hint, Miss Coldbrooke and Miss
Marston, who were already some little distance in advance,
went off almost on a run, doubtless intending to put my
sister's project into execution. But Mary Warren stood

firm, and Patt would not desert her friend, whatever might have been her disposition to treat me with less consideration.

"It is true, we may not be able to assist Mr. Littlepage, should violence be attempted," the first remarked; " but violence is, perhaps, what is least to be apprehended. These wretched people so little regard truth, and they will be three to one, if your brother be left alone; that it is better we stay and *hear* what is said, in order that we may assert what the facts really were, should these persons see fit to pervert them, as too often happens."

Both Patt and myself were struck with the prudence and sagacity of this suggestion; and the former now came quite near to the stile, on which I was still standing, with an air as steady and resolute as that of Mary Warren herself. Just then the three men approached. Two of them I knew by name, though scarcely in person, while the third was a total stranger. The two of whom I had some knowledge, were named Bunce and Mowatt, and were both tenants of my own; and, as I have since learned, warm anti-renters. The stranger was a travelling demagogue, who had been at the bottom of the whole affair connected with the late meeting, and who had made his two companions his tools. The three came up to the stile, with an air of great importance, nor could the dignity of their demeanour have been greater had they been ambassadors extraordinary from the Emperor of China.

"Mr. Littlepage," commenced Mr. Bunce, with a particularly important physiognomy, " there has been a meeting of the public, this morning, at which these resolutions was passed. We have been appointed a committee to deliver a copy of them to you, and our duty is now performed, by handing you this paper."

" Not unless I see fit to accept it, I presume, sir," was my answer.

" I should think no man, in a free country, would refuse to receive a set of resolutions that has been passed by a meeting of his fellow-citizens."

" That might depend on circumstances; the character of the resolutions, in particular. The freedom of the country it is, precisely, which gives one man the same right to say

33

he cares nothing about your resolutions, as it does you to pass them."

"But you have not looked at the resolutions, sir and until you do, you cannot know how you may like them."

"That is very true; but I have looked at their bearers, have seen their manner, and do not quite like the assumption of power which says any body of men can send me resolutions, whether I like to receive them or not."

This declaration seemed to strike the committee aghast! The idea that *one* man should hesitate to submit himself to a yoke imposed by *a hundred*, was so new and inconceivable to those who deem majorities all in all, that they hardly knew how to take it.* At first there was an obvious disposition to resent the insult; then came reflection which probably told them that such a course might not prove so well, the whole terminating in a more philosophical determination of getting along easily.

"Am I to understand, Mr. Littlepage, that you refuse to accept the resolutions of a public meeting?"

"Yes; of half-a-dozen public meetings put together, if those resolutions are offensive, or are offered offensively."

---

* The prevalence of the notion of the omnipotence of majorities, in America, is so wide-spread and deep, among the people in general, as to form a distinctive trait in the national character. It is doing an infinity of mischief, by being mistaken for the governing principle of the institutions, when in fact it is merely a necessary expedient to decide certain questions which must be decided by somebody, and in some mode or other. Kept in its proper sphere, the use of majorities is replete with justice, so far as justice *can* be exercised among men · abused, it opens the highway to the most intolerable tyranny. As a matter of course, the errors connected with this subject vary through all the gradations of intellect and selfishness. The following anecdote will give the reader some notion how the feeling impressed a stranger shortly after his arrival in this country.

A year or two since, the writer had in his service an Irishman who had been only two years in the country. It was a part of this man's duty to look after the welfare of certain pigs, of which one occupied the position of a 'runt.' "Has your honour looked at the pigs lately," said the honest fellow, one day. "No, not lately, Pat; is there any change." "That is there, indeed, sir, and a great change. The little fellow is getting the *majority* of the rest, and will make the best hog of 'em all!"—Editor.

"As to the resolutions, you can know nothing, having never seen them. Of the right of any number of the people to pass such resolutions as they may think proper, I presume there can be no question."

"Of that right, sir, there is a very great question, as has been settled within the last few years, in our own Courts. But, even if the right existed, and in as broad a way as you seem to think, it would not form a right to force these. resolutions on me."

"I am, then, to tell the people you refuse even to read their resolutions, 'Squire Littlepage."

"You can tell them what you please, sir. I know of no people, except in the legal sense, and under the limited powers that they exercise by law. As for this new power, which is rising up in the country, and has the impudence to call itself the people, though composed of little knots of men got together by management, and practised on by falsehood, it has neither my respect nor dread; and as I hold it in contempt, I shall treat it with contempt, whenever it comes n my way."

"I am, then, to tell the people of Ravensnest, you hold them in contempt, sir."

"I authorize you to tell the people of Ravensnest nothing, as coming from me, for I do not know that the people of Ravensnest have employed you. If you will ask me, respectfully, as if you were soliciting a favour instead of demanding a right, to read the contents of the paper you hold in your hand, I may be willing to comply. What I object to, is a handful of men's getting together, setting themselves up as the people, pretending to authority in that capacity, and claiming a right to *force* their notions on other folks."

The three committee-men now drew back a few paces, and consulted together apart, for two or three minutes. While they were thus employed, I heard the sweet gentle voice of Mary Warren say at my elbow—"Take their resolutions, Mr. Littlepage, and get rid of them. I dare say they are very silly, but you will get rid of them all the sooner, by receiving the paper." This was woman's advice, which is a little apt to err on the side of concession, when her apprehensions are aroused; but I was spared the pain of not complying with it, by the altered tone of the trio.

who now came up to the stile again, having apparently come to a final decision in the premises.

"Mr. Hugh Roger Littlepage, junior," said Bunce in a solemn voice, and in a manner as precise as if he were making some legal tender that was of the last importance, and which required set phrases, "I now ask you, in a most respectful manner, if you will consent to receive this paper. It contains certain resolutions, passed with great unanimity by the people of Ravensnest, and which may be found to affect you. I am directed respectfully to ask you, if you will accept this copy of the said resolutions."

I cut the rest of the speech short by receiving the proffered paper, and I thought all three of the worthy ambassadors looked disappointed at my having done so. This gave a new turn to my ideas, and had they now demanded their resolutions back again, they should not have had them, so long as the revolvers could do their duty. For a moment, I do believe Bunce was for trying the experiment. He and his companions would have been delighted to have it in their power to run up and down the country crying out that the aristocrat-landlord, young Littlepage, held the people in contempt, and had refused even to accept the resolutions they had deigned, in their majesty, to pass. As it was, however, I had sufficiently rebuked the presumption of these pretenders to liberty, avoided all the consequences of their clamour in that behalf, and had an opportunity to gratify a curiosity to know what the leaders of the meeting had been about, and to read their resolutions. I say, the leaders of the meeting, for it is very certain the meetings themselves, on all such occasions, have no more to do with the forming, or entertaining the opinions that are thus expressed, than if they had been in Kamtschatka, the whole time. Folding the paper, therefore, and putting it in my pocket, I bowed to the committee, saying, as I descended the stile on the other side of the fence—

"It is well, gentlemen; if the resolutions require any notice, they'll be sure to receive it. Public meetings held of a Sunday are so unusual in this part of the world, that this may have interest with that small portion of the State which does not dwell at Ravensnest."

I thought the committee was a little abashed; but the

stranger, or the travelling demagogue, caught at my words,
and answered as I walked away, in company with Patt and
Mary Warren—

"The better day, the better deed. The matter related to
the Sabbath, and no time so suitable as the Sabbath to act
on it."

I will own I was dying with curiosity to read the resolutions, but dignity prevented any such thing until we had
reached a spot where the path led through a copse, that concealed us from observation. Once under that cover, however, I eagerly drew out the paper, the two girls drawing
near to listen, with as lively an interest as that I felt myself
in the result.

"Here you may see at a glance," I cried, shaking open
the folds of the paper, "the manner in which the *people* so
often pass their resolutions! All this writing has a very
school-master air, and has been done with care and deliberation, whereas there was certainly no opportunity to make
a copy as fair as this of anything out in the highway where
the meeting was actually held. This proves that matters
have been cut and dried for the sovereign people, who, like
other monarchs, are saved a great deal of trouble by their
confidential servants."

"I dare say," said Patt, "two or three men down at the
village prepared everything, and then brought their work
up to the meeting to be read and approved, and to go forth
as public sentiment."

"If it were only honestly approved by even those who
heard it read, it would be another matter; but two-thirds of
every meeting are nothing but dough-faces, that are moulded
to look whichever way the skilful manager may choose. But
let us see what these notable resolutions are; we may like
them, possibly, after having read them."

"It is so extraordinary to have a public meeting of a
Sunday in this part of the world!" exclaimed Mary
Warren.

I now set about reading the contents of the paper, which,
at a glance, I saw had been very carefully prepared for pub-
lication, and no doubt would soon figure in some of the
journals. Fortunately, this business has been so much overdone, and so many meetings are held that flatly contradic

33*

each other, though all represent public sentiment, fire is made so effectually to fight fire, that the whole procedure is falling into contempt, and the-public is actually losing the great advantage which, under a more temperate use of its power, it might possess, by making known from time to time, as serious occasions offered, its true opinions and wishes.   As things actually are, every man of intelligence is fully aware that simulated public opinions are much the most noisy and active in the country, and he regards nothing of the sort of which he hears or reads, unless he happen to know something of the authority.   It is the same with the newspaper press generally; into such deep discredit has it fallen, that not only is its power to do evil much curtailed, but it has nearly lost all power to do good; for, by indulging in licentiousness, and running into the habit of crying "wolf," nobody is disposed to believe, were the beast actually committing its ravages in the flocks of the nation.   There are but two ways for a man to regain a position from which he has departed; the one is by manfully retracing his steps, and the other is by making a circuit so complete that all who choose to watch him may see and understand all sides of him, and estimate him accordingly.   The last is likely to be the career of demagogueism and the press; both of which have already gone so far as to render retreat next to impossible, and who can only regain any portion of public confidence by being satisfied with completing their circuit, and falling in the rear of the nation, content to follow those whom it has been their craving ambition to lead.

"At a meeting of the citizens of Ravensnest," I began to read aloud, "spontaneously convened, June 22d, 1845, in the public highway, after attending divine service in the Episcopal meeting-house, according to the forms of the established denomination of England, on the church and state system, Onesiphoras Hayden, Esquire, was called to the chair, and Pulaski Todd, Esquire, was appointed Secretary. After a luminous and eloquent exposition of the objects of the meeting, and some most pungent strictures on aristocracy and the rights of man, from Demosthenes Hewlett and John Smith, Esquires, the following expression of public senti ment was sustained by an undivided unanimity :—Resolved that a temperate expression of public opinion is useful to the

rights of freemen, and is one of the most precious privileges
of freedom, as the last has been transmitted to us in a free
country by our ancestors, who fought and bled for free and
equal institutions on free and equal grounds.

" Resolved, That we prize this privilege, and shall ever
watch over its exercise with vigilance, the price of liberty

" Resolved, That, as all men are equal in the eyes of the
law, so are they much more so in the eyes of God.

" Resolved, That meeting-houses are places constructed
for the convenience of the people, and that nothing ought to
be admitted into them that is opposed to public sentiment,
or which can possibly offend it.

" Resolved, That, in our judgment, the seat that is good
enough for one man is good enough for another ; that we
know no difference in families and races, and that pews
ought to be constructed on the principles of equality, as well
as laws.

" Resolved, That canopies are royal distinctions, and quite
unsuited to republicans ; and most of all, to republican meeting-houses.

" Resolved, That religion should be adapted to the institutions of a country, and that a republican form of government is entitled to a republican form of religion ; and that
we do not see the principles of freedom in privileged seats
in the House of God."

" That resolution has been got up as a commentary on
what has been circulated so much, of late, in the newspapers," cried Mary Warren, quickly ; " in which it has been
advanced, as a recommendation of certain sects, that their
dogmas and church-government are more in harmony with
republicanism than certain others, our own church included."

" One would think," I answered, " if this conformity be
a recommendation, that it would be the duty of men to make
their institutions conform to the church, instead of the church's
conforming to the institutions."

" Yes ; but it is not the fashion to reason in this way,
now-a-days. Prejudice is just as much appealed to in matters connected with religion, as with anything else."

" Resolved," I continued to read, " That in placing a
canopy over his pew, in St. Andrew's meeting-house, Ra-

vensnest, Gen. Cornelius Littlepage conformed to the spiri.
of a past age, rather than to the spirit of the present time,
and that we regard its continuance there as an aristocratical
assumption of a superiority that is opposed to the character
of the government, offensive to liberty, and dangerous as an
example.".

" Really that is too bad !" exclaimed Patt, vexed at heart,
even while she laughed at the outrageous silliness of the
résolutions, and all connected with them.   " Dear, liberal-
minded grandpapa, who fought and bled for that very liberty
about which these people cant so much, and who was actively
concerned in framing the very institutions that they do not
understand, and are constantly violating, is accused of being
false to what were notoriously his own principles !"

 " Never mind that, my dear ; there only remain three
more resolutions : let us hear them. ' Resolved, That we
see an obvious connection between crowned heads, patents
of nobility, canopied pews, personal distinctions, leasehold
tenures, land-LORDS, days' works, fat fowls, quarter-sales,
three-lives leases, and RENT.'

 " Resolved, That we are of opinion that, when the owners
of barns wish them destroyed, for any purpose whatever,
there is a mode less alarming to a neighbourhood than by
setting them on fire, and thus giving rise to a thousand reports and accusations that are wanting in the great merit of
truth.

 " Resolved, That a fair draft be made of these resolu
tions, and a copy of them delivered to one Hugh Roger Littlepage, a citizen of Ravensnest, in the county of Washington ; and that Peter Bunce, Esq., John Mowatt, Esq., and
Hezekiah Trott, Esq., be a committee to see that this act
be performed.

 " Whereupon the meeting adjourned, sine die. Onesi-
phorus Hayden, chairman ; Pulaski Todd, secretary."

 " Whe-e-e-w !" I whistled, " here 's gunpowder enough
for another Waterloo !"

 " What means that last resolution, Mr. Littlepage ?" asked
Mary Warren, anxiously. " That about the barn."

 " Sure enough ; there is a latent meaning there which has
its sting. Can the scoundrels intend to insinuate that I
aused that barn to be set on fire !"

" If they should, it is scarcely more than they have attempted to do with every landlord they have endeavoured to
rob," said Patt, with spirit. " Calumny seems a natural
weapon of those who get their power by appealing to numbers."

" That is natural enough, my dear sister ; since prejudice
and passion are quite as active agents as reason and facts,
in the common mind. But this is a slander that shall be
looked to. If I find that these men really wish to circulate a
report that I caused my own barn to be set on fire—pshaw !
nonsense, after all ; have we not Newcome, and that other
rascal in confinement, at this moment, for attempting to set
fire to my *house ?*"

" Be not too confident, Mr. Littlepage," said Mary, with
an anxiety so pointed that I could not but feel its flattery—
" my dear father tells me he has lost most of his confidence
in innocence, except as One above all weaknesses shall be
the judge : this very story may be got up expressly to throw
distrust on your accusations against the two incendiaries
you have taken in the act. Remember how much of the
facts will depend on your own testimony."

" I shall have *you* to sustain me, Miss Warren, and the
juror is not living, who would hesitate to believe that to
which you will testify. But here we are approaching the
house ; we will talk no more on the subject, lest it distress
my grandmother."

We found all quiet at the Nest, no report of any sort
having come from the red-men. Sunday was like any other
day to them, with the exception that they so far deferred to
our habits, as to respect it, to a certain extent, while in our
presence. Some writers have imagined that the aborigines
of America are of the lost tribes of Israel ; but it seems to
me that such a people could never have existed apart, unin-
fluenced by foreign association, and preserved no tradition,
no memorial of the Jewish Sabbath. Let this be as it may,
John, who met us at the door, which we reached just after
my uncle and grandmother, reported all quiet, so far as he
knew anything of the state of the farm-buildings.

" They got enough last night, I 'se thinking, Mr. Hugh,
and has found out by this time, that it 's better to light a fire
in one of their own cook-stoves, than come to light it on the

floor of a gentleman's kitchen. I never heard it said, sir
that the Hamericans was as much Hirish as they be Heng-
lish, but to me they seems to grow every day more like the
wild Hirishers, of whom we used to hear so much in Lun'un.
Your honoured father, sir, would never have believed that
his own dwelling would be entered, at night, by men who
are his very neighbours, and who act like burglariouses, as
if they were so many Newgate birds,—no. Why, Mr.
Hugh, this 'Squire Newcome, as they call him, is an hattor-
ney, and has often dined here at the Nest. I have 'anded
him his soup, and fish, and wine, fifty times, just as if he
was a gentleman, and to his sister, Miss Hopportunity, too;
and they to come to set fire to the house, at midnight!"

"You do Miss Opportunity injustice, John; for *she* has
not had the least connection with the matter."

"Well, sir, nobody knows anything, now-a-days—I declare, my eyes be getting weak, or there is the young lady,
at this very instant!"

"Young lady! where?—you do not mean Opportunity
Newcome, surely."

"I does though, sir, and it's she, sure enough. If that
is n't Miss Hopportunity, the prisoner that the savages has
got up in the cellar of the old farm-house, is n't her
brother."

John was quite right; there was Opportunity standing in
the very path, and at the very spot where I had last seen
her disappear from my sight, the past night. That spot
was just where the path plunged into the wooded ravine, and
so far was her person concealed by the descent, that we could
only perceive the head, and the upper part of the body. The
girl had shown herself just that much, in order to attract
my attention, in which she had no sooner succeeded, than;
by moving downward a few paces, she was entirely hid
from sight. Cautioning John to say nothing of what had
passed, I sprang down the steps, and walked in the direction
of the ravine, perfectly satisfied I was expected, and far
from certain that this visit did not portend further evil.

The distance was so short that I was soon at the verge
of the ravine, but when I reached it Opportunity had disappeared. Owing to the thicket, her concealment was easily
obtained, while she might be within a few yards from me

and I plunged downwards, bent only on ascertaining her object. One gleam of distrust shot across my mind, I will own, as I strided down the declivity; but it was soon lost in the expectation and curiosity that were awakened by the appearance of the girl.

I believe it has already been explained, that in this part of the lawn a deep, narrow ravine had been left in wood, and that the bridle-path that leads to the hamlet had been carried directly through it, for effect. This patch of wood may be three or four acres in extent, following the course of the ravine until it reaches the meadows, and it contains three or four rustic seats, intended to be used in the warmer months. As Opportunity was accustomed to all the windings and turnings of the place, she had posted herself near one of these seats, which stood in a dense thicket, but so near the main path as to enable her to let me know where she was to be found, by a low utterance of my name, as my tread announced my approach. Springing up the by-path, I was at her side in an instant. I do believe that, now she had so far succeeded, the girl sunk upon the seat from inability to stand.

"Oh! Mr. Hugh!" she exclaimed, looking at me with a degree of nature and concern in her countenance that it was not usual to see there—"Sen—my poor brother Sen—what *have* I done?—what *have* I done?"

"Will you answer me one or two questions, Miss Opportunity, with frankness, under the pledge that the replies never shall be used to injure you or yours? This is a very serious affair, and should be treated with perfect frankness."

"I will answer any thing to *you*—any question you can put me, though I might blush to do so—but," laying her hand familiarly, not to say tenderly on my arm—"why should we be *Mr.* Hugh and *Miss* Opportunity to each other, when we were so long Hugh and Op? Call me Op again, and I shall feel that the credit of my family and the happiness of poor Sen are, after all, in the keeping of a true friend."

"No one can be more willing to do this than myself, my dear Op, and I am willing to be Hugh again. But, you know all that has passed."

"I do—yes, the dreadful news has reached us, and mother would n't leave me a moment's peace till I stole out again to see you."

"Again?—Was your mother, then, acquainted with the visit of last night?"

"Yes, yes—she knew it all, and advised it all."

"Your mother is a most thoughtful and prudent parent," I answered, biting my lip, "and I shall know hereafter how much I am indebted to her. To *you*, Opportunity, I owe the preservation of my house, and possibly the lives of all who are most dear to me."

"Well, that's something, any how. There's no grief that has n't its relief. But, you must know, Hugh, that I never could or did suppose that Sen himself would be so weak as to come in his own person on such an errand! I did n't want telling to understand that, in anti-rent times, fire and sword are the law,—but, take him in general, Sen is altogether prudent and cautious. I'd a bit my tongue off before I'd a got my own brother into so cruel a scrape. No, no— do n't think so ill of me as to suppose I came to tell of Sen!"

"It is enough for me that I know how much trouble you took to warn me of danger. It is unnecessary for me to think of *you* in any other light than that of a friend."

"Ah, Hugh! how happy and merry we all of us used to be a few years since! That was before your Miss Cold-brookes, and Miss Marstons, and Mary Warrens ever saw the country. *Then* we *did* enjoy ourselves, and I hope such times will return. If Miss Martha would only stick to old friends, instead of running after new ones, Ravensnest would be Ravensnest again."

"You are not to censure my sister for loving her own closest associates best. She is several years our junior, you will remember, and was scarcely of an age to be *our* companion six years ago."

Opportunity had the grace to colour a little, for she had only used Patt as a cloak to make her assaults on me, and she knew as well as I did that my sister was good seven years younger than herself. This feeling, however, was but momentary, and she next turned to the real object of this visit.

" What am I to tell mother, Hugh?—You will let Sen off, I know !"

I reflected, for the first time, on the hardships of the case ; but felt a strong reluctance to allow incendiaries to escape.

" The facts must be known, soon, all over the town," I remarked.

" No fear of that: they are pretty much known, already. News *does* fly *fast*, at Ravensnest, all must admit."

" Ay; if it would only fly *true*. But, your brother can hardly remain here, after such an occurrence."

" Lord ! How you talk ! If the law will only let him alone, who 'd trouble him for this ? You havn't been home long enough, to learn that folks don't think half as much of setting fire to a house, in anti-rent times, as they 'd think of a trespass, under the old-fashioned law. Anti-rent alters the whole spirit."

How true was this ! And we have lads among us, who have passed from their tenth to their eighteenth and twentieth years, in a condition of society that is almost hopelessly abandoned to the most corrupting influence of all the temptations that beset human beings. It is not surprising that men begin to regard arson as a venial offence, when the moral feeling of the community is thus unhinged, and boys are suffered to grow into manhood, in the midst of notions so fatal to every thing that is just and safe.

" But the law itself will not be quite as complaisant as the folks.' It will scarcely allow incendiaries to escape ; and your brother would be compelled to flee the land."

" What of that ? How many go off, and stay off for a time; and that 's better than going up north to work at the new prison. I 'm not a bit afraid of Sen's being hanged, for these an't hanging times, in this country ; but it is *some* disgrace to a family to have a member in the state's prison. As for any punishment that is lasting, you can see how it is, as well as I. There 've been men murdered about anti-rentism, but, Lord ! the senators and assemblymen will raise such a rumpus, if you go to punish them, that it won't be long, if things go on as they have, before it will be thought more honourable to be put in jail for shooting a peace-officer, than to stay out of it, for not having done it.

34

Talk's all ; and if folks have a mind to make any thing hon
ourable, they 've only to say so often enough, to make it out."

Such were the notions of Miss Opportunity Newcome,
on the subject of modern morals, and how far was she from
the truth? I could not but smile at the manner in which
she treated things, though there was a homely and practical
common sense in her way of thinking, that was probably of
more efficiency than would have been the case with a more
refined and nicer.code. She looked at things as they are,
and that is always something towards success.

As for myself, I was well enough disposed to consider
Opportunity, in this unfortunate affair of the fire, for it
would have been a cruel thing to suffer the girl to imagine
she had been an instrument in destroying her brother. It
is true, there is no great danger of a rogue's being hanged,
now-a-days, and Seneca was not sufficiently a gentleman,
though very tenacious of the title, to endanger his neck.
Had he been a landlord, and caught lighting a fire on the
kitchen-floor of one of the tenants, the State would not grow
hemp enough for his execution ; but it was a very different
thing to catch a tenant at that work. I could not but ask
myself, how many of the " honourable gentlemen" at Albany
would interfere in *my* behalf, had matters been reversed; for
this is the true mode of arriving at the ' spirit of the institutions ;' or, rather, I have just as good a right to affirm such
is their ' spirit,' as any one has to assert that the lease-hold
tenure is opposed to them ; the laws and institutions themselves, being equally antagonist to both.

The results of the interview I had with Opportunity were,
1stly,—I kept my heart just where it was at its commencement, though I am not certain that it was in my own cus-
tody ; 2dly,—The young lady left me much encouraged on
the subject of the credit of the Newcomes, though I took
very good care not to put myself in her power, by promising to compromise felony ; 3dly,—I invited the sister tc
come openly to the Nest, that evening, as one of the means
to be employed in attaining her ends—as respects Seneca,
be it remembered, not as respects *me ;* and lastly, we parted
just as good friends as we ever had been, and entertaining
exactly the same views as regards each other. What those
views were, it may not be modest in me to record.

CHAPTER XXVI.

" If men desire the rights of property, they must take their consequences ; distinction in social classes. Without the rights of property
civilization can hardly exist ; while the highest class of improvements
is probably the result of the very social distinctions that so many decry.
The great political problem to be solved, is to ascertain if the social
distinctions that are inseparable from civilization can really exist with
perfect equality in political rights. We are of opinion they can ; and
as much condemn him who vainly contends for a visionary and impracticable social equality, as we do him who would deny to men
equal opportunities for advancement."

Political Essay.

My interview with Opportunity Newcome remained a
secret between those who first knew of it. The evening
service in St. Andrew's was attended only by the usual congregation, all the curiosity of the multitude seeming to have
been allayed by the visit in the morning. The remainder
of the day passed as usual, and, after enjoying a pleasant
even-tide, and the earlier hours of the night in the company
of the girls, I retired early to bed, and slept profoundly until
morning. My uncle Ro partook of my own philosophical
temper, and we encouraged each other in it by a short conversation, that occurred in his room before we respectively
retired to rest.

" I agree with you, Hugh," said my uncle, in reply to a
remark of my own ; " there is little use in making ourselves
unhappy about evils that *we* cannot help. If we *are* to be
burnt up and stripped of our property, we *shall* be burnt up
and stripped of our property. I have a competency secured
in Europe, and we can all live on *that*, with economy, should
the worst come to the worst."

" It is a strange thing, to hear an American talk of
seeking a refuge of any sort in the old world !"

" If matters proceed in the lively manner they have for
the last ten years, you'll hear of it often. Hitherto, the rich
of Europe have been in the habit of laying by a penny in
America against an evil day ; but the time will soon come,

unless there is a great change, when the rich of America will return the compliment, in kind. We are worse off than if we were in a state of nature, in many respects ; having *our* hands tied by the responsibility that belongs to our position and means, while those who choose to assail us are under a mere nominal restraint. They make the magistrates, who are altogether in their interests ; and they elect the sheriffs who are to see the laws executed. The theory is, that the people are sufficiently virtuous to perform all these duties well ; but no provision has been made for the case in which the people themselves happen to go astray, *en masse.*"

"We have our governors and masters at Albany, sir."

"Yes, we *have* our governors and servants at Albany, and there they are ! There has not been the time, probably, since this infernal spirit first had its rise among us, that a clear, manly, energetic, and well-principled proclamation, alone, issued by the Governor of this State, would not have aroused all the better feelings of the community, and put this thing down ; but, small as would have been that tribute to the right, it has never been paid, and, until we drop double-distilled patriots, and have recourse again to the old-fashioned, high-principled gentlemen for offices of mark, it never will be done. Heaven preserve me from extra-virtuous, patriotic, and enlightened citizens ; no good ever comes of them."

"I believe the wisest way, sir, is to make up our minds that we have reached the point of reaction in the institutions, and be ready to submit to the worst. I keep the ' revolver' well primed, and hope to escape being burnt up at least."

After a little more such discourse, we parted and sought our pillows, and I can say that I never slept more soundly in my life. If I did lose my estate, it was what other men had suffered and survived, and why might not I as well as another ? It is true, those other men were, in the main, the victims of what are called tyrants ; but others, again, had certainly been wronged by the masses. Thousands have been impoverished in France, for instance, by the political confiscations of the multitude, and thousands enriched by ill-gotten gains; profiting by the calamities of those around them ; and what has happened there might happen here. Big words ought to pass for nothing. No man was ever a whit more free because he was the whole time boasting of his liberty, and I was not now to learn that when numbers did inflict a wrong, it was always of the most intolerable character. Ordinarily, they were not much disposed to this species of crime; but men in masses were no more infallible than individuals. In this philosophic mood, I slept.

I was awoke next morning by John's appearing at my bedside, after having opened the shutter of my windows.

"I declare to you, Mr. Hugh," began this well-meaning, but sometimes officious servant, "I don't know what will come next at Ravensnest, now the evil spirit has got uppermost among the inhabitants!"

"Tut, tut, John—what you call the evil spirit is only the 'Spirit of the Institutions;' and is to be honoured, instead of disliked."

"Well, sir, I don't know what they calls it, for they talks so much about the hinstitutions in this country, I never can find out what they would be at. There was a hinstitution near where I lived in my last place, at the West End, in Lon'on, and there they taught young masters to speak and write Latin and Greek. But hinstitutions in Hamerica must mean something, for them as doesn't know any more Latin than I do seems to be quite hintimate with these Hamerican hinstitutions. But, Mr. Hugh, would you, could you, believe the people committed parricide last night?"

"I am not at all surprised at it, for, to me, they have seemed to be bent on matricide for some time, calling the country their mother."

"It's hawful, sir—it's truly hawful, when a whole people commits such a crime as parricide! I know'd you would be shocked to hear it, Mr. Hugh, and so I just came in to let you know it."

"I am infinitely obliged to you for this attention, my good fellow, and shall be still more so when you tell me all about it."

"Yes, sir, most willingly, and most unwillingly, too. But there's no use in 'iding the fact; it's gone, Mr. Hugh!"

"What is gone, John?—Speak out, my good fellow; I can bear it."

"The pew, sir—or, rather that beautiful canopy that covered it, and made it look so much like the Lord Mayor's seat

34*

in Guildhall. I 'ave hadmired and honoured that canopy
sir, as the most helegant hobject in this country, sir."

"So they have destroyed it at last, have they? Encour·
aged and sustained by an expression of public sentiment, as
proclaimed in a meeting that had a chairman and secretary,
they have actually-cut it down, I suppose?"

"They have, sir; and a pretty job they've made of it.
There it stands, up at Miller's, hover his pig-pen!"

This was not a very heroic termination of the career of
the obnoxious canopy; but it was one that made me laugh
heartily. John was a little offended at this levity, and he
soon left me to finish my toilet by myself. I dare say,
many of the honest folk of Ravensnest would have been as
much surprised as John himself, at the indifference I manifested at the fate of this dignified pew. But, certainly, so
far as my own social elevation, or social depression, were
concerned, I cared nothing about it. It left me just where I
was—neither greater nor otherwise; and as for any monu·
ments to let the world know who my predecessors had been,
or who I was at that moment, the country itself, or the part
of it in which we dwelt, was sufficient. Its history must
be forgotten, or changed, before our position could be mistaken; though I dare say, the time will come when some
extremely sublimated friend of equality will wish to extin
guish all the lights of the past, in order that there may not
exist that very offensive distinction of one man's name
being illustrated, while another man's name is not. The
pride of family is justly deemed the most offensive of all
pride, since a man may value himself on a possession to
which he has not the smallest claim in the way of personal
merit, while those of the highest personal claims are altogether deprived of an advantage, to the enjoyment of which
ancestors alone have created the right. Now, the institutions, both in their letter and their spirit, *do* favour justice,
in this particular, as far as they can; though even they are
obliged to sustain one of the most potent agents to such distinctions, by declaring, through the laws, that the child
shall succeed to the estate of the father. When we shall
get every thing straight, and as it ought to be, in this progressive country, Heaven only knows; for I find my tenants
laving stress on the fact that *their* fathers have leased my

lands for generations, while they are quite willing to forget that *my* fathers were the lessors-all the while. ·

I found all four of the girls on the piazza, breathing the air of as balmy a summer morning as a bountiful nature ever bestowed. They had heard of the fate of the canopy, which affected them differently, and somewhat according to temperament. Henrietta Coldbrooke laughed at it violently, and in a way I did not like; your laughing young lady rarely having much beyond merriment in her. I make all allowance for youthful spirits, and a natural disposition to turn things into fun; but it was too much to laugh at this exploit of the anti-renters, for quite half an hour together I liked Anne Marston's manner of regarding it better. She smiled a good deal, and laughed just enough to show that she was not insensible to the effect of an absurdity; and then she looked as if she felt that a wrong had been done. As for Patt, she was quite indignant at the insult; nor was she very backward in letting her opinions be known. But Mary Warren's manner of viewing the affair pleased me best, as indeed was fast getting to be the fact with most of her notions and conceits. She manifested neither levity nor resentment. Once or twice, when a droll remark escaped Henrietta, she laughed a little; a very little, and involuntarily; as it might be — just enough to prove that there was fun in her — when she would make some sensible-observation, to the effect that the evil temper that was up in the country was the true part of the transaction that deserved attention; and that she *felt* this as well as saw it. Nobo·'y seemed to care for the canopy — not even my excellent grandmother, in whose youth the church had been built, when distinctions of this sort were more in accordance with the temper and habits of the times, than they are to-day. I had been on the piazza just long enough to note this difference in the manner of the girls, when my grandmother joined us.

"Oh! grandmother, have you heard what those wretches of 'Injins,' as they are rightly named, have been doing with the canopy of the pew?" cried Patt, who had been at the bedside of our venerable parent; and kissed her an hour before: "they have torn it down, and placed it over the pen of the pigs!"

A common laugh, in which Patt herself now joined, interrupted the answer for a moment, old Mrs. Littlepage herself manifesting a slight disposition to make one of the amused.

"I have heard it all, my dear," returned my grandmother, "and, on the whole, think the thing is well enough gotten rid of. I do not believe it would have done for Hugh to have had it taken down, under a menace, while it is perhaps better that it should no longer stand."

"Were such things common, in your youth, Mrs. Littlepage?" asked Mary Warren.

"Far from uncommon; though less so in country than in town churches. You will remember that we were but recently separated from England, when St. Andrew's was built, and that most of the old colonial ideas prevailed among us. People, in that day, had very different notions of social station, from those which now exist; and New York was, in a certain sense, one of the most, perhaps *the* most aristocratical colony in the country. It was somewhat so under the Dutch, republicans as they were, with its patroons; but when the colony was transferred to the English, it became a royal colony at once, and English notions were introduced as a matter of course. In no other colony was there as many manors, perhaps; the slavery of the south introducing quite a different system there, while the policy of Penn and of New England, generally, was more democratic. I apprehend, Roger, that we owe this anti-rent struggle, and particularly the feebleness with which it is resisted, to the difference of opinion that prevails among the people of New England, who have sent so many immigrants among us, and our own purely New York notions."

"You are quite right, my dear mother," answered my uncle, "though New Yorkers, by descent, are not wanting among the tenants, to sustain the innovation. The last act either from direct cupidity, or to gain popularity with a set whereas, as I view the matter, the first are influenced by the notions of the state of society from which either they themselves, or their parents, were directly derived. A very large proportion of the present population of New York is of New England origin. Perhaps one-third have this extraction, either as born there, or as the sons or grandsons of those who were. Now, in New England generally, great equality of condition exists, more especially when you rise above the lower classes; there being very few, out of the large trading towns, who would be deemed rich in New York, and scarcely such a thing as a large landholder, at all. The relation of landlord and tenant, as connected with what we should term estates, is virtually unknown to New England; though Maine may afford some exceptions. This circumstance is owing to the peculiar origin of the people, and to the fact that emigration has so long carried off the surplus population; the bulk of those who remain being able to possess freeholds. There is a natural antipathy in men who have been educated in such a state of society, to anything that seems to place others in positions they do not, and cannot occupy themselves. Now, while the population of New York may be one-third, perhaps, of New England descent, and consequently more or less of New England notions, a much larger proportion of the lawyers, editors of newspapers, physicians, and active politicians, are of that class. We think little, and talk little of these circumstances; for no nation inquires into its moral influences, and what I may call its political statistics, less than the Americans; but they produce large consequences."

"Am I to understand you, sir, to say that anti-rentism is of New England origin?"

"Perhaps not. Its origin was probably more directly derived from the devil, who has tempted the tenants as he is known once to have tempted the Saviour. The outbreak was originally among the descendants of the Dutch, for they happened to be the tenants, and, as for the theories that have been broached, they savour more of the reaction of European abuses, than of anything American at all; and least of all of anything from New England, where there is generally a great respect for the rights of property, and unusual reverence for the law. Still, I think we owe our greatest danger to the opinions and habits of those of New England descent among us."

"This seems a little paradoxical, uncle Ro, and I confess I should like to hear it explained."

"I will endeavour so to do, and in as few words as possible. The real danger is among those who influence legis-

lation.   Now, you will find hundreds of men among us, who
feel the vast importance of respecting contracts, who perceive
much of the danger of anti-rentism, and who wish to see it
defeated in its violent and most offensive forms, but who
lean against the great landlords, on account of those secret
jealousies which cause most men to dislike advantages in
which they do not share, and who would gladly enough see
all leases abolished, if it could be done without a too violent
conflict with justice.   When you talk with these men, they
will make you the common-place but unmeaning profession
of wishing to see every husbandman the owner in fee of his
farm, instead of a tenant, and that it is a *hardship* to pay
rent, and quantities of such twaddle.   Henry the Fourth, in
a much better spirit, is said to have wished that each of his
subjects had " *une poule dans son pôt,*" but that wish did
not put it there.   So it is with this idle profession of wishing
to see every American husbandman a freeholder.   We all
know such a state of society never did exist, and probably
never will ; and it is merely placing a vapid pretension to
philanthropy in the fore-ground of a picture that should
rigidly represent things as they are.   For my part, I am
one of those who do not believe that this or any other country
would be any the better for dispensing with landlords and
tenants."

" Mr. Littlepage !" exclaimed Mary Warren, " you surely
do not mean that competency widely diffused, is not better
than wealth in a few hands, and poverty in a great many !"

" No, I shall not go as far as that ; but, I do say that
what this country most wants just now, is precisely the class
that is connected with the independence of character and
station, the leisure with its attendant cultivation and refinement, and the *principles* as well as taste that are connected
with all."

" Principles !, Mr. Littlepage !" added my uncle's sweet
interlocutor ; " my father would hardly uphold *that*, though
he agrees with you in so much of what you say."

" I do not know that.   I repeat the word *principles ;* for
when you have a class of men, who are removed from a
large range of temptations, without being placed above public
opinion, you get precisely those who are most likely to uphold that sort of secondary, but highly useful morals which

are not directly derived from purely religious duties.
Against the last I shall not say one word, as it comes from
the grace, which is of the power of God, and is happily as
accessible to the poor as to the rich, and more too ; but, of
men as they are, not one in a hundred regulates his life by
a standard created under such impulses ; and even when they
do, the standard itself is, in some degree, qualified by the
ordinary notions, I apprehend. The Christian morality of an
East Indian is not identical with that of a Puritan, or that
of a man of highly cultivated mind, with that of one who
has enjoyed fewer advantages. There is one class of principles, embracing all those that are adverse to the littlenesses
of daily practice, which is much the more extended among
the liberal-minded and educated, and it is to that set of principles I refer. Now we want a due proportion of that class
of men, as our society is getting to be organized ; of those
who are superior to meannesses."

" All this would be deemed atrociously aristocratic, were
it told in Gath !" exclaimed Patt, laughing.

" It is atrociously common sense, notwithstanding," answered my uncle, who was not to be laughed out of anything he felt to be true ; " and the facts will show it. New
England early established a system of common schools, and
no part of the world, perhaps, has a population that is better
grounded in intelligence. This has been the case so long
as to put the people of Connecticut and Massachusetts, for
instance, as a whole, materially in advance of the people of
any other State, New York included ; although, by taking
the system from our eastern brethren, we are now doing
pretty well. Notwithstanding, who will say that New England is as far advanced, in many material things, as the
middle States. To begin with the kitchen—her best cookery
is much below that of even the humbler classes of the true
middle States' families : take her language for another test,
it is provincial and vulgar ; and there is no exaggeration in
saying that the labouring classes of the middle States, if not
of New England origin, use better English than thousands
of educated men in New England itself. Both of these peculiarities, as I conceive, come from the fact that in one
part of the country there has been a class to give a tone
that does not exist in the other. The gentlemen of the larger

towns in the east have an influence where they live, no
doubt; but in the interior, as no one leads, all these matters
are left to the common mind to get along with, as well as it
can."

"Aristocratic, sir—rank aristocracy!"

"If it be, has aristocracy, as you call it, which. in this
instance must only mean decided social position, no advantages? Is not even a wealthy idler of some use in a nation?
He contributes his full share to the higher civilization that
is connected with the tastes. and refinements, and, in fact,
he forms it. In Europe they will tell you that a court is
necessary to such civilization; but facts, contradict the
theory. Social classes, no doubt, are; but they can exist
independently of courts, as they can, have, do, and ever will
in the face of democracy. Now, connect this class with the
landed interest, and see how much your chances for material improvement are increased. Coke, of Norfolk, probably conferred more benefit on the husbandry of England
than all the mere operatives that existed in his time. It is
from such men, indeed, from their enterprise and their
means, that nearly all the greater benefits come. The fine
wool of America is mainly owing to Livingston's connection
with land; and if you drive such men out of existence, you
must drive the benefits they confer with them. A body of
intelligent, well-educated, liberalized landlords, scattered
through New York, would have more effect in advancing
the highest interests of the community than all the 'small
potato' lawyers and governors you can name in a twelvemonth. What is more, this is just the state of society in
which to reap all the benefits of such a class, without the
evils. of a real aristocracy. They are and would be without any particular political power, and there is no danger
of corn-laws and exclusive legislation for their benefit. Rich
and poor we *must* have; and let any fair-minded man say
whether he wish a state of things in which the first shall
have no inducement to take an extended interest in real
estate, and the last no chance to become agriculturists, except as hired labourers?"

"You do not mince matters, uncle Ro," put in Patt. "and
will never go to Congress."

"That may be, my dear; but I shall retain my own self-respect by fair dealing. What I say I *mean*, while many who take the other side do not. I say that, in a country like this, in which land is so abundant as to render the evils of a general monopoly impossible, a landed gentry is precisely what is most needed for the higher order of civilization, including manners, tastes, and the minor principles, and is the very class which, if reasonably maintained and properly regarded, would do the most good at the least risk of any social caste known. They *have* always existed in New York, though with a lessening influence, and are the reason, in my judgment, why we are so much before New England in particular things, while certainly behind that quarter of the country in many others that are dependent on ordinary schooling."

"I like to hear a person maintain his opinions frankly and manfully," said my grandmother; "and this have you done, Roger, from boyhood. My own family, on my father's side, was from New England, and I subscribe to a great deal that you say; and particularly to the part that relates to the apathy of the public to this great wrong. It is now time, however, to go to the breakfast-table, as John has been bowing in the door, yonder, for the last minute or two."

To breakfast we went; and, notwithstanding incendiaries, anti-rentism, and canopies of pig-pens, a merry time we had of it. Henrietta Coldbrooke and Anne Marston never came out with more spirit, though in their several ways, than each did that morning. I believe I looked a little surprised, for I observed that my uncle stole occasional glances at me, that seemed to say — "there, my fine fellow, what do you think of that, now?" whenever either of his wards uttered anything that he fancied cleverer than common.

"Have you heard, ma'am," asked my uncle Ro of my grandmother, "that we are to have old Sus and Jaaf here at the Nest, shortly, and both in grand costume? It seems the red-men are about to depart, and there is to be smoking of pipes, and a great council, which the Trackless fancies will be more dignified if held in front of the house of his pale-face friends, than if held at his own hut."

"How did you ascertain that, Roger?"

"I have been at the wigwam, this morning, and have the
35

fact directly from the Onondago, as well as from the inter preter, whom I met there. By the way, Hugh, we must shortly decide what is to be done with the prisoners, or we shall have writs of habeas corpus served on us, to know why we detain them."

. "Is it possible, uncle Ro," for so his wards called him habitually — " to rescue a gentleman from the gallows by marrying him?" asked Henrietta Coldbrooke, demurely.

."That is so strange a question, that as a guardian I fee curious to hear its meaning."

"Tell — tell at once, Henrietta" — said the other ward, urging her companion to speak. "I will save your blushes, and act as your interpreter. Miss Coldbrooke was honoured by Mr. Seneca Newcome with this letter, within the last twenty-four hours; and, it being a family matter, I think it ought to be referred to a family council."

"Nay, Anne," said the blushing Henrietta, "this is hardly fair—nor am I sure that it would be quite lady-like in me to suffer that letter to be generally known — *particularly* known to you, it certainly is, already."

"Perhaps your reluctance to have it read does not extend to me, Henrietta?" said my uncle.

"Certainly not, sir; nor to my dear Mrs. Littlepage, nor to Martha—though I confess that I cannot see what interest Mr. Hugh can have in the subject. Here it is; take it and read it when you please."

My uncle was pleased to read it on the spot. As he proceeded, a frown collected on his brow, and he bit his lip, like one provoked as well as vexed. Then he laughed, and threw the letter on the table, where no one presumed to molest it. As Henrietta Coldbrooke was blushing all this time, though she laughed and seemed provoked, our curiosity was so great and manifest, that my grandmother felt an inclination to interfere.

"May not that letter be read aloud, for the benefit of all?" she asked.

."There can be no particular reason for concealing it," answered uncle Ro, spitefully. "The more it is known, the more the fellow will be laughed at, as he deserves to be."

"Will that be right, uncle-Ro?" exclaimed Miss Cold

brooke, hastily. "Will it be treating a gentleman as he——"

"Pshaw!—it will not be treating a gentleman, at all. The fellow is, at this moment, a prisoner for attempting to set an inhabited house on fire, in the middle of the night."

Henrietta said no more; and my grandmother took the letter, and read it for the common benefit. I shall not copy the effusion of Seneca, which was more cunning than philosophical; but it contained a strong profession of love, urged in a somewhat business manner, and a generous offer of his hand to the heiress of eight thousand a-year. And this proposal was made only a day or two before the fellow was 'taken in the act,' and at the very time he was the most deeply engaged in his schemes of anti-rentism.

"There is a class of men among us," said my uncle, after everybody had laughed at this magnificent offer, "who do not seem to entertain a single idea of the proprieties. How is it possible, or where could the chap have been bred, to fancy for an instant that a young woman of fortune and station, would marry *him*, and that, too, almost without an acquaintance. I dare say Henrietta never spoke to him ten times in her life."

"Not five, sir, and scarcely anything was said at either of those five."

"And you answered the letter, my dear?" asked my grandmother. "An *answer* ought not to have been forgotten; though it might have properly come, in this case, from your guardian."

"I answered it myself, ma'am, not wishing to be laughed at for my part of the affair. I declined the honour of Mr. Seneca Newcome's hand."

"Well, if the truth *must* be said," put in Patt, drily, "*I* did the same thing, only three weeks since."

"And I so lately as last week," added Anne Marston, demurely.

I do not know that I ever saw my uncle Ro so strangely affected. While everybody around him was laughing heartily, he looked grave, not to say fierce. Then he turned suddenly to me, and said—

"We must let him be hanged, Hugh. Were he to live a thousand years he would never learn the fitness of things."

"You'll think better of this, sir, and become more mer-

ciful. The man has only nobly dared. But I confess a
strong desire to ascertain if Miss Warren alone has escaped
his assaults."

Mary—pretty Mary—she blushed scarlet, but shook her
head, and refused to give any answer. We all saw that her
feelings were not enlisted in the affair in any way; but
there was evidently something of a more serious nature connected with Seneca's addresses to her than in connection
with his addresses to either of the others. As I have since
ascertained, he really had a sort of affection for Mary; and
I have been ready to pardon him the unprincipled and impudent manner in which he cast his flies towards the other
fish, in consideration of his taste in this particular. But
Mary herself would tell us nothing.

"You are not to think so much of this, Mr. Littlepage,"
she cried, so soon as a little recovered from her confusion,
"since it is only acting on the great anti-rent principle, after
all. In the one case, it is only a wish to get good farms
cheap—and in the other, good wives."

"In the one case, other men's farms — and in the other,
other men's wives."

"Other men's wives, certainly, if wives at all," said Patt,
pointedly. "There is no Mr. *Seneky* Newcome there."

"We must let the law have its way, and the fellow be
hanged!" rejoined my uncle. "I could overlook the attempt
to burn the Nest House, but I cannot overlook this. Fellows of his class get everything *dessus dessous*, and I do not
wonder there is anti-rentism in the land. Such a matrimo-
nial experiment could never have been attempted, as between
such parties, in any region but one tainted with anti-rentism,
or deluded by the devil."

"An Irishman would have included my grandmother in
his cast of the net; that's the only difference, sir."

"Sure enough, why have you escaped, my dearest mother?
You, who have a fair widow's portion, too."

"Because the suitor was not an Irishman, as Hugh intimated,—I know no other reason, Hodge. But a person so
devoted to the ladies must not suffer in the cruel way you
speak of. The wretch must be permitted to get off."

All the girls now joined with my grandmother in preferring this, to them, very natural petition; and, for a few

minutes, we heard of nothing but regrets, and solicitations that Seneca might not be given up to the law: " Tender mercies of the law" might not be an unapt way to express the idea, as it is now almost certain that the bigger the rogue, the greater is the chance of escape.

" All this is very well, ladies ; mighty humane and feminine, and quite in character," answered my uncle ; " but, in the first place, there is such a thing as compounding felony, and its consequences are not altogether agreeable ; then, one is bound to consider the effect on society in general. Here is a fellow who first endeavours to raise a flame in the hearts of no less than four young ladies ; failing of which, he takes refuge in lighting a fire in Hugh's kitchen. Do you know, I am almost as much disposed to punish him for the first of these offences as for the last ?"

" There 's a grand movement as is making among all the redskins, ma'am," said John, standing in the door of the breakfast parlour, " and I did n't know but the ladies, and Mr. Littlepage, and Mr. Hugh, would like to see it. Old Sus is on his way here, followed by Yop, who comes grumbling along after him, as if he did n't like the amusement any way at all."

" Have any arrangements been made for the proper reception of our guests this morning, Roger ?"

" Yes, ma'am. At least, I gave orders to have benches brought and placed under the trees, and plenty of tobacco provided. Smoking is a great part of a council, I believe, and we shall be ready to commence at that as soon as they meet."

" Yes, sir, all is ready for 'em," resumed John. " Miller has sent an 'orse cart to bring the benches, and we 've provided as much 'baccy as they can use. The servants 'opes, ma'am, they can have permission to witness the ceremony. It is n't often that civilized people *can* get a sight at real savages."

My grandmother gave an assent, and there was a general movement, preparatory to going on the lawn to witness the parting interview between the Trackless and his visiters.

" You have been very considerate, Miss Warren," I whispered Mary, as I helped her to put on her shawl," in

35*

not betraying what I fancy is the most important of al.
Seneca's love secrets."

"I confess these letters have surprised me," the dear girl
said thoughtfully, and with a look that seemed perplexed.
"No one would be apt to think, very favourably of Mr.
Newcome; yet it was by no means necessary to complete
his character, that one should think as ill as this."

I said no more,—but these few words, which appeared to
escape Mary unconsciously and involuntarily, satisfied me
that Seneca had been seriously endeavouring to obtain an
interest in *her* heart notwithstanding her poverty.

CHAPTER XXVII.

"And underneath that face like summer's dreams,
  Its lips as moveless, and its cheek as clear,
Slumbers a whirlwind of the heart's emotions,
Love, hatred, pride, hope, sorrow—all save fear."

HALLECK.

THE only singularity connected with the great age of the
Indian and the negro, was the fact that they should have
been associates for near a century; and so long intimately
united in adventures and friendship. I say friendship, for
the term was not at all unsuited to the feeling that connected
these old men together, though they had so little in common,
in the way of character. While the Indian possessed all the
manly and high qualities of a warrior of the woods, of a
chief, and of one who had never acknowledged a superior,
the other was necessarily distinguished by many of the
wickednesses of a state of servitude; the bitter consequences
of a degraded caste. Fortunately, both were temperate, by
no means an every-day virtue among the red-men who dwelt
with the whites, though much more so with the blacks. But
Susquesus was born an Onondago, a tribe remarkable for
its sobriety, and at no period of his long life would he taste

intoxicating drink, while Jaaf was essentially a sober
man, though he had a thorough 'nigger' relish for hard
cider. There can be little doubt that these two aged memorials of past ages, and almost forgotten generations, owed
their health and strength to their temperance, fortifying natural predispositions to tenacity of life. ·

. It was always thought Jaaf was a little the senior of the
Indian, though the difference in their ages could not be
great. It is certain that the red-man retained much the
most of his bodily powers, though, for fifty years, he had
taxed them the least. Susquesus never worked ; never would
work in the ordinary meaning of the term. He deemed it
to be beneath his dignity as a warrior, and, I have heard it
said, that nothing but necessity could have induced him to
plant, or hoe, even when in his prime. So long as the
boundless forest furnished the deer, the moose, the beaver,
the bear, and the other animals that it is usual for the red-
man to convert into food, he had cared little for the fruits of
the earth, beyond those that were found growing in their
native state. · His hunts were the last regular occupation
that the old man abandoned. He carried the rifle, and
threaded the woods with considerable vigour after he had
seen a hundred winters ; but the game deserted him, under
the never-dying process of clearing acre after acre, until
little of the native forest was left, with the exception of the
reservation of my own, already named, and the pieces of
woodland that are almost invariably attached to every American farm, lending to the landscape a relief and beauty
that are usually wanting to the views of older countries.
It is this peculiarity which gives so many of the views of
the republic, nay, it may be said to all of them, so much of
the character of park-scenery when seen at a distance that
excludes the blemishes of a want of finish, and the coarser
appliances of husbandry.

With Jaaf, though he had imbibed a strong relish for the
forest, and for forest-life, it was different in many respects.
Accustomed to labour from childhood, *he* could not be kept
from work, even by his extreme old age. He had the hoe,
or the axe, or the spade in his hand daily, many years after
he could wield either to any material advantage. The little
he did in this way, now, was not done to kill thought, for he

never had any to kill; it was purely the effect of habit, and
of a craving desire to be Jaaf still, and to act his life over
again.

I am sorry to say that neither of these men had any
essential knowledge, or any visible feeling for the truths of
Christianity. A hundred years ago, little spiritual care was
extended to the black, and the difficulty of making an impression, in this way, on the Indian, has become matter of
history. Perhaps success best attends such efforts when the
pious missionary can penetrate to the retired village, and
disseminate his doctrines far from the miserable illustration
of their effects, that is to be hourly traced, by the most casual
observer, amid the haunts of civilized men. That Christianity does produce a deep and benign influence on our social
condition cannot be doubted; but he who is only superficially
acquainted with Christian nations, as they are called, and
sets about tracing the effects of this influence, meets with so
many proofs of a contrary nature, as to feel a strong disposition to doubt the truth of dogmas that seem so impotent.
It is quite likely such was the case with Susquesus, who had
passed all the earlier years of his exclusive association with
the pale-faces, on the flanks of armies, or among hunters,
surveyors, runners, and scouts; situations that were not
very likely to produce any high notions of moral culture.
Nevertheless, many earnest and long-continued efforts had
been made to awaken in this aged Indian some notions of
the future state of a pale-face, and to persuade him to be
baptized. My grandmother, in particular, had kept this end
in view for quite half a century, but with no success. The
different clergy, of all denominations, had paid more or less
attention to this Indian, with the same object, though no visible results had followed their efforts. Among others, Mr.
Warren had not overlooked this part of his duty, but he had
met with no more success than those who had been before
him. Singular as it seemed to some, though I saw nothing
strange in it, Mary Warren had joined in this benevolent
project with a gentle zeal, and affectionate and tender interest, that promised to achieve more than had been even
hoped for these many years by her predecessors in the same
kind office. Her visits to the hut had been frequent, and I
learned that morning from Patt, that, "Though Mary her-

self never spoke on the subject, enough has been seen by others to leave no doubt that her gentle offices and prayers had, at last, touched, in some slight degree, the marble-like heart of the Trackless.".

As for Jaaf, it is possible that it was his misfortune to be a slave in a family that belonged to the Episcopal Church, a sect that is so tempered and chastened in its religious rites, and so far removed from exaggeration, as often to seem cold to those who seek excitement, and fancy quiet and self-control incompatible with a lively faith. 'Your priests are unsuited to make converts among the people,' said an enthusiastic clergyman of another denomination to me, quite lately. 'They cannot go among the brambles and thorns without tearing their gowns and surplices.' There may be a certain degree of truth in this, though the obstacle exists rather with the convert than with the missionary. The vulgar love coarse excitement, and fancy that a profound spiritual sensibility must needs awaken a powerful physical sympathy. To such, groans, and sighs, and lamentations must be not only audible to exist at all, but audible in a dramatic and striking form with men, in order to be groans, and sighs, and lamentations acceptable with God. It is certain, at any rate, that the practices which reason, education, a good taste, and a sound comprehension of Christian obligations condemn, are, if not *most* effective, still effective with the ignorant and coarse-minded. Thus may it have been with Jaaf, who had not fallen into the hands of the exaggerated during that period of life when he was most likely to be aroused by their practices, and who now really seemed to have lived beyond everything but the recollections connected with the persons and things he loved in youth.

As men, in the higher meaning of the term, the reader will remember that Susquesus was ever vastly the superior of the black. Jaaf's intellect had suffered under the blight which seems to have so generally caused the African mind to wither, as we know that mind among ourselves; while that of his associate had ever possessed much of the loftiness of a grand nature, left to its native workings by the impetus of an unrestrained, though savage liberty.

Such were the characters of the two extraordinary men

whom we now went forth to meet. By the time we reached
the lawn, they were walking slowly towards the piazza,
having got within the range of the shrubbery that immediately surrounds, and sheds its perfume on the house. The
Indian led, as seemed to become his character and rank.
But Jaaf had never presumed on his years and indulgencies
so far as to forget his condition. A slave he had been
born, a slave had he lived, and a slave he would die. This,
too, in spite of the law of emancipation, which had, in fact,
liberated him long ere he had reached his hundredth year.
I have been told that when my father announced to Jaaf the
fact that he and all his progeny, the latter of which was
very numerous, were free and at liberty to go and do
as they pleased, the old black was greatly dissatisfied.
"What good dat all do, Masser Malbone," he growled.
"Whey 'ey won't let well alone? Nigger be nigger, and
white gentle'em be white gentle'em. I 'speck, now, nuttin'
but disgrace and poverty come on my breed! We alway
hab been gentle'em's nigger, and why can't 'ey let us be
gentle'em's nigger, as long as we like? Ole Sus hab liberty
all he life, and what good he get? Nuttin' but poor red
sabbage, for all dat, and never be any t'ing more. If he
could be gentle'em's sabbage, I tell him, *dat* war' somet'ing;
but, no, he too proud for dat! Gosh! so he only he own
sabbage!"

The Onondago was in high costume; much higher even
than when he first received the visit of the prairie Indians.
The paint he used, gave new fire to eyes that age had certainly dimmed, though they had not extinguished their light;
and fierce and savage as was the conceit, it unquestionably
relieved the furrows of time. That red should be as much
the favourite colour of the redskin is, perhaps, as natural as
that our ladies should use cosmetics to imitate the lilies and
roses that are wanting. A grim fierceness, however, was
the aim of the Onondago; it being his ambition, at that moment, to stand before his guests in the colours of a warrior.
Of the medals and wampum, and feathers, and blankets, and
moccasins, gay with the quills of the porcupine, tinged half
a dozen hues, and the tomahawk polished to the brightness
of silver, it is not necessary to say anything. So much has

been said, and written, and seen, of late, on such subjects, that almost every one now knows how the North American warrior appears, when he comes forth in his robes.

Nor had Jaaf neglected to do honour to a festival that was so peculiarly in honour of his friend. Grumble he would and did, throughout the whole of that day; but he was not the less mindful of the credit and honour of Susquesus. It is the fashion of the times to lament the disappearance of the red-men from among us; but, for my part, I feel much more disposed to mourn over the disappearance of the "nigger." - I use the Doric, in place of the more modern and mincing term of 'coloured man;' for the Doric alone will convey to the American the meaning in which I wish to be understood. I regret the "nigger;" the old-fashioned, careless, light-hearted, laborious, idle, roguish, honest, faithful, fraudulent, grumbling, dogmatical slave; who was at times good for nothing, and, again, the stay and support of many a family. But, him I regret in particular is the domestic slave, who identified himself with the interests, and most of all with the *credit* of those he served; and who always played the part of an humble privy counsellor, and sometimes that of a prime minister. It is true, I had never seen Jaaf acting in the latter capacity, among us; nor is it probable he ever did exactly discharge such functions with any of his old masters; but, he was a much indulged servant always and had become so completely associated with us, by not only long services, but by playing his part well and manfully in divers of the wild adventures that are apt to characterize the settlement of a new country, that we all of us thought of him rather as an humble and distant relative, than as a slave. Slave, indeed, he had not been for more than four-score years, his manumission-papers having been signed and regularly recorded as far back as that, though they remained a perfect dead letter, so far as the negro himself was concerned.

The costume of Yop Littlepage, as this black was familiarly called by all who knew anything of his existence, and his great age, as well as that of Susquesus, had got into more than one newspaper, was of what might be termed the old school of the ' nigger !' The coat was scarlet, with buttons of mother-of-pearl, each as large as a half-dollar;

his breeches were sky blue ; the vest was green ; the stock-
ings striped blue and white, and the legs had no other peculiarities about them, than the facts that all that remained of
the calves were on the shins, and that they were stepped
nearer than is quite common to the centre of the foot ; the
heel-part of the latter, being about half as long as the part
connected with the toes. The shoes, indeed, were somewhat conspicuous portions of the dress, having a length, and
breadth, and proportions that might almost justify a natural-
ist in supposing that they were never intended for a human
being. But, the head and hat, according to Jaaf's own notion, contained the real glories of his toilette and person.
As for the last, it was actually laced, having formed a part
of my grandfather, Gen. Cornelius Littlepage's uniform in
the field, and the wool beneath it was as white as the snow
of the hills. This style of dress has long disappeared from
among the black race, as well as from among the whites ;
but vestiges of it were to be traced, my uncle tells me, in
his boyhood; particularly at the pinkster holidays, that peculiar festival of the negro. Notwithstanding the incongruities
of his attire, Yop Littlepage made a very respectable figure
on this occasion, the great age of both him and the Onondago being the circumstances that accorded least with
their magnificence.

 Notwithstanding the habitual grumbling of the negro, the
Indian always led when they made a movement. He
had led in the forest, on the early hunts and on the war-
paths; he had led in their later excursions on the neighbouring hills ; he always led when it was their wont to
stroll to the hamlet together, to witness the militia musters
and other similar striking events; he even was foremost
when they paid their daily visits to the Nest ; and, now, he
came a little in advance, slow in movement, quiet, with lips
compressed, eye roving and watchful, and far from dim, and
his whole features wonderfully composed and noble, considering the great number of years he had seen. Jaaf followed at the same gait, but a very different man in demeanour and aspect. *His* face scarce seemed human, even
the colour of his skin, once so glistening and black, having
changed to a dirty grey, all its gloss having disappeared
while his lips were, perhaps, the most prominent feature

These, too, were in incessant motion, the old man working his jaws, in a sort of second childhood ; or as the infant bites its gums to feel its nearly developed teeth, even when he was not keeping up the almost unceasing accompaniment of his grumbles.

As the old men walked towards us, and the men of the prairies had not yet shown themselves, we all advanced to meet the former. Every one of our party, the girls included, shook hands with Susquesus, and wished him a good morning. He knew my grandmother, and betrayed some strong feeling, when he shook her hand. He knew Patt, and nodded kindly in answer to her good wishes. He knew Mary Warren, too, and held her hand a little time in his own, gazing at her wistfully the while. My uncle Ro and I were also recognised, his look at me being earnest and long. The two other girls were courteously received, but his feelings were little interested in them. A chair was placed for Susquesus on the lawn, and he took his seat. As for Jaaf, he walked slowly up to the party, took off his fine cocked-hat, but respectfully refused the seat he too was offered. Happening thus to be the last saluted, he was the first with whom my grandmother opened the discourse.

" It is a pleasant sight, Jaaf, to see you, and our old friend Susquesus, once more on the lawn of the old house."

" Not so berry ole house, Miss Duss, a'ter all," answered the negro, in his grumbling way. " Remem'er him well 'nough ; only built tudder day."

" It has been built three-score years, if you call that the other day. I was then young myself ; a bride—happy and blessed far beyond my deserts. Alas ! how changed have things become since that time !"

" Yes, you won'erful changed — must say dat for you, Miss Duss. I some time surprise myself so young a lady get change so berry soon."

" Ah ! Jaaf, though it may seem a short time to you, who are so much my senior, four-score years are a heavy load to carry. I enjoy excellent health and spirits for my years ; but age will assert its power."

" Remem'er you, Miss Duss, like dat young lady dere," pointing at Patt — " now you do seem won'erful change. Ole Sus, too, berry much alter of late—can't hole out much

36

longer, I do t'ink. But Injin nebber hab much raal grit in 'em."

"And you, my friend," continued my grandmother, turning to Susquesus, who had sat motionless while she was speaking to Jaaf—"do you also see this great change in me? I have known you much longer than I have known Jaaf; and *your* recollection of me must go back nearly to childhood—to the time when I first lived in the woods, as a companion of my dear, excellent old uncle, Chainbearer."

"Why should Susquesus forget little wren? Hear song now in his ear. No change at all in little wren, in Susquesus' eye."

"This is at least gallant, and worthy of an Onondago chief. But, my worthy friend, age will make its mark even on the trees; and we cannot hope to escape it for ever!"

"No; bark smooth on young tree — rough on ole tree. Nebber forget Chainbearer. He's same age as Susquesus —little ole'er, too. Brave warrior—good man. Know him when young hunter—he dere when *dat* happen."

"When *what* happened, Susquesus? I have long wished to know what drove you from your people; and why you, a red-man in your heart and habits, to the last, should have so long lived among us pale-faces, away from your own tribe. I can understand why you like *us*, and wish to pass the remainder of your days with this family; for I know all that we have gone through together, and your early connection with my father-in-law, and *his* father-in-law, too; but the reason why you left your own people so young, and have now lived near a hundred years away from them, is what I could wish to hear, before the angel of death summons one of us away."

While my grandmother was thus coming to the point, for the first time in her life, on this subject, as she afterwards told me, the Onondago's eye was never off her own. I thought he seemed surprised; then his look changed to sadness; and bowing his head a little, he sat a long time, apparently musing on the past. The subject had evidently aroused the strongest of the remaining feelings of the old man, and the allusion to it had brought back images of things long gone by, that were probably reviewed not altogether without pain. I think his head must have been bowed, and his face riveted on the ground, for quite a minute.

"Chainbearer nebber say why?" the old man suddenly asked, raising his face again to look at my grandmother. "Ole chief, too—he know; nebber talk of it, eh?"

"Never. I have heard both my uncle and my father-in-law say that they knew the reason why you left your people, so many long, long, years ago, and that it did you credit; but neither ever said more. It is reported here, that these red-men, who have come so far to see you, also know it, and that it is one reason of their coming so much out of their way to pay you a visit."

Susquesus listened attentively, though no portion of his person manifested emotion but his eyes. All the rest of the man seemed to be made of some material that was totally without sensibility; but those restless, keen, still penetrating eyes opened a communication with the being within, and proved that the spirit was far younger than the tenement in which it dwelt. Still, he made no revelation; and our curiosity, which was getting to be intense, was completely baffled. It was even some little time before the Indian said anything more at all. When he did speak, it was merely to say—

"Good. Chainbearer wise chief—Gin'ral wise, too. Good in camp—good at council-fire. Know when to talk—know what to talk."

How much further my dear grandmother might have been disposed to push the subject, I cannot say, for just then, we saw the redskins coming out of their quarters, evidently about to cross from the old farm to the lawn, this being their last visit to the Trackless, preparatory to departing on their long journey to the prairies. Aware of all this, she fell back, and my uncle led Susquesus to the tree, where the benches were placed for the guests, I carrying the chair in the rear. Everybody followed, even to all the domestics who could be spared from the ordinary occupations of the household.

The Indian and the negro were both seated; and chairs having been brought out for the members of the family, we took our places near by, though so much in the back-ground as not to appear obtrusive.

The Indians of the prairies arrived in their customary marching order, or in single files. Manytongues led, followed by Prairiefire; Flintyheart and Eaglesflight came next, and the rest succeeded in a nameless but perfect order. To our surprise, however, they brought the two prisoners with them, secured with savage ingenuity, and in a way to render escape nearly impossible.

- It is unnecessary to dwell on the deportment of these strangers, as they took their allotted places on the benches, it being essentially the same as that described in their first visit. The same interest, however, was betrayed in their manner, nor did their curiosity or veneration appear to be in the least appeased, by having passed a day, or two, in the immediate vicinity of their subject. That this curiosity and veneration proceeded, in some measure, from the great age and-extended experience of the Trackless was probable enough, but I could not divest myself of the idea that there lay something unusual behind all, which tradition had made familiar to these sons of the soil, but which had become lost to us.

The American savage enjoys one great advantage over the civilized man of the same quarter of the world. His raditions ordinarily are true, whereas, the multiplied means of imparting intelligence among ourselves, has induced so many pretenders to throw themselves into the ranks of the wise and learned, that blessed, thrice blessed is he, whose mind escapes the contamination of falsehood and prejudice. Well would it be for men, if they oftener remembered that the very facilities that exist to circulate the truth, are just so many facilities for circulating falsehood; and that he who believes even one-half of that which meets his eyes, in his daily inquiries into passing events, is most apt to throw away quite a moiety of even that much credulity, on facts that either never had an existence at all, or, which have been so mutilated in the relation, that their eye-witnesses would be the last to recognise them.

The customary silence succeeded the arrival of the visiters; then Eaglesflight struck fire with a flint, touched the tobacco with the flame, and puffed at a very curiously carved pipe, made of some soft stone of the interior, until he had lighted it beyond any risk of its soon becoming extinguished

This done, he rose, advanced with profound reverence in his air, and presented it to Susquesus, who took it and smoked for a few seconds, after which he returned it to him from whom it had been received. This was a signal for other pipes to be lighted, and one was offered to my uncle and myself, each of us making a puff or two; and even John and the other male domestics were not neglected. Prairiefire, himself, paid the compliment to Jaaf. The negro had noted what was passing, and was much disgusted with the niggardliless which required the pipe to be so soon returned. This he did not care to conceal, as was obvious by the crusty observation he made when the pipe was offered to him. Cider and tobacco had, from time immemorial, been the two great blessings of this black's existence, and he felt, at seeing one standing ready to receive his pipe, after a puff or two, much as he might have felt had one pulled the mug from his mouth, after the second or third swallow.

"No need wait here"—grumbled old Jaaf—"when I done, gib you de pipe, ag'in; nebber fear. Masser Corny, or Masser Malbone, or Masser Hugh—dear me, I nebber knows which be libbin' and which be dead, I get so ole, now-a-day! But nebber mind if he be ole; can smoke yet, and don't lub Injin fashion of gibbin' t'ings; and dat is gib him and den take away, ag'in. Nigger is nigger, and Injin is Injin; and nigger best. Lord! how many years I *do* see— I do see—most get tire of libbin' so long. Don't wait, Injin; when I done, you get pipe again, I say. Best not make ole Jaaf *too* mad, or he dreadful!"

Although it is probable that Prairiefire did not understand one-half of the negro's words, he comprehended his wish to finish the tobacco, before he relinquished the pipe. This was against all rule, and a species of slight on Indian usages, but the red-man overlooked all, with the courtesy of one trained in high society, and walked away as composedly as if everything were right. In these particulars the high-breeding of an Indian is always made apparent. No one ever sees in his deportment, a shrug, or a half-concealed smile, or a look of intelligence; a wink or a nod, or any other of that class of signs, or communications, which it is usually deemed underbred to resort to in company. In

36*

all things, he is dignified and quiet, whether it be the effec'
of coldness, or the result of character.

The smoking now became general, but only as a ceremony; no one but Jaaf setting to with regularity to finish
his pipe. As for the black, his opinion of the superiority of
his own race over that of the red-man, was as fixed as his
consciousness of its inferiority to the white, and he would
have thought the circumstance that the present mode of
using tobacco was an Indian custom, a sufficient reason
why he himself should not adopt it. The smoking did not
last long, but was succeeded by a silent pause. Then
Prairiefire arose and spoke.

"Father," he commenced, "we are about to quit you.
Our squaws and pappooses, on the prairies, wish to see us;
it is time for us to go. They are looking towards the great
salt lake for us; we are looking towards the great fresh-
water lakes for them. There the sun sets — here it rises;
the distance is great, and many strange tribes of pale-faces
live along the path. Our journey has been one of peace.
We have not hunted; we have taken no scalps; but we
have seen our Great Father, Uncle Sam, and we have seen
our Great Father, Susquesus; we shall travel towards the
setting sun satisfied. — Father, our traditions are true; they
never lie. A lying tradition is worse than a lying Indian.
What a lying Indian says, deceives his friends, his wife, his
children; what a lying tradition says, deceives a tribe. Our
traditions are true; they speak of the Upright Onondago.
All the tribes on the prairies have heard this tradition, and
are very glad. It is good to hear of justice; it is bad to
hear of injustice. Without justice an Indian is no better
than a wolf. No; there is not a tongue spoken on the
prairies which does not tell of that pleasant tradition. We
could not pass the wigwam of our father without turning
aside to look at him. Our squaws and pappooses wish to
see us, but they would have told us to come back, and turn
aside to look upon our father, had we forgotten to do so. —
Why has my father seen so many winters? It is the will
of the Manitou. The Great Spirit wants to keep him here
a little longer. He is like stones piled together to tell the
hunters where the pleasant path is to be found. All the red

men who see him think of what is right. No; the Great
Spirit cannot yet spare my father from the earth, lest red-
men forget what is right. He is stones piled together."

Here Prairiefire ceased, sitting down amidst a low murmur
of applause. . He had expressed the common feeling, and
met with the success usual to such efforts. Susquesus had
heard and understood all that was said, and I could perceive
that he felt it, though he betrayed less emotion on this occasion than he had done on the occasion of the previous interview. Then, the novelty of the scene, no doubt, contributed
to influence his feelings. A pause followed this opening
speech, and we were anxiously waiting for the renowned
orator, Eaglesflight, to rise, when a singular and somewhat
ludicrous interruption of the solemn dignity of the scene occurred. In the place of Eaglesflight, whom Manytongues
had given us reason to expect would now come forth with
energy and power, a much younger warrior arose and spoke,
commanding the attention of his listeners in a way to show
that he possessed their respect. We were told that this
young warrior's name, rendered into English, was Deersfoot, an appellation obtained on account of his speed, and
which we were assured he well merited. Much to our surprise, however, he addressed himself to Jaaf, Indian courtesy
requiring that something should be said to the constant friend
and tried associate of the Trackless. The reader may be
certain we were all much amused at this bit of homage,
though every one of us felt some little concern on the subject of the answer it might elicit. Deersfoot delivered himself, substantially, as follows : —

" The Great Spirit sees all things ; he makes all things.
In his eyes, colour is nothing. Although he made children
that he loved of a red colour, he made children that he loved
with pale-faces, too. He did not stop there. No ; he said,
' I wish to see warriors and men with faces darker than the
skin of the bear. I will have warriors who shall frighten
their enemies by their countenances.' He made black men.
My father is black ; his skin is neither red, like the skin of
Susquesus, nor white, like the skin of the young chief of
Ravensnest. It is now grey, with having had the sun shine
on it so many summers ;. but it was once the colour of the
crow. Then it must have been pleasant to look at.—My

black father is very old. They tell me he is even older than
the Upright Onondago. The Manitou must be well pleased
with him, not to have called him away sooner. He has left
him in his wigwam, that all the black men may see whom
their Great Spirit loves.—This is the tradition told to us by
our fathers. The pale men come from the rising sun, and
were born before the heat burned their skins. The black
men came from under the sun at noon-day, and their faces
were darkened by looking up above their heads to admire
the warmth that ripened their fruits. The red men were
born under the setting sun, and their faces were coloured
by the hues of the evening skies. The red man was born
here ; the pale man was born across the salt lake ; the black
man came from a country of his own, where the sun is always above his head. What of that ?. We are brothers.
The Thicklips (this was the name by which the strangers
designated Jaaf, as we afterwards learned) is the friend of
Susquesus. They have lived in the same wigwam, now,
so many winters, that their venison and bear's-meat have
the same taste. They love one another. Whomsoever Susquesus loves and honours, all just Indians love and honour.
I have no more to say."

It is very certain that Jaaf would not have understood a
syllable that was uttered, in this address, had not Manytongues first given him to understand that Deersfoot was
talking to him in particular, and then translated the speaker's language, word for word, and with great deliberation,
as each sentence was finished. Even this care might not
have sufficed to make the negro sensible of what was going
on, had not Patt gone to him, and told him in a manner and
voice to which he was accustomed, to attend to what was
said, and to endeavour, as soon as Deersfoot sat down, to
say something in reply. Jaaf was so accustomed to my
sister, and was so deeply impressed with the necessity of
obeying her, as one of his many ' y'ung missuses,'—*which*
he scarcely knew himself,—that she succeeded in perfectly
arousing him ; and he astonished us all with the intelligence
of his very characteristic answer, which he did not fail to
deliver exactly as he had been directed to do. Previously
to beginning to speak, the negro champed his toothless
gums together, like a vexed swine ; but ' y'ung missus' had

told him he *must* answer, and answer he *did*. It is probable, also, that the old fellow had some sort of recollection
of such scenes, having been present, in his younger days,
at various councils held by the different tribes of New York;
among whom my grandfather, Gen. Mordaunt Littlepage,
had more than once been a commissioner.

"Well," Jaaf began, in a short, snappish manner, "s'pose
nigger *must* say somet'in'. No berry great talker, 'cause I
no Injin. Nigger hab too much work to do, to talk all 'e
time. What you say 'bout where nigger come from, isn't
true. He come from Africa, as I hear 'em say, 'long time
ago. Ahs, me! how ole I do get! Sometime I t'ink poor
ole black man be nebber to lie down and rest himself. It
do seem dat ebberybody take his rest but old Sus and me.
I berry strong, yet; and git stronger and stronger, dough
won'erful tired; but Sus, he git weaker and weaker ebbery
day. Can't last long, now, poor Sus! Ebberybody *must*
die, sometime. Ole, ole, ole Masser and Missus, fust dey
die. Den Masser Corny go; putty well adwanced, too.
Den come Masser Mordaunt's turn, and Masser Malbone,
and now dere anudder Masser Hugh. Well, dey putty
much all de sames to me. I lubs 'em all, and all on 'em
lubs me. Den Miss Duss count for somet'in', but she be
libbin', yet. Most time she die, too, but don't seem to go.
Ahs, me! how ole I *do* git! Ha! dere comes dem debbils
of Injins, ag'in, and dis time we *must* clean 'em out! Get
your rifle, Sus; get your rifle, boy, and mind dat ole Jaaf
be at your elbow."

Sure enough, there the Injins *did* come; but I must reserve an account of what followed for the commencemen
of the next Chapter.

CHAPTER XXVIII.

"Hope—that thy wrongs will be by the Great Spirit
Remember'd and revenged when thou art gone;
Sorrow—that none are left thee to inherit
Thy name, thy fame, thy passions, and thy throne."

Red Jacket.

IT was a little remarkable that one as old and blear-eyed
as the negro, should be the first among us to discover the
approach of a large body of the Injins, who could not be
less than two hundred in number. The circumstance was
probably owing to the fact that, while every other eye was
riveted on the speaker, his eyes were fastened on nothing.
There the Injins did come, however, in force; and this time,
apparently, without fear. The white American meets the
red-man with much confidence, when he is prepared for the
struggle; and the result has shown that, when thrown upon
his resources, in the wilderness, and after he has been al-
lowed time to gain a little experience, he is usually the most
formidable enemy. But a dozen Indians, of the stamp of
those who had here come to visit us, armed and painted, and
placed in the centre of one of our largest peopled counties,
would be sufficient to throw that county into a paroxysm of
fear. Until time were given for thought, and the opinions
of the judicious superseded the effects of rumour, nothing
but panic would prevail. Mothers would clasp their children to their bosoms, fathers would hold back their sons
from the slaughter, and even the heroes of the militia would
momentarily forget their ardour in the suggestions of prudence and forethought.

Such, in fact, had been the state of things in and about
Ravensnest, when Flintyheart so unexpectedly led his companions into the forest, and dispersed the virtuous and oppressed tenants of my estate on their return from a meeting
held with but one virtuous object; viz., that of transferring
the fee of the farms they occupied, from me to themselves.
No one doubted, at the moment, that in addition to the other
enormities committed by me and mine, I had obtained a

body of savages from the far West, to meet the forces already levied by the tenants, on a principle that it would not do to examine very clearly. If I *had* done so, I am far from certain that I should not have been perfectly justified in morals; for an evil of that nature, that might at any time be put down in a month, and which is suffered to exist for years, through the selfish indifference of the community, restores to every man his natural rights of self-defence; though I make no doubt, had I resorted to such means, I should have been hanged, without benefit of philanthropists; the 'clergy' in this country not being included in the class, so far as suspension by the neck is concerned.

But the panic had disappeared, as soon as the truth became known concerning the true object of the visit of the redskins. The courage of the "virtuous and honest" revived, and one of the first exhibitions of this renewed spirit was the attempt to set fire to my house and barns. So serious a demonstration, it was thought, would convince me of the real power of the people, and satisfy us all that their wishes are not to be resisted with impunity. As no one likes to have his house and barns burned, it must be a singular being who could withstand the influence of such a manifestation of the "spirit of the Institutions;" for it is just as reasonable to suppose that the attempts of the incendiaries came within their political category, as it is to suppose that the attempt of the tenants to get a title beyond what was bestowed in their leases, was owing to this cause.

That habit of deferring to externals, which is so general in a certain class of our citizens, and which endures in matters of religion long after the vital principle is forgotten, prevented any serious outbreak on the next day, which was the Sunday mentioned; though the occasion was improved to coerce by intimidation, the meeting and resolutions having been regularly digested in secret conclave, among the local leaders of anti-rentism, and carried out, as has been described. Then followed the destruction of the canopy, another demonstration of the "spirit of the Institutions," and as good an argument as any that has yet been offered, in favour of the dogmas of the new political faith. Public opinion is entitled to some relief, surely, when it betrays so much excitement as to desecrate churches and to destroy private property. · This circumstance of the canopy had been much dwelt on, as a favourite anti-rent argument, and it might now be considered that the subject was carried out to demonstration.   ·   ·

By the time all this was effected, so completely had the "Injins" got over their dread of the Indians, that it was with difficulty the leaders of the former could prevent the most heroic portion of their corps from · following their blow at the canopy by a *coup de main* against the old farm-house, and its occupants. Had not the discretion of the leaders been greater than that of their subordinates, it is very probable blood would have been shed, between these quasi belligerents. But the warriors of the Prairies were the guests of Uncle Sam, and the old gentleman, after all, has a long arm, and can extend it from Washington to Ravensnest without much effort. He was not to be offended heedlessly, therefore; for his power was especially to be dreaded in this matter of the covenants, without which Injins and agitation would be altogether unnecessary to attaining the great object, the Albany politicians being so well disposed to do all they can for the "virtuous and honest." Uncle Sam's Indians, consequently, were held a good deal more in respect than the laws of the State, and they consequently escaped being murdered in their sleep.

When Jaaf first drew our attention to the Injins, they were advancing, in a long line, by the highway, and at· a moderate pace; leaving us time to shift our own position, did we deem it necessary. My uncle was of ·opinion it would never do to remain out on the lawn, exposed to so great a superiority of force, and he took his measures accordingly. In the first place, the females, mistresses and maids—and there were eight or ten of the last—were requested to retire, at once, to the house. The latter, with John at their head, were directed to close all the lower, outside shutters of the building, and secure them within. This done, and the gate and two outer doors fastened, it would not be altogether without hazard to make an assault on our fortress. As no one required a second request to move, this part of the precautions was soon effected, and the house placed in a species of temporary security.

While the foregoing was in the course of execution, Susquesus and Jaaf were induced to change their positions, by transferring themselves to the piazza. That change was made, and the two old fellows were comfortably seated in their chairs, again, before a single man of the redskins moved a foot. There they all remained, motionless as so many statues, with the exception that Flintyheart seemed to be reconnoitring with his eyes, the thicket that fringed the neighbouring ravine, and which formed a bit of dense cover, as already described, of some considerable extent.

" Do you wish the redskins in the house, Colonel ?" asked the interpreter, coolly, when matters had reached to this pass ; " if you do, it 's time to speak, or, they 'll soon be off, like a flock of pigeons, into that cover. There 'll be a fight as sartain as they move, for there 's no more joke and making of faces about them critturs, than there is about a mile-stone. So, it 's best to speak in time."

No delay occurred after this hint was given. The request of my uncle Ro that the chiefs would follow the Upright Onondago, was just in time to prevent a flight; in the sense of Manytongues, I mean, for it was not very likely these warriors would literally run away. It is probable that they would have preferred the cover of the woods as more natural and familiar to them, — but, I remarked, as the whole party came on the piazza, that Flintyheart, in particular, cast a quick, scrutinizing glance at the house, which said in pretty plain language that he was examining its capabilities as a work of defence. The movement, however, was made with perfect steadiness; and, what most surprised us all, was the fact that not one of the chiefs appeared to pay the slightest attention to their advancing foes ; or, men whom it was reasonable for them to suppose so considered themselves to be. We imputed this extraordinary reserve to force of character, and a desire to maintain a calm and dignified deportment in the presence of Susquesus. If it were really the latter motive that so completely restrained every exhibition of impatience, apprehension, or disquietude, they had every reason to congratulate themselves on the entire success of their characteristic restraint on their feelings.

The Injins were just appearing on the lawn as our arrangements were completed. John had come to report

37

every shutter secure, and the gate and little door barred.
He also informed us that all the men and boys who could
be mustered, including gardeners, labourers, and stable people, to the number of five or six, were in the little passage,
armed; where rifles were ready also for ourselves.   In
short, the preparations that had been made by my grandmother, immediately after her arrival, were now of use, and
enabled us to make a much more formidable resistance, sustained as we were by the party from the Prairies, than I
could have ever hoped for on so sudden an emergency. -

 . Our arrangement was very simple.   The ladies were
seated near the great door, in order that they might be
placed under cover the first, in the event of necessity ; Susquesus and Jaaf had their chairs a little on one side, but
quite near this group, and the men from the far West occupied the opposite end of the piazza, whither the benches had
been removed, for their accommodation.   Manytongues
stood between the two divisions of our company, ready to
interpret for either ; while my uncle, myself, John, and two
or three of the other servants took position behind our aged
friends.   Seneca and his fellow-incendiary were in the
midst of the chiefs.

 It was just as the Injins had got fairly on the lawn that
we heard the clattering of hoofs, and every eye was turned
in the direction whence the sound proceeded. This was on
the side of the ravine, and to me it seemed from the first
that some one was approaching us through that dell.   So it
proved, truly ; for soon Opportunity came galloping up the
path, and appeared in sight.   She did not check her horse
until under the tree, where she alighted, by a single bound,
and hitching the animal to a hook in the tree, she moved
swiftly towards the house. My sister Patt advanced to the
steps of the piazza to receive this unexpected guest, and I
was just behind her to make my bow. But the salutations
of Opportunity were hasty and far from being very composed.   She glanced around her, ascertained the precise condition of her brother,—and, taking my arm, she led me into
the library with very little, or, indeed, with no ceremony;
for, to give this young woman her due, she was a person of
great energy when there was anything serious to be done.
The only sign of deviating, in the slightest degree, from the

object in view, was pausing one instant, in passing, to make
her compliments to my grandmother.

"What, in the name of wonder, do you mean to do with
Sen ?" demanded this active young lady, looking at me intently, with an expression half-hostile, half-tender. "You
are standing over an earthquake, Mr. Hugh, if you did but
know it."

Opportunity had confounded the effect with the 'cause,
but that was of little moment on an occasion so interesting. . She was much in earnest, and I had learned by experience that her hints and advice might be of great service
to us at the Nest.

"To what particular danger do you allude, my dear Opportunity ?"

"Ah, Hugh! if things was only as they used to be, how
happy might we all be together here at Ravensnest! But,
there is no time to talk of such things; for, as Sarah Soothings says, ' the heart is most monopolized when grief is the
profoundest, and it is only when our sentiments rise freely
to the surface of the imagination, that the mind escapes the
shackles of thraldom.' But, I haven't a minute for Sarah
Soothings, even, just now. Don't you see the Injins ?"

"Quite plainly; and they probably see my ' Indians.' "

"Oh! they don't regard them now the least in the
world. At first, when they thought you might have hired
a set of desperate wretches to scalp the folks, there was
some misgivings; but the whole story is now known, and
nobody cares a straw about them. If anybody's scalp is
taken, 't will be their own. Why, the whole country is up,
and the report has gone forth, far and near, that you have
brought in with you a set of blood-thirsty savages from the
prairies to cut the throats of women and children, and drive
off the tenants, that you may get all the farms into your
own hands before the lives fall in. Some folks say, these
savages have had a list of all the lives named in your leases
given to them, and that they are to make way with all
such people first, that you may have the law as much as
possible on your side. You stand on an earthquake, Mr.
Hugh;—you do, indeed!"

"My dear Opportunity," I answered, laughing, "I am
infinitely obliged to you for all this attention to my interests,

and freely own that on Saturday night you were of great
service to me; but I must now think that you magnify the
danger—that you colour the picture too high."

"Not in the least. I do protest, you stand on an earthquake; and as your friend, I have ridden over here to tell
you as much, while there is yet time."

"To get off it, I suppose you mean. But how can all
these evil and blood-thirsty reports be abroad, when the
characters of the Western Indians are, as you own yourself,
understood, and the dread of them that did exist in the
town has entirely vanished? There is a contradiction in
this."

"Why, you know how it is, in anti-rent times. When
an excitement is needed, folks don't stick at facts very
closely, but repeat things, and make things, just as it happens to be convenient."

"True; I can understand this, and have no difficulty in
believing you now. But have you come here this morning
simply to let me know the danger which besets me from
this quarter?"

"I believe I'm always only too ready to gallop over to
the Nest! But everybody has some weakness or other, and
I suppose I am to be no exception to the rule," returned Opportunity, who doubtless fancied the moment propitious to
throw in a volley towards achieving her great conquest,
and who reinforced that volley of words with such a glance
of the eye, as none but a most practised picaroon on the
sea of flirtation could have thrown. "But, Hugh — I call
you Hugh, Mr. Littlepage, for you seem more like Hugh to
me, than like the proud, evil-minded aristocrat, and hard-
hearted landlord, that folks want to make you out to be —
but I never could have told you what I did last night, had
supposed it would bring Sen into this difficulty."

"I can very well understand how unpleasantly you are
situated as respects your brother, Opportunity; and your
friendly services will not be forgotten in the management of
his affairs."

"If you are of this mind, why won't you suffer these
Injins to get him out of the hands of your real savages,"
returned Opportunity, coaxingly. "I'll promise for him

that Sen will go off, and stay off for some months, if you
insist on 't; when all is forgotten, he can come back again."

" Is the release of your brother, then, the object of this
visit from the Injins ?"

" Partly so — they 're bent on having him. He 's in all
the secrets of the anti-renters, and they 're afraid for their
very lives, so long as he 's in your hands. Should he get
a little scared, and give up only one-quarter of what he
knows, there 'd be no peace in the county for a twelvemonth."

At this instant, and before there was time to make an answer, I was summoned to the piazza, the Injins approaching so near as to induce my uncle to step to the door and
call my name in a loud voice. I was compelled to quit
Opportunity, who did not deem it prudent to show herself
among us, though her presence in the house, as an inter-
cessor for her brother, could excite neither surprise nor resentment.

When I reached the piazza, the Injins had advanced as
far as the tree where we had first been posted, and there
they had halted, seemingly for a conference. In their rear,
Mr. Warren was walking hurriedly towards us, keeping the
direct line, regardless of those whom he well knew to be
inimical to him, and intent only on reaching the house
before it could be gained by the ' disguised and armed.'
This little circumstance gave rise to an incident of touching
interest, and which I cannot refrain from relating, though
it may interrupt the narration of matters that others may
possibly think of more moment.

Mr. Warren did not pass directly through the crowd of
rioters — for such those people were, in effect, unless the
epithet should be changed to the still more serious one of
rebels — but he made a little détour, in order to prevent a
collision that was unnecessary. When about half-way between the tree and the piazza, however, the Injins gave a
discordant yell, and many of them sprang forward, as if in
haste to overtake, and probably to arrest, him. Just as we
all involuntarily arose, under a common feeling of interest
in the fate of the good rector, Mary darted from the piazza,
was at her father's side and in his arms so quickly, as to
seem to have flown there. Clinging to his side, she ap-

37*

peared to urge him towards us. But Mr. Warren adopted
a course much wiser than that of flight would have been.
Conscious of having said or done no more than his duty,
he stopped and faced his pursuers.   The act of Mary Warren had produced a check to the intended proceedings of
these lawless men; and the calm, dignified aspect of the
divine completed his conquest.   The leaders of the Injins
paused, conferred together, when all who had issued from
the main body returned to their companions beneath the
tree, leaving Mr. Warren and his charming daughter at
liberty to join us unmolested, and with decorum.

The instant Mary Warren left the piazza on her pious
errand, I sprang forward to follow her with an impulse I
could not control.   Although my own power over this im-
pulsive movement was so small, that of my uncle and grandmother was greater.   The former seized the skirt of my
frock, and held me back by main strength, while the light
touch of the latter had even greater power.   Both remon-
strated, and with so much obvious justice, that I saw the
folly of what I was about in an instant, and abandoned my
design.   Had *I* fallen into the hands of the anti-renters
their momentary triumph, at least, would have been complete.

Mr. Warren ascended the steps of the piazza with a mien
as unaltered, and an air as undisturbed, as if about to enter
his own church. · The good old gentleman had so schooled
his feelings, and was so much accustomed to view himself
as especially protected, or as so ready to suffer, when in
the discharge of any serious duty, that I have had occasions
to ascertain fear was unknown to him. · As for Mary, never
had she appeared so truly lovely, as she ascended the steps,
still clinging fondly and confidingly to his arm.   The excitement of such a scene had brought more than the usual
quantity of blood into her face, and the brilliancy of her
eyes was augmented by that circumstance, perhaps; but I
fancied that a more charming picture of feminine softness,
blended with the self-devotion of the child, could not have
been imagined by the mind of man.

Patt, dear, generous girl, sprang forward to embrace her
friend, which she did with warmth and honest fervour, and
my venerable grandmother kissed her on both cheeks, while

the other two girls were not backward in giving the customary signs of the sympathy of their sex. My uncle Ro
even went so far as gallantly to kiss her hand, causing the
poor girl's face to be suffused with blushes, while poor Hugh
was obliged to keep in the back-ground, and content himself with looking his admiration. I got one glance, however, from the sweet creature, that was replete with consolation, since it assured me that my forbearance was understood, and attributed to its right motive.

In that singular scene, the men of the prairies alone appeared to be unmoved. Even the domestics and workmen
had betrayed a powerful interest in this generous act of
Mary Warren's, the females all screaming in chorus, very
much as a matter of course. But, not an Indian moved.
Scarce one turned his eyes from the countenance of Susquesus, though all must have been conscious that something
of interest was going on so near them, by the concern we
betrayed; and all certainly knew that their enemies were
hard by. As respects the last, I have supposed the unconcern, or seeming unconcern of these western warriors, ought
to be ascribed to the circumstance of the presence of the
ladies, and an impression that there could be no very imminent risk of hostilities while the company then present remained together. The apathy of the chiefs seemed to be
extended to the interpreter, who was coolly lighting his pipe
at the very moment when the whole affair of the Warren
episode occurred; an occupation that was not interrupted
by the clamour and confusion among ourselves.

As there was a delay in the nearer approach of the Injins,
there was leisure to confer together for a moment. Mr.
Warren told us, therefore, that he had seen the 'disguised
and armed' pass the rectory, and had followed in order to
act as a mediator between us and any contemplated harm.

"The destruction of the canopy of Hugh's pew, must
have given you a serious intimation that things were coming
to a head," observed my grandmother.

Mr. Warren had not heard of the affair of the canopy, at
all. Although living quite within sound of a hammer used
in the church, everything had been conducted with so much
management, that the canopy had been taken down, and
removed bodily, without any one in the rectory's knowing

the fact. The latter had become known at the Nest, solely
by the circumstance that the object which had so lateiy
canopied aristocracy in St. Andrew's, Ravensnest, was now
canopying pigs up at the farm-house. The good divine
expressed his surprise a little strongly, and, as I thought
his regrets a little indifferently. He was not one to countenance illegality and violence, and least of all that peculiarly
American vice, envy; but, on the other hand, he was not
one to look with favour on the empty distinctions, as set up
between men equally sinners and in need of grace to redeem
them from a common condemnation, in the house of God.
As the grave is known to be the great leveller of the human
race, so ought the church to be used as a preparatory step
in descending to the plain that all must occupy, in spirit at
least, before they can hope to be elevated to any, even of
the meanest places, among the many mansions of our Father's house !

. There was but a short breathing time given us, however,
before the Injins again advanced. It was soon evident they
did not mean to remain mere idle spectators of the scene
that was in the course of enactment on the piazza; but that
it was their intention to become actors, in some mode or
other. Forming themselves into a line, that savoured a
great deal more of the militia of this great republic than
of the warriors of the west, they came on tramping, with
the design of striking terror into our souls. Our arrangements were made, however, and on our part every thing was
conducted just as one could have wished. The ladies, influenced by my grandmother, retained their seats, near the
door; the men of the household were standing, but continued stationary, while not an Indian stirred. As for Susquesus, he had lived far beyond surprises and all emotions
of the lower class, and the men of the prairies appeared to
take their cues from him. So long as he continued immovable, they seemed disposed to remain immovable also. ·

· The distance between the tree and the piazza, did not
much exceed a hundred yards, and little time was necessary
to march across it. I remarked, however, that, contrary to
the laws of attraction, the nearer the Injins' line got to its
goal, the slower and more unsteady its movement became.
It also lost its formation, bending into curves, though its

tramps became louder and louder, as if those who were in
it, wished to keep alive their own courage by noise. When
within fifty feet of the steps, they ceased to advance at all,
merely stamping with their feet, as if hoping to frighten us
into flight. I thought this a favourable moment to do that
which it had been decided between my uncle and myself
ought to be done by me, as owner of the property these lawless men had thus invaded. Stepping to the front of the
piazza, I made a sign for attention. The tramping ceased
all at once, and I had a profound silence for my speech.

"You know me, all of you," I said, quietly I know, and
I trust firmly; "and you know, therefore, that I am the
owner of this house and these lands. As such owner, I
order every man among you to quit the place, and to go
into the highway, or upon the property of some other person. Whoever remains, after this notice, will be a trespasser, and the evil done by a trespasser is doubly serious
in the eyes of the law."

I uttered these words loud enough to be heard by every
body present, but I cannot pretend that they were attended
by much success. The calico bundles turned towards each
other, and there was an appearance of a sort of commotion,
but the leaders composed the people, the omnipotent people
in this instance, as they do in most others. The sovereignty
of the mass is a capital thing as a principle, and once in a
long while it evinces a great good in practice; in a certain
sense, it is always working good, by holding a particular
class of most odious and intolerable abuses in check; but,
as for the practice of every-day political management, their
imperial majesties, the sovereigns of America, of whom I
happen to be one, have quite as little connection with the
measures they are made to seem to demand, and to sustain,
as the Nawab of Oude; if the English, who are so disinterested as to feel a generous concern for the rights of mankind, whenever the great republic adds a few acres to the
small paternal homestead, have left any such potentate in
existence.

So it was with the decision of the "disguised and armed,"
on the occasion I am describing. They decided that no
other notice should be taken of my summons to quit, than a
contemptuous yell, though they had to ascertain from their

leaders what they had decided before they knew themselves.
The shout was pretty general, notwithstanding, and it had
one good effect; that of satisfying the Injins, themselves,
that they had made a clear demonstration of their contempt
of my authority, which they fancied victory sufficient for
the moment; nevertheless, the demonstration did not end
exactly here. Certain cries, and a brief dialogue, succeeded,
which it may be well to record.

"*King* Littlepage," called out one, from among the ' disguised and armed,' what has become of your throne? St.
Andrew's meeting-'us' has lost its monarch's throne!"

"His pigs have set up for great aristocrats of late; presently they'll want to be patroons."

"Hugh Littlepage, be a man; come down to a level with
your fellow-citizens, and don't think yourself any better
than other folks. You're but flesh and blood, a'ter all."

"Why don't you invite me to come and dine with you,
as well as priest Warren? I can eat, as well as any man
in the county, and as much."

"Yes, and he'll *drink*, too, Hugh Littlepage; so provide
your best liquor the day he's to be invited."

All this passed for wit among the Injins, and among that
portion of the "virtuous and honest and hard-working," who
not only kept them on foot, but on this occasion kept them
company also; it having since been ascertained that about
one-half of that band was actually composed of the tenants
of the Ravensnest farms. I endeavoured to keep myself
cool, and succeeded pretty well, considering the inducements
there were to be angry. Argument with such men was out
of the question,—and knowing their numbers and physical
superiority, they held my legal rights in contempt. What
was probably worse than all, they knew that the law itself
was administered by the people, and that they had little to
apprehend, and did apprehend virtually nothing from any
of the pains and penalties it might undertake to inflict, should
recourse be had to it at any future day. Ten or a dozen
wily agents sent through the country to circulate lies, and
to visit the county town previously to, and during a trial, in
order to raise a party that will act more or less directly on
the minds of the jurors, with a newspaper or two to scatter
untruths and prejudices, would at least be as effective, at

the critical moment, as the law, the evidence, and the right.
As for the judges, and their charges, they have lost most of
their influence, under the operation of this nefarious system,
and count but for very little in the administration of justice
either at Nisi Prius or at Oyer Terminer. These are melancholy truths, that any man who quits his theories and
descends into the arena of practice will soon ascertain to bo
such, to his wonder and alarm, if he be a novice and an
honest man. A portion of this unhappy state of things is a
consequence of the legislative tinkering that has destroyed
one of the most healthful provisions of the common law, in
prohibiting the judges to punish for contempt, unless for out-
rages committed in open court. The press, in particular,
now profits by this impunity, and influences the decision of
nearly every case that can at all enlist public feeling. All
these things men feel, and few who are wrong care for the
law; for those who are right, it is true, there is still some
danger. My uncle Ro says America is no more like what
America was in this respect twenty years since, than Kamtschatka is like Italy. For myself, I wish to state the truth;
exaggerating nothing, nor yet taking refuge in a dastardly
concealment.

Unwilling to be browbeaten on the threshold of my own
door, I determined to say something ere I returned to my
place. Men like these before me can never understand that
silence proceeds from contempt; and I fancied it best to
make some sort of a reply to the speeches I have recorded,
and to twenty more of the same moral calibre. Motioning
for silence, I again obtained it.

"I have ordered you to quit my lawn, in the character
of its owner," I said, "and, by remaining, you make yourselves trespassers. As for what you have done to my
pew, I should thank you for it, had it not been done in violation of the right; for it was fully my intention to have
that canopy removed as soon as the feeling about it had
subsided. I am as much opposed to distinctions of any
sort in the house of God as any of you can be, and desire
them not for myself, or any belonging to me. I ask for
nothing but equal rights with all my fellow-citizens; that
my property should be as much protected as theirs, but not

more so. But, I do not conceive that you or any man has a right to ask to share in my world's goods any more than I have a right to ask to share in his; that you can more justly claim a portion of my lands than I can claim a share in your cattle and crops. It is a poor rule that does not work both ways."

"You're an aristocrat," cried one from among the In- jins, " or you'd be willing to let other men have as much land as you've got yourself. You're a patroon; and all patroons are aristocrats, and hateful."

. " An aristocrat," I answered, " is one of a few who wield political power. The highest birth, the largest fortune, tho most exclusive association would not make an aristocrat, without the addition of a narrow political power. In this country there are no aristocrats, because there is no narrow political power. There is, however, a spurious aristocracy which you do not recognize, merely because it does not happen to be in the hands of gentlemen. Demagogues and editors are your privileged classes, and consequently your aristocrats, and none others. As for your landlord aristo- crats, listen to a true tale, which will satisfy you how far they deserve to be called an aristocracy. Mark! what I now tell you is religious truth, and it deserves to be known far and near, wherever your cry of aristocracy reaches. There is a landlord in this State, a man of large means who became liable for the debts of another to a considerabl. amount. At the very moment when *his* rents could not be collected, owing to *your* interference and the remissness of those in authority to enforce the laws, the sheriff entered *his* house, and sold its contents, in order to satisfy an execution against *him!* There is American aristocracy for you, and I am sorry to add American justice, as justice has got to be administered among us."

I was not disappointed in the effect of this narration of what is a sober truth. Wherever I have told it, it has con- founded even the most brawling demagogue, and momenta- rily revived in his breast some of those principles of right which God originally planted there. American aristocracy, in sooth! Fortunate is the gentleman that can obtain even a reluctant and meagre justice.

CHAPTER XXIX.

" How far that little candle throws his beams;
So shines a good deed in a naughty world."
SHAKSPEARE.

I HAVE said that my narrative of the manner in which justice is sometimes meted out among us was not without its effect on even that rude band of selfish and envious rioters : rude, because setting at naught reason and the law; and selfish, because induced so to do by covetousness, and the desire to substitute the tenants for those whom they fancied to be better off in the world than they were themselves. A profound stillness succeeded; and after the bundles of calico had whispered one with another for a moment or two, they remained quiet, seemingly indisposed, just then, at least, to molest us any farther. I thought the moment favourable, and fell back to my old station, determined to let things take their own course. This change, and the profound stillness that succeeded, brought matters back to the visit of the Indians, and its object.

During the whole time occupied by the advance of the " Injins," the men of the prairies and Susquesus had conti-nued nearly as motionless as so many statues. It is true that the eyes of Flintyheart were on the invaders, but he managed to take good heed of them without betraying any undue uneasiness or care. Beyond this, I do affirm that I scarce noted a single sign of even vigilance among these extraordinary beings; though Manytongues afterwards gave me to understand that they knew very well what they were about; and then I could not be watching the red-men the whole time. Now that there was a pause, however, every body and thing seemed to revert to the original visit, as naturally as if no interruption had occurred. Manytongues, by way of securing attention, called on the Injins, in an authoritative voice, to offer no interruption to the proceedings of the chiefs, which had a species of religious sanctity, and was not to be too much interfered with, with impunity.

38

' So long as you keep quiet, my warriors will not molest
you," he added ; " but if any man amongst you has ever
been on the prer-ies, he must understand enough of the natur
of a redskin to know that when he 's in 'airnest he *is* in
'airnest. Men who are on a journey three thousand miles
in length, don't turn aside for trifles, which is a sign that
serious business has brought these chiefs here."

Whether it was that this admonition produced an effect,
or that curiosity influenced the " disguised and armed," or
that they did not choose to proceed to extremities, or that
all three considerations had their weight, is more than I can
say ; but it is certain the whole band remained stationary,
quiet and interested observers of what now occurred, until
an interruption took place, which will be related in propei
time. Manytongues, who had posted himself near the centre
of the piazza, to interpret, now signified to the chiefs that
they-might pursue their own purposes in tranquillity. After
a decent pause, the same young warrior who had " called
up" Jaaf, in the first instance, now rose again, and with a
refinement in politeness that would be looked for in vain in
most of the deliberative bodies of civilized men, adverted to
the circumstance that the negro had not finished his address,
and might have matter on his mind of which he wished to
be delivered. This was said simply, but distinctly ; and it
was explained to the negro by Manytongues, who assured
him not one among all the chiefs would say a word until
the last person " on his legs" had an opportunity of finishing his address. This reserve marks the deportment of
those whom we call savages ; men that have their own
fierce, and even ruthless customs, beyond all controversy,
but who possess certain other excellent qualities that do not
appear to flourish in the civilized state.

It was with a good deal of difficulty that we got old Jaaf
up again ; for, though a famous grumbler, he was not much
of an orator. As it was understood that no chief would
speak, however, until the black had exhausted his right, my
dear Patt had to go, and, laying one of her ivory-looking
hands on the shoulder of the grim old negro, persuade him
to rise and finish his speech. He knew her, and she succeeded ; it being worthy of remark, that while this aged
black scarce remembered for an hour what occurred, con

founding dates fearfully, often speaking of my grandmother
as Miss Dus, and as if she were still a girl, he knew every
one of the family then living, and honoured and loved us
accordingly, at the very moments he would fancy we had
been present at scenes that occurred when our great-grand-
parents were young people. But to the speech—

"What all dem fellow want, bundle up in calico, like so
many squaw?" growled out Jaaf, as soon as on his legs,
and looking intently at the Injins, ranged as they were in
a line four deep, quite near the piazza. "Why you let 'em
come, Masser Hugh, Masser Hodge, Masser Malbone, Masser Mordaunt—which you be here, now, I don't know, dere
so many, and it so hard to 'member ebbery t'ing? Oh! I
so ole!—I do won'er when my time come! Dere Sus, too,
he good for nuttin' at all. Once he great walker — great
warrior—great hunter—pretty good fellow for redskin; but
he quite wore out. Don't see much use why he lib any
longer. Injin good for nuttin' when he can't hunt. Sometime he make basket and broom; but dey uses better broom
now, and Injin lose *dat* business. What dem calico debbil
want here, eh, Miss Patty? Dere redskin, too—two, t'ree,
four — all come to see Sus. Won'er nigger don't come to
see *me!* Ole black good as ole red-man. Where dem fellow get all dat calico, and put over deir face? Masser
Hodge, what all dat mean?"

"These are anti-renters, Jaaf," my uncle coldly answered. "Men that wish to own your Master Hugh's farms,
and relieve him from the trouble of receiving any more rent.
They cover their faces, I presume, to conceal their blushes,
the modesty of their natures sinking under the sense of
their own generosity."

Although it is not very probable that Jaaf understood
the whole of this speech, he comprehended a part; for, so
thoroughly had his feelings been aroused on this subject, a
year or two earlier, when his mind was not quite so much
dimmed as at present, that the impression made was indeli-
ble. The effect of what my uncle said, nevertheless, was
most apparent among the Injins, who barely escaped an
outbreak. My uncle has been blamed for imprudence, in
having resorted to irony on such an occasion; but, after all,
I am far from sure good did not come of it. Of one thing,

I am certain; nothing is ever gained by temporizing on the subject of principles; that which is right, had better always be freely said, since it is from the sacrifices that are made of the truth, as concessions to expediency, that error obtains one-half its power. Policy, or fear, or some other motive kept the rising ire of the Injins under, however, and no interruption occurred, in consequence of this speech.

"What you want here, fellow?" demanded Jaaf, roughly, and speaking as a scold would break out on some intrusive boy. "Home-wid ye!—get out! Oh! I *do* grow so ole!—I wish I was as I was when young for your sake, you varmint! What you want wid Masser Hugh's land?—why dat you t'ink to get gentle'em's property, eh? 'Member 'e time when your fadder come creepin' and beggin' to Masser Mordy, to ask just little farm to lib on, and be he tenant, and try to do a little for he family, like; and now come, in calico bundle, to tell *my* Masser Hugh dat he shan't be masser of he own land. Who *you*, I want to know, to come and talk to gentle'em in dis poor fashion? Go home —get out—off wid you, or you hear what you don't like."

Now, while there was a good deal of "nigger" in this argument, it was quite as good as that which was sometimes advanced in support of the "spirit of the Institutions," more especially that part of the latter which is connected with "aristocracy" and "poodle usages." The negro had an idea that all his "massers," old and young, were better than the rest of the human race; while the advocates of the modern movement seem to think that every right is concentrated in the lower half of the great "republican family." Every gentleman is no gentleman; and every blackguard, a gentleman, for one postulate of their great social proposition; and, what is more, every man in the least elevated *above* the mass, unless so. elevated by the mass, who consequently retain the power to pull him down again, has no rights at all, when put in opposition to the cravings of numbers. So, that after all, the negro was not much more ou of the way, in his fashion of viewing things, than the philosophers of industrious honesty! Happily, neither the reasoning of one of these parties, nor that of the other, has much influence on the actual state of things. Facts are facts, and the flounderings of envy and covetousness can no more shut men's eyes to their existence, and prove that black is white, than Jaaf's long-enduring and besetting notion that the Littlepages are the great of the earth, can make us more than what we certainly are. I have recorded the negro's speech, simply to show some, who listen only to the misstatements and opinions of those who wish to become owners of other men's farms, that there are two sides to the question; and, in the way of argument, I do not see but one is quite as good as the other.

One could hardly refrain from smiling, notwithstanding the seriousness of the circumstances in which we were placed, at the gravity of the Indians during the continuance of this queer episode. Not one of them all rose, turned round, or manifested the least impatience, or even curiosity. The presence of two hundred armed men, bagged in calico, did not induce them to look about them, though their previous experience with this gallant corps may possibly have led them to hold it somewhat cheap.

The time had now come for the Indians to carry out the main design of their visit to Ravensnest, and Prairiefire slowly arose to speak. The reader will understand that Manytongues translated, sentence by sentence, all that passed, he being expert in the different dialects of the tribes, some of which had carried that of the Onondagoes to the prairies. In this particular, the interpreter was a somewhat remarkable man, not only rendering what was said readily and without hesitation, but energetically and with considerable power. It may be well to add, however, that in writing out the language I may have used English expressions that are a little more choice, in some instances, than those given by this uneducated person.

"Father," commenced Prairiefire, solemnly, and with a dignity that it is not usual to find connected with modern oratory; the gestures he used being few, but of singular force and significance—"Father—the minds of your children are heavy. They have travelled over a long and thorny path, with moccasins worn out, and feet that were getting sore; but their minds were light. They hoped to look at the face of the Upright Onondago, when they got to the end of the path. They have come to the end of that path, and they see him. He looks as they expected he would look. He

38*

is like an oak that lightning may burn, and the snows cover
with moss, but which a thousand storms and a hundred
winters cannot strip of its leaves.   He looks like the oldest
oak in the forest.   He is very grand.   It is pleasant to look
on him.   ·When we see him, we see a chief who knew our
fathers' fathers, and *their* fathers' fathers.   That is a long
time ago.   He is a tradition, and knows all things.   There
is only one thing about him, that ought not to be.   He was
born a red-man, but has lived so long with the pale-faces,
that when he does go away to the Happy Hunting-Grounds,
we are afraid the good spirits will mistake him for a pale-
face, and point out the wrong path.   Should this happen,
the red-men would lose the Upright of the Onondagoes, for
ever.   It should not be   My father does not wish it to
be.   He will think better.   He will come back among his
children, and leave his wisdom and advice among the people of his own colour.   I ask him to do this.

"It is a long path, now, to the wigwams of red-men.   It
was not so once, but the path has been stretched.   It is a
very long path.   Our young men travel it often, to visit the
graves of their fathers, and they know how long it is.   My
tongue is not crooked, but it is straight ; it will not sing a
false song — it tells my father the truth.   The path is very
long.   But the pale-faces are wonderful !   What have they
not done ?   What will they not do ?   They have made
canoes and sledges that fly swift as the birds.   The deer
could not catch them.   They have wings of fire, and never
weary.   They go when men sleep.   The path is long, but
it is soon travelled with such wings.   My father can make
the journey, and not think of weariness.   Let him try it.
His children will take good care of him.   Uncle Sam will
give him venison, and he will want nothing.   Then, when
he starts for the Happy Hunting-Grounds, he will not mistake the path, and will live with red-men for ever."

A long, solemn pause succeeded this speech, which was
delivered with great dignity and emphasis.   I could see that
Susquesus was touched with this request, and at the homage
paid his character, by having tribes from the prairies —
tribes of which he had never even heard through traditions
in his younger days — come so far to do justice to his
character ; to request him to go and die in their midst.   I·

is true, he must have known that the fragments of the old
New York tribes had mostly found their way to those distant regions; nevertheless, it could not but be soothing to
learn that even they had succeeded in making so strong an
impression in his favour, by means of their representations.
Most men of his great age would have been insensible to feelings of this sort. Such, in a great degree, was the fact with
Jaaf; but such was not the case with the Onondago. As he
had said in his former speech to his visiters, his mind dwelt
more on the scenes of his youth, and native emotions came
fresher to his spirit, now, than they had done even in middle
age. All that remained of his youthful fire seemed to be
awakened, and he did not appear that morning, except when
compelled to walk and in his outward person, to be a man
who had seen much more than his three-score years and ten.

- As a matter of course, now that the chiefs from the prai
ries had so distinctly made known the great object of their
visit, and so vividly portrayed their desire to receive back,
into the bosom of their communities, one of their colour
and race, it remained for the Onondago to let the manner
in which he viewed this proposition be known. The profound stillness that reigned around him must have assured
the old Indian how anxiously his reply was expected. It
extended even to the 'disguised and armed,' who, by this
time, seemed to be as much absorbed in the interest of this
curious scene as any of us who occupied the piazza. I do
believe that anti-rentism was momentarily forgotten by all
parties—tenants, as well as landlords; landlords, as well as
tenants. I dare say, Prairiefire had taken his seat three
minutes ere Susquesus arose; during all which time, the
deep stillness, of which I have spoken, prevailed.

- " My children," answered the Onondago, whose voice
possessed just enough of the hollow tremulousness of age
to render it profoundly impressive, but who spoke so distinctly as to be heard by all present—" My children, we do
not know what will happen when we are young — all is
young, too, that we see. It is when we grow old, that all
grows old with us. Youth is full of hope; but age is full
of eyes; it sees things as they are. I have lived in my
wigwam alone, since the Great Spirit called out the name
of my mother, and she hurried away to the Happy Hunting-

Grounds to cook venison for my father, who was called
first.   My father was a great warrior. - You did not know
him.   He was killed by the Delawares, more than a hundred winters ago.

"I have told you the truth. When my mother went
to cook venison for her husband, I was left alone in my
wigwam."

Here a long pause succeeded, during which Susquésus
appeared to be struggling with his own feelings, though he
continued erect, like a tree firmly rooted.   As for the
chiefs, most of them inclined their bodies forward to listen,
so intense was their interest; here and there one of their
number explaining in soft guttural tones, certain passages
in the speech to some other Indians, who did not fully comprehend the dialect in which they were uttered.   After a
time, Susquesus proceeded : " Yes, I lived alone.   A young
squaw *was* to have entered my wigwam and staid there.
She never came.   She wished to enter it, but she did not.
Another warrior had her promise, and it was right that she
should keep her word.   Her mind was heavy at first, but
she lived to feel that it is good to be just.   No squaw has
ever lived in any wigwam of mine.   I did not think ever to
be a father : but see how different it has turned out !   I am
now the father of all red-men !   Every Indian warrior is
my son.   *You* are my children ; I will own you when we
meet on the pleasant paths beyond the hunts you make to-
day.   You will call me father, and I will call you sons.

" That will be enough.   You ask me to go on the long
path with you, and leave my bones on the prairies.   I have
heard of those hunting-grounds.   Our ancient traditions
told us of them.   ' Towards the rising sun,' they said,
' is a great salt lake, and towards the setting sun, great
lakes of sweet water.   Across the great salt lake is a distant country, filled with pale-faces, who live in large villages, and in the midst of cleared fields.   Towards the setting sun were large cleared fields, too, but no pale-faces, and
few villages.   Some of our wise men thought these fields
were the fields of red-men following the pale-faces round
after the sun ; some thought they were fields in which the
pale-faces were following them.   I think this was the truth.
The red-man cannot hide himself in any corner, where the

pale-face will not find him. The Great Spirit will have it so. It is his will; the red-man must submit.'

" My sons, the journey you ask me to make is too long for old age. I have lived with the pale-faces, until one-half of my heart is white; though the other half is red. One-half is filled with the traditions of my fathers, the other half is filled with the wisdom of the stranger. I cannot cut my heart in two pieces. It must all go with you, or all stay here. The body must stay with the heart, and both must remain where they have now dwelt so long. I thank you, my children, but what you wish can never come to pass.

" You see a very old man, but you see a very unsettled mind. There are red traditions and pale-face traditions. Both speak of the Great Spirit, but only one speak of his son. A soft voice has been whispering in my ear, lately, much of the Son of God. Do they speak to you in that way on the prairies? I know not what to think.—I wish to think what is right; but it is not easy to understand."

Here Susquesus paused; then he took his seat, with the air of one who was at a loss how to explain his own feelings. Prairiefire waited a respectful time for him to continue his address, but perceiving that he rose not, he stood up, himself, to request a further explanation.

" My father has spoken wisdom," he said, " and his children have listened. They have not heard enough; they wish to hear more. If my father is tired of standing, he can sit; his children do not ask him to stand. They ask to know where that soft voice came from, and what it said?"

Susquesus did not rise, now, but he prepared for a reply. Mr. Warren was standing quite near him, and Mary was leaning on his arm. He signed for the father to advance a step or two, in complying with which, the parent brought forth the unconscious child also.

" See, my children," resumed Susquesus. " This is a great medicine of the pale-faces. He talks always of the Great Spirit, and of his goodness to men. It is his business to talk of the Happy Hunting-Ground, and of good and bad pale-faces. I cannot tell you whether he does any good or not. Many such talk of these things constantly among the whites, but I can see little change, and I have lived among them, now, more than eighty winters and summers—yes,

near ninety. The land is changed so much, that I hardly
know it; but the people do not alter. See, there; here are
men—pale-faces in calico bags. Why do they run about,
and dishonour the red-man by calling themselves Injins? I
will tell you."

There was now a decided movement among the 'virtuous
and industrious,' though a strong desire to hear the old man
out, prevented any violent interruption at that time. I
question if ever men listened more intently, than we all lent
our faculties now, to ascertain what the Upright of the Onondagoes thought of anti-rentism. I received the opinions he
expressed with the greater alacrity, because I knew he was
a living witness of most of what he related, and because I
was clearly of opinion that he knew quite as much of the
subject as many who rose in the legislative halls to discuss
the subject.

"These men are not warriors," continued Susquesus.
"They hide their faces and they carry rifles, but they frighten
none but the squaws and pappooses. When they take a scalp,
it is because they are a hundred, and their enemies one.
They are not braves. Why do they come at all?—What
do they want? They want the land of this young chief.
My children, all the land, far and near, was ours. The
pale-faces came with their papers, and made laws, and said
'It is well! We want this land. There is plenty farther
west for you red-men. Go there, and hunt, and fish, and
plant your corn, and leave us this land.' Our red brethren
did as they were asked to do. The pale-faces had it as
they wished. They made laws, and sold the land, as the
red-men sell the skins of beavers. When the money was
paid, each pale-face got a deed, and thought he owned all
that he had paid for. But the wicked spirit that drove out
the red-man is now about to drive off the pale-face chiefs.
It is the same devil, and it is no other. He wanted land
then, and he wants land now. There is one difference, and
it is this. When the pale-face drove off the red-man there
was no treaty between them. They had not smoked together, and given wampum, and signed a paper. If they had,
it was to agree that the red-man should go away, and the
pale-face stay. When the pale-face drives off the pale-face,
there is a treaty; they have smoked together, and given

wampum, and signed a paper. This is the difference. Indian will keep his word with Indian ; pale-face will not keep
his word with pale-face."

Susquesus stopped speaking, and the eye of every chief
was immediately, and for the first time that morning, turned
on the " disguised and armed" — the " virtuous and hard-
working." A slight movement occurred in the band, but
no outbreak took place ; and, in the midst of the sensation
that existed, Eaglesflight slowly arose. The nature, dignity
and ease of his manner more than compensated for his personal appearance, and he now seemed to us all one of those
by no means unusual instances of the power of the mind to
overshadow, and even to obliterate, the imperfections of the
body. Before the effect of what Susquesus had just said
was lost, this eloquent and much-practised orator began his
address. His utterance was highly impressive, being so
deliberate, with pauses so well adjusted, as to permit Manytongues to give full effect to each syllable he translated. ··

" My brethren," said Eaglesflight, addressing the Injins
and the other auditors, rather than any one else, " you have
heard the words of age. They are the words of wisdom.
They are the words of truth. The Upright of the Onon-
dagos cannot lie. He never could. The Great Spirit made
him a just Indian ; and, as the Great Spirit makes an Indian, so he is. My brethren, I will tell you his story ; it
will be good for *you* to hear it. We have heard your story ;
first from the interpreter, now from Susquesus. It is a bad
story. We were made sorrowful when we heard it. What
is right, should be done ; what is wrong, should not be done.
There are bad red-men, and good red-men ; there are bad
pale-faces, and good pale-faces. The good red-men and
good pale-faces do what is right ; the bad, what is wrong.
It is the same with both. The Great Spirit of the Indian
and the Great Spirit of the white man are alike; so are the
wicked spirits. There is no difference in this.

" My brethren, a red-man knows in his heart when he
does what is right, and when he does what is wrong. He
does not want to be told. He tells himself. His face is
red, and he cannot change colour. The paint is too thick.
When he tells himself how much wrong he has done, he

goes into the bushes, and is sorry. When he comes out, he is a better man.

" My brethren, it is different with a pale-face. He is white, and uses no stones for paint. When he tells himself that he has done wrong, his face can paint itself. Everybody can see that he is ashamed. He does not go into the bushes; it would do no good. He paints himself so quickly that there is no time. He hides his face in a calico bag. This is not good, but it is better than to be pointed at with the finger.

" My brethren, the Upright of the Onondagoes has never run into the bushes because he was ashamed. There has been no need of it. He has not told himself he was wicked He has not put his face in a calico bag; he cannot paint himself, like a pale-face.

" My brethren, listen; I will tell, you a story. A long time ago everything was very different here. The clearings were small, and the woods large. Then the red-men were many, and the pale-faces few. Now it is different. You know how it is, to-day.

" My brethren, I am talking of what was a hundred winters since. We were not born, then. Susquesus was then young, and strong, and active. He could run with the deer, and battle with the bear. He was a chief, because his fathers were chiefs before him. The Onondagoes knew him and loved him. Not a war-path was opened, that he was not the first to go on it. No other warrior could count so many scalps. No young chief had so many listeners at the Council-Fire. The Onondagoes were proud that they had so great a chief, and one so young. They thought he would live a long time, and they should see him, and be proud of him for fifty winters more.

" My brethren, Susquesus has lived twice fifty winters longer; but he has not lived them with his own people. No; he has been a stranger among the Onondagoes all that time. The warriors he knew are dead. The wigwams that he went into, have fallen to the earth with time; the graves have crumbled, and the sons' sons of his companions walk heavily with old age. Susquesus is there; you see him; he sees you. He can walk; he speaks; he sees: he is a living tradition! Why is this so? — The Great Spirit

has not called him away. He is a just Indian, and it is
good that he be kept here, that all red-men may know how
much he is loved. · So long as he stays, no red-man need
want a calico bag. ·

."My brethren, the younger days of Susquesus, the
Trackless, were happy. When he had seen twenty -win-
ters, he was talked of in all the neighbouring tribes. The
scalp notches were a great many. When he had seen thirty
winters, no chief of the Onondagoes had more honour, or
more power. He was first among the Onondagoes. There
was but one fault in him. He did not take a squaw into
his wigwam. Death comes when he is not looked for; so
does marriage. At length my father became like other
men, and wished for a squaw. It happened in this way.

"My brethren, red-men have laws, as well as the pale-
faces. If there is a difference, it is in keeping those laws.
A law of the red-men gives every warrior his prisoners. If
he bring off a warrior, he is his; if a squaw, she is his.
This is right. · He can take the scalp of the warrior; he
can take the squaw into his wigwam, if it be empty. A
warrior, named Waterfowl, brought in a captive girl of the
Delawares. She was called Ouithwith, and was handsomer
than the humming-bird. The Waterfowl had his ears open,
and heard how beautiful she was. He watched long to take
her, and he did take her. She was his, and he thought to
take her into his wigwam when it was empty. Three moons
passed, before that could be. In the meantime, Susquesus
saw Ouithwith, and Ouithwith saw Susquesus. Their eyes
were never off each other. - He was the noblest moose of
the woods, in her eyes; she was the spotted-fawn, in his.
He wished to ask her to his wigwam; she wished to go.

"My brethren, Susquesus was a great chief; the Waterfowl was only a warrior. One had power and authority ·
the other had neither. But there is authority among red-
men beyond that of the chief. It is the red-man's law.
Ouithwith belonged to the Waterfowl, and she did not belong to Susquesus. A great council was held, and men differed. Some said that so useful a chief, so renowned; a
warrior as Susquesus, ought to be the husband of Ouithwith
some said her husband ought to be the Waterfowl, for he
had brought her out from among the Delawares. A great

39

difficulty arose on this question, and the whole Six Nations
took part in it. Many warriors were for the law, but most
were for Susquesus. They loved him, and thought he would
make the best husband for the Delaware girl. For six
moons the quarrel thickened, and a dark cloud gathered
over the path that led among the tribes. Warriors who had
taken scalps in company, looked at each other, as the pan-
ther looks at the deer. Some were ready to dig up the
hatchet for the law ; some for the pride of the Onondagoes,
and the Humming-Bird of the Delawares. The squaws took
sides with Susquesus. Far and near, they met to talk together, and they even threatened to light a Council-Fire,
and smoke around it, like warriors and chiefs.

"Brethren, things could not stand so another moon.
Ouithwith must go into the wigwam of the Waterfowl, or
into the wigwam of Susquesus. The squaws said she should
go into the wigwam of Susquesus; and they met together,
and led her to his door. As she went along that path,
Ouithwith looked at her feet with her eyes, but her heart
leaped like the bounding fawn, when playing in the sun.
She did not go in at the door. The Waterfowl was there,
and forbade it. He had come alone ; his friends were but
few, while the heads and arms of the friends of Susquesus
were as plenty as the berries on the bush.

"My brethren, that command of the Waterfowl's was
like a wall of rock before the door of the Trackless's wigwam. Ouithwith could not go in. The eyes of Susquesus
said ' no,' while his heart said ' yes.' He offered the Waterfowl his rifle, his powder, all his skins, his wigwam ; but
Waterfowl would rather have his prisoner, and answered,
' no.' ' Take my scalp,' he said ; ' you are strong and can
do it ; but do not take my prisoner.'

"My brethren, Susquesus then stood up, in the midst of
the tribe, and opened his mind. ' The Waterfowl is right,'
he said. ' She is his, by our laws; and what the laws of
the red-man say, the red-man must do. When the warrior is about to be tormented, and he asks for time to go
home and see his friends, does he not come back at the day
and hour agreed on ? Shall I, Susquesus, the first chief of
the Onondagoes, be stronger than the law ? No—my face
would be for ever hid in the bushes, did that come to pass.

It should not be — it *shall* not be. Take her, Waterfowl; she is yours. Deal kindly by her, for she is as tender as the wren when it first quits the nest. I must go into the woods for a while. When my mind is at peace, Susquesus will return.

"Brethren, the stillness in that tribe, while Susquesus was getting his rifle, and his horn, and his best moccasins, and his tomahawk, was like that which comes in the darkness. Men saw him go, but none dare follow. He left no trail, and he was called the Trackless. His mind was never at peace, for he never came back. Summer and winter came and went often before the Onondagoes heard of him among the pale-faces. All that time the Waterfowl lived with Ouith-with in his wigwam, and she bore him children. The chief was gone, but the law remained. Go you, men of the pale-faces, who hide your shame in calico bags, and do the same. Follow the example of an Indian——be honest, like the Upright of the Onondagoes!"

While this simple narrative was drawing to a close, I could detect the signs of great uneasiness among the leaders of the "calico bags." The biting comparison between themselves and their own course, and an Indian and his justice, was intolerable to them, for nothing has more conduced to the abuses connected with anti-rentism than the wide-spread delusion that prevails in the land concerning the omnipotency of the masses. The error is deeply rooted which persuades men that fallible parts can make an infallible whole. · It was offensive to their self-conceit, and menacing to their success. A murmur ran through the assembly, and a shout followed. The Injins rattled their rifles, most relying on intimidation to effect their purpose; but a few seemed influenced by a worse intention, and I have never doubted that blood would have been shed in the next minute, the Indians now standing to their arms, had not the sheriff of the county suddenly appeared on the piazza, with Jack Dunning at his elbow. This unexpected apparition produced a pause, during which the 'disguised and armed' fell back some twenty yards, and the ladies rushed into the house. As for my uncle and myself, we were as much astonished as any there at this interruption.

CHAPTER XXX.

" Strong sense, deep feeling, passions strong,
    A hate of tyrant and of knave,
    A love of right, a scorn of wrong,
    Of coward and of slave."

                                    Halleck's Wild Rose of Alloway

ALTHOUGH experience has shown that the appearance of
a sheriff is by no means a pledge of the appearance of a
friend of the law in this anti-rent movement, in our instance
the fact happened to be so.   It was known to the ' disguised
and armed' that this functionary was disposed to do his duty.*
One of the rank absurdities into which democracy has fallen,
and democracy is no more infallible than individual democrats, has been to make the officers of the militia, and the
sheriffs of counties, elective.   The consequences are, that
the militia is converted into a farce, and the execution of the
laws in a particular county is very much dependent on the
pleasure of that county to have them executed or not.   The
last is a capital arrangement for the resident debtor, for instance, though absent creditors are somewhat disposed to
find fault.   But all this is of no great moment, since the
theories for laws and governments in vogue just now are of
such a character as would render laws and governments
quite unnecessary at all, were they founded in truth.   Re-

---

* The editor may as well say here, that, for obvious reasons, the
names, counties, &c., used in these manuscripts are feigned, the real
localities being close enough to those mentioned for the double purposes of truth and fiction.   As one of the " honourable gentlemen" of
the Legislature has quoted our references to '*provincial*' feelings and
notions, with a magnificence that proves how thoroughly he is a man
of the world himself, we will tell all the rest of the human race, who
may happen to read this book, that we have made this explanation lest
that comprehensive view of things, which has hitherto been so eager,
because a street and a house are named in the pages of a fiction, to
suppose that everybody is to believe they know the very individual who
dwelt in it, should fancy that our allusions are to this or that particular
functionary.—EDITOR.

straints of all kinds can only be injurious when they are imposed on perfection!

The instant the commotion commenced, and the ladies
fled, I took Seneca and his fellow-prisoner by the arm, and
led them into the library. This I did, conceiving it to be
unfair to keep prisoners in a situation of danger. This I
did, too, without reflecting in the least on anything but the
character of the act. Returning to the piazza immediately,
I was not missed, and was a witness of all that passed.

As has been intimated, this particular sheriff was known
to be unfavourable to the anti-rent movement, and, no one
supposing he would appear in their midst unsupported, in such
a scene, the Injins fell back, thus arresting the danger of an
immediate collision. It has since been privately intimated
to me, that some among them, after hearing the narrative of
Eaglesflight, really felt ashamed that a red-skin should have
a more lively sense of justice than a white man. Whatever
may be said of the hardships of the tenants, and of " poodlo
usages," and of 'aristocracy,' and ' fat hens,' by the leaders
in this matter, it by no means follows that those leaders believe in their own theories and arguments. On the contrary,
it is generally the case with such men, that they keep themselves quite free from the excitement that it is their business
to awaken in others, resembling the celebrated John Wilkes,
who gravely said to George III., in describing the character
of a former co-operator in agitation, " *He* was a Wilksite,
sir ; *I* never was."

The unexpected appearance of Dunning, the offending
agent, too, was not without its effect, — for they who were
behind the curtains found it difficult to believe that he would
dare to show himself at Ravensnest without a sufficient support. Those who thought thus, however, did not know
Jack Dunning. He had a natural and judicious aversion
to being tarred and feathered, it is true ; but, when it' was
necessary to expose himself, no man did it more freely. Tho
explanation of his unlooked-for arrival is simply this.

Uneasy at our manner of visiting Ravensnest, this trust-
worthy friend, after the delay of a day or two, determined
to follow us. On reaching the county he heard of the firing
of the barn, and of the attempt on the house, and went in
quest of the sheriff without a moment's delay. As the ob
39*

ject of Dunning was to get the ladies out of the lion's den
he did not wait for the summoning of the *posse comitatus;*
but, hiring a dozen resolute fellows, they were armed, and
all set out in a body for the Nest.   When within a mile or
two of the house, the rumour reached the party that we
were besieged ; and it became expedient to have recourse to
some manœuvring, in order to throw succour into the gar-
rison.   Dunning was familiar with all the windings and
turnings of the place, having passed many a month at the
Nest with my uncle and father, both as man and boy, and
he knew the exact situation of the cliff, court, and of the
various peculiar features of the place.   Among other arrangements that had been made of late years, a door had been
opened at the end of the long gallery which led through one
of the wings, and a flight of steps been built against the
rocks, by means of which certain paths and walks that
meandered through the meadows and followed the windings
of the stream might be reached.   Dunning determined to
attempt an ascent from this quarter, trusting to making himself heard by some one within, should he find the door fastened.   Everything succeeded to his wishes, — the cook,
alone, of all the household, being at her post in the other
wing, and seeing him the instant he presented himself on
the upper part of the steps.   Jack Dunning's face was so
well known at the Nest, that the good woman did not hesitate a moment about admitting him, and he thus penetrated
into the buildings, followed by all his party.   The last he
kept concealed by sending them into the chambers, while
he and the sheriff drew near the door, and heard most of
the speech of Eaglesflight, the attention of everybody being
given to the narrative.   The reader knows the rest.

I might as well say at once, however, that Opportunity,
who, by her position, had seen the entrance of Dunning
and his party, no sooner found herself alone with the prisoners, than she unbound them, and showed them the means
of flight, by the same passage, door and steps.   At least,
such has been my supposition, for the sister has never been
questioned on the subject.   Seneca and his co-rascal vanished, and have not since been seen in our part of the
country.   In consequence of the flight, no one has ever
complained of either for arson.   The murder of Steele, the

deputy-sher.ff of Delaware, has given a check to the ' Injin' system, and awakened a feeling in the country that was not to be resisted, in that form at least, by men engaged in a scheme so utterly opposed to the first principles of honesty as anti-rentism.

When I regained the piazza, after thrusting Seneca into the library, the Injins had fallen back to the distance of twenty or thirty yards from the piazza, in evident confusion; while the Indians, cool and collected, stood to their arms, watchful as crouching panthers, but held in hand by the calmness with which their leaders watched the progress of events. The sheriff now required the first to disperse, as violaters of the law; with the penalties of which he menaced them, in a voice sufficiently clear and distinct to make itself audible. There was a moment during which the Injins seemed undecided. They had come with the full intent to inflict on my uncle and myself the punishment of the tar-bucket, with the hope of frightening us into some sort of a compromise; the cowardly expedient of a hundred men's attacking and annoying one being particularly in favour with a certain class of those ultra-friends of liberty, who fancy that they alone possess all the public virtue of the nation, which public virtue justifies any of their acts. All of a sudden, the entire body of these virtuous citizens, who found it necessary to hide their blushes beneath calico, fell rapidly back; observing a little order at first, which soon degenerated, however, into confusion, and shortly after into a downright, scampering flight. The fact was, that Dunning's men began to show themselves at the windows of the chambers, thrusting muskets and rifles out before them, and the ' disguised and armed,' as has invariably been the case in the anti-rent disturbances, exhibited a surprising facility at the retreat. If he is ' thrice-armed who hath his quarrel just,' ten times is he a coward who hath his quarrel unjust. This is the simple solution of the cowardice that has been so generally shown by those who have been engaged in this ' Injin' warfare; causing twenty to chase one, secret attempts on the lives of sentinels, and all the other violations of manly feeling that have disgraced the proceedings of the heroes.

As soon as released from all immediate apprehension or

the score of the Injins, we had time to attend to the Indians.
These warriors gazed after those who were caricaturing
their habits, and most of all their spirit, with silent contempt; and Prairiefire, who spoke a little English, said to me
with emphasis, " Poor Injin—poor tribe—run away from
own whoop!" This was positively every syllable the men
of the prairies deigned to bestow on these disturbers of the
public peace, the agents of covetousness, who prowl about
at night, like wolves, ready to seize the stray lamb, but are
quick to sneak off at the growl of the mastiff. One cannot express himself in terms too harsh of such wretches,
who in no instance have manifested a solitary spark of the
true spirit of freemen; having invariably quailed before
authority when that authority has assumed in the least the
aspect of its power, and as invariably trampled it under foot,
whenever numbers put danger out of the question.

· Old Susquesus had been a quiet observer of all that
passed. He knew the nature of the disturbance, and understood everything material that was connected with the out-
breaks. As soon as order was restored on the piazza, he
rose once more to address his guests.

· " My children," he said, solemnly, " you hear my voice
for the last time. Even the wren cannot sing for ever.
The very eagle's wing gets tired in time. I shall soon cease
to speak. When I reach the happy hunting-grounds of the
Onondagoes, I will tell the warriors I meet there of your
visit. Your fathers shall know that their sons still love
justice. Let the pale-faces sign papers, and laugh at them
afterwards. The promise of a red-man is his law. If he is
made a prisoner, and his conquerors wish to torment him,
they are too generous to do so without letting him go to his
tribe to take leave of his friends. When the time is reached,
he comes back. If he promises skins, he brings them,
though no law can follow into the woods to force him to do
so. His promise goes with him; his promise is stronger
than chains—it brings him back.

" My children, never forget this. You are not pale-faces,
to say one thing and do another. What you say, you do.
When you make a law, you keep it. This is right. No
red-man wants another's wigwam. If he wants a wigwam,
he builds one himself. It is not so with the pale-faces.

The man who has no wigwam tries to get away his neighbour's. While he does this, he reads in his bible and goes
to his church. I have sometimes thought, the more he reads
and prays, the more he tries to get into his neighbour's wigwam. So it seems to an Indian, but it may not be so.

" My children, the red-man is his own master. He goes
and comes as he pleases. If the young men strike the war-
path, he can strike it, too. He can go on the war-path, or
the hunt, or he can stay in his wigwam. All he has to do,
is to keep his promise, not steal, and not to go into another
red-man's wigwam unasked. He is his own master. He
does not *say* so; he *is* so. How is it with the pale-faces?
They say they are free when the sun rises; they say they
are free when the sun is over their heads; they say they
are free when the sun goes down behind the hills. They
never stop talking of their being their own masters. They
talk of *that* more than they read their bibles. - I have lived
near a hundred winters among them, and know what they
are. They do that; then they take away another's wigwam. They talk of liberty; then they say you shall have
this farm, you shan't have that. They talk of liberty, and
call to one another to put on calico bags, that fifty men may
tar and feather one. They talk of liberty, and want everything their own way.

" My children, these pale-faces might go back with you
to the prairies, and learn to do what is right. I do not
wonder they hide their faces in bags. They feel ashamed;
they ought to feel ashamed.

" My children, this is the last time you will hear my voice.
The tongue of an old man cannot move for ever. This is
my counsel: do what is right. The Great Spirit will tell
you what that is. Let it be done. What my son said of
me is true. It was hard to do; the feelings yearned to do
otherwise, but it was not done. In a little time peace came
on my spirit, and I was glad. I could not go back to live
among my people, for I was afraid of doing what was
wrong. I staid among the pale-faces, and made friends here.
My children, farewell; do what is right, and you will be
happier than the richest pale-face who does what is wrong."

Susquesus took his seat, and at the same time each of the
redskins advanced and shook his hand. The Indians make

few professions, but let their acts speak for them.   Not a
syllable was uttered by one of those rude warriors as he
took his leave of Susquesus.   Each man had willingly paid
this tribute to one whose justice and self-denial were celebrated in their traditions, and having paid it, he went his
way satisfied, if not altogether happy.   Each man shook
hands, too, with all on the piazza, and to us they expressed
their thanks for their kind treatment.   My uncle Ro had
distributed the remains of his trinkets among them, and they
left us with the most amicable feelings.   Still there was
nothing dramatic in their departure.   It was simple as
their arrival.   They had come to see the Upright of the
Onondagoes, had fulfilled their mission, and were ready to
depart.   Depart they did, and as I saw their line winding
along the highway, the episode of such a visit appeared to us
all more like a dream than reality.   No interruption occurred
to the return of these men, and half an hour after they had
left the piazza we saw them winding their way up the hill,
descending which we had first seen them.

" Well, Hodge," said Jack Dunning, two or three hours
later, " what is your decision ; will you remain here, or will
you go to your own place in Westchester."

" I will remain here until it is our pleasure to depart ;
then we will endeavour to be as free as Indians, and go
where we please, provided always we do not go into our
neighbour's wigwam against his will."

Jack Dunning smiled, and he paced the library once or
twice before he resumed.

" They told me, as soon as I got into the county, that
you, and all belonging to you, were preparing to retreat tho
morning after the attempt to fire your house."

" One of those amiable perversions of the truth that so
much embellish the morality of the whole affair.   What
men wish, they fancy, and what they fancy, they say.   The
girls, even, protest they would not quit the house while it
has a roof to cover their heads.   But, Jack, whence comes
this spirit ?"

" I should think that was the last question a reasonably
informed man need ask," answered Dunning, laughing.   " It
is very plain where it comes from.—It comes from the devil
and has every one of the characteristics of his handywork.

In the first place, love of money, or covetousness, is at its root. Then lies are its agents. Its first and most pretending lie is that of liberty, every principle of which it tramples under foot. Then come in the fifty auxiliaries in the way of smaller inventions, denying the facts of the original settlement of the country; fabricating statements concerning its progress, and asserting directly in the teeth of truth, such statements as it is supposed will serve a turn.* There can be no mistaking the origin of such contrivances, or all that has been taught us of good and evil is a fiction. Really, Hodge, I am astonished that so sensible a man should have asked the question."

"Perhaps you are right, Jack; but to what will it lead?"

"Ay, that is not so easily answered. The recent events in Delaware have aroused the better feelings of the country, and there is no telling what it may do. One thing, however, I hold to be certain; the spirit connected with this affair must be put down, thoroughly, effectually, completely, or we are lost. Let it once be understood, in the country, that men can control their own indebtedness, and fashion contracts to suit their own purposes, by combinations and numbers, and pandemonium would soon be a paradise com-

---

* The frightful propensity to effect its purposes by lying, has come to such a head in the country, as seriously to threaten the subversion of all justice. Without adverting to general facts, two circumstances directly connected with this anti-rent question, force themselves on my attention. They refer to large estates that were inherited by an Englishman, who passed half of a long life in the country. In public legislative documents it has been pretended that the question of his title to his estates is still open, when the published reports of the highest court of the country show that a decision was made in his favour thirty years since; and, in reference to his heir, it has been officially stated that he has invariably refused to give any leases but such as run on lives. Now, it is of little moment whether this be true or not, since the law allows every man to do as he may please in this respect. But the fact, as I understand from the agent who draws the leases, is precisely the reverse of that which has been openly stated in this legislative document; THE PRESENT POSSESSOR OF THE ESTATE IN QUESTION, HAVING BEEN EARNESTLY SOLICITED BY THE TENANTS TO GRANT NEW LEASES ON LIVES, AND ABSOLUTELY REFUSED TO COMPLY! In this instance the Legislature, doubtless, nave been deceived by the interested representations of anti-renters.— EDITOR.

pared to New York. There is not a single just ground of complaint in the nature of any of these leases, whatever hardships may exist in particular cases; but, admitting that there were false principles of social life, embodied in the relation of landlord and tenant, as it exists among us, *it would be a far greater evil to attempt a reform under such a combination, than to endure the original wrong.*"

"I suppose these gentry fancy themselves strong enough to thrust their interests into politics, and hope to succeed by that process. But anti-masonry, and various other schemes of that sort have failed, hitherto, and this may fail along with it. That is a redeeming feature of the institutions, Jack; you may humbug for a time, but the humbuggery is not apt to last for ever. It is only to be regretted that the really upright portion of the community are so long in making themselves felt; would they only be one-half as active as the miscreants, we should get along well enough."

"The result is unknown. The thing *may* be put down, totally, effectually, and in a way to kill the snake, not scotch it; or it may be met with only half-way measures; in which case it will remain like a disease in the human system, always existing, always menacing relapses, quite possibly to be the agent of the final destruction of the body."

My uncle, nevertheless, was as good as his word, and did remain in the county, where he is yet. Our establishment has received another reinforcement, however, and a change occurred, shortly after our visit from the Injins, in the policy of the anti-renters, the two giving us a feeling of security that might otherwise have been wanting. The reinforcement came from certain young men, who have found their way across from the springs, and become guests at the Nest. They are all old acquaintances of mine, most of them schoolfellows, and also admirers of the young ladies. Each of my uncle's wards, the Coldbrooke and the Marston, has an accepted lover, as we now discovered, circumstances that have left me unobstructed in pursuing my suit with Mary Warren. I have found Patt a capital ally, for she loves the dear girl almost as much as I do myself, and has been of great service in the affair. I am conditionally accepted, though Mr. Warren's consent has not been asked. Indeed, I much question if the good rector has the least suspicion of what is in the

wind.   As for my uncle Ro, he knew all about it, though I
have never breathed a syllable to him on the subject.   Fortunately, he is well satisfied with the choice made by his two
wards, and this has somewhat mitigated the disappointment.

My uncle Ro is not in the least mercenary; and the circumstance that Mary Warren has not a cent, gives him no
concern.   He is, indeed, so rich himself that he knows it is
in his power to make any reasonable addition to my means,
and, if necessary, to place me above the dangers of anti-
rentism.   The following is a specimen of his humour, and
of his manner of doing things when the humour takes him.
We were in the library one morning, about a week after the
Injins were shamed out of the field by the Indians, for that
was the secret of their final disappearance from our part of
the country; but, one morning, about a week after their last
visit, my grandmother, my uncle, Patt and I were seated in
the library, chatting over matters and things, when my
uncle suddenly exclaimed —

"By the way, Hugh, I have a piece of important news to
communicate to you; news affecting your interests to the
tune of fifty thousand dollars."

"No more anti-rent dangers, I hope, Roger?" said my
grandmother, anxiously.

"Hugh has little to apprehend from that source, just now.
The Supreme Court of the United States is his buckler, and
it is broad enough to cover his whole body.   As for his future leases, if he will take my advice, he will not grant one
for a term longer than five years, and then his tenants will
become clamorous petitioners to the legislature to allow them
to make their own bargains.   Shame will probably bring
your free-trade-men round, and the time will come when
your double-distilled friends of liberty will begin to see it is
a very indifferent sort of freedom which will not permit a
wealthy landlord to part with his farms for a long period, or
a poor husbandman to make the best bargain in his power.
No, no; Hugh has nothing serious to apprehend, just now
at least, from that source, whatever may come of it hereafter.   The loss to which I allude is much more certain, and
to the tune of fifty thousand dollars, I repeat."

"That is a good deal of money for me to lose, sir," I
answered, but little disturbed by the intelligence; ' and it
40

might embarrass me to raise so large a sum in a hurry
Nevertheless, I confess to no very great concern on the
subject, notwithstanding your announcement. I have no
debts, and the title to all I possess is indisputable, unless it
shall be decided that a *royal* grant is not to be tolerated by
republicans."

"All very fine, Master Hugh, but you forget that you are
the natural heir of my estate. Patt knows that she is to
have a slice of it when she marries, and I am now about to
make a settlement of just as much more on another young
lady, by way of marriage portion."

"Roger!" exclaimed my grandmother, "you surely do
not mean what you say! Of as much more!"

"Of precisely that money, my dear mother. I have
taken a fancy to a young lady, and as I cannot marry her
myself, I am determined to make her a good match, so far
as money is concerned, for some one else."

"But why not marry her yourself?" I asked. "Older
men than yourself marry every day."

"Ay, widowers, I grant you; *they* will marry until they
are a thousand; but it is not so with us bachelors. Let a
man once get fairly past forty, and it is no easy matter to
bring him to the sacrifice. No, Jack Dunning's being here
is the most fortunate thing in the world, and so I have set
him at work to draw up a settlement on the young lady to
whom I refer, without any rights to her future husband, let
him turn out to be whom he may."

"It is Mary Warren!" exclaimed my sister, in a tone of
delight.

My uncle smiled, and he tried to look demure; but I cannot say that he succeeded particularly well.

"It is—it is—it is Mary Warren, and uncle Ro means to
give her a fortune!" added Patt, bounding across the floor
like a young deer, throwing herself into her guardian's lap,
hugging and kissing him, as if she were nothing but a child,
though a fine young woman of nineteen. "Yes, it is Mary
Warren, and uncle Hodge is a delightful old gentleman —
no, a delightful young gentleman, and were he only thirty
years younger he should have his own heiress for a wife
himself. Good, dear, generous, sensible uncle Ro.—This

is so like him, after all his disappointment; for I know, Hugh, his heart was set on your marrying Henrietta."

"And what has my marrying, or not marrying Henrietta, to do with this settlement of fifty thousand dollars on Miss Warren? The young ladies are not even connected, I believe."

"Oh! you know how all such things are managed," said Patt, blushing and laughing at the passing allusion to matrimony, even in another; "Mary Warren will not be Mary Warren always."

"Who will she be, then?" demanded uncle Ro, quickly.

But Patt was too true to the rights and privileges of her sex to say anything directly that might seem to commit her friend. She patted her uncle's cheek, therefore, like a saucy minx as she was, coloured still higher, looked archly at me, then averted her eyes consciously, as if betraying a secret, and returned to her seat as demurely as if the subject had been one of the gravest character.

"But are you serious in what you have told us, Roger?" asked my grandmother, with more interest than I supposed the dear old lady would be apt to feel on such a subject. "Is not this settlement a matter of fancy?"

"True as the gospel, my dear mother."

"And is Martha right? Is Mary Warren really the favoured young lady?"

"For a novelty, Patt is right."

"Does Mary Warren know of your intention, or has her father been consulted in the matter?"

"Both know of it; we had it all over together, last evening, and Mr. Warren consents."

"To what?" I cried, springing to my feet, the emphasis on the last word being too significant to be overlooked.

"To receive Hugh Roger Littlepage, which is my own name, recollect, for a son-in-law; and what is more, the young lady 'is agreeable.'"

"We all know that she is more than agreeable," put in Patt; "she is delightful, excellent; agreeable is no word to apply to Mary Warren."

"Pshaw, girl! .If you had travelled, now, you would know that this expression is cockney English for agreeing to a thing. Mary Warren agrees to become the wife of Hugh

Roger Littlepage, and I settle fifty thousand dollars on her in consideration of matrimony."

"This Hugh Roger Littlepage," cried Patt, throwing an arm around my neck; "not that Hugh Roger Littlepage. Do but add that, dearest, dearest uncle, and I will kiss you for an hour."

"Excuse me, my child; a fourth of that time would bo as much as I could reasonably expect. I believe you are right, however, as I do not remember that *this* Hugh Roger had any connection with the affair, unless it were to give his money. I shall deny none of your imputations."

Just as this was said, the door of the library was slowly opened, and Mary Warren appeared. The moment she saw who composed our party, she would have drawn back, but my grandmother kindly bade her " come in."

" I was afraid of disturbing a family party, ma'am," Mary timidly answered.

Patt darted forward, threw her arm around Mary's waist, and drew her into the room, closing and locking the door. All this was done in a way to attract attention, and as if the young lady wished to attract attention. We all smiled but Mary, who seemed half pleased, half frightened.

" It *is* a family party," cried Patt, kissing her affianced sister, " and no one else shall be admitted to it, unless good Mr. Warren come to claim his place. Uncle Ro has told us all about it, and we know all."

Mary hid her face in Patt's bosom, but it was soon drawn out by my dear grandmother to kiss it; then my uncle had his turn, and Patt her's. After this, the whole party, except Mary and I, slid out of the room, and — yes, and then it was *my* turn.

We are not yet married, but the day is named. The same is true with respect to the two wards, and even Patt blushes, and my grandmother smiles, occasionally, when gentlemen who are travelling in Egypt just now, are named. The last letters from young Beekman, they tell me, say that he was then there. The three marriages are to take place in St. Andrew's church, Mr. Warren being engaged to officiate.

The reader will be surprised to hear two things. My engagement with the daughter of a poor clergyman has pro-

duced great scandal among the anti-renters, they who so
loudly decry aristocracy! The objection is that the match
is not equal! That equality which is the consequence of
social position, connections, education and similarity of
habits, thoughts, and, if you will, prejudices, is all thrown
away on these persons. They have no notion of its existence; but they can very well understand that the owner of
an unencumbered and handsome estate is richer than the
heiress of a poor divine, who can just make the year meet
on $500 per annum. I let them grumble, as I know they
must and will find fault with something connected with myself, until they have got away my land, or are satisfied it is
not to be had. As for Opportunity, I have been assured that
she threatens to sue me for a "breach of promise;" nor
should I be at all surprised were she actually to make the
attempt. It is by no means unusual, when a person sets his
or her whole soul on a particular object, to imagine circumstances favourable to his or her views, which never had an
existence; and Opportunity may fancy that what I have
heard has been "the buzzing in her own ear." Then the
quackery of legislatures has set the ladies at work in earnest,
and he will soon be a fortunate youth who can pass through
his days of celibacy without some desperate assault, legal or
moral, from the other sex. Besides, nothing can be out of
the way, when it is found that the more popular and most
numerous branch of the Legislature of New York really
believes it can evade that solemn provision of the Constitution of the United States, which says "no state shall pass
any law impairing the obligations of contracts," by enacting,
as they can regulate the statute of descent, that whenever a
landlord dies, the tenant, by applying to the chancellor, can
have his leasehold tenure converted into a mortgage, on discharging which the land will be his, unencumbered! We
have heard of a "thimble-rig administration" in England,
and really that industrious nation seems to have exported
the breed to this country. How many of those who voted
for such a law will like to see the ays and noes on the
journals of the assembly ten years hence? If there should
be one such man left in the state, he will be an object of
humane commiseration. We have had many efforts at
legislative chicanery, and some that have been tolerably clever,

40*

but this is a palpable experiment in the same way, made for a reason that everybody understands, that has not even the negative merit of ingenuity. Our own courts will probably disregard it, should the Senate even concur ; and as for those of the United States, they will, out of all doubt, treat it as it ought to be treated, and brand it with ignominy. The next step will be to pass a law regulating descents, as it is called, under the provisions of which the debtors of the deceased can meet his obligations with a coin technically called " puppies."

Jaaf drivels away. The black occasionally mumbles out his sentiments concerning past events, and the state of the country. An anti-renter he regards as he would a thief, and makes no bones of saying so. Sometimes he blunders on a very good remark in connection with the subject, and one he made no later than yesterday, is worthy of notice.

" What dem feller want, Masser Hugh ?" he demanded. " Dey 's got one half of deir farms, and now dey wants tudder half. S'pose I own a cow, or a sheep, in par'nership, what right I got to say I will have him all ? Gosh ! dere no sich law in ole time. Den, who ebber see sich poor Injin ! Redskin mis'rubble enough, make 'e bess of him, but dis Injin so mis'rubble dat I doesn't won'er you can't bear him. Oh ! how ole I do git—I do t'ink ole Sus can't last much longer, too !"

Old Susquesus still survives, but an object of great hatred to all the anti-renters, far and near. The 'Injin' system has been broken up, temporarily at least, but the spirit which brought it into existence survives under the hypocritical aspect of " human rights." The Upright of the Onondagoes is insensible of the bad feeling which is so active against him, nor is it probable that most of those who entertain this enmity are conscious of the reason ; which is simply the fact that he is a man who respected laws to the making of which he was a party, and preferred to suffer rather than to be guilty of an act of injustice.

NOTE BY THE EDITOR.

Here the manuscript of Mr. Hugh Roger Littlepage, jun., terminates. That gentleman's feelings have probably forbidden his relating events so recent as those which have since occurred. It remains, therefore, for us to add a few words.

Jaaf died about ten days since, railing at the redskins to the last, and talking about his young massers and missuses as long as he had breath. As for his own descendants, he had not been heard to name *them*, for the last forty years.

Susquesus still survives, but the " Injins" are all defunct. Public opinion has, at last, struck that tribe out of existence, and it is hoped that their calico bags have been transmitted to certain politicians among us, who, as certain as the sun rises and sets, will find them useful to conceal their own countenances, when contrition and shame come, as contrition and shame will be sure to succeed such conduct as theirs.

It may be well to add a word on the subject of the tone of this book. It is the language of a man who feels that he has been grievously injured, and who writes with the ardour of youth increased by the sense of wrong. As editors, we have nothing more to do with that than to see, while calling things by their right names, that language too strong for the public taste should not be introduced into our pages. As to the moral and political principles connected with this matter, we are wholly of the side of the Messrs. Littlepages, though we do not think it necessary to adopt all their phrases — phrases that may be natural to men in their situations, but which would be out of place, perhaps, in the mouths of those who act solely in the capacity of essayists and historians.

To conclude : — Mr. Littlepage and Mary Warren were married, in St. Andrew's church, a very few days since. We met the young gentleman, on his wedding tour, no later than yesterday, and he assured us that, provided with such a companion, he was ready to change his domicile to any other part of the Union, and that he had selected Washington, for the express purpose of being favourably situated for trying the validity of the laws of the United States, as opposed to the "thimble-rigging" of the New York Legislature. It is his intention to have every question connected with the covenants of his leases, that of taxing the landlord for property on which the tenant has covenanted to pay all taxes; that of distress for rent, when distress must precede the re-entry stipulated for by the leases; and that of any other trick or device which the brains of your "small-potato" legislator may invent in order to wrong him out of his property. As for ourselves, we can only say, God give him success! for we are most deeply impressed that the more valuable parts of the institutions of this country can be preserved only by crushing into the dust this nefarious spirit of cupidity, which threatens the destruction of all moral feeling, and every sense of right, that remains among us.

In our view, Oregon, Mexico, and Europe, united against us, do not threaten this nation with one-half as much real danger as that which menaces it at this moment, from an enemy that is now in possession of many of its strong-holds, and which is incessantly working its evil under the cry of liberty, while laying deeper the foundation of a most atrocious tyranny.

I forgot to add, Mr. Littlepage significantly remarked, at parting, that should Washington fail him, he has the refuge of Florence open, where he can reside among the other victims of oppression, with the advantage of being admired as a refugee from republican tyranny.

THE END.

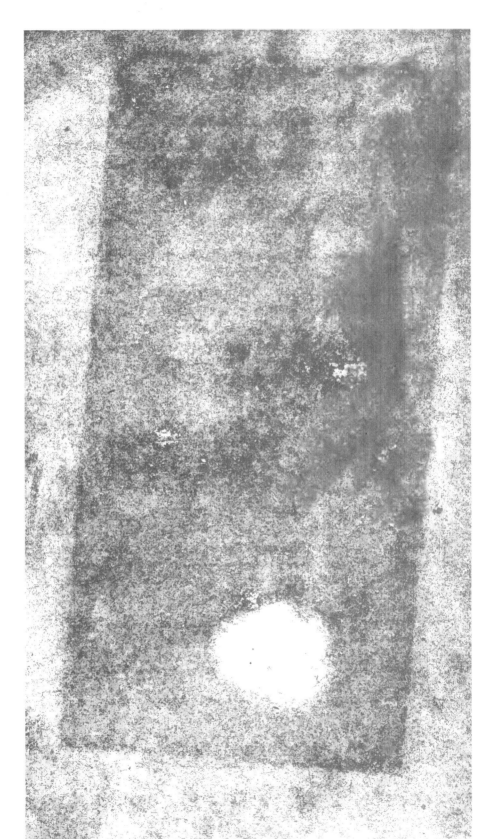

955
CM78
V.28

Cooper

H R 122

ImTheStory.com

Personalized Classic Books in many genre's

Unique gift for kids, partners, friends, colleagues

Customize:

- Character Names
- Upload your own front/back cover images (optional)
- Inscribe a personal message/dedication on the
  inside page (optional)

Customize many titles Including
- Alice in Wonderland
- Romeo and Juliet
- The Wizard of Oz
- A Christmas Carol
- Dracula
- Dr. Jekyll & Mr. Hyde
- And more...

CPSIA information can be obtained at www.ICGtesting.com
Printed in the USA
BVOW05s1758270414

351857BV00009B/59/P

9 781314 538533